THE SUFFERINGS
AND THE GLORIES OF
THE MESSIAH

THE SUFFERINGS AND THE GLORIES OF THE MESSIAH

AN EXPOSITION OF PSALM 18 & ISAIAH 52:13-53:12

JOHN BROWN

BAKER BOOK HOUSE

Grand Rapids, Michigan 49506

Reprinted 1981 by
Baker Book House Company
from the 1953 edition published by
Robert Carter & Brothers

ISBN: 0-8010-0792-5

PHOTOLITHOPRINTED BY CUSHING - MALLOY, INC.
ANN ARBOR, MICHIGAN, UNITED STATES OF AMERICA

PREFACE

It is more than thirty years since the passages of Old Testament Scripture, to the illustration of which the following pages are devoted, first attracted my attention; and the result of inquiry into them, with such helps as were then possessed, was at the time committed to writing. During the long interval which has elapsed, these notes have been repeatedly revised, and such additions and alterations made as were suggested by a further study of the sacred text, and a wider acquaintance with what had been done for its interpretation. Within the last few months, the whole, after a thorough review, has been re-written.

It will appear from the margin, that the original Hebrew, and the principal translations and commentaries, have been constantly before me; and from the text, that, while many interpreters have been respectfully consulted, no one has been slavishly followed. Among the multitude of expositors to whom I have been indebted, Peirce on the Eighteenth Psalm, and Hengstenberg on the Oracle in Isaiah, deserve to be named as my principal benefactors.

In writing on those subjects, as on others, I have indeed consulted all authors from whom I expected assistance, being, as Dr. Donne says, " willing to go all the way with company, and to take light from others, as well

in the journey as at the journey's end. And if in the
multiplicity of citations there appears vanity or ostenta-
tion, my honesty must make my excuse; for I acknowledge with Pliny, 'that to chuse rather to be taken in a
theft than to give every man his due, *est obnoxii animi
et infelicis ingenii.*'"

If any light has been thrown on these Divine oracles,
and an exemplification given of the right application of
the principles of interpretation to the exposition of
Scripture, my purpose in this publication will be gained.
The object of a great deal of interpretation of Scripture, has been (unconsciously, we doubt not) to find as
much as possible of the interpreter's already formed
opinions there,—not simply to discover what is there,
whether confirmatory or condemnatory of those opinions.
It has been my sincere desire to bring out of the inspired
words what is really in them, and to put nothing into
them that is not really there,—impressed with the conviction, that imaginary exposition is one of the worst
ways of adding to " the words of the prophecy of this
book," and that he who thus adds to God's word, " de-
ceiving and being deceived," is in great danger of " proving himself a liar." How far I have succeeded where
so many have failed, must be determined by the com-
petent judges.

The recurrence of the brief recapitulatory statements
may appear in some cases unnecessary; but as the Discourses are not likely to be always, or perhaps usually,
read in series, it was thought best that each Lecture
should contain in itself what was necessary to its being
understood. These *resumés* are studiously short, and can
easily be passed over when they are felt not to be required.

These Expositions are not offered as entirely, or indeed
principally, the result of my own personal researches in

the wide, and interesting, and difficult field of the Criticism and Interpretation of the Old Testament Scriptures. They are a specimen of what a moderate stock of information on these subjects[1] may do, in enabling a man to turn to account the labors of abler and more learned men. If the book have any merit, it is not that of originality : it is that of the resolution of the principal interpretations into their elements by a careful analysis, and the reconstruction of an exposition of the whole Oracle out of such of those elements as best stood the rather severe trial to which they were exposed. It will not mortify me, to tell me that I have merely compiled an Exposition, if it be but admitted that the compilation is more satisfactory than any *one* of the originals from which it has been made. If it be not, I have failed in my object ; but even in this case, I may not have altogether labored in vain.

In passing through the press, the proof-sheets have had the advantage of the careful supervision of my kinsman, the Rev. John B. Johnston of Kirkcaldy.

JOHN BROWN.

Author's Lodge, Newington,
December 1852.

---

[1] " Ego unus sum inter Hebraismi non *peritos* sed *studiosos,* qui minimos progressus in ea lingua facerim."—Jos. Scaliger, Ep. ccxliv. *ad* Buxtorff.

" As, it is owned, the whole scheme of Scripture is not yet understood; so, if it ever comes to be understood before the 'restitution of all things,' and without miraculous interpositions, it must be in the same way as natural knowledge is come at: by particular persons attending to comparing and pursuing intimations scattered up and down it, which are overlooked and disregarded by the generality of the world.—Nor is it at all incredible, that a book that has been so long in the possession of mankind should contain many truths as yet undiscovered. For all the same phenomena, and the same faculties of investigation, from which such great discoveries in natural knowledge have been made in the present and last age, were equally in the possession of mankind several thousand years before."—BUTLER, *Analogy*, Part II., Chap. III.

CONTENTS

PART I—AN EXPOSITION OF PSALM XVIII

LECTURE I

INTRODUCTORY

OUTLINE

LECTURE II

I.—PROEM OF THE PSALM

TEXT

PSALM XVII. 1–3.—" I will love Thee, O Lord, my strength. The Lord is my
rock, and my fortress, and my deliverer ; my God, my strength, in whom I will
trust ; my buckler, and the horn of my salvation, and my high tower. I will call
upon the Lord, who is worthy to be praised : so shall I be saved from mine
enemies."

OUTLINE

LECTURE III

II.—THE MESSIAH'S SUFFERINGS AND THE EXERCISE OF HIS MIND UNDER THEM

TEXT

Page

PSALM XVIII. 4–6.—" The sorrows of death compassed me, and the floods of ungodly men made me afraid.   The sorrows of hell compassed me about ; the snares of death prevented me.   In my distress I called upon the Lord, and cried unto my God : He heard my voice out of his temple, and my cry came before Him, *even* into his ears."

OUTLINE

LECTURE IV

III.—PRETERNATURAL DELIVERANCE OF THE MESSIAH FROM HIS SUFFERINGS

TEXT

PSALM XVIII. 7–19.—" Then the earth shook and trembled ; the foundations also of the hills moved and were shaken, because He was wroth.   There went up a smoke out of his nostrils, and fire out of his mouth devoured : coals were kindled by it.   He bowed the heavens also, and came down : and darkness was under his feet.   And He rode upon a cherub, and did fly ; yea, He did fly upon the wings of the wind.   He made darkness his secret place ; his pavillion round about Him were dark waters and thick clouds of the skies.   At the brightness that was before Him his thick clouds passed ; hailstones and coals of fire.   The Lord also thundered in the heavens, and the Highest gave his voice ; hailstones and coals of fire. Yea, He sent out his arrows, and scattered them ; and He shot out lightnings, and discomfited them.   Then the channels of waters were seen, and the foundations of the world were discovered at thy rebuke, O Lord, at the blast of the breath of thy nostrils.   He sent from above, He took me, He drew me out of many waters. He delivered me from my strong enemy, and from them which hated me : for they were too strong for me.   They prevented me in the day of my calamity : but the Lord was my stay.   He brought me forth also into a large place ; He delivered me, because He delighted in me."

OUTLINE

LECTURE V

IV —THE MESSIAH'S DELIVERANCE THE WORK OF JEHOVAH— A WORK ILLUSTRATIVE OF HIS RIGHTEOUSNESS AND BENIGNITY

Text

Psalm xviii. 20-24.—" The Lord rewarded me according to my righteousness ; according to the cleanness of my hands hath He recompensed me. For I
have kept the ways of the Lord, and have not wickedly departed from my God.
For all his judgments were before me, and I did not put away his statutes from
me. I was also upright before Him, and I kept myself from mine iniquity.
Therefore hath the Lord recompensed me according to my righteousness, according to the cleanness of my hands in his eye-sight."

Outline

LECTURE VI

IV *Continued*

THE CONDUCT OF JEHOVAH TO THE MESSIAH AND TO HIS ENEMIES

Text

Psalm xviii. 25, 26.—" With the merciful Thou wilt show thyself merciful ;
with an upright man Thou wilt show thyself upright ; with the pure Thou wilt
show thyself pure ; and with the froward Thou wilt show thyself froward."

Outline

LECTURE VII

IV *Continued*

FARTHER VIEWS OF JEHOVAH'S CONDUCT TO THE MESSIAH HIS PEOPLE AND HIS ENEMIES

TEXT

Page

PSALM XVIII. 27–31.—" For Thou wilt save the afflicted people ; but wilt bring down high looks. For Thou wilt light my candle : the Lord my God will enlighten my darkness. For by Thee I have run through a troop ; and by my God have I leaped over a wall. As for God, his way is perfect : the word of the Lord is tried ; He is a buckler to all those that trust in Him. For who is God save the Lord ? or who is a rock save our God ?"

OUTLINE

Illustration of verses 27–31—A description of Christ's people—" The afflicted people."—A description of his enemies—They who have " proud looks."—The conduct of Jehovah with regard to the first class—" He saves them."—The conduct of Jehovah with regard to the second class—" He brings down their high looks."—Two figurative views of the deliverance of the Messiah—(1.) The re-lighting his extinguished lamp, verse 28—Meaning of the figure, and proof of its realisation—(2.) The giving him victory over his enemies, and possession of their fortresses, verse 29—Meaning of the figure and proof of its realisation. An acknowledgment by the Messiah of the perfect righteousness of the Divine dispensations in reference to him, and of the incomparable excellence of Jehovah, verses 30, 31.—Reflections 126

LECTURE VIII

V, VI —THE MESSIAH'S SUCCESSFUL WARFARE AND EXTENSIVE AND ETERNAL KINGDOM

TEXT

PSALM XVIII. 32–50.—" It is God that girdeth me with strength, and maketh my way perfect. He maketh my feet like hinds' feet, and setteth me upon my high places. He teacheth my hands to war, so that a bow of steel is broken by mine arms. Thou hast also given me the shield of thy salvation ; and thy right hand hath holden me up, and thy gentleness hath made me great. Thou hast enlarged my steps under me, that my feet did not slip. I have pursued mine enemies, and overtaken them ; neither did I turn again till they were consumed. I have wounded them, that they were not able to rise : they are fallen under my feet. For Thou hast girded me with strength unto the battle : Thou hast subdued under me those that rose up against me. Thou hast also given me the necks of mine enemies, that I might destroy them that hate me. They cried, but there was none to save them ; even unto the Lord, but He answered them not. Then did I beat them small as the dust before the wind ; I did cast them out as the dirt in the streets. Thou hast delivered me from the strivings of the people ; and Thou hast made me the head of the heathen : a people whom I have not known shall serve me. As soon as they hear of me, they shall obey me ; the strangers shall submit themselves unto me. The strangers shall fade away, and be afraid out of their close places. The Lord liveth ; and blessed be my Rock ; and let the God of my salvation be exalted. It is God that avengeth me, and subdueth the people under me. He delivered me from mine enemies ;

PART II —AN EXPOSITION OF ISAIAH LII. 13—LIII.12

LECTURE I

INTRODUCTORY

OUTLINE

Introductory remarks. Opinions of Hengstenberg, Luther, Musculus, and Cappellus.—Subject of the Oracle—THE SERVANT OF JEHOVAH.—Summary of what is said of him in the Oracle itself.—The ancient Jewish interpreters refer the Oracle to the Messiah.—The Modern Jewish interpreters deny this reference, and explain it variously.—Christian interpreters united in referring it to Christ till the time of Grotius.—Opinions of the Fathers Augustine and Theodoret— Of the reformers Zwingle and Luther.—The anti-Messianic interpreters

LECTURE II

OPENING PROCLAMATION OF JEHOVAH

Text

ISAIAH LII. 13–15.—" Behold, my servant shall deal prudently, he shall be exalted and extolled, and be very high. As many were astonished at thee: (his visage was so marred more than any man, and his form more than the sons of men ;) so shall he sprinkle many nations; the kings shall shut their mouths at him: for that which had not been told them shall they see; and that which they had not heard shall they consider."

Outline

LECTURE III

THE COMPLAINT OF THE PRIMITIVE EVANGELISTS.

Text

ISAIAH LIII. 1.—" Who hath believed our report ? and to whom is the arm of the Lord revealed ?"

Outline

LECTURE IV

STATEMENT AND PROFESSION OF THE JEWISH CONVERTS

Text

ISAIAH LIII. 2–4.—" For he shall grow up before Him as a tender plant, and as a root out of a dry ground: he hath no form nor comeliness ; and when we shall see him, there is no beauty that we should desire him. He is despised and re-

jected of ·men ; a man of sorrows, and acquainted with grief; and we hid as it
were our faces from him : he was despised, and we esteemed him not. Surely
he hath borne our griefs, and carried our sorrows : yet we did esteem him
stricken, smitten of God, and afflicted."

OUTLINE

LECTURE V

STATEMENT AND PROFESSION OF THE JEWISH CONVERTS—
CONTINUED

TEXT.

ISAIAH LIII. 5.—" But he was wounded for our transgressions, he was bruised
for our iniquities : the chastisement of our peace was upon him ; and with
his stripes we are healed."

OUTLINE

LECTURE VI

STATEMENT AND PROFESSION OF THE JEWISH CONVERTS—
CONTINUED

TEXT

ISAIAH LIII. 6.—" All we, like sheep, have gone astray ; we have turned every
one to his own way ; and the Lord hath laid on him the iniquity of us all."

LECTURE VII

STATEMENT AND PROFESSION OF THE JEWISH CONVERTS—CONTINUED

TEXT

ISAIAH LIII. 7.—"He was oppressed, and he was afflicted; yet he opened not his mouth: he is brought as a lamb to the slaughter, and as a sheep before her shearers is dumb, so he openeth not his mouth."

OUTLINE

LECTURE VIII

STATEMENT AND PROFESSION OF THE JEWISH CONVERTS—CONTINUED

TEXT

ISAIAH LIII. 8, 9.—"He was taken from prison and from judgment: and who shall declare his generation? for he was cut off out of the land of the living: for the transgression of my people was he stricken. And he made his grave with the wicked, and with the rich in his death; because he had done no violence, neither was any deceit in his mouth."

OUTLINE

LECTURE IX

STATEMENT AND PROFESSION OF THE JEWISH CONVERTS— CONCLUDED

Text

ISAIAH, LIII. 10.—" Yet it pleased the Lord to bruise him; He hath put him to grief: when Thou shalt make his soul an offering for sin, he shall see his seed, he shall prolong his days, and the pleasure of the Lord shall prosper in his hand."

Outline

LECTURE X

THE CLOSING PROCLAMATION OF JEHOVAH, CONFIRMATORY OF THE STATEMENT OF THE JEWISH CONVERTS

Text

ISAIAH, LIII. 11. 12.—" He shall see of the travail of his soul, and shall be satisfied: by his knowledge shall my righteous servant justify many; for he shall bear their iniquities. Therefore will I divide him a portion with the great, and he shall divide the spoil with the strong; because he hath poured out his soul unto death: and he was numbered with the transgressors ; and he bare the sin of many, and made intercession for the transgressors."

Outline

THE

SUFFERINGS AND GLORIES

OF

THE MESSIAH

PART I

AN EXPOSITION OF PSALM XVIII

"Pluribus quidem reipublicæ philologiæ proceribus, hæc vaticiniorum de Messiah Ennarationes, quæ mihi verisimillimæ videntur, parum probantur; verum et meo mihi uti licebit judicio. Sententias quas de his lucubrationibus in Ephemeridibus literariis ferent, placide expecto. Laudem non anhelo, et vituperium non perhorresco; nam et illam et hoc æquo animo ferre didici. Fundamentum aliud nemo potest ponere præter id, quod positum est, MESSIAS JESUS. An superstruxerim aurum, argentum, et lapides preciosos, an vero lignum, fœnum, et stipulas, tempus docebit."—Ἡμέρα δηλώσει. JAHN.

THE

SUFFERINGS AND GLORIES

OF

THE MESSIAH

PART I

AN EXPOSITION OF PSALM XVIII

LECTURE I

INTRODUCTORY—SUBJECT OF THE PSALM

FEW men have excited so deep an interest, and exercised so
powerful and extensive an influence, during so many ages, and
continue to do so, as David, the king of Israel. This is owing
to various causes. But among the numerous and strong claims
which that distinguished man possesses on the grateful remembrance and high veneration of his fellow-men in every age, un-
questionably the highest are those which are derived from his
character as an inspired writer. His personal qualities command our reverence and draw forth our affection ; but it is his
poetry which has enshrined him in the hearts of the pious in all
ages. His history is in no ordinary degree interesting, but his
writings are the main foundation of his immortal and world-
wide fame. It is less as the undaunted hero and the wise
monarch, than as the sweet psalmist, that, after the lapse of
nearly three thousand years, he still excites the admiration,
and ministers to the improvement, of innumerable men of almost " every nation under heaven."

That book of sacred odes which bears his name, and of many
of which he was the author, though at least one of them belongs

to a much earlier age, and others of them belong to a much later period, is certainly one of the most delightful and useful portions of the Old Testament Scriptures.[a] The poetical merit of these divine hymns is of the highest order. In variety and richness of imagery—in sublimity and beauty, both of thought and language—and it may be, too, in symmetry of structure, if not in harmony of numbers,—they rival, they surpass, the most admired lyrical productions of Greek or of Roman genius.

But poetical merit constitutes but an inconsiderable part of their praise. Like all the other Scriptures, they are "given by the inspiration of God ;" for the Spirit of the Lord spake by their gifted writers, and His word was on their tongue, and they are therefore "profitable for doctrine and for reproof, for correction and instruction in righteousness, that the man of God may be perfect, fully furnished to every good work."

They breathe a spirit of the most elevated and rational, yet childlike and affectionate, devotion. They indicate a mind equally under the influence of veneration and love—a temper alien alike from the scepticism of the philosopher and the credulity of the vulgar. They are full of deep thought, but every thought is instinct with corresponding feeling ; they are full of strong emotion, but the emotion is never unnatural, for its subject always fully warrants it. Their sublimity has nothing in common with the undefinable abstractions of mysticism, nor do their raptures ever degenerate into the ravings of an unenlightened enthusiasm.

They form a body of religious experience admirably calculated for strengthening the faith, animating the hope, purifying and elevating the affections, and guiding the actings both of the inner and the outer man. Though written under the influence of a comparatively obscure dispensation of divine truth and grace, many of them have a reference to that better order of things which "came by Jesus Christ ;" and in most of them we meet with the expressions of that faith, and hope, and gratitude, and reverence, which are sentiments not peculiar to any dispensation, but are common to all good men, in every country and in every age.

It is also deserving of notice, that the remarkable vicissitudes to which David was exposed, in the course of his singularly chequered life, have been overruled as the means of communicat-

[a] See Note A.

ing a superadded value to his compositions, as they have naturally
given origin to a variety in the psalms wonderfully suited to the
diversity of situation in which good men may be placed, each
characterized by its own responsibilities, and difficulties, and
temptations. There are few shades of devotional feeling which
the saint will not find here accurately delineated; and it would
not be easy to imagine a conjuncture of circumstances in which
a good man may be placed, for which the book of Psalms does
not furnish appropriate warning, direction, and consolation.

It has been said, with equal truth and beauty, that this little
volume, " like the paradise of Eden, affords us in perfection,
though in miniature, everything that groweth elsewhere—'every
tree that is pleasant to the sight and good for food;' and, above
all, what was there lost, but is here restored—'the tree of life,
which was in the midst of the garden."—" Composed upon particular occasions, yet designed for general use; delivered out as
services for Israelites under the Law, yet no less adapted to the
circumstances of Christians under the Gospel; they present religion to us in the most engaging dress; communicating truths
which philosophy could never discover, in a style which poetry
can never equal; while history is made the vehicle of prophecy,
and creation lends all its charms to paint the glories of redemption. Calculated alike to profit and to please, they inform the
understanding, elevate the affections, and entertain the imagination. Indited under the influence of Him to whom all hearts are
known and all events foreknown, they suit mankind in all situa-
tions, grateful as the manna which descended from above, and
conformed itself to every palate. The fairest productions of
human wit, after a few perusals, wither in our hands, like
gathered flowers, and lose their fragrancy; but these unfading
plants of paradise become, as we are accustomed to them, still
more and more beautiful; their bloom appears to be daily
heightened; fresh odors are emitted, and new sweets extracted
from them. He who has once tasted their excellences will desire to taste them yet again, and he who tastes them oftenest
will relish them best."[1]

It has been observed of this book by one of its later interpreters, Bishop Horsley, that, "of all the books of the Old Testament, the book of Psalms is most universally read, but, it is to

---

[1] Bp. Horne.

be feared, as little as any understood. This cannot be ascribed
to any extraordinary obscurity of these sacred songs; for of all
the prophetic parts of Scripture, they are certainly the most
perspicuous. But it is owing partly, I fear, to some dulness of
the faculties of the natural man on spiritual subjects, and partly to the misapplied labors of modern expositors, who have
employed much learning and ingenuity to find the immediate
subject of each psalm either in the history of the Jewish nation,
or in the occurrences of the life of David." There can be no
doubt that there is much truth in these observations; yet it is
necessary to remark, that while the greater part of later expositors have erred in this way, not a few have run into the opposite extreme,—the learned and acute interpreter just quoted,
among the foremost of them; and by the violence which they
have done to the sacred text, and to the principles of sound interpretation, in making all the Psalms refer immediately and
solely to the Messiah—to the traits of *his* character, and the
events of his life on earth and reign in heaven—they have excited in men of sober minds strong prejudices against viewing
any of them as direct predictions of the sufferings of Christ and
of the glory which should follow, and have led them, in their
turn, frequently to employ as much violence in explaining of
the illustrious monarch of Israel, what was certainly meant to
refer entirely to his still more illustrious Son and Lord.[1]

---

[1] After all that has been written, a full satisfactory discussion of the "Messianic
Prophecies" is still a desideratum. One of the most important and not least difficult
parts of such a work, would be the settlement of the question respecting what has
been called "the double sense,"—a question, the clear statement of which would go a
good way towards its right resolution. The following principles seem to stand on
safe ground: '(1.) All passages in Scripture referring to the future may be considered
as prophetic. (2.) Many of these prophecies are expressed in such general and comprehensive terms, as to find fulfilment in an endless variety and infinite number of
events; but such prophecies have but one, and that often a very plain, meaning.
The principles of the Divine government are unchangeable; and in really similar circumstances, similar events will transpire.—It is chiefly, if not exclusively, to the interpretation of such predictions that Lord Bacon's remark can safely be applied:—
"They have a springing and germinant accomplishment through many ages, though
the height and fulness of them may refer to one age." "The kingdom of God," as
Neander says, "in the course of its development from beginning to end, forms a
connected whole, and it strives towards its completion according to sure and certain
laws." (3.) Many predictions which have been supposed to be Messianic have no such
reference, but predict events which took place comparatively soon after the prophecy
was published. (4.) Many predictions are Messianic, and solely Messianic, in their

This has been, I am persuaded, very much the case with regard to that sublime and beautiful psalm which now lies before us for explication. The extreme unsatisfactoriness of all attempts to find, in the events of David's life and reign, an adequate correspondence to the statements in this psalm, has led me to inquire whether there is not reason to suppose that this is one of those psalms, in which, to use the language of the apostle Peter, "the patriarch David," "being a prophet, and knowing that God had sworn with an oath to him, that of the fruit of his loins, according to the flesh, He would raise up Christ, to sit on his throne : he, seeing this before, spake"[1] of Him who was to be at once his Son and his Lord ; and the result of this inquiry is a persuasion that a greater than David is here—that, so far as the subject of the psalm is concerned, David is not here at all, except, it may be, in the way of allusive illustration—and that this psalm is, equally with the second, the sixteenth, the twenty-second, the fortieth, and the hundred-and-tenth, to mention no more, a Messianic Psalm.

A brief statement of the evidence which has led me to this conclusion, will not only form an appropriate and necessary introduction to the illustration of the various parts of the inspired

reference, which have been applied to events under the former dispensation, because their language and imagery have been borrowed from that dispensation. (5.) Predictions in reference to typical persons, like narratives in reference to such persons, are fitted and intended to lead the mind to the correspondence in the antitype ; but the prediction, no more than the narrative, has anything but one meaning. It is the fact that the subject of the prediction or narrative is an image, a type of "Him that was to come," or "a shadow of the good things to come," not the words, which lead the mind to the Messiah and the events of his reign. The system of interpretation that, in such predictions, passes from the type to the antitype, when the subject of the psalm is plainly one, referring the prediction to the latter when it promises to bring out what is thought to be an interesting or edifying sense,—and then reverting to the former to avoid a difficulty, which, being disposed of, there is a return to the latter,— is extremely unsatisfactory. Where the subject is a typical person, everything that is true in a higher sense of the antitype, must in a lower sense be true of the type. Dr. Owen's maxim is full of good sense: "If the Scripture has more than one meaning, it has no meaning at all;" and it is just as applicable to the prophecies as to any other portion of Scripture.' The effect of this method of multiplying senses is very graphically stated by Mr. Douglas : "Thus revelation has come to resemble Virgil's mystical tree at the mouth of Avernus, thickly covered with visionary leaves, and on every leaf a dream :—

> 'In medio ramos annosáque brachia pandit
> Ulmus opaca, ingens ; quam sedem Somnia volgò
> Vana tenere ferunt, foliisque sub omnibus hærent.' "—*Æn.* vi. 282-284.

[1] Acts, ii. 29-31.

ode, which, proceeding on this principle, I mean to lay before you in a few lectures, but will also, I trust, furnish you with the means of satisfactorily determining for yourselves a question which is of much importance to the reading of the Psalms with intellectual satisfaction and spiritual profit,—'What are those psalms, or portions of psalms, in which it is written of Christ?'

I am fully persuaded that there is much more of Christ in the Psalms than many Christians are aware of, and that their ignorance and misapprehension on this subject are calculated materially to diminish the pleasure and the advantage they derive from the study of these inspired poems; but I am equally convinced that this advantage is not to be secured by a practice which has prevailed but too extensively—the allegorising at will—the applying to Christ all such passages as, when taken apart from their connection, admit of a plausible accommodation to Him. This has often been done, not only in the absence of all evidence that the inspiring Spirit intended them to be so understood, but where there was abundant evidence, if it had only been looked at, proving that they have, that they can have, no such reference. Such a mode of interpretation is a most unbecoming and presumptuous "meddling with God"—a making Him say what He never said—a substitution of a human dream for a divine revelation. It affords facilities for infidels in their attacks on revelation, and materially impedes the edification of Christians. A sound judgment is of far more importance in such matters than a lively imagination; and if we will be at the pains to seek for them, we shall assuredly find, in the divine revelation itself, the means of rightly interpreting it—of properly fixing both its meaning and its reference.

There are two great principles, on one or both of which all right interpretation of passages in the Psalms, as referring to the Messiah, must proceed—principles which bear their own evidence along with them, and which, though requiring consideration and caution in applying them, will, in every case, bring us to a safe and satisfactory conclusion.

The first of the principles to which I refer may be thus stated: 'That passages in the Psalms, which in the New Testament are expressly represented as predictions of the Messiah, are to be considered as having been originally intended to be so, and are to be interpreted accordingly.' I refer to such passages as Psalm cx. 1, as quoted by our Lord, Matt. xxii. 44 ; and Psalm xvi. 10, as quoted by the apostle Peter, Acts ii. 25. This principle rests on the most solid foundation ; for if it is not admitted, we are compelled to allow, either that the New Testament writers did not understand the Old Testament Scriptures, or that, though understanding them, they wilfully misinterpreted them. We must charge them with such a want, either of information or integrity, as would equally, if established, destroy their claim to inspiration.

This principle carries us farther than, at first view, may appear. These quoted passages are to be viewed in their connection, and in this way they become the key to the whole psalm in which they occur. If the speaker in a psalm, or if the subject of a psalm, is obviously the same from the beginning to the end, and if a portion of such a psalm is, in the New Testament, expressly referred to the Messiah, the whole is to be considered as applicable to him. Nor is this all. Many of the Psalms plainly refer to the same subject, and are composed on a common plan ; so that when you satisfactorily establish that one of such a class of psalms is Messianic, you cannot reasonably doubt of the reference of those which obviously stand in the same class.

The second principle referred to may be thus stated : 'That when, in the Psalms, we meet with descriptions of a perfection of character and conduct—a depth and complication of suffering —a suddenness and completeness of deliverance—a height of dignity, and an extent of dominion, to which we can find no adequate correspondence in David, or in any of the great and good men commemorated in the Jewish history,—we are war- ranted to hold that they refer to the Messiah.' This principle rests on the statement made by our Lord, " that in the Psalms it is written of him "'[1]—a statement which obviously means much more than that there are a few detached references to him there— which, indeed, cannot reasonably be understood to mean less than that *he* is one of the principal subjects of those inspired poems. This certainly not only warrants, but requires us, when we meet with passages which cannot, without extreme violence, if at all, be made to comport with facts in reference to David, or any other individual, but which admit of an easy interpretation if

[1] Luke xxiv. 43.

viewed as referring to the Messiah, to consider them as intended predictions of "Him who was to come." In this respect it has been said, with a pardonable accommodation of scripture phraseology, that "Christ has 'the key of David;' for, without reference to him, much of what David says would be unintelligible—a locked-up treasure."

These are the principles on which psalms or portions of them, must be determined to belong, or not to belong, to "the testimony of Jesus" yielded by "the Spirit of prophecy," speaking by the holy psalmists. Let us endeavor to apply them to the psalm before us. For reasons obvious to every considerate mind, it will be found advantageous to reverse the order in which we have stated these principles of interpretation, in our application of them in the inquiry we are about to institute.

The extreme difficulty of finding anything that even approximates to a satisfactory correspondence between many of the statements in this psalm, and the incidents of David's life, making the most liberal allowances for the peculiar characteristics of oriental poetry, has been found by all, and acknowledged by the best, expositors.

Look, first, at the character of the subject of the psalm, as sketched from the 20th to the 26th verse. Could David have said, what is there said of the speaker, of himself? or could any one else have truly said it of him? Does it not describe a perfection of character and conduct, which was never found but in him who was "holy, harmless, undefiled, and separate from sinners"?

Then look at the variety and depth of his sufferings, as these are described in the 4th and 5th verses. David was exposed to numerous and severe sufferings; but when did "the sorrows of death" compass him but on his death-bed? when did "the cords of Sheol"—the separate state—bind him, but when he actually died? The plain meaning of these expressions—and all expressions are to be understood in their plain meaning, unless there be a good reason why they should be understood otherwise —is, that the person who speaks had died and gone into the state of the dead previously to his deliverance and exaltation. This is not true of David, but it is true of David's Son.

Look, next, at the account of the deliverance, as described from the 6th to the 9th verse. David was often wonderfully delivered; but when did anything occur to him that, even in the exaggerated language of eastern poetry, could be truly described in such lofty strains as these? A feeling like shame comes over us when we find learned men seeking, and thinking that they had found, in a thunderstorm, which they suppose may have taken place when Saul sent men to David's house to kill him, and which may have facilitated his escape out of their hands, the event described here, in language not inferior in grandeur to that in which the solemnities of Sinai are represented.[1] Whether the words are to be understood literally or figuratively, they are no exaggerated account of the Divine deliverance of the Messiah from all his enemies.

Look, again, at the account of the successful warfare of the subject of the psalm, from the 25th to the 42d verse. Could David, who wrote the beautiful lamentation on the death of Saul, speak of his triumph over *him* in such language? and is the description of entire discomfiture of all enemies, in these verses, nothing more than a victory over the neighboring Philistine, Edomitish, Moabitish, and Ammonitish tribes?

Finally, when was David made "the head of the heathen"? when did he, among them, give thanks to Jehovah, and sing praises to His name? Besides, there is obviously a striking similarity in plan between this psalm and psalm xl., which is undoubtedly Messianic, and psalm cxvi., which probably is so. On this ground, then, that there is much in the psalm that cannot be applied to David—that there is nothing in it but what can be applied to Christ—conjoined with the admitted facts that Christ is a leading subject of the Psalms, and that there is a general resemblance in it to psalms undoubtedly referring to the Messiah, we should consider ourselves as warranted to consider this as a Messianic psalm.

But if we apply the other principle announced above to the interpretation of the psalm, we will obtain much additional evidence that this is the only satisfactory view that can be taken of it. There are allusions to, and quotations from, this psalm in the New Testament, which clearly show that the apostles considered it as referring to the Messiah. The expression used by Peter in his Pentecostal address—"Whom God raised up, having loosed the

---

[1] Delany.

pains of death ; because it was not possible that he should be
holden of it"¹—is plainly an allusion to the 4th verse of the
psalm ; and, in the Epistle to the Hebrews, when proving that,
according to the ancient prophets, the Messiah was to be a real
man, the apostle seems to quote the words in the 2d verse—"In
whom I will trust." Words of similar import, indeed, occur
in the prophet Isaiah, and in the immediate neighborhood of
other words which the apostle cites ; but the use of the formula,
"again," seems rather to intimate that the two quotations were
made from separate parts of Scripture.²

Whatever there may be in this, the psalm is explicitly quoted
by the apostle Paul in the fifteenth chapter of the Epistle to the
Romans, in a way which can be satisfactorily explained only on
the supposition that the Messiah is throughout the subject of the
psalm. The passage to which I refer occupies the 8th and 9th
verses. "Jesus Christ was a minister of the circumcision for
the truth of God, to confirm the promises made unto the fathers :
and that the Gentiles might glorify God for his mercy ; as it is
written, For this cause I will confess to thee among the Gentiles,
and sing unto thy name." The passage here cited is the 49th
verse of the psalm. It is plain that the apostle's object, in quoting these words, is to show that the Gentiles, according to the
ancient prophecies, were to form a part of the Messiah's kingdom ; and therefore, if the quotation has any bearing on his
object, it must be considered as the words of the Messiah. For
certainly no human ingenuity will bring out of the words a
proof of what the apostle obviously brings them forward to
prove, if they only mean that it was David's purpose, after
being deliveren from his enemies, to maintain the worship of
Jehovah, and, in the midst of the Gentile tribes he had subdued,
proclaim His true and sole divinity. It is thus as clear as can
well be conceived, that the apostle Paul, an infallible commentator, considered the 49th verse of this psalm as the words of
the Messiah ; and if this be admitted, it follows, of course, that
he is the speaker in the whole psalm.

"The whole psalm," as one of its acutest interpreters³ remarks, "runs in one continued style of the same person from
the beginning to the end of it ; and whoever would suppose that

---

¹ Acts ii. 24.   ² Peirce.   ³ Peirce.

one part is to be understood as spoken by one person, and another part by another, will find it very difficult to assign the different parts to their supposed respective speakers ; or at least he will find it difficult to assign any convincing or even tolerably plausible reasons for his making such a distinction."[1] In this case we have no alternative, if we are to consider Paul as an infallible interpreter, but to consider this psalm, like the sixteenth and the twenty-second, and a number of other psalms, as spoken throughout in the person of the Messiah. Such is the positive evidence in behalf of the Messianic reference of this psalm.

It ought not, however, to be concealed that there are difficulties connected with this view of the subject. These are of two kinds. Some of them arise from the contents ; others from the history of the psalm.

There are particularly two passages in the psalm which, at first sight, seem irreconcilable with the Messianic reference— the 50th and the 23d verses. The first of these seems, in express terms, to refer it to David ; and the second of them seems to prove, by implication, that it cannot be referred to Christ.

In the first case, the words are, "Great deliverance giveth He to his king ; and showeth mercy to his anointed, to David, and to his seed for evermore." Here the difficulty is only an apparent one. It is no uncommon thing in the prophetic writings to term the Messiah David. Of such a use of the word, which signifies 'beloved,' the following are instances :—"Afterward," i. e., after having abode many days without a king, and without a prince, and without a sacrifice, and without an image, and without an ephod, and without teraphim—"shall the children of Israel return, and seek the Lord their God, and David their king." "It shall come to pass that Israel and Judah, when the Lord brings again their captivity, and saves them out of their trouble, shall serve the Lord their God, and David their king." "I will set up one Shepherd over them, and he shall feed them, even my servant David ; he shall feed them, and he shall be their shepherd. And I the Lord will be their God, and my servant David a prince among them : I the Lord have spoken it." "And David my servant shall be king over them ; and they all shall have one shepherd : they shall also walk in my

---

[1] VAN TIL, a pedantic and injudicious interpreter, has attempted this, but the result has been a complete failure.

judgments, and observe my statutes, and do them. And they shall dwell in the land that I have given unto Jacob my servant, wherein your fathers have dwelt; and they shall dwell therein; even they, and their children, and their children's children, for ever; and my servant David shall be their prince for ever."[1] The prophets now cited all lived long after the death of David, and two of them after the final overthrow of the Jewish kingdom; and there can be no reasonable doubt that, in these oracles, *David* is an appellation of the Messiah. It seems also very probable that the words in psalm lxxxix. 20, 35, "I have found David my servant; with my holy oil I have anointed him. Once have I sworn by my holiness, that I will not lie unto David;" and in Isaiah lv. 3, "I will make an everlasting covenant with you, even the sure mercies of David,"—refer not to the literal but to the mystical David. These passages clearly show that the use of the name David has no force as an objection against the Messianic reference of the psalm.

The difficulty, originating in the second passage referred to, is of a more serious kind. It seems, at first view, to say, 'To whomsoever this oracle may refer, it cannot refer to him who is "the holy One of God."' The passage in question is the 23d verse: "I was also upright before Thee, and *I kept myself from mine iniquity.*" It may be asked, Was he not "without sin"? Was not that which was born of the virgin "a holy thing"? and did he not live and die "holy, harmless, undefiled"? "He knew no sin." What sin, then, could be called *his?* This seems an insurmountable difficulty. Let us examine it a little.

It deserves notice, that there are at least as startling statements in psalms which are undoubtedly Messianic. For example, in the fortieth psalm, He who says, "Lo, I come: in the volume of the book it is written of Me, I delight to do thy will, O my God; yea thy law is within my heart;" and who by the apostle in the tenth chapter of the Epistle to the Hebrews, is identified with Jesus Christ, says also (v. 12), "innumerable evils have compassed me about; mine iniquities have taken hold upon me, so that I am not able to look up: they are more than the hairs of mine head; therefore my heart faileth me;" and in the forty-first psalm, "He whose familiar friend, to whom he had

---

[1] Hosea iii. 5. Jer. xxx. 9. Ezek. xxxiv. 23, 24; xxxvii. 24, 25.

committed a trust, who ate of his bread, lifted up his heel against him," whom our Lord in the thirteenth chapter of the gospel of John identifies with himself, says (v. 4), "Lord be merciful to me; heal my soul, for I have sinned;" I am guilty " before Thee." This is not the same difficulty as that before us, but it is assuredly an equally great one. Yet it is removed by the undoubtedly true principle—the principle which, above all others, gives Christianity its peculiar character—" He who knew no sin, was made sin;" " On his righteous servant, Jehovah made to fall the iniquities of us all." In this sense, " innumerable iniquities compassed him " —the iniquities made to fall on him—made "his" as to their liabilities—by Divine appointment laid hold of him. In the sense of *culpa*—blame-worthiness—he had no sin. In the sense of *reatus*—liability to the penal effects of sin—never had any one so much sin to bear as he—" He bare the sins of many."

The difficulty before us is not the same as in the cases we have alluded to; but let us see if it may not be just as satisfactorily disposed of. If it refer to Jesus Christ, it cannot mean, 'I preserved myself from my sin'—in the sense of, 'the sin to which I was peculiarly prone;' for in his nature there was no tendency to any sin— there was the strongest possible repugnance to every sin. But it has been supposed by some learned men,[1] that the word *sin* here is equivalent to calamity, and that the meaning is, 'I was upright before Him, therefore I was kept from my trouble;' and it has been supposed that the words are parallel with, "He was heard" —delivered—"in that he feared,"[2] *i.e.*, because of his piety. We not only consider this as a misinterpretation of the passage in the Epistle to the Hebrews, but we hold that the word rendered "iniquity"[3] never signifies calamity but as the punishment of sin, and our Lord did not keep himself from this—he most willingly submitted to it; he "stedfastly set his face to go up to Jerusalem;" he "set his face as a flint;" he "gave his back to the smiters, and his cheeks to them who plucked off the hair; he hid not his face from shame and spitting." It is a more probable account of the matter, that the expression, "my iniquity," refers to the sin to which the Messiah was specially tempted; and that was, to use worldly means to accomplish his object—to employ his miraculous powers in raising himself to worldly distinction—the sin to

[1] Peirce.   [2] Heb. v. 7.   [3] עון.

which the great tempter urged him in various forms. From this
he kept himself; and when his favorite disciple, Peter, became
his tempter to it, he showed how he kept himself from it by bid-
ding him get behind Him as an adversary and a stumbling-block.
But what seems to me the true resolution of the difficulty, is
that given by a learned interpreter,[1] who, however, applies the
passage to David. He renders the words,—" I kept myself, that
sin might not be mine;" in which case it is nearly equivalent
to our Lord's question to his Jewish enemies,—" Which of you
convinceth me of sin?" When his faults were sought for, they
could not be found. "I find," said the judge who condemned
him, "I find no fault in him."

Having thus, as we trust, satisfactorily disposed of the objections to the Messianic reference of this psalm from its contents;
let us shortly consider the objection which originates in its history. We have an abstract of its history in its title, which is
the most minute and circumstantial of all the titles of the
Psalms.—"A psalm of David, the servant of the Lord, who
spake unto the Lord the words of this song in the day that the
Lord delivered him from the hand of all his enemies, and from
the hand of Saul." Learned men are by no means of one mind
as to the antiquity and authority of the titles of the Psalms,[2]
some of which are exceedingly difficult of interpretation; but
although their claim to inspiration were more doubtful than it
is, though it were even satisfactorily disproved, that could be of
no use in relieving us from the objection; for we have the same
piece of history in very nearly the same words in a sacred book,
the inspiration of which is undoubted. In the beginning of the
twenty-second chapter of the Second Book of Samuel, we have
these words, "And David spake unto the Lord the words of this
song, in the day that the Lord had delivered him out of the
hand of all his enemies, and out of the hand of Saul," followed by
what is substantially the same poem we have here. The dif-
ferences are just such as might be expected in a hymn originally
composed for private use, when fitted for the public services of
the temple, and put into the hand of the chief musician. The title
as it stands in the book of Psalms has been thus translated by

---

[1] Geier. De Wette takes the same view of the phrase.
[2] There is an excellent article "On the Titles of the Psalms," in Dr. Kitto's "Daily
Bible Illustrations," Evening Series, vol. i. p. 313.

Peirce and Bishop Horsley,—"To the Giver of Victory. A psalm of the servant of Jehovah the beloved,[1] who spake unto Jehovah the words of this song, in the day that Jehovah delivered him from the hand of all his enemies, and from the power of Sheol," *i.e.*, the separate state. This is a correct enough translation of the original text, with merely the change of the points in the word rendered "Saul" in our version. Such a rendering would exactly suit the following hymn as referring to the Messiah. But the corresponding passage in the Second Book of Samuel convinces us that the words before us are rightly rendered by our translators, and that they state the author and date of the poem, that David was the writer of the psalm, and that it was composed when he had been delivered from all his enemies.

But the fixing of the writer and the date of the poem does not necessarily determine its subject. Circumstances in David's life seem often to have been the occasion of the utterance of Messianic oracles. The truth seems to be, David, full of pious gratitude to Jehovah for his goodness in his deliverance from his enemies, is visited with an impulse of the inspiring Spirit and rapt into future ages when his Son and Lord was to be delivered from deeper afflictions than his, and raised to higher honors. The true history of this psalm seems just to be that already referred to, which Peter gives of the sixteenth psalm, the title of which is "Michtam of David," and which, like this psalm, is spoken in the first person from beginning to end. "David speaketh of Jesus of Nazareth."—"Being a prophet and knowing that God had sworn with an oath to him, that of the fruit of his loins, according to the flesh, He would raise up Christ to sit on his throne ; he seeing this before, spoke thus of him, of his sufferings, and of the glory which should follow." It is a common thing for poets—and the prophets were poets—to compose poems, especially odes, as in the person of another. How many of Isaiah's oracles are spoken, not in his own person, but in that of Jehovah, or the Messiah, or the church, and that without any intimation but what is found in the nature of the oracle itself. That David expected the Messiah, and knew well enough, when he was "in the spirit," whether he was speaking of himself or of his Son, there can be no reasonable doubt ; and that he attached

[1] The Messiah is, by way of emphasis, "the Servant,"—"the beloved Servant of the Lord."—Isa. xlii. 1 ; lii. 13, etc.

general ideas to the words to which he was led to give utterance, seems equally plain, though the precise nature of the
events predicted, their concomitant circumstances, and the period when they were to take place, were but dimly, if at all, discerned by him. When uttering such an oracle as that before us,
or the sixteenth, the twenty-second, the fortieth, the forty-fifth,
the seventy-second, and the hundred-and-tenth psalm, to him,
"searching what and what manner of time the Spirit of Christ
which was in him did signify, testifying beforehand the sufferings of Christ and the glory that should follow," "it was," no
doubt, "revealed, that not unto himself" and his contemporaries,
"but to those in a future age," did he "minister the things
which have been reported to us by them who preached the Gospel with the Holy Ghost sent down from heaven."[1]

This view of the subject of this psalm is not the common one,
but in adopting it, we follow in the steps of ancient and illustrious
interpreters. The ancient Chaldee paraphrast refers the psalm to
the Messiah. On the 32d verse he says, "Because of the miracle
and redemption which Thou shalt show to thy Messiah and to the
relics of thy people, all the people, nations, and languages shall
give praises to Thee;" and on the 49th verse he says, "Thou shalt
rescue me from Gog," the great opposer of the Messiah, according
to the Jews. The title given to the psalm in the ancient Syriac
version is, "Of the ascension of Christ." Augustine and Jerome,
the one the most profound, the other the most learned, of the
Latin fathers, held this view; and so did Luther, and Bugen-
hagen, and Brentz,[2] among the reformers; and Cocceius and
Van Til of a succeeding age. In our own country, Ainsworth,
who holds a very high rank among interpreters, says, "of
Christ and of his kingdom, this psalm is chiefly intended."
James Peirce of Exeter has defended this view with great acute-
ness in a separate dissertation.[3] Bishop Horne says, "The sub-

---

[1] 1 Pet. i. 11, 12.

[2] "De Christo uno literaliter et proxime hic psalmus intelligendus est."—BRENTIUS.

[3] "I desire the reader to observe what I take to be the nature and design of this
psalm in general; and that is, that it is our Saviour's hymn or song of praise to God
—(1) for raising him from the dead; and (2) for making him victorious over his
enemies, and particularly over the Jews, in whose destruction he took vengeance on
them for what they had done against him; and (3) for giving him a people among
the Gentiles. To these three heads, the several things said in the psalm may be
easily reduced. I am persuaded that an entire comment upon the song, according
to this account of it, might be to good service; but that would soon swell to a

limity of the figures used in this psalm, and the consent of
ancient commentators, even Jewish as well as Christian, but
above all, the citations made from it in the New Testament,
evince that the kingdom of the Messiah is pointed at. The
psalm, it is apprehended, should now be considered as a glorious
epinikion or triumphal hymn to be sung by the church risen and
victorious in Christ their head." Bishop Horsley takes the same
view; and so does a man of much sounder judgment, the late
Dr. John Erskine of this city.[1] Indeed, so impracticable is it to
apply many things in the psalm to any one else than Christ, that,
besides those with whom we go along, who consider it as directly
and solely referring to him, not a few who hold that it is primarily
spoken by David in his own person, consider much in it as, in its
highest sense, referring to Christ. Amyraut considers the ele-
mental storm as leading the mind to the shaking of the heavens and
the earth by which the introduction of the new dispensation was
accompanied, and on the 58th verse says, "That this psalm refers
to Christ is clear from this very verse, cited by Paul to confirm
the call of the Gentiles." Crusius, though advocating what we
consider as a loose and erroneous system of interpretation, says,
"There are many sayings in this psalm so magnificent, that they
become Christ better than David."[2] And De Sacy, one of the
best of Roman Catholic expositors, says, in reference to the 43d
and 44th verses, "If these words can be explained literally of
David, they apply much more naturally to Jesus Christ, who
has been delivered from the strivings of the Jewish people;
when, after the terrible opposition he met with on their part, to
the establishment of the Gospel, he was made the head of the
Gentiles, who were a strange people, and whom he had not formerly acknowledged as his, but who nevertheless obeyed him
with astonishing readiness as soon as they heard his voice."[3]

---

treatise."—Peirce. After an interval of more than a century, the first attempt to
realize the ingenious author's idea has been made in these pages.

[1] Notes on the Eighteenth Psalm. *Religious Monitor* for 1806, vol. iv. pp. 14–19.

[2] "Multa in hoc psalmo tam magnifice dicta sunt ut loquentem Christum magis
deceant quam Davidem."—*Hypomnemata.*

[3] It is right to remark, that most of the interpreters who consider the psalm as
having a reference to the Messiah, consider that reference as merely secondary.
David, in spirit, transfers what directly concerns himself to the Messiah, and speaks
as the present type of the coming Deliverer. But how are we to know when the
transition is made?—or is the whole to be understood as referring both to the type

The general argument[1] of the psalm may be thus stated : It is a magnificent eucharistic ode. It begins with a celebration of the glorious perfections of the Divinity, whose assistance the speaker had so often experienced. He describes, or rather he delineates, his perils, the power of his enemies, his sudden deliverance from them, and the indignation and power of his divine Deliverer manifested in their overthrow. He paints these in so lively colors, that while we read we seem to see the lightning, to hear the thunders, to feel the earthquake. He afterwards describes his victories, so that we seem to be eye-witnesses of them, and take part in them. He predicts a wide-extended empire, and concludes with a lofty expression of grateful adoration of Jehovah, the author of all his deliverances and triumphs.

The style[2] is highly oratorical and poetical, sublime and full of uncommon figures of speech. It is the natural language of a person of the highest mental endowments, under a divine inspiration, deeply affected by remarkable divine benefits, and filled with the most lofty conceptions of the Divine character and dispensations.

There is a very natural reflection from the manner in which we have spent this hour, which I wish to impress on your minds. There is much more important and interesting truth contained in many passages of Scripture than there seems to be on first

---

and the antitype? There is all but a limitless liberty given here to the fancy of the interpreter. There is much force in Hengstenberg's words in reference to this system of interpretation : "Such an exposition I cannot but regard as perfectly inconceivable. How David could extend his own consciousness to that of his illustrious Descendant cannot be conceived, without confusion of the life of souls, and destruction of personal identity."

[1] "Magnificum Eucharisticon quod poeta orditur celebratione numinis, cujus auxilium et insignem opem tum sæpe fuerit expertus. Sua igitur pericula et hostium ingentem vim poetice describit aut depingit potius; moxque suam liberationem ac vehementem præpotentis Dei in hostibus evertendis iram, eo scribendi genere et iis figuris amplificat ut, pæne, adhuc inter legendum, cœlum ipsum et terram, Dei fulminantis ictibus conquassum ac prope incendio ardere videamus. Postea victorias quas de hostibus reportavit ita describit, ut qui legit illas sub oculis habere se putet. Regni quoque mirum in modum prolatos terminos prædicit. Tandem læta cum acclamatione Jovam celebrat quem peculiarem sui curam gerere agnoscit."—ROSENMULLER.

[2] "Stylus est plane oratorius et poeticus, sublimis et figuris minime vulgaribus plenus. Spirat virum divinum sensu beneficiorum Dei vividissime affectum, et in sublimes cogitationes evectum. Nihil hic vulgare, nihil humile, sed cuncta magnifica et excelsa."—VENEMA.

sight; and it requires serious consideration and earnest search to bring it out. The Scriptures are at once the plainest and the deepest of all books. They resemble those tracts of country where gold is to be found on the surface, but the richest veins are in the bowels of the earth. A man may get much good from this psalm, though he be quite in the dark as to who is the subject of it. But there can be no doubt that he who sees in it, and sees in it as exhibited by the inspiring Spirit, the person and work, the toils and triumphs, the sufferings and glories, of the incarnate Son of God, will find in it treasures of wisdom and knowledge peculiarly valuable.

Let us, then, my brethren, search this Scripture. It requires search,—it will reward search.. Let us search this Scripture: Christ is in it,—it "testifies of him." If we search *it* aright, we will find *him;* and, in finding him, we will find life—eternal life; for " he that findeth me," says the Wisdom of God, "findeth life, and shall obtain favor of the Lord." May we be enabled so to prosecute our inquiries, that this " word of Christ may dwell in us richly, in all wisdom." There is depth, as well as truth and beauty, in the remark of George, Prince of Anhalt, one of the fairest ornaments of the Reformation :—" The Scriptures are the swaddling-bands[1] of God's holy child Jesus; but we must unfold them if we would wish to see him, or make him be seen."

Thus have I finished this inquiry into the meaning and structure of this magnificent ode. The views I have been led to entertain are considerably different from those usually taken by commentators; but they are such as the evidence produced seems to me satisfactorily to support.[2]

I conclude with supplicating, in the well-chosen words of one of the greatest of the schoolmen, the guidance of the true Author of this psalm, in my attempt to explain it: " Ineffabilis Deus,

---

[1] τὰ σκάρυανα.

[2] "Judicium Dei magis timeo quam hominum. Video enim sentioque, posse commentatorem revera meliora solidiora, pulchriora, utiliora dicere, quam multi ante aut post eum commentatores, et tamen a precisa veritate divina, a decore Dei verbique divini subtilissimo, ab abysso profunditatis scripturariæ, ab ea in Scripturis facultate, quæ virilis et regalis sit et adversitatem igne excocta, longe adhuc abesse. Agnoscenda et celebranda est longanimitas qua tractat Deus homines verba suæ majestatis tractantes. Eam quisquis sacros versat libros et implorare debet in deprecanda sua imbecillitate, et imitari in ferendis proximorum judiciis, erroribus, detorsionibus."— Burkius, Præf. in Gnom. Psalm. § xviii.

vere fons luminis et sapientiæ atque supereminens principium,
da mihi intelligendi acumen, retinendi capacitatem, interpre-
tandi subtilitatem, addiscendi facultatem, loquendi gratiam co-
piosam : gressum instruas, processum dirigas, et egressum com-
pleas.   Amen."[1]

NOTE A, p. 22

DESCRIPTIVE CHARACTER OF THE PSALMS

" THE Psalms are an epitome of the Bible, adapted to purposes of devotion.   They treat occasionally of the creation and formation of the world;
the dispensations of providence and the economy of grace; the transac-
tions of the patriarchs; the exodus of the people of Israel; their journey
through the wilderness and settlement in Canaan; their law, priesthood,
and ritual; the exploits of their great men, wrought through faith; their
sins and captivities; their repentance and restorations; the sufferings and
victories of David; the peaceful and happy reign of Solomon; the advent
of the Messiah, with its effects and consequences,—his incarnation, birth,
life, passion, death, resurrection, ascension, kingdom, and priesthood;
the effusion of the Spirit; the conversion of the nations; the rejection
of the Jews; the establishment, increase, and perpetuity of the Christian church; the end of the world; the general judgment; the condemnation of the wicked, and the final triumph of the righteous, with their
Lord and King.   These are the subjects here presented to our medita-
tion.

" We are instructed how to conceive of them aright, and to express the
different affections which, when so conceived of, they must excite in our
minds.   They are, for this purpose, adorned with the figures and set off
with all the graces of poetry, that so delight may prepare the way to improvement, and pleasure become the handmaid of wisdom, while every tur-
bulent passion is calmed, and the evil spirit still dispossessed by the harp
of the son of Jesse.

" That which we read as matter of speculation in the other Scriptures, is reduced to practice when we recite the Psalms: in those,
repentance and faith are described; in these, they are acted.   By a perusal of the former, we learn how others served God; but by using

[1] Thomas Aquinas.

the latter, we serve Him ourselves. 'What is there necessary for man to know,' says the judicious Hooker, 'which the Psalms are not able to teach? They are to beginners an easy and familiar introduction—a mighty augmentation of all virtue and knowledge, to such as are entered before—a strong confirmation to the most perfect among others. Heroical magnanimity, exquisite justice, grave moderation, exact wisdom, repentance unfeigned, unwearied prudence, the mysteries of God, the sufferings of Christ, the terrors of wrath, the comforts of grace, the works of Providence over the world, and the promised joys of that world which is to come; all good necessarily either to be known, done, or had, this one celestial fountain yieldeth. Let there be any grief or disease incident unto the mind of man, any wound or sickness named, for which there is not in this treasure-house a present, comfortable remedy at all times to be found.'

" In the language of this divine book, therefore, the prayers and praises of the church have been offered up to the throne of grace from age to age. And it appears to have been the manual of the Son of God in the days of his flesh—who, at the conclusion of the last supper, is generally supposed, and that upon good grounds, to have sung a hymn taken from it—who pronounced on the cross the beginning of the twenty-second psalm, ' My God, my God, why hast Thou forsaken me ?'—and expired with a part of the thirty-first psalm in his mouth, ' Into thy hands I commend my spirit.' Thus, he who had not the Spirit by measure, in whom were hid all the treasures of wisdom and knowledge, and who spake as never man spake, yet choose to conclude his life, to solace himself in his greatest agony, and at last to breathe out his soul, in the psalmist's form of words rather than his own. ' No tongue of man or angel,' as Dr. Hammond justly observes, ' can convey a higher idea of any book, and of their felicity who use it aright.' "—-HORNE, *Pref. to Com. on Psalm*, pp. i.–iv.

" These songs of Zion express not only the most remarkable passages which have occurred in the spiritual experience of the most gifted saints, but are the record of the most wonderful dispensations of God's providence unto his church, containing pathetic dirges sung over her deepest calamities, jubilees over her mightiest deliverances, songs of sadness for her captivity, and songs of mirth for her prosperity, prophetic announcements of her increase to the end of time, and splendid anticipations of her ultimate glory. Not, indeed, the exact narrative of the events as they happened or are to happen, nor the prosaic improvement of the same to the minds of men; but the poetical form and monument of the event, where it is laid up and embalmed in honorable wise, after it has been incensed and perfumed, with the spiritual odors or the souls of inspired men.

" And if they contain not the code of the Dvine law as it is written in

the books of Moses, and more briefly, yet better, written in our Lord's
Sermon on the Mount, they celebrate the excellency and glory of the law,
its light, life, wisdom, contentment, and blessedness, with the joys of the
soul that keepeth it, and the miseries of the soul that keepeth it not. And
if they contain not the argument of the simple doctrines, and the detail of
the issues of the Gospel, to reveal which the Word of God became flesh
and dwelt among us; yet, now that the key is given and the door of spiritual life is opened, where do we find such spiritual treasures as in the book
of Psalms, wherein are revealed the depths of the soul's sinfulness, the stout-
ness of her rebellion against God, the horrors of spiritual desertion, the
agonies of contrition, the blessedness of pardon, the joys of restoration, the
constancy of faith, and every other variety of Christian experience? And
if they contain not the narrative of Messiah's birth, and life, and death,
or the labors of his apostolic servants, and the strugglings of his infant
church as these are written in the books of the New Testament; where, in
the whole Scriptures, can we find such declarations of the work of Christ,
in its humiliation and its glory, the spiritual agonies of his death, and glorious issues of his resurrection, the wrestling of his kingdom with the powers
of darkness, its triumph over the heathen, and the overthrow of all its
enemies, until the heads of many lands shall have been wounded, and the
people made wllling in the day of his power?

   " And where are there such outbursting representations of all the attributes of Jehovah, before whom, when He rideth through the heavens, the
very heavens seem to rend in twain, to give the vision of his going forth,
and we seem to see the haste of the universe to do her homage, and to hear
the quaking of nature's pillars, the shaking of her foundations, and the horrible outcry of her terror? And oh, how sweet it is, in the midst of these
soarings into the third heaven of vision, to feel that you are borne upon the
words of a man, not upon the wings of an archangel—to hear, ever and
anon, the frail but faithful voice of humanity making her trust under the
shadow of his wings, and her hiding-place in the secret of his tent, and say·
ing to Him in faithful strains, ' For, as the heaven is high above the earth,
so great is his mercy to them that fear Him. As far as the east is from
the west, so far has He removed our transgresions from us. Like as a
father pitieth his children, so the Lord pitieth them that fear Him.' So
that, as well by reason of the matter which it contains, as of the form in
which it is expressed, the book of Psalms, take it all in all, may be safely
pronounced one of the divinest books of all the Scriptures—which hath exercised the hearts and lips of all saints, and become dear in the sight of the
church—which is replenished with the types of all possible spiritual feelings,
and suggests the forms of all God-ward emotions, and furnishes the choice
expressions of all true worship, the utterances of all Divine praise, the

confession of all spiritual humility, with the raptures of all spiritual joy."—IRVING.

"The Psalms, as to their *form*, include all varieties of lyric composition. They are of every character as to the nature of their subjects, and of all shades and colors of poetic feeling; but as to their *essence*, they are as a light from heaven, or an oracle from the sanctuary : they discover secrets, divine and human ; they lay open the holy of holies of both God and man, for they reveal the hidden things belonging to both, as the life of the one is developed in the other.   The Psalms are the depositories of the mysteries, the records of the struggles, the wailings when worsted, the pæans when triumphant, of that life.   They are the thousand-voiced heart of the church, uttering from within, from the secret depths and chambers of her being, her spiritual consciousness,—all that she remembers, experiences, believes— suffers from sin and flesh—fears from earth or hell—achieves by heavenly succor—and hopes from God and his Christ.   They are for all time.   They never can be outgrown.   No dispensation, while the world stands, and con- tinues what it is, can ever raise us above the reach or the need of them. They describe every spiritual vicissitude ; they speak to all classes of minds ; they command every natural emotion.   They are penitential, jubi- lant, adorative, deprecatory ; they are tender, mournful, joyous, majestic ; soft as the descent of dew ; low as the whispers of love ; loud as the voice of thunder ; terrible as the almightiness of God.

"There was often, we believe, a natural harmony between the personal qualities of individuals, and the work to which they were called of God. It was thus with Paul ; it was thus with David.   His comely person and "fair countenance" indicated the harmoniously-constituted dwelling-place of a soul endowed with clearness and melody, and fitted to become the favored channel of heavenly thought.   The shepherd boy was bold and brave, manly and magnanimous, and had in him, from the first, the slumbering elements of a hero and a king.   His harp was the companion of his early prime.   Its first inspirations were caught from the music of brooks and groves, as he lay on the verdant and breathing earth, was smiled on through the day by the bright sky, or watched at night by the glowing stars. Even then, probably, he had mysterious minglings of the Divine Spirit with the impulses of his own ; was conscious of cogitations with which none could intermeddle, which would make him at times solitary among num- bers, and which were the prelude and prophecy of his future greatness.   He became a soldier before he was twenty.   Ten years afterwards he was king by the suffrages of his own tribe.   During most of the interval, his life was of a nature seriously to peril his habits and principles.   He was obliged to use rude, lawless, and uncongenial agents.   He had to live precariously by gifts or spoil. 'He was hunted like a partridge on the mountains.' By day providing for sustenance or safety, and sleeping by night in cave or rock, field or forest. And yet this man—in the heat of youth, with a brigand's reputation and a soldier's license—watched carefully his inner-self; learned from it as a pupil, and yet ruled it as a king; and found for it congenial employment in the composition of some of the most striking of his psalms. When his companions in arms were carousing or asleep, he sat by his lamp in some still retreat, or 'considered the heavens,' as they spread above him, or meditated on the law, or engaged in prayer, or held intimate communion with God, and composed and wrote (though he thought not so) what shall sound in the church, and echo through the world, to all time! There is nothing more wonderful, in either sacred or profane litera-ture, than the combination of the circumstances and employment of David from his twenty-fifth to his thirtieth year. Even beyond that, his life was not tranquil. It is sad to think that his years of calm enjoyment were few, and that the cup of life, after being filled for him by God to overflowing, and made pure and sweet by previous suffering and self-restraint, should have been recklessly poisoned by his own hand. Till near forty he had to struggle hard for secular success. Even as a king, *twice* crowned, he had some about him that troubled his repose. But his worst enemy at length was himself. A short period of regal security bred indolence, luxury, and lust. At forty-eight he tarnished the virtue of as many years, and, in one day, sowed the seeds of a rank harvest of blood and bitterness for his after-life. Certain of God's great gifts—such, especially, as distinguished David—are often associated with such accessories as expose to more than ordinary peril. Inspiration itself, when it chose Genius as the channel of its song, did not alter the terms on which it had been conferred. Nothing can be an excuse or apology for sin; yet, by God's mercy, it may be turned to account, and made to produce the opposite to itself. To some men's errors the world has been indebted for their richest lessons and ripest fruit. Worsted in battle, their wounds and bruises have festered and mortified, till, spreading into the flesh, *it* has become, to their better nature, as soil to seed. In the constitution of things, a quick sensibility to physical impress-ions is often associated with a moral idealism, and with a living conscience of infinite memory and ceaseless voice; and when such persons are 'alive unto God,'—have 'tasted of his grace,' and yet 'tarnished their garments,' —their burning shame, bitter tears, prostrate humiliation, settled sorrow and slow hope, render them often the most memorable instructors. Natural impulses and spiritual neglect were associated in the sin, natural qualities and spiritual aids combined in the grief and re-conversion, of the psalmist. To the lamentable lapse, the penitence and the punishment of David, we owe some of the most subduing, the most spiritually instructive and consolatory of his psalms—psalms that have taught Despair to trust, and have turned the heart of flint to a fountain of tears !

"It is impossible to refer, however, to his compositions· themselves ; it must suffice to remark his own personal and enthusiastic delight in psalmody. He felt ' praise' to be ' comely and pleasant.' His ' psaltery and harp' were his ' glory' and delight. *Every day* he praised God. ' He showed forth his loving-kindness in the *morning*, and his faithfulness *every night.*' *During* the night he would 'rise and give thanks ;' *in* the night ' God's song was with him.' ' When old and gray headed' his harp and psaltery were still his joy—sources of pleasure and instruments of usefulness.[1] His ' last words' were prompted by the Spirit of prophetic song. He was then permitted to lay claim to the highest inspiration, and to assume to himself the title by which he has been celebrated.[2] At length, he fell asleep. Harp and lute, psaltery and psalm, were heard no more. ' The prayers of David, the son of Jesse, were ended.' But he commenced with their close, and will continue forever, 'the service of song' in the upper world."— BINNEY.

[1] Psal. lxxi.　　　　　　　　[2] 2 Sam. xxiii. 1, 2.

LECTURE II

PROEM OF THE PSALM

Psalm xviii. 1–3.—" I will love Thee, O Lord, my strength. The Lord is my rock, and my fortress, and my deliverer; my God, my strength, in whom I will trust; my buckler, and the horn of my salvation, and my high tower. I will call upon the Lord, who is worthy to be praised: so shall I be saved from mine enemies."

In interpreting scripture prophecy, it is of primary importance that we form a just judgment respecting the subject of each particular prediction. Without this, we are likely to wander in an endless maze of perplexities and errors. The question of the Ethiopian eunuch to the Christian evangelist must often be proposed by the interpreter of the inspired oracles—" Of whom speaketh the prophet this? of himself, or of some other man?" This question has been proposed and answered at considerable length, in reference to that sublime prediction which lies before us; and it has been made, we trust, satisfactorily evident, that the subject of this oracle is HE to whom " Moses and all the prophets from Samuel, and those that follow after," bear testimony. It is my design, therefore, in the illustration which I am about to lay before you of its various parts, " to preach unto you Jesus" —the grand theme of the gospel ministry—"the only name given under heaven among men, whereby we must be saved."

Next to correct views with regard to the subject of a prediction, a clear apprehension of the structure of the prophetic discourse is of greatest importance to the right understanding and the satisfactory interpretation of the Divine oracles. Sometimes the prediction is made in a simple form. The prophet, in his own person, declares future events—narrates what is to come as the historian narrates what is past. At other times, future events are predicted by an account of a vision presented by the inspiring spirit to the prophet's mind, or by a series of emblema-

tical actions on the part of the prophet, performed in obedience
to Divine appointment. Not unfrequently, particularly in the
Psalms, predictions are given under the form of dialogues
between persons sustaining particular characters.

The prophetic discourse before us differs from all these classes.
It is a hymn of victory[1]—spoken not in the person of the prophet
himself, David, but in the person of his illustrious Son and Lord,
Messiah the Prince—referring to events all of them in a distant
futurity when the psalm was composed, but spoken of as some of
them past, some of them present, and some of them future at
the period when this song was to be sung " in the midst of the
congregation," in the temple above.

To understand the hymn, then, it is obviously very desirable
to fix the period when the Messiah was placed in the circumstances in which this psalm represents him. If this can be done,
we obtain an elevated and fixed station, from which we can, with
greater ease and certainty, look both backwards and forwards,
to the past and to the future, and perceive what are the particular events in the history of the Messiah and of his kingdom,
to which the various parts of the prophetic hymn refer.

Nor does it seem difficult, on satisfactory grounds, to arrive at
a general conclusion on this subject. The psalm itself furnishes
us with materials which, if rightly applied, will give us all the
information we need, to ascertain where the Messiah is, and in
what circumstances he is placed, when he utters this sublime
hymn of thanksgiving and triumph to Jehovah. The Messiah is
" in a large place"—delivered from all his sufferings—rewarded
for his righteousness, avenged of his enemies—the head of the
heathen, and going forth conquering and to conquer the Gentile
nations. The Father has placed him at his right hand. All
power in heaven and in earth has been conferred on him. His
cause has obtained a triumph, but has greater triumphs yet before it. He is reigning, " expecting" that all his enemies shall
be made his footstool. The psalm is the expression of the mind
and heart of the glorified God-man at the right hand of the
Majesty in the heavens, when, by divine power, himself and his
cause had been made triumphant over their numerous and
powerful enemies. Not only are the resurrection and the ascen-

[1] ἐπ νίκιον.

sion past, but by the spirit of his grace many of his enemies
have been converted into friends, and by the power of his providence multitudes of his irreclaimable enemies have received
condign punishment. His churches are numbered by thousands,
his people by myriads. Jerusalem, the bloody city, is a desolation; and Rome, no longer pagan, adores the crucified. He
is setting judgment on the earth, and the isles are waiting for
his law. The beloved Servant of the Lord is delivered out of
the hands of all his enemies. These seem to be the circumstances
in which we are to consider the Messiah as singing this new song
to Jehovah,—rehearsing, in the language of heaven, the depth
of his debasement, the severity of his sufferings, the completeness of his deliverance, the height of his exaltation, the rapidity
of his conquests, and the extent of his dominions.

Keeping these remarks in view, we proceed to the illustration
of the various parts of the psalm. It seems naturally to resolve
itself into six parts,—First, the preface or proem of the song,
verses 1–3; Second, an account of the deep distress of the
speaker, verses 4, 5; Third, a description of a miraculous deliverance, verses 4–19; Fourth, a solemn thanksgiving, verses
20–31; Fifth, an account of successful warfare, verses 32–42;
and, Finally, an account of the extent and permanence of
Messiah's kingdom, verses 43-50.

Let us, then, turn our attention to the introduction to the
poem. "I will love thee, O Lord, my strength. The Lord is my
rock, and my fortress, and my deliverer; my God, my strength,
in whom I will trust; my buckler, and the horn of my salvation, and my high tower. I will call upon the Lord, who is
worthy to be praised: so shall I be saved from mine enemies."

The whole of this psalm is spoken by the Son of God as the
Father's servant in the great work of human redemption. That
man has read the Bible either with little attention, or under the
blinding and misleading influence of very powerful prejudice,
who has not seen in it the doctrine of the true deity of Jesus
Christ. This doctrine is written as in characters of light in both
volumes of the book of God. The Messiah of the Old Testament
is "the mighty God," "Jehovah our righteousness," "Immanuel,
God with us." Jesus of the New Testament is "God"—"the
great God"—"the first and the last and the living One"—"God
over all, blessed forever." But it is equally plain, that Messiah

of the Old Testament and Jesus of the New, is represented as possessed of a created nature, an official character, a subordinate station; as sent by the Father to accomplish a great work attended with much labor and suffering; as receiving from the Father his commission and qualifications; as conforming himself to the Father's will; as sustained by the Father amid his labors, and delivered by Him from all his sufferings; as rewarded by Him for his fidelity; as thanking Him for that state of dignity and blessedness to which He has raised him; and as employing all the power with which he has been invested—power supreme in reference to creatures, but still power subordinate in reference to essential Deity—in doing the Father's will and promoting His glory. Even when, as the reward of having glorified God on the earth, he is "glorified by God in himself with the glory he had with Him before the foundation of the world," having "power over all flesh," he still glorifies the Father by bestowing on all whom He has given him, that eternal life which consists in the knowledge of "the only true God, and of Jesus Christ whom He has sent." [1] The only satisfactory way of reconciling these apparently inconsistent representations, is to be found in that double view of the Saviour's person and character which we so often meet with in Scripture, and which is so fully and clearly exhibited in the words of the apostle to the Philippian Christians. He who was "in the form of God, did not think it robbery to be equal with God "—did not treat the equality with God which he possessed in the form of God as if it were a prey, but "made himself of no reputation "—emptied himself—" took upon him the form of a servant, and was made in the likeness of men: and being found in fashion as a man, he humbled himself, and became obedient unto death, even the death of the cross. Where-fore God also hath highly exalted him, and given him a name which is above every name: that at the name of Jesus every knee should bow, of things in heaven and things in earth, and things under the earth; and that every tongue should confess that Jesus Christ is Lord, to the glory of God the Father." [2] He who is essentially equal with his Father became officially inferior to Him, and this official inferiority is not confined to that state of humiliation which was necessary to gain the objects of

[1] John, xvii. 1–4.   [2] Phil. ii. 6–11.

his assumption of an official character, but continues in that state of exaltation to which, in his assumed inferior nature and office, he has been raised. When all things were put under him, He, as a matter of course, was excepted who put all things under him; and even in his state of exaltation, "the Son is subject to the Father."[1] The principle which pervades the whole mediatorial economy is, "the Father is greater than the Son"—"God is all in all."

It is, then, in his official character—in his exalted state—that we are to consider the Messiah as speaking, when he is introduced as singing this song to Jehovah. The object of the Messiah's adoration, the subject of his song, is JEHOVAH: the Being—the independent, eternal, infinite, immutable Centre and Source of existence, and power, and holiness, and felicity, who was and is, and will be all in all,—"of whom, through whom, to whom are all things; the only living and true God."[2] He acknowledges *Him* as the source of all his blessings. He owns *Him* as his "strength," his "rock," his "fortress," his "deliverer," his "God," the "object of his confidence," his "buckler," the "horn of his salvation," and his "high tower." Let us inquire into the meaning of these varied representations of the relations and corresponding feelings of the exalted Messiah to JEHOVAH, *i. e.*, to the Father sustaining the honors of essential Deity.

He acknowledges Him as his "strength," *i. e.*, the author of his strength; He who had "made him strong," and would preserve him strong "for himself," for doing his will, for promoting his glory. The expression intimates equally a consciousness of strength, and a conviction that this strength comes from Jehovah. It is explained in psalm cxlii., "my strength, which teacheth my hands to war and my fingers to fight;" — "I am strong, strong *in* Thee." It is a common idiom in the Hebrew language to give to God, as an epithet, the name of the blessings He bestows; for example, "The Lord is my light and my salvation; whom shall I fear? the Lord is the strength of my life; of whom shall I be afraid?"[3]

Then he calls Him his "rock."[4] The reference here is to the

---

[1] 1 Cor. xv. 27, 28.

[2] "Whenever we sing this psalm, let us think we are singing it in conjunction with our Saviour, newly risen from the dead."—HORNE.

[3] Psal. xxvii. 1.   [4] מָלְעִי.

rocky eminences surrounded by precipices, accessible only by
one difficult path, with which Palestine abounds, affording a
safe retreat from enemies however numerous and powerful.
This appellation is equal to, 'The author of my security.' 'He
who has protected me, does protect me, will protect me, from
all my enemies.' This was a figurative representation very
likely to occur to the mind of one who had occasion to resort to
such strongholds.

Then he calls Him his "fortress."[1] We find this word used
along with that in the former clause in the book of Isaiah, where
the dwelling of the just is said to be "the munition," the fortress of the "rocks." It seems to bear the same relation to
"rock" as "citadel" does to the walled and fortified city. 'He
who gives me the completest security, such security that I cannot
even dream of danger.'

Then he calls Him his "deliverer;"[2] literally, 'He who enables me to go forth.' One of the best of the Jewish interpreters[3] thus explains this term: "He who betook himself to
one of these inaccessible retreats, was sometimes obliged by
famine to surrender to his enemy, who lay in wait for him beneath; but Jehovah gives him not only security but liberty;
not only preserves him, as it were, in an inaccessible retreat,
but at the same time enables him to go forth in safety."

Then he calls Him his "God"—the object of his worship—
Jesus, the God-man mediator, worships the Father. He is the
God as well as the Father of our Lord Jesus Christ. "I ascend
to my Father and your Father; to my God and your God."[4]
We find him often worshipping the Father on earth, "in the
days of his flesh;" and in this psalm, and in other psalms, we
find him represented as worshipping Him in heaven in the days
of his glory. "My God," is equivalent to, 'He who acts the
part of a God to me, who performeth all things for me; He
whom I regard and treat as my God,—regarding Him with supreme love, veneration, and confidence, and yielding to Him
unreserved obedience and most cheerful submission.' What an
emphasis in that word uttered on the cross—uttered before the
throne—"*my God!*" The attribute of power which the radical

---

[1] מצודתי. This word is used along with the preceding one, Isa. xxxiii. 16, and
bears the same relation to it that "citadel" does to "fortress."

[2] מפלטי.   [3] Jarchi.   [4] John, xx.

word expresses, seems to have been especially before the mind
—‘infinite power, infinite power to save, infinite power to save
me.’ This word does not occur in the edition of the psalm in
second book of Samuel. The previous word there, however, is
given with peculiar emphasis.[1] “My own deliverer.” ‘He
who never delivered any as He has delivered me.’

He then calls Him his “strength.”[2] This is a different word
from that used in the first verse, and literally signifies, “my
rock;” but it is also a different word from that which in the beginning of this verse is rendered “rock.” It is the word used
when Moses says, “ their rock is not as our rock ;” and in this
psalm, at verse 31, “who is a rock save our God?” and is rendered, Isaiah, xxx. 29, “the mighty One.” “My strength,” is
an expression of faith in the Divine power, and of confidence
that that power will be exercised on his behalf.

The words that follow, “in whom I will trust”—words, as I
showed in last lecture, which are probably quoted by the apostle,
Hebrews, ii. 13—may be more literally and more naturally and
impressively rendered simply, ‘I will trust in Him .’[3]—‘my rock,
I will trust in Him ;’ equivalent to, ‘ I have trusted, I do trust, I
will trust, in Him. In whom should I trust but in my Rock?’
“The Lord is upright, He is my rock, and there is no unrighteousness in Him.”

Then he calls Him his “ buckler” or “shield.”[4] It is still the
idea of protection. ‘His power, wisdom, and grace secure my
safety amid all dangers.’ It is the same thought as, “He will
cover thee with his feathers, and under his wings shalt thou
trust: His truth shall be thy shield and buckler.”

He then calls Him “the horn of his salvation.” The allusion
here is doubtful. Some have supposed the reference to be to the
horns of animals by which they defend themselves and attack
their enemies.[5] ‘God is to me—does for me—what their horns

---

[1] Amos ii. 13. Psal. cxliv. 2.

[2] צוּרִי,—literally, ‘ my rock,’ ‘my defence,’ ‘ my defender.’—Deut. xxxii. 30: 1 Sam.
ii. 2; verse 31 *infra;* Isa. xxx. 29.

[3] There is no need to suppose an ellipsis of the pronoun. It is more the language
of nature, “My God, I will trust in Him,” than—“ My God, in whom I will trust.”

[4] The LXX. render this term very accurately, so far as the signification is concerned—ὑπερασπιστής μου,—‘ He who by stretching out a shield protects me.’

[5] “Τὸ δὲ κέρας σωτηρίας τέθεικεν ἐκ μεταφορᾶς τῶν ζώων, τών τοῖς κέρασι τοὺς πολε-
μίους ἀμυνομένων.”—THEODORET.

do for them.' Others consider it as referring to the well-established fact, that warriors were accustomed to place horns, or
ornaments like horns, on their helmets.[1] The horn stands for
the helmet; and "the helmet of salvation" is an expression
equivalent to, 'a saving, a protecting helmet.' Others consider
the reference as to the corners or handles of the altar in the court
of the tabernacle or temple, which are called its horns.[2] Others
suppose the reference to be to the highest point of a lofty and
precipitous mountain,[3] which we are accustomed to call its peak.
No doubt, in the Hebrew language, horn is used for mountain,
as in Isaiah, chap. v. 1. A very fertile mountain is called a
horn of oil. The sense is substantially the same, whichever of
these views we take of the reference of the words; though, from
the connection with "shield" or "buckler," I am induced to
consider the second of these views as the most probable. It
seems the same idea as that expressed, psalm cxl. 7, "Thou hast
covered," and Thou wilt cover, "my head in the day of battle."

Finally, he calls Him his "high tower."[4] The word connected
with it, in 2 Samuel, "my refuge," brings out the meaning.
These passages are parallel. "Thou hast been a shelter for me,
and a strong tower from the enemy. Be Thou my strong habitation, for a rock of habitation, to which I may continually resort. Thou hast given commandment to save me, for thou art
my rock and my fortress." Under all this variety of beautiful
poetical imagery, there are two leading ideas: 'Jehovah *de-
fends* amidst, and *delivers* from, all enemies and dangers.
Jehovah is all, and infinitely more than *all*, that these figurative expressions naturally suggest, and He is all this to *me*.'

The designations here given to God contain, on the part of
the speaker, an expression of confidence for the future, as well
as of gratitude for the past. 'The Lord has been, is, and will
be, all this to me.' The relation referred to is a standing relation, out of which will come all good for the future, as out of it

---

[1] Nösselt, in Diss. Inscript, "Jesus Christus." "Το κέρας τῆς σωτηρίας.".—*Ad. loc.*
Luc. i. 69.

> "Duces—qui capitibus cornua
> Suis ligant, ut conspicuum in prœliis
> Haberent signum."—Phædrus.

[2] Fischer. Exod. xxvii. 2; 1 Kings, i. 50; xi. 28.   [3] Paulus.

[4] משגבי. All the words employed are just such as were likely to suggest themselves (for inspiration did not interfere with the great laws of thought) to David. We
find them, 1 Sam. xxiii. 25 ; xxiv. 2.

has come all good for the past. It is justly said by a late interpreter,[1] "That the designation must be understood in this way,
appears, first of all, from the expression in the next verse, ' I
am delivered'—not ' I was delivered ;' and it is clear, from the
whole body of the Psalm, which refers not only to the past, but
also to the future." How exactly does this wonderful passage
harmonize with another prophecy respecting the Messiah,—
" He shall cry unto me, Thou art my Father, my God, and the
Rock of my salvation."[2]

Jehovah was all this in himself—all this to his beloved Servant ; and therefore, says he, " I will love THEE, O Jehovah."
The word rendered "love"[3] is a peculiarly expressive one. It
is derived from a term indicative of what is most inward in
man. It is equivalent to, ' In the heart of my heart do I love
Thee.' " It appears as if David had made the word for himself," says one of the most learned interpreters ; " no existing
term was sufficient for the expression of his feelings. Another
compares the feeling to that of an infant reposing on the bosom
of its mother—entire love, perfect confidence ; she is its whole
world, and it wishes no more.

We are not to take the words, " I *will* love," as exclusively
future. The indefinite, in Hebrew, is expressed by the future ;
and the expression is equivalent to, ' Thou art the object of my
supreme, constant, entire love. I have thus loved Thee ; I do
thus love Thee ; I ever will thus love Thee.' There is an ineffable affection between the Son and the Father as divine persons, and also between the Son, as God-man mediator, and the
Father, as " Him who appointed him." While the Father loves
the Son, the Son also loves the Father, for all that He is in himself—for all that He is, and has done, and is to do, to and for

---

[1] Hengstenberg.   [2] Psal. lxxxix. 26.

[3] Interpreters differ as to the meaning of the verb רחם. Some consider it as equivalent to—' I ask mercy from,' or—' will cry to Thee, O Jehovah.' This is the opinion
of Aben Ezra ; and he is followed by Bucer, who renders it—' I will trust in thy
fatherly kindness, and always implore it.' The sense given by our translators is that
given by Jarchi, and by the LXX. and the Chaldee Paraphrast. The original meaning of the word is ' tenderly to cherish,' as the hen does her eggs, or the mother the
embryo infant. It is often used to describe God's kind regard for his people, and to
express generally tender, strong, benevolent affection. Burk, the pious and learned
son-in-law of the pious and learned Bengel, finely says, " Talis sensus in animo habet
aliquid ineffabile. Imaginem ejus mihi videre videor in puello, infante qui simpliciter, placide, cum bona mora, a collo matris suæ pendet, cætera, omnia oblitus."

him and his.   Luther paraphrases the words thus :—" I have a
sincere and childlike longing toward Thee. He confesses, he
says, his warmest love, and that he has a desire after the Lord
God, for he has found his kindness to be unspeakable. It is
from this constraining desire and love, that he ascribes to God
so many names as follow."[1]   Oh, how deep does this let us see
into the Messiah's heart! What meaning, what emphasis, belong to these words as spoken by him,—"I will love thee, O
Lord, my strength. The Lord is my rock, and my fortress, and
my deliverer : my God, my strength, in whom I will trust; my
buckler, and the horn of my salvation, and my high tower!"
Some interpreters would render the phrase, " I will love Thee,"
' I ask, or will ask, mercy of Thee;' but we prefer the sense
which our translators, following as they usually do the best
Jewish and Christian interpreters, have given it.

What Jehovah is to his Son—the exalted Mediator, the Redeemer of men, the substitute of his people—He is to all the
redeemed. "I ascend," said the risen Saviour—"I ascend to
my Father, and to your Father ; to my God, and to your God."
" My Father," says he, " shall love you."   " The Father himself also," says the apostle, " has loved us."   He is in them,
and they are in him, sons of God, heirs of God, because they are
Christ's, and Christ is God's. They are the dear children of
God in Christ Jesus. On the ground of this union, every believer may claim God in all the characters, and address Him
by all the endearing appellations, which are here employed by
his Son.   " He that sanctifieth and they who are sanctified are
all of one; so that he is not ashamed to call them brethren."
And, if he calls them brethren, they need not be afraid either
to call him brother, or to call his Father their Father. If they
are "joint heirs with Christ," then it follows that they are
" heirs of the kingdom," " heirs of the world," and, what is infinitely more than this, " heirs of God."[2]

How happy are those who are united to Christ! Jehovah,
infinitely powerful, wise, righteous, kind, and faithful, is their
God, *God to* them,—and will be and do *for* them everything that
a God can be expected to be and do. He is their rock, higher
than they, to which they may continually resort—standing on

---

[1] Psal. lxxiii. 25, 26.   " Amo te, Domine, plus quam mea, meos, me."—BERNHARD.
[2] Heb. ii. 11-13.   Rom. iv. 13; viii. 17.

which they may defy the universe. He is their fortress, which neither earthly nor hellish power can invade. He is their deliverer, who gives them freedom as well as safety. He is their strength, well may they trust in Him. He is their shield, broad and strong, to protect them from the deathful sword, or envenomed arrows of their foes. He is their helmet of salvation; He is their high tower. He preserves them *amidst*, He will deliver them *from*, all hazards and enemies. They are, indeed, in themselves weak, and exposed to many enemies, but they are in no danger. Jehovah is theirs *really*, theirs *immutably*, theirs *eternally*. He is theirs, for he is their Lord's. While He continues to be *his* God, He will—He must—continue to be *theirs*.' "The eternal God is their refuge, and underneath are the everlasting arms :" 'Israel then shall dwell in safety alone: the fountain of Jacob shall be upon a land of corn and wine; also his heavens shall drop down dew. Happy art thou O Israel: who is like unto thee, O people saved by the Lord, the shield of thy help, and who is the sword of thy excellency !" "There is none like unto the God of Jeshurun, who rideth upon the heaven in thy help, and in his excellency on the sky."[1]

Brethren of the Messiah ! acknowledge, gratefully acknowledge, that he has been all this to you ; and humbly, yet confidently, trust that he will be all this to you forever and ever. Can you take this view of the Divine character—can you think of what He is, and what He does, and what He promises to do, without being sweetly constrained to say, "I will love Thee, O Jehovah" ? "O love the Lord, all ye his saints." Love Him with all your heart, and soul, and strength, and mind. Love him, for He is infinitely lovely ; love Him, for He is—He will be—kind exceeding abundantly, above all that you can think or ask.

We come now to the interpretation of the 3d verse. It has been translated by some very learned interpreters, so as to bring out a sense considerably different from that expressed in our version. "In distress I will call on the Lord, so shall I be saved from my enemies." I am disposed, however, to prefer the rendering of our translators,—"I will call on Him who is worthy to be praised, so shall I be saved from my enemies."[2]

---

[1] Deut. xxxiii. 27–29.
[2] מהֻלָּל אקרא יהוה. The meaning of מהֻלָּל is doubtful: the root is sometimes used

The appellation here given to the Divine Being is striking—Him who is praised, or " who is worthy to be praised." Who that has ever had the eye of his mind opened to the truth about God, can doubt the appropriateness of this appellation ? He is praised. All his works are praising Him, *i. e.*, manifesting his excellences—proclaiming the truth about Him ; and his saints, his holy ones, on earth and in heaven, are blessing Him. And He is worthy of all praise, for He is possessed of all excellence. " Who is like unto Thee, O Lord, among the gods ?" "glorious in holiness, fearful in praises, doing wonders." " Who is a God like unto thee, that pardoneth iniquity, and passed by the transgression of the remnant of his heritage ? He retaineth not his anger forever, because He delighteth in mercy." " Who shall not fear Thee, O Lord, and glorify thy name? for Thou only art holy."[1]

The expression translated " I will call," admits of two somewhat different interpretations, according as it is considered as applying to the past or to the future. The same word, in the 6th verse, is rendered, " I called on the Lord ;" and the whole verse may be fairly enough rendered, " I called on the Lord, who is worthy to be praised, so was I delivered from mine enemies." In this case the 3d verse is a short enunciation of the

---

to signify 'to be deranged in mind,' Eccles. vii. 7 ; Isa. xliv. 24 ; Job, xii. 17. Understood in this way, the word must refer to the state of the suppliant when he called on God,—' Distracted, I called on Jehovah,' and is nearly of equivalent meaning with the phrase translated "in my haste," Psal. cxvi. 11. This is the view given by Geier and Dathé,—the first, one of the best commentators, the second, one of the best translators, of the Psalms. Michælis and Geddes also adopt it. Understanding the word in its more common meaning of ' praising,'—a mode of interpretation greatly recommended by the circumstance that מהלל is an epithet given to God in many other psalms, e. g., xlviii. 1, xcvi. 4, cxiii. 3, cxlv. 3,—there can be no doubt that it refers to Jehovah, though the particular manner in which it refers to Him is somewhat doubtful. Some would render it, ' I call,' or ' will call, on Jehovah, praised by me ;'—i. e., as Jarchi explains it, " I will call on Him, having praised Him, or given Him thanks ; being so secure of his assistance, that before I receive it, I thank Him for it ;" or, " Praising for what is past, I will pray to Him for what is to come.' In this case, the expression is similar to the Latin phrase, "laudatum dimisit,"—' He dismissed him, being praised ;' i. e., He first praised him, and then dismissed him. Others render it, ' The praiseworthy One,' ' the Blessed,'—ὁ εὐλογητὸς, Mark, xiv. 61. Others, ' Praised,' will I cry, ' be Jehovah.' Others, Dr. Durell in particular,—' I will call on the Lord with praise.' I am not aware that any mode of construing or interpreting the words is superior to that adopted by our translators.

[1] Exod. xv. 11. Mic. vii. 18. Rev. xv. 4.

events described more at length in the succeeding part of the psalm—a kind of prefatory argument. If we follow the rendering of our translators, the meaning is, 'I will continue to call on the Lord, who is worthy to be praised, for having heard my former prayers; so shall I continue to be saved from mine enemies.'

We rather think that here, as in a former case, the Hebrew future is used as the indefinite, and that the words indicate what had been, was, and would be, the practice of the Messiah, and what had been, was, and would be, its result.[1] His habitual practice was calling on Jehovah, and the habitual result was deliverance from his enemies. It has been justly and strikingly said, "Faith knows no past and no future. What God has done, and will do, is present to it."[2] The exalted Redeemer has many enemies, human and diabolical. When he was a man among men, they attacked him personally; and, when he had to endure their contradiction against himself, he betook himself to prayer.[3] "In prayer and supplication, he made his requests known to God." "With strong crying and tears," he offered up prayers "to Him that was able to save him from death, and he was heard in that he feared."[4] Of his prayers, and their effect, we have an account in the sequel, as well as in the twenty-second and fortieth psalms. "Be not Thou far from me, O Lord: O my strength, haste Thee to help me. Deliver my soul from the sword; my darling from the power of the dog. Save me from the lion's mouth: for Thou hast heard me from the horns of the unicorns." "I waited patiently for the Lord, and He inclined unto me, and heard my cry. He brought me up also out of an horrible pit, out of the miry clay, and set my feet upon a rock, and established my goings." On his exaltation, Christ was placed, personally, far, far beyond the reach of his enemies. But they continue to attack his people and his cause, which he identifies with himself. From all these enemies, he is to be delivered; for "he must reign, till He"—that is, the Father—"hath put all enemies under his feet."[5]

---

[1] "The apparent future tense, in which many verbs occur in this psalm, has occasioned many commentators and translators to despoil the poem of its beauty; but these apparent futures are aoristical or indefinite verbs."—WEISS.

[2] Hengstenberg.   [3] Psal. cix. 4.   [4] Heb. v. 6, 7.   [5] 1 Cor. xv. 25.

Prayer to the Father is to be the grand means of their being destroyed. He is pledged to destroy them. "The Lord said unto our Lord"—when he had finished the work He had given him to do on earth,—"Sit thou at my right hand, until *I* make thine enemies thy footstool." But for this thing, He must be inquired of by his servant to do it for him. The established order is, "He shall call on Me, and I will answer him. "Ask, and I will give thee." "He asked for life, and it was given him, even length of days forever and ever." The saving omnipotence of the Saviour is grounded on his intercession. He is "able to save to the uttermost all coming to God by him, seeing he ever liveth to make intercession for them."[1]

The connection between the Messiah's prayers, and deliverance from his enemies—the enemies of his cause and people,—is very strikingly pointed out in two passages of Scripture, both of them prophetical, the one in the Old, and the other in the New Testament. "Ask of Me, and I shall give thee the heathen for thine inheritance, and the uttermost parts of the earth for thy possession. Thou shalt break them with a rod of iron; thou shalt dash them in pieces like a potter's vessel. Be wise now, therefore, O ye kings; be instructed, ye judges of the earth. Serve the Lord with fear, and rejoice with trembling. Kiss the Son, lest he be angry, and ye perish from the way, when his wrath is kindled but a little. Blessed are all they that put their trust in him." "And another angel came and stood at the altar, having a golden censer; and there was given unto him much incense, that he should offer it with the prayers of all saints upon the golden altar which was before the throne. And the smoke of the incense, which came with the prayers of the saints, ascended up before God out of the angel's hand. And the angel took the censer, and filled it with fire of the altar, and cast it into the earth: and there were voices, and thunderings, and lightnings, and an earthquake."[2]

Is any saint delivered from the temptations of Satan? it is because Christ has prayed for him. Is any saint delivered from all his enemies by death? it is because Christ has called on Him who is worthy to be praised, and said, "Father, I will that they also whom Thou hast given me be with me where I am;

---

[1] Psal. cx. 1; xc. 15; ii. 8–12.   [2] Rev. viii. 3–5.

that they may behold my glory, which Thou hast given me : for Thou lovedst me before the foundation of the world."[1] What a delightful thought, that in all the afflictions and distresses of his people (which he considers as his own—for "he who touches them, touches the apple of his eye"—inasmuch as men either help or harm them, he considers it as done to himself), the exalted Redeemer calls on his and their Father, and "him the Father heareth always"!

Does not our exalted Lord here "set us an example, that we should follow his steps"? Is it not the duty of all saints, when pressed with suffering and surrounded with foes, to call on "Him who is worthy to be praised"! and have they not abundant reason to believe that, in doing so, they will be delivered from their enemies? God has promised to deliver his people from all their enemies. Satan shall be bruised under their feet shortly; and the last enemy, death, shall be destroyed. "Faithful is He who hath promised; who also will do it." But for all these things, our Father must be inquired of by his children to do it for them. "Ask, and ye shall receive; seek, and ye shall find; knock, and it shall be opened unto you. For every one that asketh, receiveth; and he that seeketh, findeth; and to him that knocketh, it shall be opened." Let past deliverances, for which Jehovah is "worthy to be praised," encourage us to make known our request to Him in every future calamity. *He* is "the same yesterday, to-day, and for ever." "His mercy endures for ever, his truth to all generations."

But in all our prayers, let us have a respect to the prayers of Him who is our "Advocate with the Father; and let us expect the answer of our prayers only on the ground of the efficacy of his all-perfect atonement—the true cause of the success of his all-prevalent intercession.

The account of the Messiah's deep humiliation and severe suffering, and of his miraculous deliverance, must be reserved as the subject of another discourse.

[1] John, xvii. 24.

LECTURE III

THE MESSIAH'S SUFFERINGS AND THE EXERCISE OF HIS MIND UNDER THEM

Psalm xviii. 4–6.—"The sorrows of death compassed me, and the floods of ungodly men made me afraid. The sorrows of hell compassed me about; the snares of death prevented me. In my distress I called upon the Lord, and cried unto my God: He heard my voice out of his temple, and my cry came before Him, *even* into his ears."

The subject, the structure, and the arrangement of the prophetic oracle, of which these words form a part, have already at some length been considered by us.

By applying to the psalm before us, the two principles on which it is to be determined, whether psalms are or are not to be considered as referring to the Messiah, we have arrived at the conclusion, that this is one of the psalms in which it is written of Christ. There are to be found in it descriptions of a perfection of character, an intensity of suffering, a depth of debasement, a suddenness and completeness of deliverance, a height of exaltation, an extent of dominion, to which no adequate correspondence can be found in the character and history of David, or of any of his royal successors, but which are fully verified in the character and history of his Son and Lord. There are repeated allusions to the psalm in the New Testament, which strengthen the conclusion to which the consideration just noticed leads, and every reasonable doubt vanishes when we find the Apostle Paul quoting the 49th verse as a proof "that Jesus Christ was a minister for the truth of God to confirm the promises, and that the Gentiles might glorify God for his mercy." The only two objections of weight against this view of the subject—the one derived from the inspired history of the ode, and the other from a statement contained in the 23d verse—were examined, and found capable of satisfactory explanation, in perfect consistency with the direct and sole Messianic reference of the psalm.

As to the structure of the oracle, it is obviously a triumphal hymn, uttered in the person of the Messiah from beginning to end, and referring to a period when both he and his cause had obtained a remarkable deliverance, and had before them still farther triumphs.

The hymn, on being closely examined, was found to resolve itself into six divisions. The first of these divisions—the proem of the psalm—has already been explained. It is intended to devote this discourse to the exposition of the second—the account of the Messiah's sufferings, and of his conduct under them. That is contained in the following words—" The sorrows of death compassed me, and the floods of ungodly men made me afraid. The sorrows of hell compassed me about; the snares of death prevented me. In my distress I called upon the Lord, and cried unto my God: He heard my voice out of his temple, and my cry came before Him, even into his ears."

These words bring before our minds the Messiah's sufferings, his exercise under those sufferings, and the result of this exercise. To these points we will attend in their order. And, first, let us consider the account here given us of the Messiah's sufferings —"The sorrows of death compassed me, and the floods of ungodly men made me afraid. The sorrows of hell compassed me about; the snares of death prevented me."

Even without going into anything like a minute examination of these words—which, however, they require, and must receive —every attentive reader must see in them a statement that the Messiah's sufferings were to be violent, severe, numerous, varied, fatal, and penal.

The sufferings here described are plainly *violent:* they do not originate in inward decay or disease—they come from without. So it was with the Messiah. Neither in the body nor in the soul of the Messiah were there, as in the case of every other man, those seeds of sufferings which require only time and occasion to make them bring forth bitter fruit—fruit unto death. His sufferings did not come in the ordinary course of things. We never read of our Lord being sick. He did not die of disease, nor of natural decay. He was " taken, and with wicked hands crucified and slain."

Then the sufferings here described are not only violent in reference to their origin, but *severe* in their degree. It is no common suffering that is indicated by these words. And the sufferings of the Messiah were no common sufferings. The infamy heaped on him was not common reproach. The pain of the Roman scourge, and of the cross, was no ordinary pain. The anguish of spirit which made him exceedingly sorrowful—sorrowful even to death—was no ordinary anguish. The temptations to which he was exposed were no ordinary temptations.

Still farther, the sufferings here described are *numerous* sufferings. The number of sufferings is indicated by the number of the figurative representations, and by the nature of some of them—the bands of death, the floods of Belial, the sorrows of hell, the snares of death. And were not the sufferings of the righteous One many? Who can count them,—from the inconveniences of the stable in Bethlehem, to the agonies of the cross on Calvary?

The description before us further intimates that the sufferings of the speaker were *varied*—not only many in number, but diverse in kind. Not only did the same calamity or calamities of the same general kind often recur, but Christ experienced all the sad variety of suffering, bodily and mental, which innocent humanity could endure,—bodily pain, mental anguish, poverty and contempt, neglect and reproach, the unkindness of friends, the virulence of enemies.

Yet again, the sufferings here described are *fatal* sufferings. The sufferer is bound by the cords, entangled in the snares of death, fettered by the bands of the separate state. And did not Christ *die* according to the Scriptures? Did he not become "obedient unto death, even the death of the cross"—did he not lie in the grave—did he not enter into the region of separate souls?

Finally, the sufferings here described are penal sufferings. For death, in man, is the wages of sin—physical evil is the punishment of moral evil. These leading characters of the Messiah's sufferings are marked with sufficient distinctness; and when we take into consideration the absolute perfection of character, that in the subsequent part of the psalm is claimed by the speaker, we must come to the conclusion that these sufferings must have been *vicarious* and *expiatory*.

But we must not rest satisfied with such a general view of our Lord's sufferings. We must endeavor distinctly to apprehend what each of the expressions in the passage before us is intended to teach us. Let us endeavor, first, to fix the meaning of the words, and to form a distinct idea of the figurative representations; and then to discover the great truths which these figurative representations are intended to shadow forth.

The word rendered "sorrows," both in the 4th and 5th verses, properly signifies 'cords' or 'bands.'[1] "The bands of death"—"the bands of hell" encircled me.[2] In the other version of the psalm in 2d Samuel, a different word occurs in the 5th verse—a word signifying severe breaking pains, like the pangs of childbirth.

The word "Belial," rendered "ungodly men," according to the view taken of its derivation, signifies what is useless and unprofitable, or what is abject and contemptible.[3] Hence it comes to signify wickedness in the abstract, as that which is of all things the most unprofitable and vile; and then, sometimes with the adjunct "sons of," and sometimes, as in the case before us, simply by itself, it signifies the wicked, perhaps sometimes the wicked one. Here the word *men* is a supplement; and it would have been better to have retained the original word, or to have rendered it simply 'the wicked,' including evil angels as well as evil men. It has been supposed that the word is sometimes used to signify the evil place—Hell, Gehenna—into which all the refuse of the universe is to be cast; in which case the parallel between

---

[1] Instead of חֶבְלֵי, the other edition of the psalm in Samuel has מִשְׁבְּרֵי. The primary notion of שׁבר is to 'break.' The derivative noun comes to signify 'severe pains,' which, as it were, break the patient in pieces; and also 'waves,' which, impelled by the tempest against the rocks, are broken in pieces. Jon, ii. 4.

[2] אֲפָפוּנִי. Some would render this—'set themselves against me,'—face to face; others, 'terrified me.' There can be no reasonable doubt that our translators, following the ancient interpreters, the LXX., the Chaldee, and the Syriac, give the true meaning, 'surround, encircle.'

[3] Some deriving it from הֹעִיל and בְּלִי; others, from יַעַל and בְּלִי. Others derive it from עוּל, 'a yoke,' and בְּלִיו, 'one who has cast off the yoke, who is *ex lex*—a lawless one.' Drusius remarks,—"Vocabulum Belial quærens uno Latino vocabulo rationem nominis exprimere aptius, non inveni quam *nequam* ut enim ex *ne* et *quidquam*, media extrita syllaba, *nequam* fit sic ex בְּלִי et יַעַל compositum est Belial, unoque significatur *homo nihili*, neque rei, neque frugis bonæ. Quod genus Græci fere, ἄσωλον ἢ ἀκόλαστον, ἢ ἀχρεῖον, ἢ ἄχρηστον, ἢ κακότροπον ἢ μιαρόν, dicunt." In later times it seems to have come to be used as a name of the devil,—2 Cor, vi. 15, "τίς δὲ συμφώνησις Χριστῷ πρὸς Βελίαλ."

the two clauses would have been more complete : 'The cords of death surrounded me'—'The floods of hell made me afraid.' There is no sufficient ground, however, for this suggestion.

The word "floods" properly signifies torrents. If descriptive of agents, whether human or diabolical, it indicates their number, power, and violence; if descriptive of afflictions, it signifies their severity, their overwhelming nature. The term translated "made me afraid," is expressive of vehement consternation; as in Job, xviii. 11, "Terrors shall make him afraid on every side, and shall drive him to his feet;" Job, vii. 14, "Thou scarest me with dreams, and terrifiest me through visions."[1]

The word translated "hell,"[2] as I have often had occasion to remark to you, signifies, not the place of torment, but the state of the dead. "Hell" and "death," or the grave, in the Old Testament, do not differ essentially: the one refers to the state of the soul after death, as separated from the body; the other to the state of the body, as separated from the soul. It is often used as the designation of the place where the separate souls are, and is viewed as divided, by an impassable gulf, into the regions of the blessed and the regions of the condemned. The rich man and Lazarus are equally in the region of separate souls, but they cannot come at each other. It is viewed as the repository

---

[1] Isa. xxi. 4.   Job, xv. 24.   Est. vii. 6.

[2] " שְׁאוֹל et מוֹת rei ipsius respectu non differunt, nisi quod prior ad animæ statum post mortem, posterior ad corporis dissolutionem nos ducat."—VENEMA. " It signifies," says Dr. Campbell, " the state of the dead in general. The word, in its radical meaning, expresses what is secret or concealed." Its signification, as used in the Old Testament, is illustrated by the following passages:—Gen. xxxvii. 35; xlii. 38; Psal. xvi. 10. Many critics suppose that שְׁאוֹל and קֶבֶר are synonyms; but this is a mistake. No doubt you may substitute קֶבֶר for שְׁאוֹל in the first two of the passages just referred to without altering the general sentiment; but it does not follow that therefore the words are synonymous, any more than that, because for an accident or disease, to bring a man to his shroud, to his coffin, to his grave, are expressions of the same import,—shroud, coffin, and grave, are synonymous words. It is of great importance to understand distinctly the difference between the *sensus* and the *significatio* of a word. קֶבֶר is never rendered by the Greek translators by ᾅδης, nor שְׁאוֹל by τάφος or μνῆμα. קֶבֶר is often used in the plural; שְׁאוֹל never. There are many קְבוֹרִים; but there is only one שְׁאוֹל, though it is divided into two regions, Paradise and Gehenna,—a receptacle for the righteous, and a receptacle for the wicked, impassably divided from each other. In our Lord's parable of the rich man and Lazarus, both are in שְׁאוֹל. The Greeks and Romans had similar notions. Horace (*Od.* ii. 13, 23) speaks of "sedes discretas piorum;" and every schoolboy knows that Erebus, the region of the shades, was divided into Elysium and Tartarus. קֶבֶר admits of the possessive pronoun; שְׁאוֹל, as the repository of all the dead, does not.

of the spirits of all who have died. In the Song of Solomon, it is said to be "cruel," rather "inexorable." This is substantially the idea here. To be bound with the cords of Scheol, or the separate state, is to be in that state from which there is no return, without a miracle, to the state of living men.

The word "snares,"[1] signifies such traps or gins as are laid for birds and wild beasts. The English word "prevent" has changed its meaning in some measure since our authorized translation of the Bible was made. Its original meaning is to "come before." It is now almost restricted to one sense ;—to prevent an event, is to hinder an event from taking place ; to prevent a person from doing or suffering anything, is to keep him from doing and suffering it by as it were coming before him—coming between him and it. It is used in its original meaning here. 'The snares of death came before me, so that I could not escape them.' In this way it very well expresses the force of the original Hebrew word, Psalm cxix. 147, "I prevented the dawning of the morning." 'I got before the dawn with my prayers.' Some interpreters prefer the signification 'met,' as in Isaiah, xxi. 14, "they prevented with their bread him that fled." The meaning here is, 'They met me, so that I could not escape from them.'

Such are the figures, and they are very striking and appropriate ones. The Messiah is represented as overwhelmed with floods, bound with fetters, entangled with snares. Let us now endeavor to bring out distinctly what is meant by these figurative expressions.

"The bands or cords of death encompassed" him. It is not very easy to fix the precise meaning of the phrase, "bands" or "cords" of death.[2] It may either be considered as equivalent to, 'the bands by which the dead are bound,' in which case, to be encircled with the bands of death is just a figurative expression for being dead ; or it may be considered as equivalent to, the bands by which a person is bound in the prospect of a violent death, and by which his violent death is secured, he being pre-

---

[1] Amos, iii. 5. Psal. lxiv. 6 ; cxl. 6.

[2] Geierus thus paraphrases the clause :—" Ejusmodi periculis mortiferis eram cinctus, qualia præ oculis sentiunt damnati ad mortis supplicium, vinculisque jam constricti, atque ad locum illum infamem abducti." He adds, " Vel Mors per prosopopœiam introducitur quasi carnifex qui vincula jam injecerit Davidi. Aut metaphora petitur a jumentis vel bestiis quæ, si vinculis ligantur, non amplius suæ sunt potestatis, sed alterius arbitrio parere coguntur."

vented from escaping. It has been supposed by some, that the allusion is to the ancient mode of hunting wild animals. A considerable tract of country was surrounded with strong ropes. The circle was gradually contracted, till the object of pursuit was so confined as to become an easy prey to the hunter. These cords were the cords of death, securing the death of the animal. The phrase is applicable to our Lord in both senses; but as the floods of wickedness, or the wicked, are represented as making him afraid subsequently to his being encircled with the cords of death, I am disposed to understand it in the latter of these two senses.

In two points of view, the Messiah may be considered as bound with the cords of death. His being made "under the law" in the room of men, under its curse as well as under its precept, in consequence of his own most voluntary engagement, rendered his violent death as the victim for human transgressions absolutely certain. This was the bond of adamant which, as it were, bound the great sacrifice before being laid on the altar. Having taken the place he occupied, " it *behoved* him" thus to suffer and die. Then, in the second place, the various schemes of his enemies, whether human or infernal, from the commencement of his ministry till they consummated their nefarious design, may be considered as cords by which they endeavored to draw the object of their malignity within their reach. How often did they seek to entangle him in his talk, that they might accuse him to the Roman government! How frequently did they take counsel to take him and put him to death! There is just one circumstance which would lead me to suppose, that being encompassed by the cords of death, means death, rather than that which renders death certain, and that is the way in which the phrase, borrowed either from this place or from Psalm cxvi., is used by the apostle Peter,[1] "Whom God raised up, having loosed the pains,"—rather ' cords'—" of death, because it was not possible that he should be holden of it," *i. e.*, permanently bound by them. At the same time, this passage is by no means irreconcilable with the view which, from the context, I think the more probable one; and the reference is a strong corroboration of our general principle, that the psalm refers not to David but to Jesus.

"The floods of the ungodly made me afraid." The floods of

[1] Acts, ii. 24.

the ungodly may either refer to the enemies of our Lord, or to
the sufferings which befell him.   In the first case they are called
" floods," to mark their number, their power, and their violence.
During the whole of his humbled life, Messiah was surrounded
by enemies ; but these words are peculiarly applicable to the
closing scene of his sufferings.   Herod and Pontius Pilate, with
the Gentiles and the people of Israel, were " gathered together"
against God's holy child Jesus.   What a troubled ocean of ungodliness raged around his cross—mocking scribes and a murderous rabble !   Nor were they his only, or his worst, enemies.
" Then was the hour and the power of darkness."   "The foun-
tains of the great deep were broken up."   " Hell opened its
mouth."   The prince of this world and his legions were then full
of malignity and fury.   " Then did the floods lift up their voice ;
they lifted up their waves."   The Saviour had all the innocent
feelings of a man, and this tremendous concourse of enemies,
seen and unseen,—so numerous, so powerful, so fierce,—made
him afraid,—afraid, not of the issue of the enterprise, for he well
knew that would be the victory, but of the agony of the conflict,
which he knew would task to the uttermost the capacities of
endurance of the man, God's fellow, made strong for this very
purpose.   We find the suffering Saviour speaking of the same
events under a different set of figures in the twenty-second
psalm, verses 12, 16, " Many bulls have compassed me : strong
bulls of Bashan have beset me round.   They gaped upon me
with their mouths ;" they " compassed me ; the assembly of the
wicked have enclosed me."

In the second case, " the floods of the wicked," is an expression equivalent to, ' the floods by which the wicked are to be
overwhelmed "[1]—the penal evils due to the sons of men.   They
deserved them ; but Jehovah made them to fall on him.   He
was treated as if he had been a sinner, the greatest of sinners.
The evils which sin deserved were coming on him, and the
prospect was terrible.   " He feared."   "Father, if it be possible,
let this cup pass from me."   "Now is my soul troubled, and
what shall I say !"   " Then the waters came in unto his soul ;
then he sunk in deep mire, where there was no standing : then
he came into deep waters, where the floods overflowed him :

[1] Venema.

then did innumerable evils compass him about ; the iniquities laid hold on him, took hold on him, so that he was not able to look up ; his heart failed him." This fearful commotion of angry billows continued till he cried with a loud voice " It is finished," and gave up the ghost. Then the Lord on high, " who is mightier than the noise of many waters, yea, than the mighty waves of the sea," made the storm a calm, and the waves thereof were still. The worn-out body found rest in Joseph's sepulchre, and the weary spirit in the bosom of God.

In the 5th verse, the Messiah is represented as in the state of the dead. " The sorrows," or rather the ' bands,' the ' cords,' " of hell compassed me about ; the snares of hell prevented me." That our Lord, in the ordinary sense of the words, descended into hell—the place of the condemned, and continued there till his resurrection, though held by some divines, seems a notion altogether irreconcilable with our Lord's declaration on the cross, " It is finished," and his promise to the penitent malefactor expiring at his side, " To-day shalt thou be with me in paradise." To avoid the necessity of admitting this to be the meaning of the words before us, some have supposed that they refer to the inward sufferings for sin, which our Lord endured in the room of his people, and which have been represented as substantially what otherwise they must have in hell endured forever. That our Lord's mental sufferings were inconceivably severe, and that, in the estimation of Infinite righteousness, they are available to save innumerable multitudes from the pit of perdition, there is no reason to doubt ; but that these sufferings were of the same nature as those of the condemned in hell, is what no reflecting person will very readily admit, as conscious desert of punishment and self-reproach, neither of which could have any place in the case of our Lord, form principal ingredients in the misery of the finally condemned.

A better sense may be got out of these words by keeping in view the fact already stated, that the word before us is the word ordinarily used in the Old Testament Scripture to signify, not the place of torment, but the state of the dead. By the bands or cords of the separate state surrounding him, we understand that he not only died, but for a season remained dead. He entered into the state from which, in the ordinary course of things, there is no return to this world. He had passed through the gates that open only inward. While his body was buried, his soul went to paradise. For a part of three days did the cords of the separate state hold the Lord of life.

"The snares of death prevented" him. The mighty hunter, death, had caught him in his snare, out of which, to mankind, there is usually no escape. He was brought into a state from which there is ordinarily no return to the regions of embodied life.

While these words are strictly applicable to the Messiah personally, they may be considered also as suggesting, and as intended to suggest, the apparently hopeless state of his cause. Indeed, the two things are closely connected. The foundations of the kingdom he came to establish seemed completely dug up. His disciples were dispersed, and the opening prospect of the deliverance of man appeared closed in the blackness of darkness for ever. The mortal enemies of the Saviour triumphed ; and if ever there was joy in hell, it must have been when the incarnate Son expired on a cross, or lay a lifeless corpse in a sepulchre. And even after he had risen, his cause had to struggle with many difficulties—to encounter many enemies— to be exposed to many dangers—from the virulence of apostate Judaism, and the power of all-prevalent Paganism, before he became the head of the heathen, and the isles waited for his law.

Such is the view given us, in these words, of the sufferings of the Messiah. How obviously impossible it is to find anything in David's history that answers this description ! How true to the letter is the description, viewed as referring to Jesus !

And now, "holy brethren, partakers of the heavenly calling, let us consider this apostle and high-priest of our profession." Contemplate, Christians, your suffering Lord. See him encircled by his enemies, insulted, scourged, and crucified. Behold how the waves and billows pass over him—how the yawning deep threatens to swallow him up. See him bound by the bands of death, and laid, in weakness and dishonor, in a sepulchre.

And, while you survey the amazing scene, say, 'He dies, the just for the unjust ; he is " wounded for our transgressions, bruised for our iniquities, the chastisement of our peace is on him ;" he " bears our sins in his own body on the tree ;" he dies for sin once, that we may live forever to God ; he descends into the grave, and remains there for a season, that that lonely loathsome abode should not be our everlasting dwelling-place. By dying, he is destroying death, and him that has the power of death.'

Think how he has loved you; and love him who has so loved you, as to conflict with and overcome all your enemies—as to bear your punishment—as to purchase your salvation.

Disciples of a suffering Saviour, count on suffering; reckon it not as a strange thing that you should be attacked by Satan and his emissaries—Belial and his sons. "Is it not enough that the disciple be as his teacher, and the servant as his master?"

Be not afraid of suffering; he has conquered, and so shall you. He has conquered for you—he will conquer in you. In the world—from the world—you must have tribulation; but be of good cheer, he has overcome the world, so that in HIM you may have peace, as through him you shall have victory. You shall be "more than conquerors through him that loved you."

Fear not to go down to the grave. It is "the place where the Lord lay." He brake the bands of death; it was not possible he should continue to be bound by them; and his deliverance secured yours. "Because he lives, ye shall live also." His grave is empty; and the graves of all his people shall, in due time, be empty too.

Amid the inward sorrows and the outward afflictions of life— amid the agonies of death, think of him—how he suffered, how he triumphed. Think, too, how he conducted himself under his unparalleled sufferings, and, as he has left you an example, follow in his steps.

This remark leads me to the second great topic of consideration which the text brings before our minds—the exercise of the Messiah under his sufferings. We have an account of this in the first part of the 6th verse: "In my distress I called on the Lord, and cried unto my God."

The Messiah was a magnanimous sufferer. His, however, was not that bastard greatness of soul which considers suffering as something that is to be despised, and holds that manly courage requires us to act as if we did not feel pain. He felt his sufferings in all their bitterness. He bowed to them as the appointment of God, and *in* Him he sought help—*from* Him he sought deliverance. He called on Jehovah, the only living and true God—the all powerful, righteous, wise, and benignant disposer of all things. His prayer was addressed to Him as HIS

God,—"the God, as well as the Father, of our Lord Jesus Christ."
He remembered the word on which he had been caused to hope,
—"Fear thou not, for I am with thee; be not dismayed, for I
am thy God: I will strengthen thee, yea, I will help thee, yea,
I will uphold thee with the right hand of my righteousness."[1]
The life of the God-man on earth was a life of faith. Believing
the promise, he prayed for its fulfilment. And these prayers
were fervent prayers: "I *cried*[2] to my God." The evangelist
tells us that, on one occasion, "being in an agony, he prayed
more earnestly;" and the apostle tells us that "in the days of
his flesh he offered up prayers and supplications, with strong
crying and tears, to Him who was able to save him from death."
Jesus was remarkably a man of prayer during the whole of his
mortal life. On one occasion, "rising up in the morning, a
great while before day, he went out, and departed into a solitary
place, and there prayed;" and on another occasion, "he went
out into a mountain to pray, and continued all night in prayer
to God;"[3] and his prayers seem to have increased in frequency
and fervor as his sufferings approached their consummation.
"O my God," says he, "I cry in the day time, and in the night
season, and am not silent." "As for me, I will call upon God,
and the Lord will save me." "As for me, my prayer is unto
Thee, O Lord, in an acceptable time."[4]

The best way of illustrating this part of our subject, is just to
quote some of his prayers, as predicted by the prophets, or narrated by the evangelists. Let us hear first the testimony of the
spirit of prophecy: "Be not far from me, for trouble is near;
for there is none to help." "Be not Thou far from me, O Lord:
O my strength, haste Thee to help me. Deliver my soul from
the sword; my darling from the power of the dog. Save me
from the lion's mouth: for Thou hast heard me from the horns
of the unicorns." "Withhold not Thou thy tender mercies
from me, O Lord: let thy loving-kindness and thy truth continually preserve me." "Be pleased, O Lord, to deliver me:
O Lord, make haste to help me." "Deliver me out of the mire,
and let me not sink: let me be delivered from them that hate

---

[1] Isa. xli. 10.

[2] The word used in reference to the Messiah when they pierced his hands and his
feet.—Psalm xxii. 25.

[3] Luke, v. 16; vi. 12.   [4] Psal. lxix. 13.

me, and out of the deep waters. Let not the water-flood overflow me, neither let the deep swallow me up, and let not the
pit shut her mouth upon me." "Hear me, O Lord; for thy
loving-kindness is good: turn unto me according to the multitude of thy tender mercies. And hide not thy face from thy
servant; for I am in trouble: hear me speedily. Draw nigh
unto my soul, and redeem it: deliver me, because of mine enemies." "I am poor and sorrowful: let thy salvation, O God,
set me up on high." "O Lord, be merciful unto me, and raise
me up." "Do thou for me, O God the Lord, for thy name's
sake: because thy mercy is good, deliver Thou me. For I am
poor and needy, and my heart is wounded within me." "Help
me, O Lord my God: O save me according to thy mercy."[1]
Such is the testimony of the Spirit of prophecy to the prayers
of the Messiah.

Let us now attend to the witness of those who were chosen to
be his companions when on the earth. These are some of his
prayers, as recorded by them :—"Now is my soul troubled; and
what shall I say? Father, save me from this hour: but for
this cause came I unto this hour. Father, glorify thy name."
"Father, the hour is come; glorify thy Son, that thy Son also
may glorify Thee: as Thou hast given him power over all flesh,
that he should give eternal life to as many as Thou hast given
him. And this is life eternal, that they might know Thee the
only true God, and Jesus Christ, whom Thou hast sent. I have
glorified Thee on the earth; I have finished the work which
Thou gavest me to do. And now, O Father, glorify Thou me
with thine own self with the glory which I had with Thee before
the world was." "O my Father, if it be possible, let this cup
pass from me: nevertheless, not as I will, but as Thou wilt."
"O my Father, if this cup may not pass away from me, except
I drink it, thy will be done." "Abba, Father, all things are
possible unto Thee. Take away this cup from me: nevertheless, not what I will, but what Thou wilt." "My God, my God,
why hast Thou forsaken me?"[2] This calling on God was habitual; it was not a transient cry. The prayers were not immediately heard; but he waited patiently on the Lord. Such was
the exercise of the Messiah amid his sufferings; so fervent, so

---

[1] Psal. xxii. 11, 19-21 ; xl. 11, 13 ; lxix. 14-18, 29 ; xli. 10 ; cix. 21-23, 26.

[2] John, xii. 27, 28 ; xvii. 1-5. Matth. xxvi. 39, 42. Mark, xiv. 36. Matth. xxvii. 46.

persevering his devotion, so firm his faith, so intense his desire, so entire his submission. From the order of the clauses, it seems intimated that, even in the separate state, he would cry to Jehovah. When dead, "he asked for life, and God gave it him, even length of days forever and ever."

"He shall call on me, and I will answer him," said the ancient oracle : "I will be with him in trouble ; I will deliver him, and honor him. With long life will I satisfy him, and show him my salvation."[1] And so it was. Faithful is He who promised. "This poor man" (he who "was rich, yet for our sakes became poor") "cried, and the Lord heard him, and saved him out of all his troubles." He was "heard in that"—in reference to that—which "he feared."[2]

This is the last topic to which the text turns our attention,—the results of the Messiah's sufferings, and of his exercise under them. "He"—'the Lord my God'—"heard my voice out of his temple, and my cry came before Him, even into his ears."

Though uttered on earth, or in the state of the dead, the voice of his prayer was heard in heaven ; though unheeded by men, they were listened to by God. Heaven is here represented, as in other places of Scripture, as a magnificent building,—the palace of the great King,—the "temple" of the only living and true God. "The Lord is in his holy temple : let all the earth keep silence before Him."[3] "The Lord is in his holy temple ; his throne is in heaven." Yet He sits there no unconcerned observer of what is going on in the earth. "His eyes behold, his eye-lids try the children of men." "The Lord trieth the righteous one ;" but when He has tried him, He brings him out like gold ; while upon his enemies He will, as is stated in the following context, "rain snares, fire and brimstone, and an horrible tempest : this shall be the portion of their cup." But He will show that "the righteous Lord loveth righteousness ;" and that "his countenance doth behold the upright." "His eyes are upon the righteous, and his ears are open unto their cry."[4]

The petitions of the Messiah were heard and answered. How could it be otherwise? His prayers proceeded not from "feigned lips." He asked but for what had been promised him; he asked but for what his obedience to the death, in the cause of God's

---

[1] Psal. xci. 15, 16.   [2] Psal. xxxiv. 6.   Heb. v. 7.
[3] Hab. ii. 20.   [4] Psal. xi. 4–7 ; xxxiv. 15.

glory and man's salvation, richly merited. His prayers, both
in matter and manner, were entirely in conformity with the will
of God, dictated as they were by that Spirit who knows the will
of God.

The manner in which the Messiah's prayers were answered is
detailed in the sublime description that follows, on the illustration of which we cannot at present enter.

Let Christians learn, from their Lord, in their distress to call
on Jehovah, and to cry to their God. Let them not be insensi-
ble under affliction,—let them not be self-confident in affliction
—let them recognize the hand of God in their affliction,—let
them humble themselves under his mighty hand,—let them, in
faith and resignation, seek support under, deliverance from,
their affliction, when and how God pleases.

Let them come with affectionate fervor to Jehovah as *their*
God,—" God in Christ, reconciling the world to himself,"—the
God of the whole earth,—the God and portion of every believ-
ing sinner. He cannot deny himself. He would be ashamed
to be called our God, were He not ever ready to do all for us a
God alone can do.

And let them rejoice that the success of the Saviour's prayers
secures the success of theirs. Whatsoever they ask in his name,
believing, they will assuredly receive. He will pray for what
they pray, and "him the Father heareth always." "This is
our confidence that we have in Him, that if we ask anything according to his will, He heareth us." We know that the Lord
has saved his Anointed One,—our Surety, our Saviour ; He has
heard from his holy heaven,—with the saving strength of his
right hand ; and because He has heard him, He will hear us if
we are *his*. Everything depends on this. If we have not his
Spirit, "the Spirit of grace and supplication," we are none of
his ;—if we have this Spirit, we are *his*. This Spirit is received
by faith. It can be obtained, it can be retained, it can be
increased, in no other way. He who wants it, may have it if
he but believe ; he who has it can preserve it only in believing ;
he who would have more of it, can obtain it only in believing.
Oh, the transcendent importance of the *faith* of " the *truth* as it
is in *Jesus*"! Lord, increase our faith.

LECTURE IV

PRETERNATURAL DELIVERANCE OF THE MESSIAH FROM HIS SUFFERINGS

Psalm xviii. 7–19.—"Then the earth shook and trembled; the foundations also of the hills moved and were shaken, because He was wroth. There went up a smoke out of his nostrils, and fire out of his mouth devoured: coals were kindled by it. He bowed the heavens also, and came down: and darkness was under his feet. And He rode upon a cherub, and did fly; yea, He did fly upon the wings of the wind. He made darkness his secret place; his pavilion round about Him were dark waters and thick clouds of the skies. At the brightness that was before Him his thick clouds passed; hailstones and coals of fire. The Lord also thundered in the heavens, and the Highest gave his voice; hailstones and coals of fire. Yea, He sent out his arrows, and scattered them; and He shot out lightnings, and discomfited them. Then the channels of waters were seen, and the foundations of the world were discovered at thy rebuke, O Lord, at the blast of the breath of thy nostrils. He sent from above, He took me, He drew me out of many waters. He delivered me from my strong enemy, and from them which hated me; for they were too strong for me. They prevented me in the day of my calamity: but the Lord was my stay. He brought me forth also into a large place; He delivered me, because He delighted in me."

"All things are of God." "Of *Him*, and through *Him*, and to *Him*, are all things." "*He* worketh all things according to the counsel of his own will;" and of every being that comes into existence, and of every event which occurs, it may be justly said, "This also cometh forth from the Lord of Hosts, who is wonderful in counsel, and excellent in working." He is the great, and, in the highest sense of the word, the only agent in the universe. "In Him" all creatures have their being, and in Him the living live, and the moving move.

Yet, while He is the ultimate author of all the changes, minute and mighty, which are constantly taking place throughout the universe, his usual mode of operation is characterized by a solemn silence and a steady uniformity, which strikingly harmonize with the spirituality, the invisibility, and the unchangeableness of his nature. It is He who makes the grass to grow, and the flowers to spring. It is He who covers the heavens with clouds, and refreshes the earth with showers. It is He who shuts up the sea as with doors, and restrains the fury of the whirlwind. It is He who keeps the planets in their orbits, and impels and guides them in their journeys round the sun. Yet all these amazing operations go on so steadily and so silently that they attract little attention; and it is only on reflection that our thoughts turn to the infinite wisdom, and power, and goodness, in which they originate. "The heavens declare the glory of God, and the firmament showeth his handiwork;" but "there is no speech nor language—their voice is not heard."

But though this is the general character of the Divine dispensations, both in the natural and moral world, there have been occasional and striking exceptions. The Supreme Agent has sometimes broken the awful silence He usually preserves, made bare that arm of might which ordinarily works unseen, and drawn aside for a moment the clouds which commonly veil the manner of his working and the splendors of his majesty. He has "come forth out of his place," "caused his glorious voice to be heard, and showed the lighting down of his arm with the indignation of his anger, and with the flame of a devouring fire, with scattering, and tempest, and hailstones."

Such a visible display did He make of his power and majesty, in those dispensations of his providence of which we have so impressive a description in the paragraph which lies before us for explication :—"Then the earth shook and trembled;' the foundations also of the hills moved, and were shaken,² because He was wroth.³ There went up a smoke out of his nostrils, and fire out of his mouth devoured :⁴ coals were kindled by it. He bowed the heavens also, and came down : and darkness was

---

¹ "Voces sunt emphaticæ et selectæ quæ vehementissimum murmur et gravissimam concussionem vivide depingunt."—VENEMA.

² Nah. i. 5 ; Jer. iv. 24 ; Isa. xxiv. 18 ; Psal. cxiv. 4. In the corresponding passage in 2d Samuel, we have " the foundations of the heavens," instead of " the foundations of the hills." The reference is probably to the line of the horizon, on which the heavens as a canopy seem to rest.

³ The phrase in the original is elliptical—' there was kindling to him,' or ' in him,' —לוֹ must be supplied. The LXX. mistook the meaning when they rendered the phrase, " ὅτι ὠργίσθη αὐτοῖς ὁ Θεός."

⁴ Anger induces rapid breathing; and in the case of lions, horses, and other animals of a generous spirit, the breath takes the form of smoke or vapor. We have similar figurative representations, Psal. lxxiv. 1 ; Deut. xxix. 49 ; Isa. xxx. 27, 33.

under his feet. And he rode upon a cherub, and did fly; yea, He did fly upon the wings of the wind. He made darkness his secret place; his pavilion round about Him were dark waters and thick clouds of the skies. At the brightness that was before Him his thick clouds passed; hailstones and coals of fire. The Lord also thundered in the heavens, and the Highest gave his voice; hailstones and coals of fire.[b] Yea, He sent out his arrows, and scattered them; and He shot out lightnings, and discomfited them. Then the channels of waters were seen, and the foundations of the world were discovered at thy rebuke, O Lord, at the blast of the breath of thy nostrils. He sent from above, He took me, He drew me out of many waters.[1] He delivered me from my strong enemy, and from them which hated me; for they were too strong for me. They prevented me in the day of my calamity: but the Lord was my stay. He brought me forth also into a large place: He delivered me, because He delighted in me."

To the question, "Of whom speaketh the prophet this? of himself, or of some other man?" I have already, at some length, endeavored to furnish a satisfactory reply; and that reply substantially was this, "David being a prophet, and knowing that God had sworn with an oath to him, that of the fruit of his loins, according to the flesh, He would raise up Christ to sit upon his throne: he, seeing this before, spake of the resurrection of Christ, that his soul was not left in hell, neither did his flesh see corruption." This is the song which the beloved Servant of the Lord, the mystical David, spake unto the Lord, "in the day that the Lord delivered him out of the hands of all his enemies, and from the power of the grave." I endeavored to show you that there is abundant evidence that this is one of the psalms in which it is written of Christ, and that here "the Spirit of prophecy is the testimony of Jesus." Proceeding on this principle, I have already illustrated the introduction of the hymn contained in the first three verses of the psalm, and the account of the Messiah's humiliation and sufferings contained in the following three verses.

[b] See Note B.

[1] Calamities are very often, by the Hebrew poets, spoken of under the figure of *waters*, in which a person is in danger of sinking, or being overwhelmed by,—Psal. xxxii. 6; lxix. 1, 2; Isa. xxviii. 2; xliii. 2. Indeed, the figure is found in all languages.

The third part of the hymn of triumph—the account of the Messiah's miraculous deliverance—comes now to be considered.

It is worthy of remark, that the wonderful events detailed are represented as the effect—the answers of the Messiah's prayers. "I called upon the Lord, and cried unto my God: He heard my voice out of his temple, and my cry came before Him, even into his ears. *Then* the earth shook and trembled." It seemed but the voice of a feeble, suffering, dying man, but that was the voice of Him of whom it is said, "His voice then shook the earth," at Sinai, and this was the fulfilment of what he had promised, "Yet once more I shake not the earth only, but also heaven."[1]

The general idea it is not difficult to recognize. A tremendous preternatural agitation of the elements of nature takes place, produced by the power of Jehovah, influenced by his regard for his beloved servant, and his indignation against his enemies, amid which, and by means of which, they are punished, and he is delivered. The first thing to be done, in order to a satisfactory exposition of this paragraph, is to endeavor to form a distinct idea of the picture which the inspired poet brings before the mind, and makes the vehicle of his prediction of the deliverance of the Messiah, and the discomfiture of his enemies.

It has been very generally supposed that the imagery here has been borrowed from the Mosaic narrative of the passage of the Red Sea by the Israelites, and of the giving of the law.[2] This opinion seems to rest on no sufficient foundation. "The imagery," as Michaelis justly remarks, "is derived from nature, not from history."[3] There were earthquakes and thunders at the giving of the law; but there have been many earthquakes, and it often has thundered. There is nothing in the storm here described peculiar to that which took place at Sinai. It is a description of a more terrific storm than earth ever witnessed, emblematic of the tremendous dispensations which characterized the deliverance of Messiah in his person and in his cause. The most dreadful appearances of nature, exalted by the divinely-excited

---

[1] Heb. xii. 26.   [2] Exod. xiv. 19–30; xix. 16–25; xx. 18–21.

[3] "Tota imago ex natura petita est non ex historia. Lata quidem inter tonitrua lex est: sed sæpius tonuit. Neque hic ulla latæ legis mentio, nihil quod illi procellæ privum fuerit. Describitur autem gravior tempestas, non qualis est, et intelligitur a naturæ peritis, sed qualis poetis esse videtur."—*Notæ ad Lowthum*, N. xliv.

imagination of the psalmist, are assembled together in one picture, and the impression is indefinitely increased by these appearances being represented as produced by the direct agency of the present Divinity.

Jehovah had for a season permitted the enemies of his beloved Servant to triumph ; but, from his dwelling-place, his eye was on them and on him, regarding him with infinite complacency—them with holy displeasure. And now, in the hour of their apparent triumph and his utter discomfiture, He comes out of his place to punish them and deliver him. "The Lord is a man of war, Jehovah is his name." He comes as the Lord of hosts, the supreme ruler of all the elements. The figure is not, as has been supposed, that of a warrior mounted on his war-horse—a figurative view never given of the Divinity in Scripture—but of a warrior sitting in his war-chariot, drawn by fleet and powerful coursers.[1] He comes in the thunder-cloud moved by angelic instrumentality. He rides on the cherub—the singular being, according to a Hebrew usage, employed for the plural, the cherubim.[2] "The chariots of God are twenty thousand, even

---

[1] Milton had this among other passages of Scripture in his eye, in the following description :—

> —— "Forth rush'd, with whirlwind sound,
> The chariot of paternal Deity,
> Flashing thick flames, wheel within wheel, undrawn,
> Itself instinct with spirit ; but convoyed
> By fair cherubic shapes."—*Par. Lost*, vi.

[2] 'Cherub' is a word expressive of strength. It is applied to unembodied spirits higher in the scale of being than man. When described as wearing a visible form, they unite the appearance of a man, an ox, a lion, and an eagle, Ezek. i. 10 ; Rev. iv. 6, 7. The symbol, no doubt, intimates their possession, in a high degree, of the qualities of all these. The singular, 'cherub,' is probably here used for the plural, 'cherubim,'—more ordinarily used in such a case. It is common in Hebrew to use the singular for the plural of multitude.—Exod. viii. 6,—The frog for multitudes of frogs ; Numb. xxi. 7,—the serpent, for multitudes of serpents ; Exod. x. 4,—the locust ; Exod. xxiii. 28,—the hornet. The same usage prevails in other languages. Virgil says, in reference to the Trojan horse,—

> ——"Uterumque armato *milite* complent."

We, in the same way, use 'the horse' for 'cavalry ;' and say, 'the swallow has arrived,'—'the caterpillar has attacked the fruit trees.' "The cherub is such a being as, standing upon the highest stage of the creaturely life, and combining in itself the most perfect kinds of creaturely life, is the most complete manifestation of God, and of the divine life. It is an image of the creature in its highest form,—an ideal creature. The powers of life, which are divided amongst the creatures that occupy the highest place in the visible creation, are in it combined and individualized."—BAEHR, *Symbolik. Theol.* l. p. 341, ap. Hengstenberg.

thousands of angels."[1] The first indication of his presence is that most dreadful of all physical phenomena—the earthquake. No sooner does his chariot touch the earth, than the great globe trembles to its centre—the foundations of the hills, notwithstanding their superincumbent weight, are moved. "The mountains quake at Him;" and, while the mountains are trembling, and all the hills moving lightly, a thick, livid, sulphurous gloom overspreads the earth, from which ever and anon break forth flashes of the forked lightning, the smoke out of *his* nostrils, the devouring fire out of his mouth. Coals are kindled at it—rather firebrands, thunderbolts, go forth from it. "Behold, the name of the Lord cometh from far, burning with his anger: his lips are full of indignation, and his tongue as a devouring fire."[2] The pillared firmament seems crushed down—"He bows the heavens and comes down;" a preternatural gloom pervades the earth—"darkness is under his feet;" the thunder-clouds are, in wild commotion, moving in all directions—"HE flies on the wings of the wind," or, as the old paraphrast has it,

> "On the wings of all the winds,
> Comes flying all abroad."

In the midst of that darkness, Jehovah dwells as in a tabernacle. "He made darkness his secret place: his pavilion round about Him dark waters and clouds of the skies." The storm now rages in all its fury. By the bright flashes of the lightning the clouds are broken, and hail, mingled with fire, is poured out on the earth. And still the thunder rolls on high, and still the lightnings flash forth, and the hail descends. The clouds pour out water,—the skies send forth a sound,—his arrows go abroad,—the voice of his thunder is in the heavens,—his lightnings lighten the world,—the earth trembles and shakes. The enemies of Messiah and his cause are represented as set in battle array against Jehovah and his Anointed One. In the unequal conflict they are utterly routed and overcome. "He sent out his arrows, and scattered them; He shot out lightnings, and discomfited them." "Thou, even Thou, art to be feared; and who may stand in thy sight, when once Thou art angry? Thou didst cause judgment to be heard from heaven; the earth feared, and was still, when God arose to judgment, to save all the meek of the earth."[3] By

---

[1] Psal. lxviii. 17.   [2] Isa. xxx. 27.   [3] Psal. lxxvi. 7–9.

these tremendous commotions, great changes are produced. The channels of rivers and seas are laid bare, and the foundations of the earth, which, according to the Hebrew mode of viewing things, was founded on the waters, were discovered. The whole aspect of nature is altered. What was sea is dry land, and what was dry land is a wide waste of waters.

Amid these strange changes, and by means of them, Jehovah delivered the Messiah and his cause from depression, and suffering, and danger, while He overwhelmed with disappointment and ruin his enemies. *His* deliverance of the Messiah is described by a variety of figures. He was in deep waters, and in danger of being overwhelmed by them, and Jehovah sent from above, laid hold of him, and brought him forth[1] from the devouring deeps. He was in the hands of strong and malignant enemies, and Jehovah delivered him out of their hands. In the day of his calamity, when those enemies came before him, and met him in whatever direction he turned, Jehovah was his stay and helper, and ultimately removed him far beyond the reach of their malice and power. He brought him from a state of confinement into a large place. He thus delivered him, for He delighted in him.

In seeking for the events in the history of the Messiah, in which these prophetic representations have found, or are to find, their accomplishment, we are to remember that the oracle has the ordinary character of Messianic prophecies. It refers to the Messiah both in his person and his cause; and it has had, and will have, its fulfilment, not in one event or in one age, but in a series of events during successive ages, till the mystery of God is finished, and Messiah and his cause become finally and completely triumphant, being "delivered from all their enemies, and from the power of the grave." To attempt to find anything like an adequate correspondence to the description before us in the events of David's life, is a hopeless undertaking.[2] How

---

[1] Hengstenberg supposes there is a reference to Exod. ii. 10, and that David marks himself as the second Moses. משה occurs nowhere else except here and in the original passage. Luther also notices the circumstance.

[2] He is really easily reconciled to an interpretation who is satisfied with Rosenmuller's remark,—and I am not aware that any of those who hold the Davidical reference have said, or can say, anything better,—" Hic poetica εἰδωλοποιία videtur, quæ simpliciter hoc dicit, ' Deum iratum hostibus Davidis, et precibus ejus contra hos excitatum, subvenisse invocanti ope mirabili atque gloriosa.' "

accurately it answers to what has taken place, and will yet take place, in reference to Christ and his cause, I shall now endeavor to make evident.   The general statement in the oracle is, that the Messiah and his cause should be delivered from degradation and suffering, amid and by events of an extraordinary character, disordering the common course of nature.   We will find that, whether the words are understood literally or metaphorically, this is their meaning, and that, both literally and metaphorically, they have been verified.[1]

Let us first endeavor to show that this oracle has been fulfilled with respect to the Messiah personally.   His humiliation reached its lowest point when he died on the cross, and was laid in the sepulchre.   Then " the sorrows of death compassed him, the floods of Belial made him afraid ;" then the " cords of the separate state surrounded him, and the snares of death entangled him."   He appears utterly vanquished, and his enemies more than conquerors.   But the preparation for *his* deliverance and *their* overthrow was now completed in heaven.   The "prayers and supplications, with strong crying and tears, to Him who was able to save him from death," have not been offered in vain.   The displeasure of the Almighty at the enemies of the Messiah, and his approbation of him and his cause, were testified as the Almighty only can do.   While Jesus hung on the cross, a preternatural " darkness covered all the land ;" and no sooner had he yielded up his spirit, than " the vail of the temple was rent in twain from the top even to the bottom, and the earth did quake, and the rocks rent, and the graves were opened ; and many bodies of the saints that slept arose, and came out of the graves, after his resurrection, and went into the holy city, and appeared unto many."   So evident was the Divine hand in these events, that the Roman centurion exclaimed, "Truly this was a righteous man ;" " truly this was the Son of God."[2]   He, however, still continues in the state of the dead ; he lies in the sepulchre ; but

---

[1] " Nihil prohibet, quominus hic cogitemus de illa rerum omnium commotione de qua post prophetam Aggæum loquitur apostolus,—Heb. xi. 26."—AMYRAUT.   It is of importance to remark, that what is done by subordinate agents, is in Scripture represented as done by God ; as in the destruction of Sodom and Gomorrah, Gen. xix. 13, 24 ; in the destruction of the first-born in Egypt, Exod. xi. 4,—xii. 12, 2 3 ; in the destruction of the Egyptians at the Red Sea, Exod. xiii. 21,—xiv. 19, 24 ; and in the wars with the Canaanites, Josh. v. 13-15,—x. 11.   *Vide* Weiss, *ad loc.*

[2] Matth. xxvii. 45, 51-54.   Luke, xxiii. 47.

" in the end of the Sabbath, as it began to dawn toward the first day of the week," "there was a great earthquake; for the angel of the Lord descended from heaven, and came and rolled back the stone from the door, and sat upon it. His countenance was like lightning, and his raiment white as snow: and for fear of him the keepers did shake, and became as dead men."[1] Thus did God send from above, and take him and draw him out of the depths. Thus did He deliver him from his strong enemy; and not only raising him from the dust of death, but taking him up into heaven, and setting him at his own right hand, made him both Lord and Christ. Messiah thus exchanged the prison of the grave for the palace and throne of the universe.

But though he is personally delivered, and exalted, and placed far beyond the reach of his enemies, he has a people and a cause on the earth with which he identifies himself. "Saul, Saul, why persecutest thou ME?" "Inasmuch as ye did it to the least of these my brethren, ye did it unto me." The glorified Head in heaven sympathises with the suffering body on earth: their enemies are his enemies; and he will not consider his own victory complete till they, through him, are made more than conquerors. Let us endeavor to trace the fulfilment of this oracle in reference to the triumph of his cause, and the destruction of his enemies, since " he sat down on the right hand of God, from henceforth expecting till his enemies be made his footstool."

The first remarkable fulfilment we meet with is in the destruction of our Lord's Jewish enemies, and the deliverance of his church from their persecutions. Many of the particular predictions, in the following part of the psalm, seem to have a special reference to these events. It is remarkable that these events are predicted both by the Old Testament prophets and by our Lord, in language very similar to that of the oracle under consideration. Thus Isaiah—"Judgment also will I lay to the line, and righteousness to the plummet; and the hail shall sweep away the refuge of lies." "The Lord shall rise up as in mount Perazim, He shall be wroth as in the valley of Gibeon, that He may do his work, his strange work; and bring to pass his act, his strange act." " A voice of noise from the city, a voice from the temple, a voice of the Lord that rendereth recompense to his

---

[1] Matth. xxviii. 1–4.

enemies."[1]   Thus Joel—"And I will show wonders in the heavens and in the earth, blood, and fire, and pillars of smoke. The sun shall be turned into darkness, and the moon into blood, before the great and the terrible day of the Lord come."[2]   Thus Malachi—"The day cometh that shall burn as an oven ; and all the proud, yea, and all that do wickedly, shall be stubble : and the day that cometh shall burn them up, saith the Lord of hosts, that it shall leave them neither root nor branch."[3]   Thus our Lord—"Nation shall rise against nation, and kingdom against kingdom; and there shall be famines, and pestilences, and earthquakes, in divers places ;" "and fearful sights and great signs shall there be from heaven." "These are the beginning of sorrows." "Then shall be great tribulation and distress in the land, and wrath upon this people, such as was not from the beginning of the creation, which God created, unto this time ; no, nor ever shall be. And there shall be signs in the sun, and in the moon, and in the stars ; and upon the earth distress of nations, with perplexity ; the sea and the waves roaring ; men's hearts failing them for fear, and for looking after those things which are coming on the earth."[4]

Of the fulfilment of the oracle in the destruction of Jerusalem, and of its guilty inhabitants, the most inveterate enemies of Christ and his cause, Josephus, their own unbelieving historian, furnishes abundant evidence. I shall cite a few passages from his "History of the Jewish Wars." "In the night in which the Idumeans lay before Jerusalem, there arose a prodigious tempest and fierce winds, with most vehement rains, frequent lightnings, and terrible thunderings, and great roarings of the shaken earth ; and it was manifest that the state of the universe was disordered at the slaughter of men ; so that one might guess that these were signs of no small calamity." "At the day of Pentecost, when the priests, by night, went into the inner temple, according to their custom, to execute their office, they said they perceived, first of all, a shaking and a noise, and after that a sudden voice, 'Let us go hence.'" "A few days after the feast of unleavened bread, a strange and almost incredible sight was seen, which would, I suppose, be taken for a

---

[1] Isa. xxviii. 17, 21 ; lxvi. 6.   [2] Joel, ii. 30.   [3] Mal. iv. 1.
[4] Matth xxiv. 7, etc. Mark, xiii. 8, etc.   Luke, xxi. 10, etc.

mere fable, were it not related by such as saw it, and did not
the miseries which followed appear answerable to the signs : for,
before the sun set, were seen on high, in the air, all over the
country, chariots and armed regiments moving swiftly in the
clouds, and encompassing the city."[1] How Jehovah sent out
his arrows and scattered that guilty people, how He shot out his
lightnings and scattered them, is known to every reader of history. And not less remarkable was the deliverance thus wrought
for the people and cause of Christ. They who persevered were
most wonderfully delivered, when the great body of their countrymen were destroyed. An opportunity was strangely afforded
to the Christians in Jerusalem to comply with their Lord's command to withdraw from the doomed city ; and, all over the
Roman empire, the Christian churches generally obtained rest
from the harassing persecutions of the Jews.

The next great event, in which we find a farther verification
of the oracle, is the destruction of the pagan Roman empire, and
the deliverance of the people and cause of Christ from persecution by this means. The events which were to prepare the way
for the general establishment of Christianity among the nations,
are predicted both in the Old and New Testament under images
similar to those employed in the passage under consideration.
Take, for example, Psalm xcvii., which, we know, is an account of
Jehovah "bringing in his First-begotten into the world"—putting
him in possession of his promised inheritance of the heathen.
" Clouds and darkness are round about Him : righteousness and
judgment are the habitation of his throne. A fire goeth before
Him, and burneth up his enemies round about. His lightnings enlightened the world ; the earth saw, and trembled.
The hills melted like wax at the presence of the Lord : at the
presence of the Lord of the whole earth. The heavens declare
his righteousness, and all the people see his glory. Confounded
be all they that serve graven images, that boast themselves of
idols : worship Him, all ye gods. Zion heard, and was glad ;
and the daughters of Judah rejoiced because of thy judgments."
" Light is sown for the righteous, and gladness for the upright
in heart." Take, as another example, the passage in Hagai, ii.
6, 7 :—" Yet once, it is a little while, and I will shake the

---

[1] Jos. de Bell. Jud. iv. 17 ; vii. 31.

heavens, and the earth, and the sea, and the dry land; and I will shake all nations, and the Desire of all nations shall come." Look, now, at the still more graphic description of John the divine, when the events were comparatively near at hand:— "And when he had opened the fifth seal, I saw under the altar the souls of them that were slain for the word of God, and for the testimony which they held; and they cried with a loud voice, saying, How long, O Lord, holy and true, dost thou not judge and avenge our blood on them that dwell on the earth?" "And I beheld when he had opened the sixth seal, and, lo, there was a great earthquake; and the sun became black as sackcloth of hair, and the moon became as blood; and the stars of heaven fell unto the earth, even as a fig-tree casteth her untimely figs, when she is shaken of a mighty wind; and the heaven departed as a scroll when it is rolled together; and every mountain and island were moved out of their places. And the kings of the earth, and the great men, and the rich men, and the chief captains, and the mighty men, and every bond man, and every free man, hid themselves in the dens, and in the rocks of the mountains; and said to the mountains and rocks, Fall on us, and hide us from the face of Him that sitteth on the throne, and from the wrath of the Lamb: for the great day of his wrath is come; and who shall be able to stand?"[1]

How fearfully the enemies of Christianity were punished at the time referred to, when the empire ceased to be pagan, and how remarkably Christianity and Christians were delivered from persecution, is known to every one at all acquainted with history. "The ruin of the pagan religion," says the infidel Gibbon, "is described by the sophists as a dreadful and amazing prodigy, which covered the earth with darkness, and restored the ancient dominion of chaos and of night."

These three stages of fulfilment are long ago past. There remain yet two behind, very distinctly marked in the sure word of prophecy. The next, on the borders of which many appearances seem to indicate that we now stand, is the course of events which is to terminate the reign of antichrist, and introduce the glories of the millennial age.[2] The prayers of the saints, which

[1] Rev. vi. 9, 10, 12–17.

[2] "I cannot resist the feeling that a greater than David is here, and that the description applies more to the final conflict dimly portrayed in the Book of Revelation,

are at once the result of the influence of the Spirit of Christ, and the subject of his intercession, are ascending for the full coming of the kingdom of Messiah the Prince. On these prayers being presented by the angel who stands at the altar, having a golden censer, he is represented as taking the censer, and filling it with the fire of the altar, and casting it on the earth, and "there are voices, and thunderings, and lightnings, and an earthquake." At the same period, "the nations are angry, and God's wrath is come;" "and there are lightnings, and voices, and thunderings, and an earthquake, and great hail." "And there came a great voice out of the temple of heaven, from the throne, saying, It is done. And there were voices, and thunders, and lightnings; and there was a great earthquake, such as was not since men were upon the earth, so mighty an earthquake, and so great. And the great city was divided into three parts, and the cities of the nations fell: and great Babylon came in remembrance before God, to give unto her the cup of the wine of the fierceness of his wrath. And every island fled away, and the mountains were not found. And there fell upon men a great hail out of heaven, every stone about the weight of a talent."[1] It is not for us minutely to decipher the symbols of unfulfilled prophecy; but this obviously is to be another stage in the accomplishment of the oracle before us, intimating that, amid and by strange appearances, physical and political, Christ and his cause are to become triumphant, while their obstinate enemies are to be covered with discomfiture and ruin. Then the Lord God Almighty is "to take to himself his great power and reign," and "the kingdoms of this world are to become the kingdom of our Lord and his Christ." The long battle between the Lamb and the kings of the Latin earth is to terminate in their overthrow. "These shall make war with the Lamb, and the Lamb shall overcome them: for he is Lord of lords, and King of kings."[2]

This oracle, like so many more, is to find its complete accomplishment at the time of the consummation of all things. The

---

and which terminates in an overthrow of the powers of darkness, and the ushering in of the 'new heavens and the new earth, wherein dwelleth righteousness.' . . . It may also be held as applying to that mysterious conflict when Christ spoiled principalities and powers, and was drawn out of the agony which well nigh overwhelmed him."—Dr. CHALMERS, *Daily Scripture Readings*, iii. pp. 15, 16.

[1] Rev. viii. 5; xi. 13, 18, 19; xvi. 17–21.　　　　　[2] Rev. xvii. 14.

Messiah and his cause are, during the millennium, to occupy a
far higher place on earth than during any former period ; and
their enemies are to be reduced to comparative insignificance.
Yet, even then, the material part of millions of his chosen ones
lies under the dominion of death. "And when the thousand
years are expired, Satan shall be loosed out of his prison, and
shall go out to deceive the nations which are in the four quar-
ters of the earth, to gather them together to battle."[1] This is
to be the final conflict. "Fire shall come down from God out
of heaven to consume them." And now, amid the piercing
notes of the last trumpet, the voice of the archangel, and the
thunders of a dissolving world, the great white throne appears,
and the Servant of the Lord, once so humbled, sits on it the
judge of the universe ; and at his all-powerful word the wicked
—his irreclaimable enemies—go away into everlasting punishment; and the righteous—his saved ones,—in bodies like unto
his glorious body, go with him into life eternal.

The beloved Servant of the Lord, with all his faithful followers, are thus, by this wonderful succession of extraordinary divine
dispensations, delivered from all his and their enemies, and from
the hand of the grave; and then, in a song forever new, will he,
during the ages of eternity, declare Jehovah's name to his
brethren, and in the midst of the great congregation praise
Him, saying, "I will love Thee, O Lord, my strength. The
Lord is my rock, and my fortress, and my deliverer ; my God,
my strength, in whom I will trust; my buckler, and the horn of
my salvation, and my high tower." In these events—in no
other—do the magnificent descriptions of the prophetical oracle
find an adequate and complete realization.

All these glorious events are but the manifestation of the complacential delight Jehovah has in the person, character, and
work of his beloved Servant,—the meritorious result of his voluntary humiliation and suffering. "He brings him forth into a
large place ; He delivers him, because He delights in him."
Well He may. This sentiment forms the text, as it were, of the
fourth section of this triumphal hymn, which will, if it please
God, form the subject of our next discourse.

Meanwhile, we conclude with a few reflections.—How obviously

---

[1] Rev. xx. 7, 8.

are Christ and Christianity the objects of the Divine complacency and care! " The heathen have raged ; the people have imagined many a vain thing. The kings of the earth have set themselves, and the rulers have taken counsel together, against the Lord, and against his Anointed." " He that sitteth in the heavens has laughed : the Lord has had them in derision." No weapon formed against Christianity has prospered ;—every tongue that has risen up in judgment against it, God has condemned.

How foolish, how criminal, how dangerous, to disregard *Him*, or to oppose *it !* How absolutely certain the overthrow of all systems based on unchristian, antichristian principles, by whatever measure of worldly wisdom and power they are sustained ! How complete and hopeless the ruin of individuals who, by continuing unbelieving and disobedient to him, persist in despising the Divine grace, and braving the Divine vengeance ! Oh, that the united voice of history and prophecy could but find its way to the ears and hearts of the rulers of the earth,—" Be wise now, O ye kings ; be instructed, ye judges of the earth. Serve the Lord with fear, and rejoice with trembling." Oh, that the merciful warning may produce its proper effect on every one of *us*, —" Kiss the Son, lest he be angry, and ye perish from the way, when his wrath is kindled but a little. Blessed are all they that put their trust in him."

Note B, p. 78

The following attempts to transfuse into other languages the striking description contained in the 9th and following verses may be interesting to some readers :—

> " Οὐρανόθεν κατέπαλτο πόλον φλογοειδέα κλίνας
> Ἀθανάτου πεφόρητο γνόθος παρὰ ποσσὶ θεοῖο
> Ἐμβεβαὼς ὀχέεσσιν ἑοῖς πεκότητο χερουβίμ
> Ἵπτατο βυκτάων ἀνέμων πτερύγεσσιν ἀερθεὶς
> Κευθόμενος κνέφαι. τὸ γὰρ ἤθελεν ἄλκαρ ἐλέσθαι."

This is from the first metrical version of the psalms we are acquainted with. The author is Apollinarius, who lived in the fourth century, and who, when Julian forbade the study of the classics by Christians, wrote poems taken from the Old Testament history for their use.

The Latin translation which follows, is also very ancient. It is corrected by Sylburgūs :—

> " De Cœlo descendit, cœlum ignitum inclinnas :
> Immortalis ferebatur caligo sub pedibus Dei :
> Ascendens curribus suis volavit super cherubim :
> Volavit velocium ventorum pennis elevatus,
> Tectus caligine : hoc enim voluit auxilium capere."

STERNHOLD, 1549.

> " The Lord descended from above,
> 　　And bow'd the heavens high,
> And underneath his feet He cast
> 　　The darkness of the sky.

> " On cherubs and on cherubims
> 　　Full royally He rode,
> And on the wings of mighty winds,
> 　　Came flying all abroad."

BUCHANAN, 1565.

> " Utque suum Dominum terræ demittat in orbem
> Leniter inclinat jussum fastigia cœlum :
> Succedunt pedibus fuscæ caliginis umbræ.
> Ille vehens curru volucri, cui flammeus ales
> Lora tenens levibus ventorum adremigat alis ;
> Se circum furvo nebularum involvit amictu,
> Prætenditque cavis piceas in nubibus undas."

ARCHBISHOP PARKER, 1567.

> " The heavens full low He made to bow,
> 　　And down did He ensue ;
> And darkness great was underset,
> 　　His feet in clouds of hue.

> " He rode on high, and did so fly
> 　　Upon the cherubims ;
> He came in sight, and made his flight
> 　　Upon the wings of winds ;

> " The Lord from heaven sent down his leven,
> 　　And thunder'd thence in ire ;
> He thunder cast in wondrous blast,
> 　　With hail and coals of fire."

SIR PHILIP SYDNEY, *written* before 1586, first printed, 1823.

> " He bow'd the heavens, and from the bow'd heavens did descend
> With angry darkness, which aboute his feet did węnd ;
> The cherubim their backes, the windes did yield their winges,
> To bear his sacred flight ; in secret place then clos'd,
> About which He dimme clouds like a pavilion brings :
> Cloudes even of waters, dark and thickest aire compos'd ;
> But straight his shining eyes this misty masse dissolv'd ;
> Then haile, then fire-coales, then thunder'd heavenly Sire ;
> Then spake He his loude voice, then hailstone, coles, and fire.

AINSWORTH, 1612.

" And he bowed the heavens and came down, and gloomy darkness was under his feet; and he rode upon the cherub and did fly; and He flew swiftly on the wings of the wind. He set darkness his secret place, round about Him his pavilion,—darkness of waters, thick clouds of the skies."

KING JAMES, 1631.

" He also did bow down the heavens, and did in state descend ;
And darkness did in threatening clouds under his feet attend ;—
And He upon a cherub rode, and did most swiftly fly ;
Yea, on the wings of all the winds, his flight was raised high.

" He darkness made his secret place ; his tent Him round about
Dark waters were, and clouds most thick, from skies in state stretch'd out ;
And as the glorious brightness there, that did go Him before ;
Thick clouds did pass with hailstones join'd, and coals of fire in store."

SANDYS, 1636.

" In his descent, bow'd heaven with earth did meet,
And gloomy darkness roll'd beneath his feet ;
A golden winged cherub He bestrid,
And on the swiftly-flying tempest rid.

" He darkness made his secret cabinet ;
Thick fogs and dropping clouds about him set ;
The beams of his bright presence these expel,
Whence showers of burning coals and hailstones fell."

ARTHUR JOHNSTON, 1637.

" Æthere diducto, solio descendit ab alto
Nubila sidereos implicuere pedes
Ventorum volucris humeris circumdedit alas,
Scandit et ætherei flammea terga chori.
Quaque volat nubes glomerans se condidit umbris
Et circumfusis undique texit aquis."

BARTON, 1644.

" The Almighty Lord the heavens bow'd,
And downward did descend ;
Beneath his feet a sable cloud
Of darkness did extend.

" A cherub chariot did Him bear,
Whose plumes He made his sail ;
The winds He made his winged carre,
And darkness was his vail."

ROUS, 1645.

" He bow'd the heavens, came down, below his feet did darkness lie ;
He rode on cherub and did fly—on wings of wind did fly ;
Darkness He made his secret place ; about him for his tent
Darkness of waters were, and clouds thick of the firmament.

Scotch Version, 1649.

" He also bowed down the heavens,
　　And thence he did descend ;
And thickest clouds of darkness did,
　　Under his feet attend.

" And He upon a cherub rode,
　　And thereon he did fly ;
Yea, on the swift wings of the wind,
　　His flight was from on high.

" He darkness made his secret place ;
　　About Him for his tent
Dark waters were, and thickest clouds
　　Of the airy firmament."

Tate and Brady, 1698.

" He left the beauteous realms of light,
　　While heaven bow'd down its awful head ;
Beneath his feet substantial night
　　Was like a sable carpet spread.

" The chariot of the King of kings,
　　Which active troops of angels drew,
On a strong tempest's rapid wing,
　　With most amazing swiftness flew."

Watts, 1719.

" When God, our leader, shines in arms,
　　What mortal heart can bear,
The thunder of his loud alarms,
　　The lightning of his spear !

" He rides upon the winged wind,
　　And angels in array,
In millions wait to know his mind,
　　And swift as flames obey."

Lowth, 1753.

" Inclinat cœlos et descendit : sub pedibus ejus caligo densa :
　Et inequitat cherubo et volat ; et fertur super alis venti.
　Facit tenebras penetrale suum, tabernaculum sibi circum undique ;
　Tenebras aquarum, densa nubium.

Houbigant, 1753.

" Inclinavit cœlos atque descendit ; caligo sub pedibus ejus. Equitavit super cherubim et volavit ; volavit super alas ventorum. Posuit tenebras latebram circum se ; tabernaculum suum, conglomerationem aquarum, nubis cœlorum. Præ fulgore ejus diffluxerunt nubes ejus ; accensa sunt grando et ignei carbones."

Michælis, 1758.

" Inclinat cœlum et descendit, et nimbus est sub pedibus ejus,
　Equo tonante vehitur volatque, et fertur alis venti
　Caliginem ponit latibulum suum, circa se tabernaculum suum
　Tenebras aquarum nubes conglomeratas."

MERRICK, 1765.

" Incumbent on the bending sky,
  The Lord descended from on high ;
  And bade the darkness of the pole,
  Beneath his feet tremendous roll.

" The cherub to his car He join'd,
  And on the wings of mightiest wind,
  As down to earth his journey lay,
  Resistless urged his rapid way.

" Thick woven clouds, around Him clos'd,
  His secret residence compos'd ;
  And waters, high suspended, spread
  Their dark pavilion o'er his head."

DATHE, 1794.

" Inclinavit cœlum et descendit,
  Caligo erat sub pedibus ejus,
  Vectus est cherubo et volabat,
  Volabat super alis venti.
  Fecit tenebras suum latibulum
  Tergurium quo erat cinctus
  Aquæ nigræ, nubes condensata."

MARSH, 1832.

" Then was the earth asunder riv'n,
  Shook the foundations of the heav'n,
      And trembled at his ire.
  Forth from his nostrils pass'd a smoke,
  Flames from his mouth in vengeance broke,
      And kindled coals of fire.

" The heavens were bow'd as He came down,
  Thick clouds beneath his feet were strewn.
  He on a cherub rode. He flew.
  Attendant winds their Sov'reign knew."

Among these versions, of very various degrees of merit, it is gratify-
ing to a Scotsman to perceive what a respectable place the vernacular
translation, to which he has been accustomed from his childhood, holds.
It has been the fashion with our Southern neighbors to sneer at that
version on account of its occasional baldness and harshness ; but it will
stand a comparison with any literal metrical version in any language. It
is commonly considered as little better than a reprint of Rous' version ;
but this, as appears even from the above specimens, is a mistake. It
was the result of the careful labors of a committee of the General Assembly of the Church of Scotland. An interesting history of this version
is given in the last edition of Principal Baillie's letters, by its accomplished
editor, David Laing, Esq.

LECTURE V

THE MESSIAH'S DELIVERANCE THE WORK OF JEHOVAH—A WORK
ILLUSTRATIVE OF HIS RIGHTEOUSNESS AND BENIGNITY

PSALM XVIII. 20–24.—"The Lord rewarded me according to my righteousness;
according to the cleanness of my hands hath He recompensed me. For I have kept
the ways of the Lord, and have not wickedly departed from my God. For all his judgments were before me, and I did not put away his statutes from me. I was also upright before Him, and I kept myself from mine iniquity. Therefore hath the Lord
recompensed me according to my righteousness, according to the cleanness of my
hands in his eye-sight."

To strangers to Christianity, when solicited to examine and receive it, nothing about it has generally appeared so revolting as
the doctrine of the cross ; and the conduct of the advocates of
that religion, in giving this doctrine so prominent a place in all
their representations of it, has seemed strange and unaccountable. "To the Jew" in the primitive age, "the cross"—both
the fact that the Author of Christianity died the death of a felonious slave, and the doctrine, that that death was the effectual
expiation of the sins of men—"was a stumbling-block, and to
the Greeks foolishness." They rejected the whole system with
scorn, because of its connection with a fact so disgraceful and a
dogma so paradoxical ; and could not help regarding, as consummate foolishness, the conduct of the primitive evangelists in
placing in the very foreground of their representations minute
details of the one and strong statements of the other, and their
expectations in cherishing and avowing the hope of success, not
only notwithstanding, but by means of, such representations.
It seemed to them absolute madness to anticipate in this way
the making proselytes to the new faith.

And no doubt, at first sight, the conduct of the Christian
evangelists does appear somewhat extraordinary. In the gospel
histories, our Saviour's uncommon popularity as a teacher, the

immense crowds which flocked to hear his discourse and see his miracles, and the high honors to which they were ready to raise him—these facts, so well fitted to make a favorable impression on the minds of men, are merely cursorily mentioned; while, on the other hand, every circumstance of degradation and suffering is minutely chronicled, from his birth in a stable to his death on a cross; and a singularly detailed account is given, of his being apprehended as a malefactor, condemned as an impostor, blasphemer, and traitor, and publicly executed as if he had been a felonious slave. The sermons of the apostles and their fellow-laborers were fashioned after the model of the gospel histories. The superior reasonableness of the doctrines of Christianity respecting the character and government of God, when compared with the absurdities of the popular creed, and even the most plausible speculations of the philosophical schools,—and the superior purity, simplicity, completeness, and practicability of the morality of Christianity, when compared with every other system of morals ever presented to the world, were themes on which the wisdom of the world would have taught the primitive teachers of Christianity principally, if not exclusively, to expatiate. These, however, are rather left to be inferred by the disciple than laboriously unfolded by the teacher. The doctrine of the expiation of the sins of men, through the obedience, and sufferings, and death of him who was not only a perfect man, but an incarnation of Divinity, held the first place in their discourses. In preaching the Gospel, they declared what they had received "first of all," that "Christ died for our sins according to the Scriptures." The banner they displayed was the banner of the cross. Under it they fought and they conquered. They determined to know nothing among those whom they instructed, but "Jesus Christ and him crucified." "God forbid," says one of them—and he but expressed their common faith and determination—"that I should glory save in the cross of our Lord Jesus Christ."

Strange and unaccountable, irrational and unwise, as such conduct appeared, and still appears, to men of unenlightened minds, no man who thoroughly understands the Christian system can wonder at it. The cross of Christ is the foundation of all the Christian preacher's hope for himself as an individual, and of all his hope, too, for the real improvement and happiness of

mankind in time and in eternity. He believes that, in the fullest
sense of the terms, ' the blood of the Saviour is the seed of the
church.' He is fully persuaded of the truth of our Lord's
mystic declaration,—" Except a corn of wheat fall into the
ground, and die, it abideth alone : but if it die, it bringeth
forth much fruit."[1] He believes that the bloody passion of the
Son of God has obtained eternal redemption for all who believe
in him, and for himself—supreme authority, unlimited dominion; " the heathen for his inheritance,"—" the uttermost
parts of the earth for his possession;" the worship of angels and
the control of devils ; " a name above every name "—Saviour
of the world ; Lord of all. Who can wonder, then, at the place
the cross holds in scripture representations of Christianity !
Who can wonder that Christian teachers should glory in it !
The cross was the way to the crown ; and all the authority and
power—all the honor and dominion—to which the Messiah has
been raised, are the dear-earned rewards of his mediatorial
labors and sorrows.

In this, as in every other important point, " The spirit of
prophecy is the testimony of Jesus." In the fourth section of
this Messianic psalm, which now lies before us for consideration,
we find the beloved Servant of Jehovah, delivered from all his
enemies and the power of the grave, representing, in his solemn
thanksgiving, his deliverance and exaltation as the expression of
Jehovah's entire satisfaction with his conduct, and as the merited
reward of his having become obedient—obedient even to the
death—in the execution of the great undertaking with which he
had been intrusted,—in accomplishing which he had been compassed with the sorrows of death, terrified by the floods of Belial,
surrounded by the cords of the separate state, entangled in the
snares of death,—and for accomplishing which, Jehovah, by
wonderful displays of divine power, had sent from above, taken
him and drawn him out of many waters, delivered him from his
strong enemy, and from them who hated him, brought him forth
into a large place and delivered him. All this was the manifestation of the delight which Jehovah had in his suffering Servant,
the pleasure which He had in his bruised One. " The Lord
rewarded me according to my righteousness ; according to the

[1] John, xii. 24.

cleanness of my hands hath he recompensed me. For I have
kept the ways of the Lord, and have not wickedly departed
from my God. For all his judgments were before me, and I did
not put away his statutes from me. I was also upright before
Him, and I kept myself from mine iniquity. Therefore hath the
Lord recompensed me according to my righteousness, according
to the cleanness of my hands in his eye-sight. With the merciful Thou wilt show thyself merciful; with an upright man Thou
wilt show thyself upright; with the pure Thou wilt show thyself
pure; and with the froward Thou wilt show thyself froward."

It is scarcely necessary to recall to your minds, that I have endeavored at length to prove that this psalm is a Messianic
oracle, referring directly and solely to the person and cause of
Jesus Christ, whom we hold to be the Messiah, in whom " we
have found him of whom Moses in the law, and the prophets did
write ;" and that on that principle I have expounded the introduction to the hymn contained in the 1st, 2d, and 3d verses; the
account of the Messiah's humiliation and sufferings, contained in
the 4th, 5th, and first half of the 6th verses; and the account of
his preternatural deliverance, contained in the last half of the
6th verse, and the following thirteen verses.

The words before us are an acknowledgment, on the part of
the delivered and rewarded Messiah, of the righteousness of
Jehovah in his deliverance and reward. The general idea is,—
These wonderful works of Jehovah, which have just been commemorated, are the merited expression of his entire righteous
approbation of, and most complacent holy delight in, his humbled and suffering Servant's person and work. 'God has in
these works proved his delight in me; the "deliverance" and
the "exaltation," are the merited rewards of what I have done
and suffered. I have perfectly done the work assigned me.
And this is the appropriate recompense.' I do not see how anything less—how anything else—can fairly be considered as the
meaning of these words. They are words which become no son
of man, but *the* Son of man. In his mouth, they are the words
of truth and soberness. In the mouth of any other man, they
are the utterance of falsehood, the offspring of pitiable self-ig-
norance and insufferable arrogance.[1]

[1] "If the psalm be prophetical, and sung in the person of the Messiah, then do
these verses no less exactly than beautifully delineate that all-perfect righteousness

They certainly are in no way suitable to David. David, though a truly good man—an eminently good man—was very far from being a perfect man. Were he, or any man, rewarded according to his own righteousness, recompensed according to the cleanness of his hands, judged of according to the standard of eternal rectitude, condemnation, not approval—punishment, not reward in the ordinary sense of the word, must be his portion. Far from claiming reward from divine justice, David implores forgiveness from Divine mercy. "Enter not into judgment with thy servant." "Pardon mine iniquity, for it is great." "Have mercy on me, O Lord, according to thy loving kindness; according to the multitude of thy tender mercies, blot out my transgressions." How do these acknowledgments and petitions comport with, "The Lord rewarded me according to my righteousness. I have kept the ways of the Lord; therefore the Lord recompensed me"? Indeed, so obviously inapplicable are the words, in their plain meaning, to David—so utterly irreconcilable with the facts of the case, the incidents of his life, and the leading features of his character,—that those interpreters who insist that the psalm refers to David, have been obliged to have recourse to the supposition that the words before us are either to be considered as describing, not David's personal character and conduct, but his cause, as the anointed of God—the chosen earthly head of the theocratic government of Israel; or, if they refer to his conduct, are to be considered as limited to his behavior in reference to Saul. But these suppositions are plainly unwarranted and arbitrary. Such a solution of the difficulty would never have been resorted to, had not the previously assumed principle, that the psalm refers to David, and not to Christ, produced the difficulty. In applying these words to the Messiah, I do not say that we shall not meet with difficulties; but certainly we shall meet with no such difficulty as this.

There is not much in the language of the paragraph that requires explication. The import of it is, 'I have been righteous. My whole character and conduct have been in conformity to the law under which I have been placed. I have, as it became me, fulfilled all righteousness. I have been—I have done—all that

wrought by the Redeemer, in consequence of which he obtained deliverance for himself and for his people."—HORNE. "Hæc uni Christo conveniunt si absolute sumantur."—AMYRAUT.

God requires. My hands have been clean;[1] my conduct has been blameless,—clean in *His* eye-sight—blameless in the estimation of the God of perfect knowledge and perfect purity. "I have kept the ways of the Lord;" I have, with undeviating rectitude, performed the duties prescribed by Him. I have in no instance violated them; I have never deviated from the straight path of this enlightened principled obedience. His judgments—all his judgments—his law, holy, just, and good, exceeding broad as it is, was constantly, in all its extent, before me, the object of my intelligent apprehension, my habitual consideration, my complacent approbation. I did not put away any of his statutes from me. I approved of them all; I obeyed them all. "I was upright."' The word expresses moral perfection in the strongest way. 'I was perfect, complete, wanting nothing —without spot, and blameless; and all this not only before[2] *men*, but before *Him*, in his estimation—as *He* saw me, who searches the heart and the reins. And the deliverance I have obtained— the dignity and felicity to which I am raised—is the meet recompense of my having thus been and done all that God required of me. In sending from above—in delivering me, in bringing me forth from the confinement of the grave to a large place, and in doing all this by a most wonderful exertion of Divine power,—God has but rewarded me according to my righteousness—but recompensed me according to the cleanness of my hands in his sight.' The passage is parallel to that undoubted Messianic oracle, the fortieth psalm, in which the being brought out of a horrible pit, out of the miry clay, and being set on a rock, and having his goings established, and a new song put in his mouth, are represented as the result of his saying, "Lo, I come" to do what sacrifice and offering have not accomplished. "I delight to do thy will; yea, thy law is in my heart." Surely there is but one servant of the Lord who, with entire truth, and without exposing himself to a just charge of undue self-estimation, could make such a declaration as this.

The concluding clause of the 23d verse seems, at first sight, to comport ill with the rest of the declaration, "I kept myself

---

[1] "Clean hands" was a proverbial expression for 'blameless, innocent, righteous conduct.'—Job, ix. 30; xxii. 30. Psal. xxiv. 4.

[2] עם is rightly rendered "before." It occurs in the same sense, Psal. xxxix. 13; 1 Sam. ii. 26.

from my iniquity." In the preliminary discourse, in which I stated at large the evidence for the Messianic reference of the psalm, I endeavored to meet the objection against that reference, grounded on these words; and I do not mean to repeat what I then said. I only remark that, among the various methods which have been adopted to remove the apparent difficulty, I am disposed to rest in that given by some of the most learned interpreters, who do not take the same view of the reference of the psalm as I do. " I kept myself so that sin was not mine,"[1]—the second parallel of the verse thus corresponding with the first—" I was perfect before Thee; I kept myself from all sin." This seems quite satisfactory; yet, though we were not able completely to remove the difficulty, that would be no sufficient reason why we should resist the evidence, so varied and so strong, that the statements in this psalm cannot, without the greatest violence, be applied to any but the Messiah.

Having thus endeavored to ascertain the import of the words in these verses, let us reduce to a few propositions the great truths, in reference to the Messiah, which they teach. These seem to be the following :—That the Messiah was a perfectly righteous person ; that, on the conclusion of his labors and sufferings, he received from God important and numerous benefits; and that these benefits were the merited recompense of these labors and sufferings. These are most important truths. Let us briefly illustrate them.

First, The Messiah was a perfectly righteous person. It was necessary he should be so; for the great design of his office was to expiate sin and save sinners. To do this, it is plain that it was absolutely necessary that he should not himself be a sinner. That he was to be a perfectly righteous person, is the testimony of Old Testament prophecy ; that he was so, is the testimony of New Testament history. The prophet David speaks of him as God's holy One ; the prophet Isaiah as one in whom Jehovah complacently delights,—his elect One, in whom his soul delights, He was, in the full extent of meaning that belongs to the term,

---

[1] Geierus, Vogel, De Wette. Geierus says, " Cavi ne peccatum aliquod fieret meum." The reader is reminded that the question respecting the meaning of this clause has been fully considered in the Introductory Discourse, as laying the foundation of one of the most plausible objections to the scheme of interpretation which we have been led to adopt.

" the man according to God's own heart, who should fulfil all his counsel." The New Testament writers tell us that that which was born of the virgin was " a holy thing ;" that " he knew no sin ;" that " in him was no sin ;" that " he was without sin"— the only thing in which he was not "made like to his brethren ;" that " he was holy, harmless, undefiled, and separate from sinners."[1]

Whether we look at our Lord personally or officially, the description in the words before us is exactly suitable to him. Personally, he was absolutely free from sin, and, in heart and life, completely conformed to the requisitions of the holy, just, and good law of God. He came into the world free from every taint of guilt—every tendency to evil ; and this original purity was never in the slightest degree stained. He kept himself unspotted from the world. He died as he lived, an entire stranger, experimentally, to guilt and depravity. But he was not only free from faults, he was full of excellence. He loved God with all his heart, and soul, and strength, and his neighbor as himself. He fully did all that God required—cheerfully suffered all that God appointed. In principle, in extent, in continuance, his obedience answered the demands of the holy law, which is exceeding broad. He was all fair, there was no spot in him. And as he was personally, so was he officially, righteous. As a prophet, he faithfully delivered the message he received from his Father. " All the words of his mouth were in righteousness, there was nothing froward or perverse in them." As a priest, he fulfilled all righteousness. He fully satisfied the demands of the law on those in whose place he stood. He obeyed its whole precept ; he bore its entire penalty ; " he finished transgression, made an end of sin, and brought in an everlasting righteousness ;" and, as a king, he reigns in righteousness—he rules in judgment. His laws and administration are equally accordant with justice. He is the true Melchizedek— " the King of righteousness"—the righteous King, as well as " the Prince of peace"—the pacific Prince.

Then, secondly, the Messiah, the righteous servant of Jehovah, on concluding his labors and sufferings, received from God numerous and important blessings. These are indicated in the context, by his being drawn out of many waters, delivered from

---

[1] Luke, i. 35.   2 Cor. v. 21.   1 John, iii 5.   Heb. iv. 15.

his strong enemy, and from those who hated him, and brought forth into a large place. If we wish to know more about these blessings, we have but to open the two volumes of prophetic and apostolic testimony. Hear the testimony of the prophets :— "The king shall joy in thy strength, O Lord; and in thy salvation how greatly shall he rejoice ! Thou hast given him his heart's desire, and hast not withholden the request of his lips. For Thou preventest him with the blessings of goodness : Thou settest a crown of pure gold on his head. He asked life of Thee, and Thou gavest it him, even length of days forever and ever. His glory is great in thy salvation : honor and majesty hast Thou laid upon him. For Thou hast made him most blessed forever : Thou hast made him exceeding glad with thy countenance. For the king trusted in the Lord; and, through the mercy of the Most High, he shall not be moved. Thine hand shall find out all thine enemies ; thy right hand shall find out those that hate Thee." "Thou hast ascended on high, thou hast led captivity captive : thou hast received gifts for men ; yea, for the rebellious also, that the Lord God might dwell among them." "The Lord said unto my Lord, Sit thou at my right hand, until I make thine enemies thy footstool. The Lord shall send the rod of thy strength out of Zion : rule thou in the the midst of thine enemies. Thy people shall be willing in the of thy power, in the beauties of holiness from the womb of the morning : thou hast the dew of thy youth. The Lord hath sworn, and will not repent, Thou art a priest forever after the order of Melchizedek. The Lord at thy right hand shall strike through kings in the day of his wrath. He shall judge among the heathen, He shall fill the places with the dead bodies ; He shall wound the heads over many countries. He shall drink of the brook in the way : therefore shall He lift up the head." "I will make him my first-born, higher than the kings of the earth. My mercy will I keep for him for evermore, and my covenant shall stand fast with him. His seed also will I make to endure forever, and his throne as the days of heaven.'" Hear now the testimony of the apostles :—"The God of peace hath brought again from the dead our Lord Jesus, that great Shepherd of the sheep, through the blood of the everlasting

---

¹ Psal. xxi. 1–8 ; ʃxviii. 18 ; cx. ; lxxxix. 27–29.

covenant." "After the"—risen—" Lord had spoken unto them, he was received up into heaven, and sat on the right hand of God." "God raised him up from the dead, and gave him glory." "He is gone into heaven, and is on the right hand of God; angels, and authorities, and powers, being made subject unto him." "According to the working of his mighty power, God raised him from the dead, and set him at his own right hand in the heavenly places, far above all principality, and power, and might, and dominion, and every name that is named, not only in this world, but also in that which is to come; and hath put all things under his feet, and gave him to be the head over all things to the church, which is his body, the fulness of Him that filleth all in all."[1]

Then, thirdly, these benefits were the merited rewards of the Messiah's labors and sufferings. They are a reward, a recompense. And for the illustration of this remark too, what can we do better than listen to the words which have been spoken by the holy prophets and apostles of our Lord Jesus? What say the prophets?—" Thou lovest righteousness, and hatest wickedness: therefore God, thy God, hath anointed thee with the oil of gladness above thy fellows." " He shall see of the travail of his soul, and shall be satisfied: by his knowledge shall my righteous Servant justify many, for he shall bear their iniquities. Therefore will I divide him a portion with the great, and he shall divide the spoil with the strong;" rather, ' therefore, will I give him the multitude for his portion, and he shall possess the strong as his prey;' " because he poured out his soul unto death: and he was numbered with the transgressors, and he bare the sins of many, and made intercession for the transgressors.'"[2] And what say the Apostles?—" When he had by himself purged our sins, he sat down on the right hand of the Majesty on high; being made so much better than the angels, as he had by inheritance obtained a more excellent name than they." " After he had offered one sacrifice for sins, forever sat down on the right hand of God; from henceforth expecting till his enemies be made his footstool." " Christ Jesus, being in the form of God, thought it not robbery to be equal with God; but made himself of no reputation, and took upon him the form of a ser-

---

[1] Heb. xiii. 20.   Mark, xvi. 19.   1 Pet. i. 21; iii. 22.   Eph. i. 19–23.
[2] Psal. xlv. 7.   Isa. liii. 11, 12.

vant, and was made in the likeness of men : and being found in fashion as a man, he humbled himself, and became obedient unto death, even the death of the cross. Wherefore God also hath highly exalted him, and hath given him a name which is above every name : that at the name of Jesus every knee should bow, of things in heaven, and things in earth, and things under the earth ; and that every tongue should confess that Jesus Christ is Lord, to the glory of God the Father."[1]

Such is the harmonious light which Old Testament prophecy and New Testament history and doctrine pour on the ancient oracle now under consideration. Thus did Jehovah's righteous Servant do His will and fulfil all righteousness, finishing the work given him to do ; and thus did Jehovah recompense him according to his righteousness, according to the cleanness of his hands in His eyesight. How perfect his righteousness to merit such a recompense ! How rich the reward which could compensate such sufferings and such labors on the part of one so exalted as the Servant, who was the Son, of Jehovah !

The words which follow, from the 25th to the 27th verses, seem a following out of the thought expressed in the words we have been illustrating. They are a direct address to Jehovah. Such transitions from statement to address are common in all poetry[2]—very common in Hebrew poetry. " With the merciful Thou wilt show thyself merciful ; with an upright man Thou wilt show thyself upright ; with the pure Thou wilt show thyself pure ; and with the froward Thou wilt show thyself froward. For Thou wilt save the afflicted people ; but wilt bring down high looks." These words have very generally been considered as a description of the great features of the Divine moral government. 'The great King of the universe deals with his subjects according to their characters. The righteous Lord judges righteously.' I am rather disposed, as the words—the merciful, the upright, the pure, the froward—are all in the singular, to consider the passage as descriptive of the Divine dispensations celebrated in the psalm, towards the Messiah, the merciful, the upright or perfect, the pure one ; and towards his great enemy, the froward, perverse, rather, perhaps, crafty one ; and towards their respective adherents, the afflicted people, and those of high

---

[1] Heb. i. 3, 4 ; x. 12, 13. Phil. ii. 6–11.   [2] Paradise Lost, iv. 720–725.

looks. I obviously have not time, in this lecture, to state the
grounds on which I prefer this mode of interpretation, or to unfold the important truths which the words thus considered
bring before the mind. This must be left as the subject of future
consideration.

Meanwhile, I conclude with remarking,—In the subject we
have been considering, we are presented at once with the ground
of our hope and the model for our imitation. The finished work
of Christ, his all-perfect righteousness, acknowledged by the supreme Judge in the deliverance vouchsafed him, and the felicities and glories conferred on him—that is the ground, the sole
ground, of our hope of pardon and salvation; and that, too, is the
faultless model according to which we should be constantly en-
deavoring to form our character and to regulate our conduct.

It is the ground of our hope. Nothing short of entire satisfaction
to the law and justice of God can lay a foundation for salvation to a
sinner. *That* the sinner cannot yield for himself; *that* no creature,
no combination of creatures, can yield for him. A meritorious
perfect obedience to the precept, and a full endurance of the penalty of the law, were required; and they are found in the obedience to death of the incarnate Son of God in the character of the
Surety of men. His obedience has done the law more honor
than the obedience of an unsinning race of men ; his sufferings
have done it more honor than the eternal misery of a sinning
race of men. He has, indeed, fulfilled all righteousness. He
was perfect before God, and the Lord was well pleased. He was
propitiated for this righteousness' sake, inasmuch as it magnified
the law and made it honorable. And this has been proved by
the recompense which he has given him for his toils and sacrifices in the cause of God's glory and man's salvation. In
Jesus, "holy, harmless, undefiled, separate from sinners," giving
himself a sacrifice for us, and now through that sacrifice—for
that sacrifice—passed through these heavens, and made higher
than all but the Highest there,—we have a sure ground of
hope. What has satisfied God's justice may well satisfy our conscience. With humble confidence may we—ought we—to look
to Jesus, the righteous One, on the cross, in the grave, on the
throne, given for our offences, raised again for our justification,
having died for us, living and reigning for us ; and to say, in
the full assurance of faith, with a distinct view of our sins in

all their aggravations, Surely, "in the Lord," "the Lord our righteousness," "have we righteousness." "In the Lord we are justified, and in the Lord we will glory."[1]

But the all-perfect righteousness of our Lord is not only the ground of our hope, the matter of our justification,—but the great exemplar we ought to copy. When he obeyed and suffered in our room, he "set us an example, that we should follow his steps." He fulfilled all righteousness, not that we might live in unrighteousness, but that we might be "righteous, even as he is righteous." He gave himself for us, that he might save us, not *in* sin, but *from* sin,—that he might "redeem us from all iniquity, and purify" us "to himself a peculiar people, zealous of good works." He died, not to deliver us from all law, but to bring us under the law to him—to God in him; and to make his law plain and pleasant, he embodied it in his own character and conduct,—so that, when we want direction and motive to duty, as well as ground of hope and consolation, we cannot do better than just look to Jesus. Let us seek to be righteous, as he was righteous; let our hearts be pure, our hands be clean, like his; let us, like him, keep the ways of our God, and not wickedly depart from our God. Let His judgments be before us; and let us not put away His statutes from us. Let us seek to be upright, perfect, before Him; and let us keep ourselves from our iniquity. Our very imperfect righteousness can never merit reward;—indeed we have merited punishment, everlasting punishment,—and we never can merit anything else. But, trusting entirely in the Saviour's righteousness as the ground of our hope; and, at a humble distance, constantly imitating his righteousness as our all-perfect model, we too shall obtain great recompense of reward. The reward is all of grace; but it is not the less secure, it is not the less glorious, on that account. To them who, trusting in the Saviour's merits, and walking in his steps, are, "through a constant continuance in well-doing, seeking for glory, honor, and immortality,"—they are not to be obtained in any other way,—God will render eternal life, glory, honor, and peace, to every one that thus worketh good. He will make us participants of our Lord's deliverance and glory. He will send from above, and take us, and draw us from the depths

[1] Isa. xlv. 24, 25.   Jer. xxiii. 6.

of the grave. He will deliver us from all our enemies, even that last enemy who was too strong for us. He will bring us to the large and wealthy place which He has prepared for all his people; and, in the completeness and permanence of our deliverance, He will show us, as He has shown him, that He delights in us. "Therefore, my beloved brethren, be ye stedfast, unmovable, always abounding in the work of the Lord, forasmuch as ye know that your labor is not in vain in the Lord."[1]

[1] 1 Cor. xv. 58.

LECTURE VI

THE CONDUCT OF JEHOVAH TO THE MESSIAH, AND TO HIS ENEMIES

PSALM XVIII. 25, 26.—" With the merciful Thou wilt show thyself merciful; with an upright man Thou wilt show thyself upright; with the pure Thou wilt show thyself pure; and with the froward Thou wilt show thyself froward."

THESE words are the conclusion of the fourth of the six sections into which the psalm, of which they form a part, is, as I have endeavored to show at length in a previous discourse, found, when carefully considered, to resolve itself. The subject of the psalm is the deliverance of the Messiah, both in his person and cause, by Divine power, from all his enemies. This is celebrated in a hymn of thanksgiving to Jehovah, the Divine deliverer. After a suitable introduction (verses 1–3), forming the first section of the psalm, we have a striking description,—first (verse 4 to middle of verse 6) of the deep and varied distresses in which the Messiah was involved; and then (verses 6 to 19) of the supernatural Divine dispensations by which he had been delivered from these distresses. These descriptions, forming the second and third sections of the psalm, are followed by an assertion of the Divine righteousness in these dispensations (verses 20–24.) The Messiah had performed the work intrusted to him in a manner perfectly satisfactory to Him who appointed him; and his deliverance and exaltation were the appropriate expression of the Divine approbation, which this fulfilling of all righteousness had merited. He had been righteous; his hands had been clean in God's sight; he had kept the ways of the Lord; he had not, in any instance, wickedly departed from his God; all His judgments had been constantly before him; he had not put away any of His statutes from him; he had been perfect before Him, and so kept himself, as never, in the slightest degree, to contract guilt—never, in any instance, to commit iniquity; and his miraculous deliverance—his high exaltation—were the deserved rewards of his perfect obedience—his entire conformity to the Divine will,—rewards conferred on him by the supreme moral Governor, who judgeth righteously, and renders to every man according to his deeds. "The Lord," says the delivered and exalted Messiah—"The Lord, in sending from above, taking me, drawing me out of many waters, delivering me from my strong enemy, and bringing me into a large place, hath shown that He delighted in me." To use the words of Bishop Horne, —" For his righteousness' sake Jehovah was well pleased, and rewarded with everlasting felicity the unspotted purity of his works. He performed an unsinning obedience to every part of the law, and swerved not from its line in a single instance. The rule was ever in his eye, and no temptation could induce him to deviate from its direction. Like the light, he passed through all things undefiled, and his garments were white as the lily ; therefore a glorious kingdom was given to him, forasmuch as in him the piercing eye of heaven could discover no blemish at all." This assertion, that the deliverance and exaltation of the Messiah were the merited reward of his righteousness, was illustrated at large in our last lecture.

The words that now come before us seem to be a following out of the same great idea, that, in the Divine dispensations, both towards the Messiah and towards his great enemy—the froward, perverse, or crafty one,—there had been, and would be, a glorious display of that perfect righteousness and consummate wisdom, which form the grand characteristic features of the moral government of Him who is " righteous in all his ways —holy in all his works ;" " wonderful in counsel—excellent in working." " With the merciful Thou wilt show thyself merciful ; with an upright man Thou wilt show thyself upright ; with the pure Thou wilt show thyself pure ; and with the froward Thou wilt show thyself froward. For Thou wilt save the afflicted people : but bring down high looks. For Thou wilt light my candle : the Lord my God will enlighten my darkness."

There is a transition here from statement to address—from speaking *about* God to speaking *to* God. "The Lord recompensed me." " With the merciful "—not ' He shows himself,' as we would have expected, but—" Thou wilt show thyself merciful." Such transitions are common in poetry—very common in Hebrew poetry. This psalm abounds in them. The psalmist begins with address, and passes to statement, in the 2d verse, which continues down to the paragraph before us. He returns to statement at the 30th verse, and again resumes direct address in the 35th verse. He again reverts to statement at the 41st verse, to return to address at the 43d. Similar transitions occur at the 44th, and in the middle of the 48th, and at the beginning of the 50th verses—the psalm thus commencing with address, and terminating with statement. In the sublime ode of praise, which forms the hundred and forty-fifth psalm, we have there alternations of address and statement, so regularly recurring as naturally to suggest the idea that the poem was composed with the intention of being sung by two separate bands of choristers.

There is a remark or two, of a grammatical kind, which must be made, to pave the way for the satisfactory interpretation of the paragraph, and which I shall endeavor to make, as little encumbered with technical phraseology as possible.[1] To an English reader, the whole paragraph must appear to refer exclusively to the future, as a prediction—not a statement of what has been or is. Thus to view it, were however to misapprehend the meaning of the inspired writer. The statement is what is called indefinite as to time. It is a description of God's habitual mode of acting towards the persons referred to. To express anything indefinitely, different tenses, as they are called, are employed in different languages. The Hebrew uses the future; we, in English, employ ordinarily the present tense. Accordingly, one of the most learned of late interpreters of the Psalms considers himself entitled to render all the Hebrew futures in this paragraph in the present. "Toward the merciful Thou art—Thou habitually art—has been—art—will be—merciful; towards the upright Thou *art* upright; towards the pure Thou art pure; and towards the froward Thou art froward ; for Thou savest the

[1] The subject of the various modifications of the Hebrew verb, so far as they have a reference to time, is still involved in some difficulty. What has been called the future tense seems a kind of aorist (Professor Lee and others consider it as a present), the time of which requires to be ascertained from the context. In the present case, the context seems to require us to understand the statements either of the past, or rather of the habitual, conduct of Jehovah towards his "righteous servant." On this subject, the article "On the Sequences of the Hebrew Tenses," in the Introduction to the Rev. Mr. Paul's "Analysis and Critical Interpretation of the Book of Genesis," —a valuable addition to our helps towards an accurate knowledge of Hebrew, well deserves to be consulted.

afflicted people, and bringest down the high looks. Thou lightest my candle; the Lord God enlightens my darkness."

The words in the 25th and 26th verses have usually been
viewed by interpreters as a general description of the ordinary
course—of the great leading law of the Divine moral government. God treats every man according to his character; He
renders to every man according to his works; to the merciful
according to his mercy; to the upright according to his uprightness; to the pure according to his purity; to the froward according to his frowardness. This is no doubt truth—important
truth; and important truth which these words naturally enough
express. But, viewed in this general form, it is difficult to perceive how it stands connected either with what goes before or what
follows it. It appears to me to be the statement, not of the general
fact of the Divine strict equity, in his treatment of moral agents,
but of the exemplification of this general fact in his conduct
towards the Messiah, and his great enemy, and their respective
adherents. It deserves notice that all the words here are in the
singular. It is not merciful persons, as a body, that are spoken
of, but the merciful one; not upright persons generally, but the
upright one; not pure persons generally, but the pure one; not
froward persons generally, but the froward one. There can be
no doubt that sometimes such words, in the singular, are used
collectively—the upright man, for every upright man. But,
when we recollect that the psalm is uttered in the name of one
Individual, to whom the appellations, "merciful," "upright,"
and "pure," are applicable in a higher sense than they are to
any mere creature, human or angelic, and that the words before
us follow a description of his righteousness, and its reward, and
that it contains an account of his complete deliverance from all
his enemies, and especially from that powerful and crafty being,
his arch-enemy, who is, by way of eminence, the wicked, perverse, froward one, we can scarcely doubt that the words are to
be viewed as a declaration of the manner in which Jehovah had
treated, is treating, and will treat, the Messiah, his beloved Servant, and his great adversary.

Looking at the passage in this light, let us endeavor to ascertain the import of the appellations here given to the Messiah,
and to his great enemy, and then consider what is said with regard
to the manner in which Jehovah has treated, is treating, and

will treat them, respectively. The Messiah is spoken of as the merciful, the upright, and the pure one ; his adversary is the froward one. With the Messiah, He acts mercifully, uprightly, purely ; with his adversary, frowardly.

I

1. The Messiah is the merciful one. The word rendered "merciful" here is often translated "holy," or "saint." It is the word which, in the 10th verse of the sixteenth psalm, is rendered "thy holy One," with an undoubted reference to the Messiah. "Thou wilt not leave my soul in hell; neither wilt Thou suffer thine holy One to see corruption." It is the opinion of some[1] interpreters, that wherever this word, or the word the "right-eous," occurs in the singular, in the book of Psalms, the refer-ence is to the Messiah; but this is, to say the least, doubtful. The proper meaning of the word is ' benignantly bountiful.' It suggests the two ideas of kindness and liberality—the tender heart and the open hand. How strikingly applicable, in all its extent of meaning, is the word to the Messiah! Who can form an adequate idea of "the great love wherewith he loved men"— the love which brought him from the bosom of God, in the heaven of heavens, to the manger in Bethlehem, to the cross on Calvary, to the depths of the grave in Joseph's sepulchre; which induced the blessed One to become a curse, to redeem men from the curse,—him, who knew no sin, to become sin, that men might be made the rightousness of God ; which induced him to wash men from their sins in his own blood! "Greater love has no man, than that he lay down his life for his friend; but herein he commendeth his love to us, in that when we were enemies he died for us." Surely he is the "kind one." His love has a height and depth, and breadth and length, that pass knowledge.

And, as he is kind, so is he bountiful. His kindness finds expression in the bestowal of benefits countless in number, in-estimable in value. He gives *himself* for us, and to us (thanks be to Him for this unspeakable gift) ; and, with himself, he gives us "all things that pertain to life and godliness"—"all heavenly and spiritual blessings." "It pleased the Father that in him all fulness should dwell;" and "out of his fulness we receive grace for grace "—abundance, superabundance, of blessings. He

---

[1] Horsley.

gives grace, and He gives glory, and He withholds no good thing. The benignity and the bounty which this word expresses are strikingly described, in conjunction, in that text, "Ye know the grace"—the kindness—"of our Lord Jesus Christ, who, though he was rich, yet for our sakes became poor, that we through his poverty might be rich." He " poured out his soul unto death ;" he shed forth the Holy Ghost, in his influence and blessings, abundantly.

2. But the Messiah is not only represented as the merciful one —the kind, liberal one,—but also the upright one. The precise meaning of the original phrase is, 'the man of perfections "— ' the perfect man.' It looks back to the description contained in the preceding part of the paragraph, from the 20th to the 24th verse. That description was illustrated in our last lecture, in which it was shown that the Messiah was indeed, both personally and officially, perfect—being all, doing all, suffering all, which the law of God, under which he was made, required him to be, and do, and suffer,—yielding an obedience absolutely perfect in principle, in extent, and in duration ; and presenting himself, " through the eternal Spirit, an offering, without spot or blemish, to God."

3. Still further, the Messiah is represented as the pure one.[2] It is not easy to perceive the precise distinction between the " perfect" and the " pure" one. The one epithet seems to refer to the positive conformity of the character and conduct to the law of God, which is the rule of perfection ; the other to the entire absence of every species of disconformity in thought or action, in disposition or conduct, to that rule. He was equally

---

[1] גבר תמם. The phrase has been translated by Schultens, " Strenuus, potens integri." He explains that rather odd expression by " qui se in integro et recto omni fortem et firmum præstet."

[2] עם־גבר תתברר. These words have been variously explained : some referring them to the Messiah's great enemy, " the froward one ;" others, to the Messiah himself. In the first case, the word נבר is borrowed from an Arabic word signifying ' to swell,'—' the swelling or proud one ,' and תתברר is derived from אבר, which is supposed, from the meaning of a word of similar sound in Arabic, to signify ' to prick or puncture,'—to break by puncturing, as in the case of a purulent tumor. This interpretation of Venema is not satisfactory. The image is far-fetched and unpoetical ; and but that some such interpretation is necessary to make the 26th verse a contrasted parallel with the 25th, would never probably have been thought of. The ordinary interpretation seems to be the just one :—' Thou hast acted, or actest, to the pure one correspondingly to his character ;—Thou hast reciprocated his purity.'

a stranger to hereditary and acquired tendencies to evil. There
was nothing in thought, feeling, desire, will, or action, inconsistent with perfect holiness. He " knew no sin"—" in him was
no sin"—he was " holy, harmless, undefiled, separate from sinners." Such is the character of the Messiah.

4. Let us now consider the description given of his great adversary. The psalmist speaks of " the froward one." Did the
psalm refer to David, as many suppose, I could not doubt that
this appellation refers either to Saul or to Ahithophel. If the
word be considered as equivalent to " perverse," it would be very
descriptive of the former of these; if as equivalent to " crafty," it
would be equally characteristic of the latter of them. Considering the psalm, however, as directly and solely referring to the
Messiah, as I think I have showed the evidence compels us to do,
I can as little doubt that the expression is descriptive of his great
enemy, the enemy that was too strong for the first man, and would
have been found too strong for the Second Man, if he had not been
more than man. "The wicked one" of the first clause of Psalm
cix. 6, is identified with the Satan of the second clause. Here, as in
the first promise, the two combatants stand contrasted—the Seed
of the woman and the serpent—the benignantly bountiful, perfect,
pure One, and the froward one, whose works he came to destroy,
and who made it his great business to circumvent him whom he
feared. The literal meaning of the word is " tortuous" or
" crooked," [1] and both the ideas of perversity and cunning which
the figure naturally suggests, are very applicable to " that old
serpent the devil." From the concluding part of the sentence, I
think there is no doubt that it is the latter idea that is intended to
be conveyed. God cannot deal perversely with any one; but He
outwits the wise, and takes the cunning in their own craftiness.

This crafty one originally belonged to that order of being
whose wisdom is proverbial—" wise as an angel of God." When
he lost his moral purity, we have no reason to think that he lost
his intellectual energy. It took a new direction, but with unabated force. From the change of its object, it ceased, indeed,
to deserve the name of wisdom. Its appropriate appellation
henceforward was craft or cunning. He beguiled Eve through
his subtlety, and has deluded, to their destruction, many mil-

---

[1] Schultens ad Job, v. 14.   Prov. viii. 8.   Deut. xxxii. 5.

lions of her sons. By a course of deep policy, he endeavors to
counterwork the great designs of the holy and benignant moral
government of God. In nothing has he ever dealt more craftily
than in his conduct towards the Messiah. How admirably was
the plot laid for his seduction from his onward path, in the
temptation in the wilderness; and, finding it impossible to se-
duce him, how craftily did he work on the mind of the traitor
disciple, the Jewish rulers and populace, and the Roman governor, till he no doubt trusted he had destroyed him, when he
saw him hang a dishonored corpse on the accursed tree!

II

1. Let us now look at the view which the psalm gives us of
the Divine dispensations towards the Messiah and towards his
enemy. "With the merciful," *i. e.*, the benignantly bountiful,
"Thou showest thyself merciful," benignantly bountiful. The
Divine dispensations to the Messiah were many of them apparently neither benignant nor bountiful. He was visited with such
severe afflictions as not unnaturally led those who witnessed them
to the conclusion that he was the object of the peculiar displeasure
of God—"stricken, smitten of God, and afflicted," and, instead of
being bountifully dealt with, he was, by way of eminence, the
poor man and the destitute. "The foxes had holes, and the birds
of the air had nests" (rather lodging-places), "but the Son of man
had not where to lay his head." He was scantily furnished with
the necessaries of life—dependent on the bounty of others for
subsistence while he lived, and for a grave when he died. But
the Messiah, looking at the whole course of the Divine dealings
to him, acknowledges that in them God has manifested himself
benignantly bountiful. The Father loved him as He loved himself; and in love to him, as well as to man, originated the wondrous scheme of human salvation. He appointed him to a difficult work, but He abundantly furnished him with the necessary
qualifications. He gave him the Holy Spirit without measure.
"The Spirit of the Lord rested upon him, the spirit of wisdom
and understanding, the spirit of counsel and might, the spirit of
knowledge, and of the fear of the Lord."[1] "It pleased the
Father, that in him should all fulness" of grace and truth "dwell."

---

[1] Isa. xi. 2, 3.

"The grace of God was on him," as he "grew up before Him."
He laid on him all the labor and suffering that were necessary
to the accomplishment of the object of his appointment—and who
can measure their weight and severity?—yet when innumerable
evils compassed him about, God did not "withhold his tender
mercies from him; his loving-kindness and truth continually
preserved him," so that when he "gave his back to the smiters,
and his cheeks to those who plucked off the hair, when he hid
not his face from shame and spitting"—even then he could say,
"The Lord God will help me, therefore shall I not be confounded: therefore have I set my face like a flint, and I know
that I shall not be ashamed.   He is near that justifieth me; who
will contend with me? let us stand together; who is mine adversary? let him come near to me.   Behold, the Lord God will
help me; who is he that shall condemn me?" [1]   And the benignant bountifulness of Jehovah was still more remarkably
manifested to the benignantly bountiful One, when, after he had
fully glorified his Father on the earth, and finished the work
given him to do, He "glorified him in himself"—"glorified him
with the glory he had with Him before the world was"—"gave
him power over all flesh, that he might give eternal life to as
many as He had given."   "The Father loved him, because he
laid down his life for the sheep;" and He showed this love in a
manner worthy of his benignantly bountiful nature.   He heaped
upon him all conceivable, all possible, honors and benefits.   H
gave all things into his hand.   He prevented him with the blessings of goodness.   He blessed him for evermore, giving him a
dominion unbounded and enduring, making him "exceeding
glad with his countenance."   And the delivered and exalted
Messiah acknowledges that in all these dispensations, Jehovah
had "dealt well with his servant, according to his word."   "I
will declare thy name unto my brethren: in the midst of the
congregation will I praise Thee.   Ye that fear the Lord, praise
Him: all ye the seed of Jacob, glorify Him; and fear Him, all
ye the seed of Israel.   For He hath not despised nor abhorred
the affliction of the afflicted: neither hath He hid his face from
him; but when he cried unto Him, He heard." [2]

2. "With the upright Thou showest thyself upright," or 'With

---

[1] Isa. l. 7–9.   [2] Psal. xxii. 22–24.

the perfect Thou showest thyself perfect.' The Messiah did his work of service perfectly, and perfectly does Jehovah do his work of reward. In the one case, there is every duty performed; in the other, every promise fulfilled. In the review of all the dispensations of God to him, the delivered and exalted Messiah declares that He has done all things well. His testimony is, "The Lord is a rock; his work is perfect; all his ways are judgment; a God of truth, and without iniquity: just and right is He." The Messiah dealt righteously with Him who appointed him. He shrunk from no toil, however oppressive—from no suffering, however intense. He paid the whole debt he had charged himself with; he "finished" the work given him to do. And Jehovah dealt righteously with the Messiah: He exacted from him nothing more than the law—holy, just, and good—demanded of him in the character he had voluntarily assumed; He withheld from him no promised support; He bestowed on him the entire promised recompense. The words in the beginning of the hundred-and-eleventh psalm may be considered as a paraphrase on those before us, "With the upright Thou showest thyself upright." "I will praise the Lord with my whole heart, in the assembly of the upright, and in the congregation. The works of the Lord are great, sought out of all them that have pleasure therein. His work is honorable and glorious, and his righteousness endureth forever."

3. "With the pure Thou showest thyself pure." These words may signify, 'Thou dealest with the pure according to his purity.' In this sense, the words are not applicable to the Divine dispensations towards the Messiah during his humbled state, considered by themselves, for Jehovah treated the righteous One, as if he had been a sinner. "He made him who knew no sin to be sin in our room." But they are gloriously true of the Divine dispensations viewed complexly—of the whole treatment of the pure One by Jehovah. He gave him an opportunity of showing how pure he was, by placing him in circumstances of unparalleled difficulty and temptation; and as his purity bore the trial, He "justified" him, wiped off all the calumnies of his enemies, and, in raising him from the dead and giving him glory, proclaimed to the universe his perfect purity and the high estimation in which it was held by the Supreme Judge. "He loved righteousness and hated wickedness: therefore God, even his God, anointed him with the

oil of gladness above his fellows," and said to him, " Thy throne is forever and ever."[1] But we prefer interpreting the words on the same principle as we have done those which precede it. As purity was the character of the Messiah's conduct towards Jehovah, so it was the character of Jehovah's dispensations towards the Messiah. Spotless holiness characterized all these dispensations,—equally appearing in the sufferings inflicted on the Holy One, as the voluntarily-appointed substitute of sinners, and in the honors and felicities conferred on him as the reward of that manifestation of immaculate purity, perfect holiness, which he made in all he said, and did, and suffered. This, then, is the character of the Divine dispensations in reference to the Messiah, the merciful, the upright, the pure One. He has been treated according to his deserts. His mercifulness, uprightness, and purity, have met with a corresponding benignant bountifulness, moral perfection, and purity, on the part of Him " of whom, and through whom, and to whom, are all things."

4. Let us now, for a little, look at the Divine dispensations in reference to the Messiah's great enemy, "the froward one." " With the froward Thou showest thyself froward."[2] I have already stated that the proper force of the word is tortuous, crooked,—and that it may be considered as signifying either perverse or crafty. In both senses the word is applicable to Satan. He is the wilful, perverse one. He is determined to have his will in opposition to the will of God. God can never act frowardly or perversely, in the strict sense of the words. He never can do even Satan any wrong. Nothing can move Him from the onward, straight path of perfect righteousness. But still, in reference to his great enemy, it is true, as He says with regard to his enemies generally, " Since he walks contrary to God, God will walk contrary to him." If he opposes God, God will oppose him. If he will sin, God will punish. God is as determined to have His holy will, as the devil can be to have his wicked will; and therefore the consequence must be collision. If the devil counterwork God, God will counterwork the devil ; and as the contest is between created and uncreated wisdom and power, there can be no doubt of the ultimate result ;—wo, eter-

---

[1] Psal. xlv. 6, 7.

[2] עקש and פתל often go together,—Prov. viii. 8; Deut. xxxii. 5. " With the froward Thou wilt show thyself wry."—AINSWORTH.

nal wo, must be to the angel, as well as to the man, that con-
tends with his Maker—that defies the Omnipotent to arms.

I have no doubt, however, that it is rather to the *craftiness* of
the character, and counsels, and operations of the wicked one,
than to their *perverseness*, that there is a reference here; and
that the meaning is, 'With the crafty one, He shows himself
crafty.' Not that there is any craft or cunning, properly speaking, in any of the Divine dispensations, but that there is a depth
of wisdom, by means of which all the enterprises of Satan shall
end in disappointment, overthrow, and ruin, and indeed be
made conducive to the advancement of purposes directly opposite to those which they were designed, and which they seemed
well fitted to accomplish. God has made, and is making, and
will yet more remarkably make, all Satan's attempts to dishonor
Him,—many of them for a season apparently successful,—the
means of still more illustriously displaying his glory. How
much of what is most glorious in the Divine power, and wisdom,
and holiness, and righteousness, and especially kindness, must
have been forever unknown to men and angels, but for sin, that
work of the devil, in itself fitted to do nothing but cast a cloud
over all these attributes! In suggesting the plan for securing
the Messiah's untimely, and cruel, and ignominious death, and
urging on its accomplishment, he was the unconscious and most
guilty instrument of hastening forward that which alone could
secure—that which has effectually secured—" glory to God in
the highest, peace on earth, and good will to men," the expiation of human guilt, the vindication of Divine truth and righteousness, the destruction of the kingdom of darkness, and the
full development of the reign of God.

We meet with innumerable exemplifications of the same truth
in the history of the progress of Christianity among men. The
devil's attempts by his agents to obscure and destroy Christian
truth and its evidence by infidel philosophy, have uniformly ter-
minated in making the truth more clear, and the evidence more
obviously invincible; and the tempests of persecution designed
to eradicate Christianity, and seemingly well fitted to serve their
purpose, have often but made its roots take a still faster hold
of the soil, and scattered its seeds more widely and more speedily through surrounding regions. Were the history of God's
dispensations in reference to Satan written, and it would form a

very entertaining and very useful book, a better motto could not be found than in the words before us, " With the crafty one Thou dealest craftily;" and if additional ones are required, here are two from the books of Job and of the Psalms, " He disappointeth the devices of the crafty, so that their hands cannot perform their enterprise. He taketh the wise in their own craftiness; and the counsel of the froward is carried headlong." "Behold, he travaileth with iniquity, and hath conceived mischief, and brought forth falsehood. He made a pit, and digged it, and is fallen into the ditch which he made. His mischief shall return upon his own head, and his violent dealing shall come down upon his own pate. I will praise the Lord according to his righteousness; and will sing praise to the name of the Lord most high."[1]

It is a delightful truth, that the Messiah has not only obtained these blessings for himself by his mercifulness, uprightness, and purity, but that he has secured similar blessings to all his true followers. They are freed from guilt, and restored to the Divine favor, on the ground of his all-perfect surety-righteousness, which was the price equally of his exaltation and their salvation; and they are, through the effectual operation of his spirit, conformed to his image, and made, like him, merciful and upright, and pure. None but such are Messiah's people. The selfish and hard hearted, the dishonest and hypocritical, the impure in heart and in life, are none of his. Now, to the merciful, God is merciful; to the upright, upright; to the pure, pure. He treats them, not according to what they deserve,—not according to what they naturally were, and, apart from the influences of his Spirit, still are (for " in them, that is, in their flesh, dwelleth no good thing"), but he treats them according to what their Lord deserves; and He communicates those blessings to them in proportion to the degree in which they resemble Him, for all of which they are indebted to " grace reigning through righteousness unto eternal life through Jesus Christ our Lord." Indeed, it is just in that degree that they are capable of enjoying his best blessings—" heavenly and spiritual blessings."

How exceeding great and precious are the promises made to the merciful, the upright, and the pure ! To the merciful,—" A

---

[1] Job, v. 12, 13.   Psal. vii. 14–17.

good man who showeth favor, who is kind and merciful, surely
he shall not be moved forever." "The liberal soul shall be made
fat." "He that hath mercy on the poor, happy is he." "He
that hath a bountiful eye, shall be blessed." "The liberal who
deviseth liberal things, by liberal things shall he stand." "If
thou draw out thy soul to the hungry and satisfy the afflicted
soul, then shall thy light rise in obscurity, and thy darkness be
as the noon-day." Whosoever shall give to drink unto one of
God's little ones a cup of cold water in the name of a disciple,
"shall in nowise lose his reward." In the great day of judgment, the King will say in the presence of an assembled universe
to such, "Inasmuch as ye have done it to the least of these my
brethren, ye have done it unto me." "Come ye blessed enter
into the kingdom." "Blessed are the merciful, for they shall
obtain mercy :" To the upright,—"God has pleasure in up-
righness." "He that walketh uprightly and worketh righteousness, shall abide in God's tabernacle and dwell in his holy hill."
"The Lord is a buckler to them that walk uprightly." "Such
as are upright in their way, are the Lord's delight." "If our
heart condemn us not, then we have confidence toward God."
"He that walketh righteously and speaketh uprightly," "he
shall dwell on high; his place of defence shall be the munitions
of rocks; bread shall be given him, and his waters shall be sure;"
To the pure,—"Blessed are the pure in heart : for they shall see
God." "Truly God is good to such as are of a clean heart."
"If a man therefore purge himself," "he shall be a vessel unto
honor ; sanctified, and meet for the Master's use, and prepared
unto every good work."[3]   All those promises are yea and amen
to the glory of God in the experience of those who, through the
mind of Christ being in them, are like him, though in far inferior degree, merciful, and upright, and pure.

Let not then the afflictive, and sometimes apparently wrathful,
dispensations of Divine providence discourage such persons.
Let them trust and not be afraid. He will do for them what He
did for their great Leader. He will qualify, support, and reward

---

[1] Psal. cxii. 6.   Prov. xi. 25 ; xiv. 31 ; xxii. 9.   Isa. xxxii. 8 ; lviii. 10.   Matth. x.
42 ; xxv. 40, 34 ; v. 7.
[2] 1 Chron. xxix. 17.   Psal. xv. 1, 2.   Prov. ii. 7 ; xi. 20.   1 John, iii. 21.   Isa. xxxiii.
15, 16.
[3] Matth. v. 8.   Psal lxxiii. 1.   2 Tim. ii. 21.

them. He will supply their need according to his glorious riches, and make all grace to abound to them. He will, as the holy One, make them more and more holy, that He may make them more and more happy, and in the ultimate result of things, constrain them to acknowledge that all the paths of the Lord have been mercy and truth to them keeping his covenant and his testimonies; that all things have worked together for good ; and that He has indeed, to them and for them, as to and for their Lord, done all things well. With one heart and one voice, they will say,—The Lord has shown himself to be upright. He is our Rock, and there is no iniquity in Him.

What an encouragement it is to Christians to grow in likeness to their Lord, that they may thus, if I may use the expression, put it in the power of Him who is all bountiful, to communicate, in a consistency with the constitution of our nature and the order of his holy government, large measures of holy happiness!

What a powerful motive to those who are strangers to that mercifulness, uprightness, and purity, in connection with which alone true happiness can be enjoyed, to seek these in the only way they can be obtained,—in that union with the Saviour's person which secures the habitual influence of his sanctifying Spirit! That can be obtained only by any one—that may be obtained by every one—in the faith of the truth as it is in Jesus. It is thus only men can be justified ; it is thus only they can be sanctified ; it is thus only they can be saved.

In the manner in which God has dealt, is dealing, and will deal, with the great enemy of the Messiah, "the froward one," all the enemies of the Messiah may see what they have to expect under the righteous moral government of God. They, like their father and prince, are "froward ones." They are self-willed, perverse ones. The language of their hearts and lives is, "Who is lord over us ?" And they are often, too, characterized by a craft and cunning, which pass with themselves and their associates as wisdom. They often discover very considerable, though most misplaced, ingenuity in their schemes for opposing the progress and counteracting the influence, in themselves and in others, of the cause of the Messiah—the cause of truth, holiness, freedom, and happiness. It would be well for all such persons to reflect, that they are engaged in a hopeless struggle under a vanquished leader. With the *froward one*, the head of the rebellion in God's universe, God has showed—is showing—will show—himself froward. He has baffled his most deeply-laid schemes; He has turned his artillery against himself; He will overwhelm him with complete and everlasting destruction. And so will He deal, too, with all who obstinately support the great rebel's cause. There is no successfully opposing God. There is no outwitting infinite wisdom,—no overcoming infinite power. If men *will* not *do* his will, they *shall suffer* his will. Every man who is rejecting, every man who is neglecting, the great salvation,—every man who is living in unbelief and impenitence,—belongs to the doomed family, at the head of which is " the froward one." They resemble him in their character, and if that be not changed, they must resemble him in their destiny ;—disappointment here, damnation hereafter, must be their portion. Oh, that such men were wise, and would consider, in this the day of their merciful visitation, these true and faithful sayings of God ! " If ye walk contrary to Me, I will set my face against you; I will walk contrary to you also in fury, and chastise you seven times for your sins."[1] " Surely He scorneth the scorners." " Hear the word of the Lord ye scornful men :" " Because ye have said, we have made a covenant with death, and with hell are we at agreement; when the overflowing scourge shall pass through, it shall not come unto us ; for we have made lies our refuge, and under falsehood have we hid ourselves." " Thus saith the Lord," " Judgment will I lay to the line, and righteousness to the plummet, and the hail shall sweep away the refuge of lies, and the waters shall overflow the hiding place. And your covenant with death shall be disannulled, and your agreement with hell shall not stand." " For the Lord shall rise up," " that He may do his work, his strange work ; and bring to pass his act, his strange act. Now, therefore, be ye not mockers, lest your bands be made strong." God " *will* render to every man according to his deeds :" unto them that are contentious, and do not obey the truth"—the froward ones—" indignation and wrath, tribulation and anguish," " in the day when God shall judge the secrets of men by Jesus Christ."[2] Such must be the end of perverse opposition to God, however craftily carried on.

But why should men prosecute so hopeless a warfare ? Their

---

[1] Lev. xxvi. 21, 23, 27, 28.   Prov. iii. 34.   Isa. xxviii. 15-22.   [2] Rom. ii. 6, 8, 9, 16

offended Sovereign holds out to THEM the sceptre of mercy. They are not yet, like their leader and his angelic followers, "reserved under chains to the judgment of the great day." HE whom they wickedly, madly oppose, is proclaiming, "Turn ye, turn ye ; why will ye die ?"   What words of encouragement are these !—"If they that are pining away in their inquity " "shall confess their iniquity," "with their trespass which they tres- passed against Me, and that also they have walked contrary unto Me ; and that I also have walked contrary unto them," " then will I remember my covenant," " I will not cast them away, neither will I abhor them, to destroy them utterly, and to break my covenant with them ; for I am the Lord their God." " Only acknowledge thine iniquity," " and I will not cause mine anger to fall upon you : for I am merciful, saith the Lord, and I will not keep anger forever." [1]

These words were originally addressed to " the froward" Israel- ites, but they are applicable to all "froward ones,"in all countries, and in all ages.   It is all but certain there are such perverse ones in this assembly.   Are all here merciful, upright, pure ones,— who have nothing to fear, everything to hope, from God's deal- ings with them ?   Would God it were so!   But the most en- larged charity, if but enlightened, cannot hope for an affirma- tive answer.   They who do not belong to these classes are " fro- ward ones."   Oh, let such persons remember that " the counsel of the froward shall be carried headlong ; for the froward is abomination to the Lord."   " Let them forsake the foolish,"— all the froward are, as we have seen, fools, madmen,—"let them forsake the foolish, and live ; and go on in the way of under- standing."   " If they are wise," in complying with this call, " they shall be wise for themselves ; but if they continue fro- ward"—if they scorn—" they alone must forever bear."   *What* they alone must bear the inspired writer does not say,—human language could not express it.   " Who knows the power of HIS anger ?"   " It is a fearful thing to fall into the hands of the living God."   Oh, may none of us learn from experience on this subject, what can be learned in no other way !   It is better, on this subject, to believe than to know.   Believing would pre- vent knowing.   But he who will not believe, and act accord- ingly, must be made to know.

[1] Lev. xxvi. 39–44.   Jer. iii. 12, 13.

LECTURE VII

FARTHER VIEWS OF JEHOVAH'S CONDUCT TO THE MESSIAH HIS PEOPLE AND HIS ENEMIES

PSALM XVIII. 27-31.—"For Thou wilt save the afflicted people; but wilt bring down high looks. For Thou wilt light my candle: the Lord my God will enlighten my darkness. For by Thee I have run through a troop; and by my God have I leaped over a wall. As for God, his way is perfect: the word of the Lord is tried; He is a buckler to all those that trust in Him. For who is God save the Lord? or who is a rock save our God?"

IT is scarcely needful to put you in mind, that I consider this psalm, in the illustration of which I have been for sometime engaged, as belonging to the class of Messianic psalms, properly so called,—not one of the many psalms in which "it is written of Christ" in the way of indirect and occasional reference,—but one of the comparatively few psalms, of which the Messiah in his person and work forms the direct and the sole subject. The reasons which have established this conviction in my mind were laid before you at length in the introductory discourse; and the objections against this mode of interpretation were also fully stated, and, I trust, satisfactorily answered. This magnificent ode is, then, in my apprehension, a triumphal song, uttered by the Messiah in the midst of the great congregation of worshippers in the temple above, after he had been delivered by Jehovah from the hands of all his enemies.

The poem seems to resolve itself naturally into six parts. The first of these parts is introductory, and embraces the 1st, 2d, and 3d verses. The second, containing the next three verses, is occupied with a brief statement of the Messiah's humiliation and sufferings, his exercise under them, and his deliverance from them. In the third of these parts, reaching from the 7th to the 19th verses, we have a highly poetical account of the supernatural events by which this deliverance was effected. The fourth part, which extends from the 20th to the 31st verses, is occupied with an acknowledgment, that this deliverance was entirely the work of Jehovah,—a work gloriously illustrative of the equity and benignity which are the characteristic features of his moral administration.   The fifth part, reaching from the 32d to the 42d verses, contains an account of Messiah's successful warfare with his enemies.   And the sixth and concluding part, is occupied with a description of the extent and permanence of the Messiah's kingdom.   These parts, according to the genius of poetical compositions, are not formally divided, but beautifully rise out of and merge into each other, so that it is not easy to say precisely where the one terminates and the other begins ; but of the existence of such an order as that which I have indicated, and of its importance to the right interpretation of the psalm, there can be no reasonable doubt.

The first, second, and third of these parts have been fully considered.   We are at present engaged in the illustration of the fourth of them, to which I have already devoted two discourses. I have shown that the deliverance and exaltation of the Messiah are here represented as the merited reward of his perfect fulfilment of the great work given him to do ; that in doing that work, he had shown himself righteous, spotlessly pure in all his actions ; that he had uniformly kept the ways of Jehovah, and never in any instance departed from his God ; that *all* the Divine judgments had.been kept steadily before him as the rule of his conduct, and that he had not put any of His statutes away from him ; that he had been perfect even before God, and had kept himself from all fault ; that he had, in one word, fulfilled all righteousness, and that his deliverance and exaltation were the merited, and, so far as that was possible, the adequate reward and recompense bestowed by the righteous Judge,—the token that the Lord was "well pleased for his righteousness' sake,"— that He indeed delighted in him.   I have illustrated also the Messiah's acknowledgment,—that with him, the benignantly bountiful One, Jehovah had acted in a benignantly bountiful manner,—with him, the perfect One, He had showed himself perfect,—with him, the pure One, He had showed himself pure ; while, in reference to his great adversary, the crooked—the perverse and crafty—one, He had taken him in his own craftiness, and made his mischief return on his own head.   So far have I proceeded in the illustration of this fourth section of the psalm.

In the words of the 27th verse, with which the subject of this discourse commences, the Messiah makes a transition from the Divine mode of dealing with the Messiah and his great enemy, to the Divine mode of dealing with the two bodies of men, of which he and his great enemy are respectively the heads and leaders. " For Thou wilt save the afflicted people : but wilt bring down high looks ;" or, "Thou savest the afflicted people : but bringest down high looks." ' This is thy ordinary, thy fixed, mode of dealing with these classes. Thou hast acted, Thou dost act, Thou wilt act, in this manner towards them.'

There are plainly two classes of persons mentioned here, characterized by opposite dispositions. The afflicted people— an exclusive class of men—whom the psalmist calls elsewhere[1] " the congregation of God's poor," standing in contrast with another class just as exclusive,—the men with high looks or lofty eyes.

The word rendered " afflicted,"[2] properly signifies ' poor' or ' needy.' The persons spoken of are obviously afflicted ones, for they need to be saved or delivered ; but it is not their affliction, so much as their poverty, that is indicated by the epithet here given them ; and, from the poor being contrasted, not with the wealthy, but with the proud—for that is the meaning of the figurative expression, "the man of high looks "—it seems plain that, though the great body of the class referred to have always been found among the comparatively " poor in this world," the reference is to those poor ones whom our Lord represents as "poor in spirit." It describes that class of men who have just—that is, very lowly—sentiments and feelings respecting themselves, both as creatures and as sinners—who clearly see, deeply feel, that as creatures they are entirely dependent on God—that they are nothing that is good but what God has made them—that they have nothing that is good but what God has given them—that, as sinners, they are very guilty, thoroughly depraved—that they deserve nothing, that they never can deserve anything, from God but punishment—that for anything short of the severest suffer-ing they are capable of, they ought to be grateful—that no in-fliction, however severe, can be a reasonable ground of complaint to them—that " in them, that is, in their flesh, dwelleth no good thing "—that " their hearts are deceitful above all things, and

[1] Psal. lxxiv. 19.   [2] עָנִי

desperately wicked"—that they are indeed in themselves spiritually " poor, and blind, and naked" who consider all the
blessings they have or hope for, as the result of free grace,
sovereign kindness—and who view whatever is right and good
in their dispositions and conduct, as the result of " God working
in them, to will and to do of his good pleasure." These are the
poor ones so often spoken of in Scripture, as objects of the Divine complacency and care.

The other class, the men of high looks, includes all the rest of
mankind : for though "pride was not made for man"—though
nothing can be more incongruous than haughtiness in a creature,
still more in a sinner—men, unchanged by divine influence, are
all proud. They have no proper sense of their place as creatures,
or of their character and deserts as sinners. Their leading disposition is selfish wilfulness. They are determined to have their
own will—without reference, or in opposition, to God's will,
and without reference, or in opposition, to the rights and interests of others. The language of their prevailing desire, as
expressed in their habitual conduct, is, 'We are our own : who
is Lord over us ?' They have little or no regard to the rights
either of God or their fellow-men, when these interfere with
what they suppose they have a right to, and that is substantially the being and possessing whatever they desire.

The poverty of spirit which distinguishes the one class, and
the self-estimation which distinguishes the other, are more
strongly developed in some individuals than in others, but are
to be found in all; and the first class have at their head him
who is "meek and lowly in heart ;" and the second have at their
head him whose pride made him contest the supremacy with
the Supreme, and defy the Omnipotent to arms.

With regard to the first of these classes, the Messiah, addressing Jehovah, says, "Thou savest the poor people." The language intimates that the poor people are an afflicted people.
The perfectly safe and happy do not need to be saved. But the
poor people are exposed to many dangers and sufferings,—some
of them common to the race they belong to—some of them
peculiar to themselves, rising out of their character and circumstances—not a few of them springing from the oppression of the
men of lofty looks, who are their enemies. But whatever are
their dangers or their sufferings, God will help them under them,

and in due time completely deliver them from them. "He forgetteth not the cry of the humble." He hears not only their cry, but their desire. "He regards the prayer of the destitute: He will not despise their prayer." "He delivers the needy when he crieth : the poor also, and him that hath no helper. He spares the poor and needy, and saves the souls of the needy. He redeems their souls from deceit and violence; and precious shall their blood be in his sight."[1] Though "heaven be his throne, and the earth his footstool," and though these heavens He inhabits cannot contain Him, "He looks to, He dwells with, the man who is humble, who trembles at his word, to revive the spirit of the lowly, and to revive the heart of the contrite one."[2] His providence often remarkably interposes in their behalf; and his economy of grace is so arranged that none but they, and that every one of them, shall be made partakers of its blessings. "He that humbleth himself, shall be exalted." "Blessed are the poor in spirit, for theirs is the kingdom of heaven." God will sustain them under all their afflictions; He will prevent them from receiving any real injury from them. He will do more—He will make them conducive to their spiritual improvement and ultimate salvation. He will grant them such partial deliverances even here as He sees to be necessary or useful to them; and He will at last completely deliver them from them, and set them beyond the reach of evil, in every form and degree, forever.

With regard to the second class, the Messiah, addressing himself to Jehovah, says, 'Thou bringest down the "high looks," the men of "high looks," the proud.' "God resisteth the proud;" He sets himself to oppose him. It is impossible, in the nature of things, that God should not disapprove of pride; for it is a disposition which, in the degree in which it prevails, unfits a man for his duty to God and man,—making him a rebel to the one, and an oppressor to the other; and, in every view we can take of it, counterworks God's design to glorify himself in making his creatures happy. The Divine disapprobation of sin is marked in an endless variety of ways. In the ordinary course of his

---

[1] Psal. lxxii. 2, 4, 12–14. These words are a description of "the King's Son;" but he is his Father's image, "the express image of His person,"—so that "he who hath seen him, hath seen the Father."

[2] Isa. lxvi. 1, 2.

providential dispensations, God often brings down the men of "high looks." It has indeed become a proverb, "A haughty spirit goeth before a fall." And he has not unfrequently gone out of his ordinary course to punish the proud by degradation. See the proud king of Egypt, who asked, " Who is Jehovah, that I should obey him ?" and madly pursuing Jehovah's people through the miraculously-bared channel of the Arabian Gulf, said, "I will pursue, I will overtake, I will divide the spoil ; my lust shall be satisfied upon them ; I will draw my sword, my hand shall destroy them." See how God silenced his blasphemous boasting, and brought down his high looks,—"Thou didst blow with thy wind, the sea covered them : they sank as lead in the mighty waters."[1] See the, if possible, still prouder king of Babylon, Nebuchadnezzar, "walking in the palace of the king-dom of Babylon :" And as he walked, "he spake and said, Is not this great Babylon, that I have built for the house of the kingdom, by the might of my power, and for the honor of my majesty ?" Behold how God brought down his high looks,— " While the word was in the king's mouth, there fell a voice from heaven, saying, O king Nebuchadnezzar, to thee it is spoken : The kingdom is departed from thee ; and they shall drive thee from men, and thy dwelling shall be with the beasts of the field : they shall make thee to eat grass as oxen, and seven times shall pass over thee, until thou know that the Most High ruleth in the kingdom of men, and giveth it to whomsoever He will. The same hour was the thing fulfilled upon Nebuchad-nezzar."[2] Take a third example. "Upon a set day Herod, arrayed in royal apparel, sat upon his throne, and made an ora-tion unto them. And the people gave a shout, saying, It is the voice of a god, and not of a man. And immediately the angel of the Lord smote him, because he gave not God the glory : and he was eaten of worms, and gave up the ghost."[3] No proud man can participate in the blessings of the Christian salvation. " The rich"—those who think themselves rich, and increased with goods—" are sent empty away ;" and the result of the new economy shall be, "The lofty looks of man shall be humbled, and the haughtiness of men shall be bowed down ; and the Lord alone shall be exalted."[4] God will either, by the power of his

[1] Exod. xv. 9, 10.   [2] Dan. iv 29-33.   [3] Acts, xii. 21-23.   [4] Isa. ii. 11.

grace, humble the pride of men's hearts, or, in the power of his righteous vengeance, plunge them into the pit of perdition.   He will either bend them or break them into submission to his authority.   What an awful illustration will this passage of Scripture receive, when "the kings of the earth, and the great men, and the rich men, and the chief captains, and the mighty men," shall "hide themselves in the dens, and in the rocks of the mountains; and shall say to the mountains and rocks, Fall on us, and hide us from the face of Him that sitteth on the throne, and from the wrath of the Lamb: for the great day of his wrath is come; and who shall be able to stand!"[1]

While the words thus naturally express a great law of the Divine moral government, in regard of the poor and the proud in spirit, it is natural to suppose that they have a particular reference to its exemplification, in the events which led more immediately to the utterance of this triumphal hymn by the delivered and exalted Messiah.   The disciples of our Lord were, in both senses of the word, poor ones, and those who opposed him and his cause were men of high rank, and of overbearing haughtiness.   Most wonderfully did God help and save these poor ones.   He remarkably *saved* those of them who dwelt in Jerusalem, affording them an opportunity to escape from the beleaguered city, of which, remembering the words of their Lord, they availed themselves, and thus were delivered from those tremendous evils which befell their unbelieving brethren, when "wrath came on them to the uttermost."   By the destruction of the Jewish polity, He delivered the Christians residing in Judea from the persecutions of their countrymen.   He saved the church from being destroyed by the power and fury of her heathen persecutors, and ultimately delivered them entirely from these persecutions, by the overthrow of the pagan Roman empire.

The saving of the afflicted people, and the bringing down of the high looks, generally go together.   The latter is the cause or means of the former.   By bringing down the high looks of the proud oppressor, He saves his poor ones.   To both of these events the language of the prophet is very applicable,—" He bringeth down them that dwell on high; the lofty city, He layeth it low: He layeth it low, even to the ground; He bringeth it even to

---

[1] Rev. vi. 15–17.

the dust. The poor shall tread it down, even the feet of the poor, and the steps of the needy."[1]

It may be remarked, in passing, that the particle introducing this and some of the following verses, rendered " for,"[2] does not here indicate that what follows it assigns the reason for, or the cause of, what is stated in the preceding clause, but is intended merely to give intensity to the assertion,—being equivalent to, 'Surely Thou savest the poor people, and bringest down the high looks.'

The transition made by the Messiah from himself and his great enemy, to his people and their enemies, will not be wondered at by any who know how close is the connection between him and his people, and between his great enemy and their enemies. He is in them, and they are in him. United to his person, conformed to his character, God will deal with them as He dealt with him; and their enemies, having identified themselves with his great enemy—being " of their father the devil," animated with his spirit, and engaged in his work,—may lay their account, continuing so, with being dealt with as he is to be dealt with. He who delivered the Messiah will deliver his people; and He who mortifies, and disappoints, and destroys his enemy, will mortify, disappoint, and destroy theirs. They who take the side of the Messiah, and they who take the side of his enemy, will be treated by God in the same way as their leaders. The first shall " enter into the joy of their Lord," and the second depart " into the everlasting fire prepared for the devil and his angels."

In the 28th verse, the Messiah reverts to the Divine dispensations to himself, describing his deliverance and exaltation under the figures of rekindling an extinguished lamp, and of light being made to arise out of darkness. " For Thou wilt light my candle: the Lord my God will enlighten my darkness." Or, on the principles of interpretation formerly stated,—'Surely Thou lightest my lamp: the Lord my God enlightens my darkness.' The general meaning of these words is plain. The force of the figurative representation appears from the manner in

---

[1] Isa. xxvi. 5, 6.

[2] " The particle כִּי not unfrequently has an intensive meaning (like the Latin imo, or the German ya) in the beginning of a sentence.—Isa. xxviii. 28; viii. 23; xxxii. 13. Psal. lxxvii. 12; lxxi. 23. Exod, xxii. 22. Job, viii. 26. Ewald Gram. § 320. Ges. Lex. sub. voc."—M. STUART. In Prov. ii. 3, it is rightly translated "yea." ὅτι, in the New Testament used as the translation of the Hebrew particle, has not unfrequently the same meaning.

which it is applied in the book of Job. "The light of the wicked shall be put out, and the spark of his fire shall not shine. The light shall be dark in his tabernacle, and his candle"—or lamp—"shall be put out with him." "How oft is the candle of the wicked put out! and how oft cometh their destruction upon them! God distributeth sorrows in his anger."[1] A state of darkness is thus often emblematical of a state of obscurity and suffering; a state of light of a state of dignity and enjoyment.

The Messiah's whole state on earth had been one of obscurity, depression, inferiority, contempt, suffering, and sorrow; and his lamp had been, as it were, extinguished by death, and he himself laid in the darkness and degradation of the tomb. But, in his resurrection, God "brought him out of darkness and the shadow of death, and brake his bands asunder;" the extinguished lamp was rekindled; and, in his consequent ascension and glorification, "light was shed over the righteous One,"—for that is the meaning of the words, "Light is sown for the righteous," in the ninety-seventh psalm—a psalm referring to the same events as that which we are engaged in illustrating. The darkness of the grave is exchanged for the light of life; the sufferings of earth for the joys of heaven. From being unknown, he becomes well known; his name, from a proverb of contempt, becomes the "name above every name." The despised and rejected of men, becomes the object of worship to angels. He who was crucified in weakness, lives for ever by the power of God. He who had not where to lay his head, is acknowledged to be the proprietor of the universe. He who was exceeding sorrowful, even to death, is "made most blessed forever." The hands nailed to the cross wield the sceptre of supreme government, and the diadem of divine glory has taken the place of the crown of thorns. Such is the general import of the words. 'Thou hast changed my state of obscurity and suffering into a state of dignity and enjoyment.'

Perhaps, without straining the figure, we may find somewhat more in it. The lamp ordained for Jehovah's Anointed may be considered as emblematical of the gospel revelation, by means of which the Messiah becomes known and honored among men. In this view of the figure, the lighting of Messiah's lamp by Jehovah, and making it dispel the obscurity in which he was

---

[1] Job, xviii. 5, 6; xxi. 17.

previously involved, represents the diffusion of the Gospel throughout the world. Jehovah has thus lighted the Messiah's lamp—still keeps it burning, notwithstanding all attempts by earth and hell to extinguish it,—and will continue to make it burn with increasing brightness, till, by its means, all nations shall be made to behold, in the once humbled, but now exalted Messiah, their divine Lord and Saviour.

> "The beam that shines from Sion hill
> Shall lighten ev'ry land;
> The King who reigns in Salem's tow'rs
> Shall all the world command."

The deliverance and exaltation of the Messiah are brought before our minds under a different set of figures in the 29th verse. "For by Thee I have run through a troop; and by my God have I leaped over a wall."[1] The Messiah seems here represented as a warrior seeking to take possession of a fortified city; he breaks through the hostile bands who have come forth to attack *him*, and defend *it ;* and, passing through them by vanquishing them, he scales the walls, and takes possession of the fortress. The general idea is, 'In the face of the greatest opposition, in spite of the most powerful obstacles, the Messiah has attained that high state of dignity and enjoyment which he possesses. All the difficulties arising out of the justice of God, the guilt and depravity of man, the craft and power of evil angels, have been overcome. He has triumphed, is triumphing, will triumph, over principalities and powers, till all his enemies are made his footstool, and he is recognised Lord of all.' This is undoubtedly the general idea. It is not inconsistent with this interpretation, to recognise a fulfilment of the prophetic oracle in the Messiah triumphing over particular obstacles which lay in the way of the success of himself and his cause. Accordingly, we do not blame those who find in these words an adumbration of the events of the resurrection, or of those of the siege and capture of Jerusalem. Neither the hosts of darkness nor the Roman guard could keep him in the sepulchre : he broke through them all,—overleaped its rocky walls, and walked forth, in the power of an endless life, to take possession of his blood-bought inheritance. I cannot doubt that, in the subsequent verses, as

---

[1] Kimchi interprets this phrase as equivalent to—" I have leaped over the walls of the cities of my enemies so as to take them."

I shall endeavor to make evident when I come to illustrate them, there is a reference to the Messiah's triumph over his Jewish enemies, when their city was taken, and their polity finally destroyed; and therefore I am not prepared to consider, as altogether fanciful, the interpretation of Peirce, an acute and generally judicious commentator, who finds in these words an allusion to the siege and capture of Jerusalem. I think his words worth quoting. " By his running through a troop, I suppose is meant his overthrowing the Jewish army; but, in his leaping over a wall, we may well understand the taking Jerusalem by the Romans. A man must be a stranger to the style of Scripture that sees any difficulty in Messiah speaking of this as his doing, because it was done immediately by the Romans. Nothing is commoner than to speak of a thing as done by him who is the grand director and cause of its being done." Thus, Matth. xxii. 7—which refers to the same event to which we suppose there is an allusion in these words,—" When the king heard thereof, he was wrath, and sent forth his armies and destroyed these murderers, and burnt up their city." The Romans were God's armies,—the instruments of his vengeance; and Messiah, to whom the administration of the Divine government is committed, may be said to do what they did, in punishing the Jews. This passage had a remarkable fulfilment at the taking of Jerusalem. The city was fenced all round by three walls, one within another, except where it was secured by deep valleys. These the Romans were forced to break through, though they were strongly defended by the Jews. A minute description of this may be found in the sixth book of Josephus' " History of the Jewish Wars." One short extract is very striking. " On the 8th of September, when Titus entered the city, and admired, among other things, the fortifications and towers, he said, We have fought with God on our side; and it was God who withdrew the Jews from these strongholds; for what could the hands of men or engines do against these ?"[1] In these words we almost think we hear Messiah speaking by the mouth of the instrument of his righteous vengeance,—" By my God I have leaped over a wall."

For all his deliverances and triumphs, the Messiah repre-

---

[1] Joseph. de Bell. Jud. vi. 16, *et seq.*

sents himself as entirely indebted to Jehovah. " Thou lighest
my candle "—" the Lord God enlightens my darkness "—" by
Thee I have run through a troop "—" by my God I have leaped
over a wall." Such expressions may to some seem fitter for
David than for David's Son and Lord, who was " God manifest
in the flesh," and whose own arm brought him deliverance.
But the Son, who is essentially one with the Father, speaks here
in his mediatorial character,—in which all he does is done in
obedience to the Father's command, and in the exercise of qualifications bestowed by the Father. This is quite in accordance
with the ordinary representations both of the Old and New Testament Scriptures. It is Jehovah who makes all the enemies of
David's Lord, sitting at his right hand, to be his footstool. It is
the Father who sets the Son " far above all principality, and
power, and might, and dominion, and every name that is named,
not only in this world, but in that which is to come; and puts
all things under his feet; and gives him to be head over all
things to the church." He seeks not his own glory, but the glory
of Him who sent him. All he does on earth and in heaven, is
to the glory of God the Father, that God may be all in all.

This section of the psalm is closed in the 30th and 31st verses,
with an acknowledgment on the part of the Messiah, of the absolute perfection of the Divine dispensations in reference to
him, and of the incomparable excellence of Jehovah. " As for
God, his way is perfect; the word of the Lord is tried; He is a
buckler to all those who trust in Him. For who is God save the
Lord, or who is a rock save our God ?"

The word " way " is generally, in Scripture, used to signify a
course of conduct; as, " a man's way is right in his own eyes."
" The way of the Lord," is an expression which, taken by itself,
may signify either that course of conduct which God follows
towards men, or that course of conduct which God requires men
to follow. In the first case, it is equivalent to the dispensations
of his providence; in the second, to the injunctions of his law.
The expression is to be met with in both senses in the Bible ;—
in the first, when it is said, " The Lord is righteous in all his
ways;" in the second, when it is said, " Blessed is every one that
walketh in the way of the Lord ;" or, as in the 21st verse, " I
have kept the ways of the Lord." It is by the connection of the
passage that we are to judge which of these meanings belongs to

the phrase in any particular place; and, in most cases, there is no difficulty in determining the question. In the passage before us, it is obvious that the phrase is used in the first sense. "The way of the Lord," signifies, 'the dispensations of his providence.'

This way is said to be "perfect;" that is, the Divine providential conduct is free from fault. There is nothing in it inconsistent with wisdom, righteousness, and benignity; nothing is done without a reason—nothing without a good reason. There is nothing unwise, nothing iniquitous, nothing capricious, nothing cruel, in his providential administration. This is true with regard to all the Divine dispensations. "The Lord is the rock, his work is perfect; all his ways are judgment; a God of truth and without iniquity; just and right is He." It is very strikingly true in reference to the Divine dispensations to, and concerning, the Messiah. Many of these dispensations were very mysterious. "God's way" to his righteous Servant—his beloved Son —was often "in the sea, and his paths in the mighty waters; but justice and judgment was ever the foundation of his throne. Mercy and truth went before his face." Everything was ordered in infinite wisdom, righteousness, and mercy. The Messiah declares himself quite satisfied with them. And when we contemplate these dispensations as unfolded in their connection and purpose in the New Testament revelation, surely we must say, from the beginning to the end of the economy of mercy,— 'He has done all things well. Oh, the depth of the riches, both of the wisdom and knowledge—of the righteousness and grace—of God; how unsearchable are his judgments, and his ways past finding out.'

"The word of the Lord is tried." The word of the Lord is here plainly, 'the promise of God to the Messiah,' that He would sustain him under his labors and sufferings, deliver him from them, and reward him for them. This word is said to be "tried." It has been brought to the trial, and has stood it. Jehovah has been faithful to his word. He has shown in his conduct to the Messiah, that "He is not a man that He should lie, nor the son of man that He should repent." All the Divine promises of qualification, support, comfort, victory, and reward, are fulfilled, or in the way of being fulfilled. The Messiah proclaims Him, the "covenant-keeping God." "Thou hast dealt well with thy servant according to thy word." "Thou hast kept with thy servant that which Thou hast promised him. What Thou spakest with thy mouth, Thou hast fulfilled with thine hand." And it is true universally. The word of the Lord is tried. It has often been tried, and it has always stood the trial. Not one trusting to God's word, rightly understood and applied, has ever been disappointed.[1]

"He is a buckler or shield to all who trust in Him."[2] The language is figurative; but the meaning is plain. 'He is the protector of all who trust in Him.' The Messiah was distinguished for his trust in God. Jehovah was his buckler—his protector and defender—amid all his enemies; and what He was to him, He will be to all who, like him, " know God's name, and put their confidence in Him."

Full of admiration of the wisdom, righteousness, faithfulness, and kindness of Jehovah, as manifested in his dispensations towards himself, the Messiah declares his conviction of his supreme, infinite, unparalleled excellence in the striking interrogation, "For who is God save the Lord? Who is a rock save our God?" That is just a more energetic way of saying, 'There is no God but Jehovah. There is no rock but our God.' The great design of the Messiah, in this triumphal song, as in all he did on earth and all he does in heaven, is to manifest his Father's name, to declare his excellence, to show forth his glory, to celebrate his praise,—to give men eternal life in giving them the knowledge of Him as the only true God. One great design of the Messiah's mission, though by no means the sole design, was to diffuse throughout the world the knowledge and worship of the one true God, and to destroy idolatry in all the various forms in which it had established itself among mankind. The two truths contained in this verse, hold a most distinguished place in that system of truth which our Lord commanded his apostles to preach to every creature. There is no God but Jehovah. "There be gods many and lords many, but to us there is one God." "The Gods whom the nations worship are no gods." "They have mouths, but they

---

[1] The phrase may be intended, not so much to record the fact that the word of the Lord has often been tried and always found true, as to mark the character of his word as entire truth, nothing but truth, like pure silver,—as in Psal. xii. 6, "The words of the Lord are pure words: as silver tried in a furnace of earth, purified seven times;"—"very faithful," Psal. cxix. 138.

[2] חוסים בו, equivalent to 'who place themselves under the skirts of his garments,' referring to an ancient custom.

speak not; eyes have they, but they see not; they have ears, but they hear not; noses have they, but they smell not; they have hands, but they handle not; feet have they, but they walk not; neither speak they through their throat. They that make them are like unto them; so is every one that trusteth in them." But our God made the heavens. He is in the heavens, and He hath done whatsoever He pleaseth. "The gods that have not made the heavens and the earth, even they shall perish from the earth, and from under these heavens." But our God "is the true God, He is the living God, and an everlasting King; at his wrath the earth shall tremble, and the nations shall not be able to abide his indignation;" for "He hath made the earth by his power, He hath established the world by his wisdom, and hath stretched out the heavens by his discretion." "There is none like unto the God of Jeshurun."[1] "There is no rock," *i.e.*, no being, in whom we may safely place supreme—entire—confidence, " but our God." 'My God,' says the Messiah, 'and the God of all my people.' "I ascend," says he, "to my Father and your Father; my God and your God,"—the covenant God. The great truth taught is, 'Jehovah as God in Christ is all, and does all that can be wished for in a God. He is the immutable—eternal—protector of all who trust in Him. No other being in the universe can be so.' The words also naturally suggest the thought—Who can prevent the fulfilment of his promises, or the accomplishment of his purposes? "Vain," as Bishop Horne says, "were the idols of the ancient world, Baal and Jupiter. As vain are those of modern self-called enlightened times,—pleasure, honor, or profit. They cannot make their votaries happy even here; much less can they deliver from death, and make man's immortality of being an immortality of bliss."

We shall not wonder at these truths being introduced here, when we consider that the destruction of our Lord's Jewish enemies, and the overthrow of heathen superstitions, both of which are celebrated in this psalm, were illustrious demonstrations given by the exalted Messiah, that there was no God but Jehovah— no rock but Jehovah in Christ Jesus, man's covenant God.

The illustration of the next section of the psalm, containing an account of the exalted Messiah's successful warfare with his enemies, will form the subject of our next discourse.

---

[1] Psal. cxv. 3–8.   Jer. x. 10–16.   Deut. xxxiii. 26.

The practical reflections to which the passage explained naturally gives rise, are numerous and important. With merely indicating a few of them, I shall close the discourse.

Let us all cultivate that poverty of spirit which fixes the complacent regard of Jehovah, and mortify that pride which, in all its forms, is the object of his abhorrence. If we should share Christ's happiness, let us seek to be, like him, meek and lowly, knowing that, if we resemble the proud leader of the fallen angels, we must share in his doom.

Let us rejoice in the ever-extending fame of the once dishonored Messiah, and seek the honor of being agents, in the hand of Him who commanded the light to shine out of darkness, in enlightening a dark world by gospel truth, that so they may see and admire the glory of God in the face of Christ Jesus, "the brightness of the Father's glory—the express image of his person."

Let our Lord's past victories strengthen our faith, that "He must reign till all his enemies are made his footstool."

However painful and perplexing may be some of the dispensations of Providence (they cannot be more so than some of the dispensations in reference to the Messiah), let us rest assured that all is done in wisdom, righteousness, and benignity; and that, in the ultimate result of things, it will be made apparent that He has done all things well.

And, contemplating the incomparable grandeur, and excellence, and grace of the Divine character, especially as manifested to the Messiah and his people, let us say in our hearts, "Who is a God like unto Thee, glorious in holiness, fearful in praises, doing wonders?" "Who is a God like unto Thee, who pardoneth iniquity, and passeth by the transgression of the remnant of his heritage; who retaineth not his anger forever, because He delighteth in mercy?" "There is none like the God of Jeshurun." "This God shall be our God forever; He shall be our guide even unto death."

> "Just are thy ways, and true thy word,
>   Great Rock of my secure abode;
> Who is a God beside the Lord,
>   Or where's a refuge like our God?"

"Their rock is not like our Rock, our enemies themselves being judges."

LECTURE VIII

THE MESSIAH'S SUCCESSFUL WARFARE AND EXTENSIVE AND ETERNAL KINGDOM

PSALM XVIII. 32–50.—" It is God that girdeth me with strength, and maketh my way perfect. He maketh my feet like hinds' heet, and setteth me upon my high places. He teacheth my hands to war, so that a bow of steel is broken by mine arms. Thou hast also given me the shield of thy salvation; and thy right hand hath holden me up, and thy gentleness hath made me great. Thou hast enlarged my steps under me, that my feet did not slip. I have pursued mine enemies, and overtaken them; neither did I turn again till they were consumed. I have wounded them, that they were not able to rise: they are fallen under my feet. For Thou hast girded me with strength unto the battle: Thou hast subdued under me those that rose up against me. Thou hast also given me the necks of mine enemies, that I might destroy them that hate me. They cried, but there was none to save them; even unto the Lord, but He answered them not. Then did I beat them small as the dust before the wind; I did cast them out as the dirt in the streets. Thou hast delivered me from the strivings of the people; and Thou hast made me the head of the heathen: a people whom I have not known shall serve me. As soon as they hear of me, they shall obey me: the strangers shall submit themselves unto me. The strangers shall fade away, and be afraid out of their close places. The Lord liveth; and blessed be my Rock; and let the God of my salvation be exalted. It is God that avengeth me, and subdueth the people under me. He delivered me from mine enemies; yea, Thou liftest me up above those that rise up against me: Thou hast delivered me from the violent man. Therefore will I give thanks unto Thee, O Lord, among the heathen, and sing praises unto thy name. Great deliverance giveth He to his king; and showeth mercy to his anointed, to David, and to his seed for evermore."

WHEN I entered on the exposition of this psalm, after stating the reasons which induce me to consider it as prophetic, referring not to David, but to his Son and Lord, the Messiah,—I remarked that it seems naturally to resolve itself into six sections. The first is introductory (verses 1–3); the second contains a short account of the Messiah's humiliation and sufferings, the exercise of his mind under them, and his deliverance from them (verses 4–6); the third is a most picturesque description of those preternatural Divine dispensations by which this deliverance was effected (verses 7–19); the fourth is an acknowledgment and celebration of the Divine perfections,—the righteousness, the benignity, and faithfulness manifested in these dispensations (verses 20–31);

the fifth is a narrative of successful warfare (verses 32–42) ; and the sixth (verses 43–50) is a description of the extent and permanence of the Messiah's kingdom. We have illustrated four of these sections : we proceed now to the consideration of the fifth of them.

"It is God that girdeth me with strength, and maketh my way perfect. He maketh my feet like hinds' feet, and setteth me upon my high places. He teacheth my hands to war, so that a bow of steel is broken by mine arms. Thou hast also given me the shield of thy salvation; and thy right hand hath holden me up, and thy gentleness hath made me great. Thou hast enlarged my steps under me, that my feet did not slip. I have pursued mine enemies, and overtaken them ; neither did I turn again till they were consumed. I have wounded them, that they were not able to rise : they are fallen under my feet. For Thou hast girded me with strength unto the battle : Thou hast subdued under me those that rose up against me. Thou hast also given me the necks of mine enemies, that I might destroy them that hate me. They cried, but there was none to save them; even unto the Lord, but he answered them not. Then did I beat them small as the dust before the wind; I did cast them out as the dirt in the streets." This paragraph, all descriptive of the Messiah's successful warfare, divides itself into two parts : first, a description of the qualifications for successful warfare bestowed on him by Jehovah (verses 32–36); and, secondly, a description of his exercise of these qualifications in the defeat and destruction of his enemies (verses 37–42). Let us look at these in their order.

"It is God that girdeth me with strength." There are here two ideas : 'I am girded with strength;' and, 'it is God who has thus girded me.' To be girded with strength is a figurative expression—to be furnished with power.[1] Words expressive of clothing are often used to signify 'allotting,' or 'bestowing.'[2] The Messiah represents himself as bound round with strength as with a girdle, fitting him for work and for warfare,—the energy of which the apostle speaks, " whereby he is able to subdue all things to himself." And He ascribes his possession of this

---

[1] 'Forte in verbo latet nomen verbale ut solet : accingit me cingulo roboris."— DRUSIUS.

[2] Psal. cxxxii. 16, 18. 1 Chron. xii. 18 ; xxiv. 20, marg. Psal. xciii. 1. 1 Pet. v. 5.

strength to the gift of God : "It is God that girdeth me with strength." [1] Whatever the Son possesses as Mediator is bestowed by the Father, as the merited and promised reward of his labors and sufferings. "The Father hath committed all judgment"— all government—"unto the Son." He "hath given to the Son to have life in himself." "All things," says he, "are delivered unto me of my Father." "All power is given unto me, in heaven and in earth." "Father, glorify thy Son," "as Thou hast given him power over all flesh." He is "Lord of all ;" "angels, and authorities, and powers being made subject to him."

"He maketh my way perfect." The Messiah's "way" is his administration of the government committed to him by Jehovah —the course of his providence. That administration is "perfect," —i. e., either free from all defect or fault,—perfectly wise, perfectly righteous, perfectly benignant; or rather, perhaps, prosperous, successful. Like the parallel passage in Isa. lii. 13, both ideas may be included. Jehovah's servant deals both "prudently" and prosperously. "The pleasure of the Lord prospers in his hand." His enterprizes are always ultimately successful. None can stay his arm ; none dare say to him, "What doest thou ?" He goes forth, "conquering and to conquer." It has been said to him by Him who "speaks and it is done," "Gird thy sword upon thy thigh, O most Mighty, with thy glory and thy majesty. And in thy majesty ride prosperously, because of truth, and meekness, and righteousness ; and thy right hand shall teach Thee terrible things. Thine arrows are sharp in the heart of the King's enemies ; whereby the people fall under Thee."

"He maketh my feet like hinds' feet,[2] and setteth me upon

---

[1] "To be well girt was to be well armed, in the Greek and Latin idioms, as well as in the Hebrew."—GEDDES.

[2] מְשַׁוֶּה רַגְלַי בָּאַיָּלוֹת. Celerity of motion was considered as one of the qualities of an ancient hero. Achilles is celebrated for being ποδὰς ὠκὺς. Virgil's Nisus is hyperbolically described, "Et ventis et fulminis ocior alis;" and the men of Gad, who came to David, "men of might, and men of war fit for the battle, that could handle shield and buckler," are said to have had "faces like the faces of lions," and to have been "as swift as the roes upon the mountains,"—1 Chron. xii. 8. Asahel is described as "light of foot as a wild roe,"—2 Sam. ii. 18 ; and Saul seems called the roe (in the English translation, "the beauty") of Israel,—2 Sam. i. 19. It has been said that the legs of the hind are straighter than those of the buck, and that she is swifter than he is ; but there is no sufficient proof of this. Gataker gives the true account of it when he says, "The female formula is often used for the species." This is not uncommon in Hebrew. The female ass obviously stands for the ass species,— Gen. xii. 16 ; Job, i. 3 · xlii. 12. Some (at the head of whom is Bochart, *Hierozoicon.*

my high places." It is not easy to fix the precise meaning of
these words. It is difficult to say whether there be one or two
figurative representations. The words may describe the Messiah's suddenly obtaining complete security from the attacks of
his enemies, by being removed entirely beyond the sphere of
their power. As the fleet hind distances her pursuers, and finds
a safe refuge in the inaccessible heights of the mountains,—so,
in one day, in one hour, Messiah rose from earth to heaven, and
obtained perfect and permanent security from all the fraud and
violence of his enemies. We think it more likely that the figure
is double ;—the expression, " making his feet like hinds' feet,"
referring to the rapidity of the Messiah's conquests; and the
" setting him upon his high places," to his being raised to the
possession of that power and influence among men which was
his due, but which had long been usurped by his great enemy.
He calls these " *his* high places." The Father had " given him
the heathen as his possession." They were his

> " By ancient covenant, ere Nature's birth;
> And he had made them his by purchase since,
> And overpaid their value in his blood."[1]

That the " high places" here, are not " places of refuge," seems
plain, both from the context, and from the original passages in
ancient prophetic poetry, to which there is a reference : " He
made him to ride on the high places of the earth." " Thou
shalt tread on their high places." The whole paragraph refers,
not to secure flight, but to resistless victory. We find the fulfilment of the oracle in the rapid progress of the Gospel, and the
speedy downfall both of Judaism and Paganism. " The word of
the Lord," which is " the rod of his strength going forth out of
Zion," " had free course, and was glorified." Before the destruction of Jerusalem, Christianity was very generally known—very
extensively received. " It had come," says the apostle, in his
Epistle to the Colossians, " to all the world, as well as to them ;"
and in the course of little more than two centuries, it had in a

---

P. i. L. ii. c. 17) have supposed the reference to be to the peculiar hardness of the
hoof of the roe, which enables it to walk firmly, without danger of falling, on the
roughest and rockiest places. Virgil calls the hind " æri-pedem "—brass-footed.
Others suppose the reference to be to its agility and celerity. There is nothing to
prevent our supposing that there is a reference to both these distinguishing qualities
of the hind's feet.

[1] Cowper.

great measure supplanted Paganism, and become the dominant religion throughout and beyond the Roman empire.

Peirce expounds the verse in the following way:—" He maketh my feet like hinds' feet." The meaning probably is, ' He gives me to be swift and speedy in performing my designs:' and when it is added, He "setteth me upon my high places," I suppose the sense is, ' He dislodges my enemies, and gives me to possess, and, according to my pleasure, to dispose of those places of strength and renown which anciently belonged to me, such as Jerusalem.' The high places of any country in Scripture language being the capital cities, or those fortresses on the strength of which they chiefly depended for defence and safety against their enemies. "The high places of the Jews, the Messiah may be understood to call *his*, as he had all along been their king and protector." This is ingenious, but it is better to understand the words generally, in which case the events referred to by Peirce were a partial accomplishment of the oracle.

" He teacheth my hands to war, so that a bow of steel is broken by mine arms." The first clause of this verse is just another mode of expressing the great thought in this part of the section,—' Jehovah has every way qualified me for successful warfare.' [1] The breaking of the bow of any enemy, is equivalent to vanquishing and disarming him—wresting his weapon of offence out of his hands and rendering it useless by breaking it. The expression seems proverbial; it often occurs in Scripture. "The wicked have" "bent their bow to cast down the poor and needy;" "their bows shall be broken." "Come, behold the works of the Lord, what desolation He hath made in the earth: He maketh wars to cease unto the end of the earth; He breaketh the bow, and cutteth the spear in sunder; He burneth the chariot in the fire." "I will break the bow of Elam." "The spoiler is come up upon her, even upon Babylon, and her mighty men are taken; every one of their bows is broken." "I will break the bow of Israel." "I will break the bow and the sword." "The battle bow shall be cut off," says Zechariah, speaking of the same events, when Messiah "speaks peace unto the heathen." [2] In this case, the meaning is, — ' The

---

[1] Psal. cxliv. 1.

[2] Psal. xxxvii. 14, 15; xlvi. 8, 9. Jer. xlix. 35; li. 56. Hos. i. 5; ii. 18. Zech. ix. 10.

Messiah overcomes his enemies, and renders them incapable of opposing him.'

Some of the best interpreters give a different meaning, which brings out a different, but perhaps still more appropriate, meaning. They read, "a bow of steel"—or rather of brass—"is bent by my arms." 'Jehovah, in teaching me to war, has qualified me for wielding the mightiest and apparently most unmanageable agencies, in order to gain my objects. He has taught me how to use the Roman armies to punish my Jewish enemies.' To bend a bow of brass was a proof of great strength and dexterity, especially with the arms alone, the foot being usually called to aid in such an operation.[1]

"Thou hast given"—or givest—"me the shield of thy salvation, and thy right hand hath holden me up, and thy gentleness hath made me great." A shield of salvation is just a saving, protecting shield. The first clause is equivalent to, 'Thou protectest me;—covered with thy broad and strong shield, I am safe.' The second clause is equivalent to, 'Thou sustainest me; I am holden by thy right hand, which is all-powerful, and therefore I cannot fall. "Thy gentleness"—thy kindness—"has made me great,"[2] or multiplied me.' The Divine kindness (for the Father loveth the Son) was manifested in the high state of ex-

---

[1] To be able to bend a brazen bow was a great proof of strength. To bend the bow of Ulysses is proverbial. The LXX. render the clause—" καὶ ἔθου τόξον χαλκοῦν τοὺς βραχίονάς μου:" the Vulgate, " posuisti ut arcum æreum brachia mea." There can be no doubt that " steel " is a mistranslation. Our version has followed Kimchi, who gives no authority for interpreting it of hardened iron. Arms were anciently made of brass. Hesiod, in his "'Εργ. καὶ ἡμερ.," says,—

"Τοῖς δ' ἦν χάλκεα μέν τεύχη

——Μέλας δ' οὐκ ἔσκε σίδηρος,"—

'Their armor war of brass, for black iron did not then exist.' They had the art of hardening brass. Alcæus, who is quoted in Athenæus, speaks of greaves and swords made of brass. Lucretius (v. 1282) gives the following succinct history of the progress of society in reference to warlike instruments:—

" Arma antiqua manus, ungues, dentesque fuere;
Et lapides et item sylvarum fragmina rami:
Posterius ferri vis est et æris reperta,
Et prior æris erat quam ferri cognitus usus."

[2] Some render " Thy humiliation,"—i. e., the humiliation laid on me by Thee,—" has increased me."—HORSLEY. Others," Thy discipline has taught me."—LXX., KENNICOTT. We prefer the rendering of our translators, who follow Kimchi. His paraphrase is, "Although my enemies greatly exceed me in the number of their forces, yet I have come off conqueror; for thy benignity has enabled me, with my handful of soldiers, to overcome, as if I had had an army more numerous than that of my foes." This is too specific. The idea is that given above. " By humbling, Thou hast magnified me."—TRAPP.

altation to which He raised him, and in the vast numbers of his
followers. The idea is, 'Through thy benignity, from a very low
I am elevated to a very high situation ; and instead of a "little
flock," I have now a vast number of disciples.' He who at his
death had probably not more than five hundred adherents, in the
course of a few years numbered his followers in Jerusalem by
myriads. He who, as the Lamb, was led alone to the altar, the
victim for the sins of mankind, is seen standing on the heavenly
Zion, surrounded not only by his hundred and forty-four sealed
ones from among his ancient people, but by an innumerable company out of every kindred, and nation, and people, and tongue,
while all the angels of God worship him. And when he, whose
name is the Word of God,—whose royal style and title is, Faithful
and True, King of kings, and Lord of lords ; whose eyes are as a
flame of fire, and on whose head are many crowns ; clad in his
blood-stained vesture, with his sword on his thigh and his bow in
his hand, seated on the apocalyptic white horse, in his majesty rides
forth prosperously because of truth, and meekness, and righteousness, to judge and make war, that his arrows may be sharp in the
heart of the King's enemies, and the people may fall under him—
conquering and to conquer ; he goes not, as erst he did, alone to the
combat, "none of the people with him," but "the armies which
are in heaven follow him on white horses, clothed in fine linen,
white and clean," and the number of them is, like that of the angels,
"ten thousand times ten thousand and thousands of thousands."[1]

"Thou hast enlarged"—or enlargest—" my steps under me,"[2]
that my feet do not slip." 'Thou enablest me to take long
steps—to walk at liberty.' One takes short steps when many
stumbling-blocks and hindrances are in the way.[3] The idea is,
' Thou removest obstacles out of my way, and enablest me to
proceed steadily, rapidly, securely, in my progress towards victory.' "When he goeth, his steps are not straitened ; and
when he runneth he shall not stumble." Such is the Messiah's
acknowledgment of the qualifications for successful warfare,
which Jehovah had bestowed on him.

---

[1] Our translation here is so literal as to be obscure. The meaning is well given by
Henry Ainsworth, who, like the apostle, is "rude in speech, but not in knowledge,"
—"Thou hast widened my passage, and enlarged my pass, so that it is given me to
walk steadily and safe."—Job, xviii. 7 ; Prov. iv. 12. The ultimate ideas are, 'Thou
hast given me comfort and security instead of discomfort and danger.'

[2] Hengstenberg.   [3] Rev. vii. 4–17 ; xiv. 1, 2, etc. ; xix. 11–14 ; v. 11.

The description of the successful employment of these qualifications follows:—" I have pursued mine enemies, and overtaken them : neither did I turn again till they were consumed.
I have wounded them, that they were not able to rise; they are
fallen under my feet. For Thou hast girded me with strength
unto the battle : Thou hast subdued under me those that rose up
against me.[1] Thou hast also given to me the necks of mine
enemies,[2] that I might destroy them that hate me." These
words are plainly a description of the Messiah's triumph over
his enemies. They are very similar to other predictions which
undoubtedly refer to this subject, such as,—" Thou shalt break
them with a rod of iron; Thou shalt dash them in pieces like a
potter's vessel." " Thine hand shall find out all thine enemies :
thy right hand shall find out those that hate Thee. Thou shalt
make them as a fiery oven in the time of thine anger : the Lord
shall swallow them up in his wrath, and the fire shall devour
them. Their fruit shalt Thou destroy from the earth, and their
seed from among the children of men." " The Lord at thy
right hand shall strike through kings in the day of his wrath.
He shall judge among the heathen, He shall fill the places
with the dead bodies; He shall wound the heads over many
countries."[3]

Though the passage before us, viewed by itself, might be
considered, like those just cited, as generally descriptive of our
Lord's triumph over all his enemies, human and infernal, ye
when we look into the context, and particularly notice the 41st
verse, which is applicable only to professed worshippers of Jehovah, we shall see reason to refer them to the judgments inflicted on the impenitent Jews. *They* were, by way of eminence,
Messiah's enemies. They were " his own ;" he came to them,
but they " received him not ;" they despised and rejected him.
" They killed the Lord Jesus as they had done the prophets ;
they persecuted his apostles ; they pleased not God ; they were
contrary to all men ; they forbade the apostles to speak unto
the Gentiles, that they might be saved." Was it wonderful that

---

[1] Probably Exod. xv. 9 was present to the inspired poet's mind.

[2] The construction here is peculiar : literally, " And my enemies, Thou hast given
to me the neck." It may either be the nom. abs., " As to my enemies, Thou hast
given to me the neck;' or, ' Thou hast given to me my enemies,' *quoad verticem*.

[3] Psal. ii. 9; xxi. 8–10; cx. 5, 6.

they at last filled up the measure of their sin, and that "wrath came on them to the uttermost"?[1]

The Messiah "pursued them."[2] From his throne in the heavens he so overruled the passions and interests of men, that a series of events took place, which gradually but rapidly brought on the great crisis of their fate. It came. Messiah "overtook" them. By means of the Romans he "came with an army and destroyed these murderers, and burnt their city;" and when he had thus overtaken them, "he did not turn again till they were consumed." The meaning is not that the Jewish nation were exterminated. The slaughter was indeed dreadful. Not less than eleven hundred thousand individuals are supposed to have perished in and around Jerusalem; but we know the Jewish people still exist, and are at present perhaps as numerous as they ever have been. The meaning is, that, as efficient enemies of the Messiah, they were consumed. Their political power was taken from them, and from that time they have been unable, however willing, to oppose Christianity, or to persecute Christians. He so "wounded them that they were not able to rise: they are fallen under his feet." Any attempts made by them at after periods to regain their liberties and their independent existence as a nation have been utterly fruitless, and have served but more completely to fix them in a state of subjugation. They are under Messiah's feet,—utterly incapable of opposing his designs.

The Messiah again ascribes all the glory of this victory to Jehovah. "For Thou hast girded me with strength unto the battle: Thou hast subdued under me those that rose up against me." In the whole mediatorial economy the Son is dependent on the Father. What he does, he does by the power and according to the will of the Father. The power in heaven and earth he possesses was power given him. This is no way inconsistent with the equally clearly-revealed truth, that essentially the Father and the Son are equal, for they are one. There is great emphasis in the words, "Thou hast subdued those that rose up against me." They would not have him to rule over them, and, refusing to submit to the sceptre of his grace, they are broken

[1] 1 Thess. ii. 15, 16.

[2] Hengstenberg, in his commentary on Rev. v. 6, referring to this passage, says, "David here points to Christ, in whom he saw the highest perfection of his being and his race."

to pieces by the rod of his vengeance. His strength and their weakness are equally ascribed to Divine agency. All the Son does is to the glory of God the Father. The design of the whole economy is that God may be all in all.

According to the genius of poetry, especially oriental poetry, the description of the Messiah's victory is amplified, and image heaped on image to point out its completeness. "Thou," says he to Jehovah, "Thou hast also given me the necks of mine enemies, that I might destroy them that hate me." The expression, "Thou hast also given me the necks[1] of mine enemies," has been variously explained. There can be no doubt that the phrase here used is employed proverbially, to signify to flee in battle—to turn back. It is used in this way, Exod. xxxiii. 27; Josh. vii. 8; 2 Chron. xxix. 6. In this case the meaning is, 'Thou hast made my enemies flee before me.' Others think the meaning is, 'Thou hast placed my enemies completely in my power, so that I may either put them to death, or impose a yoke on them;' and others still, suppose there is a reference to a custom, of which we have an example recorded in the book of Joshua, x. 24, where Joshua calls on the Israelitish captains to come and put their feet on the necks of the vanquished Canaanitish kings, as a token of their complete conquest. It is probable that one or other of these last two interpretations is the correct one, for this verse seems to describe what is consequent to the army of Messiah's enemies being completely routed. The meaning is, 'Thou hast completely stripped them of their power, and subjected them to my will; Thou hast fulfilled thy promise in reference to *them*,—they are made my footstool.'

The description of the Messiah's triumph, and his enemies' entire discomfiture, is continued. "They cried, but there was none to save them;[2] even unto the Lord, but He answered them not. Then did I beat them small as the dust before the wind; I did cast them out as the dirt in the streets." This is one of the passages in the psalm which is strongly corroborative of our hypothesis that it does not refer at all to David, but entirely to

---

[1] "ערֶף is the back part of the neck, and therefore equivalent to the back, as the LXX. translate it = 'Thou puttest them to flight.'"—MUDGE.

[2] There is a paranomasia in the Hebrew words, which is happily imitated by the LXX.—"βοήσονται καὶ οὐκ ἔστι βοηθῶν." It is seldom that such a peculiarity can be transferred into another language.

the Messiah. The enemies spoken of are represented as crying to Jehovah amid their reverses. Now, to what victory of David could this representation be applicable? The whole account plainly does not at all accord with what took place at the death of Saul, or at any of the battles with the portion of Israel that for some time clave to Ishbosheth, the unfortunate son of Saul. If it refers to a victory of David at all, it must refer to a victory over some of the surrounding heathen nations. But it cannot refer to them; for assuredly, in their distress, they would cry for aid, not to Jehovah, the God of Israel, but to their own deities. On the hypothesis that the Messiah is the subject of the psalm, all is plain. History exactly corresponds with prophecy. The severity of the calamities inflicted on the Jews, as we have already seen, fully comes up to the powerful description in the passage before us. And we know, from the testimony of their own historian, that amid all these sufferings, plain indications as they were of Jehovah's displeasure, they maintained confidence in their mistaken apprehensions that He was so their God, that He would not suffer his city and his people to fall into the hands of the Gentiles. But though they cried to Jehovah, He did not save them. No; He destroyed them, for their prayer was not the prayer of faith, but of presumption; not of penitence, but of obstinacy. It was not offered in the name of the only effectual intercessor, whom they still hated with unabated inveteracy. It was too late to knock; the door was shut.

The description in the 42d verse is very striking,—" I beat them small as the dust before the wind." This is what is called a pregnant construction, and is equivalent to, 'I made them small as the dust is made small when driven before the wind.' The dust must be reduced to very minute particles in order to its being raised from the earth and carried through the air. This indicates their entire dissolution as a political body, and their wide and speedy dispersion over all the earth, like dust scattered in all directions by a whirlwind. Without ruler, civil or ecclesiastical—without king or high priest—they are wanderers among the nations; and what is said of Elam is literally true of Israel, "There is no nation whither her outcasts have not come."[1]

The degraded condition into which the Jews were to be re-

[1] Jer. xlix. 36.

duced, in consequence of their opposition to the Messiah, is graphically described in the concluding clause of the verse,—"I did cast them out[1] as the dirt in the streets." They became a by-word and a reproach among all nations whither they were scattered. According to the striking emblem of our Lord, they have been "trodden under foot of the Gentiles" for nearly eighteen centuries, and must continue to be so "till the times of the Gentiles are fulfilled."

The last section of the psalm begins at the 43d verse, and has for its subject the security, extent, and permanence of the Messiah's kingdom. With a few explicatory remarks on it we will conclude the exposition.

"Thou hast delivered me from the strivings of the people;[2] and Thou hast made me the head of the heathen : a people whom I have not known shall serve me." Some interpreters consider "people" here as used collectively for "peoples," and as synonymous with "nations" (heathen), used in the close of the verse. I think it more natural to consider "people" as bearing its ordinary meaning in the book of Psalms—the people of Israel; and, as contrasted with the heathen, the nations. In the copy of the psalm in 1 Samuel, it is "my people," and I have no doubt refers to those of whom the prophet says, "For the transgression"—by the wickedness—"of my people was he stricken." The Messiah was exposed to the strivings, the enmities of the Israelitish people, both in his person and in his cause. They strove against him personally—they hated, persecuted, and slew him. Jehovah delivered him from these strivings. He placed him beyond the reach of their fraud or violence. Taken up into heaven, and set down on the right hand of the throne of God, he was completely delivered from insult and from injury. But while he was thus personally delivered, his cause and people still were the object of their malignant strivings ; and what is done to them he considers as done to himself. Messiah in heaven calls out to the persecutors on earth, 'Why persecutest

---

[1] Instead of אריקם, as in the psalm, we have אדיקם, in the second book of Samuel : "I bruised them ; I trode them down." This seems the preferable reading.

[2] Some interpreters consider עם here, as used collectively for עמים, and as referring to the same individuals as גוים in the second clause. It is more natural to consider the word as bearing its ordinary signification and reference, and as contrasted, as it so often is, with the nations, or heathen. "Sub hoc typo Spiritus Sanctus, regnum Christi depingit."—VATABLUS.

thou *me?*' When the Jewish polity was destroyed, the cause of Christ was delivered from the strivings of the people. They had no longer the means of persecuting the Christians. They had more than enough to do in seeking security for themselves.

These words, so applicable to Messiah, are by no means so applicable to David. He was never "delivered from the strivings of the people." He was indeed delivered from many civil dissensions; but, according to God's threatening, evil was raised up against him out of his own house, and the sword never departed from it. He left his people striving about Adonijah.

But if the first clause of the verse be with difficulty capable of being explained of David, far less can the last clause be referred to any event that befel him. "Thou hast made me the head of the heathen." "Head" is often used in the Hebrew language as equivalent to "prince." We use the word in a similar way in our own language,—the head of the house. "Thou hast made me the prince of the nations."[1] We read, indeed, of David subduing some of the heathen tribes in the neighborhood of the holy land, such as the Philistines, the Moabites, the Syrians, the Ammonites, and the Edomites, but these were as nothing compared with the nations that never owned his rule, nor even heard his name.

Ainsworth is right in his annotation,—"Hereby Christ's headship over the church of the Gentiles is signified, and the contradiction of his own people the Jews. Rom. x. 10, 21." What cannot, without extreme violence, be applied to David, is most appropriate to David's Son and Lord. "For all power has been given to Him on earth" as well as "in heaven." "He is head over all things to his body the Church." "The heathen are given him for his inheritance, and the uttermost ends of the earth for his possession." And his actually becoming "the Head of the nations," was connected with his being delivered from "the strivings of the people." While delivered from "the strivings of *the* people," *a* people whom he had not known became his servants. Instead of his

---

[1] Num. xxxvi. 1. Josh. xiv. 1. Psal. cx. 6. We have the word in the Abyssinian *Ras*. The chief city in a country is its capital; the commander of a detachment of soldiers is its captain. "Many expositors, such as Calvin have justly remarked that the complete fulfilment of this and the next verse is to be found in Christ."—HENGSTENBERG.

ancient people who rejected him, and therefore had been rejected by him, from among the nations—the heathen,—he was to receive " a people to his name."[1]   " A people whom I have not known shall serve me."   This would have been very strange language in the mouth of David, just about to leave the world. But no language could be more appropriate, considered as spoken by the Messiah.   We find very similar language used in the book of the prophet Isaiah in reference to the same subject. "Behold, thou shalt call a nation that thou knowest not; and nations that know not thee shall run unto thee."   In one sense these nations were all well known to the Messiah, for he formed them and governed them all; but he had not known them as he knew Israel—he had not acknowledged them as his peculiar people.[2]   They were " aliens from the commonwealth of Israel, strangers to the covenants of promise, without God, and without hope in the world."[3]   These nations were to embrace his religion and obey his laws.

The heathen are here called not as usually " peoples," but " a people," in reference to the condition into which they were to be brought under the Messiah,—in whom there is neither " Jew, nor Greek, nor barbarian, nor bond, nor free, but one holy nation."   He " called them a people who were not a people."   He was " sought of them who aforetime asked not for him: He was found of them who sought him not."   He with power said, " Behold me, behold me," to a people which was not " called by his name."   This prediction was remarkably fulfilled when, in the primitive age, " Gentiles in the flesh, without Christ," were brought nigh in him who was their peace; " being no more strangers and foreigners, but fellow citizens with the saints, and of the household of God; built upon the foundation of the apostles and prophets, Jesus Christ himself being the chief corner stone."[4]   It has continued being fulfilled in every succeeding age; and it will yet be more remarkably fulfilled, when " all the ends of the earth shall remember and turn unto the Lord, and all the kindreds of the nations worship before him."

The rapidity with which the Gentiles should be subdued to the Messiah, and the means by which this subjection is to be accomplished, are celebrated in the next verses, " As soon as they

---

[1] Acts, xv. 14.   [2] Amos, iii. 2.   [3] Eph. ii. 12.   [4] Eph. ii. 19, 20.

hear[1] of me, they shall obey me: the strangers shall submit themselves unto me. The strangers shall fade away, and be afraid out of their close places." The people who had not previously known the Messiah were to obey him—acknowledge him as their Saviour and Lord. And they were to do this as soon as they heard of him. There are two important thoughts suggested by these words. First, That hearing of the Messiah, was to be the means of bringing the nations to submit to him. They were not to be subdued by force of arms, but by persuasion and argument. The preaching of the gospel has, in every age, been the great means of the conversion of sinners. And then, secondly, It intimates the rapidity of the conversion of the Gentiles. No sooner should they hear than they would obey. "The word of the Lord had free course. It grew and multiplied." Vast multitudes in a short time became subjects of the Redeemer; and a period will again come when, with wonder and delight, the Church shall exclaim, "Who are these that fly as a cloud, and as the doves to their windows ?"

Interpreters have found much difficulty with the words that follow, " The strangers shall submit themselves unto me." Indeed, it is the obscurest passage in the whole psalm. Some render them, "Strangers shall lie to me." A learned Jew[2] supposes an ellipsis of, "for fear of me;" and reads ' for fear of me they will falsely deny that they ever were my enemies.' Others render it, " On account of me, they have lied to their confederates," i. e., ' broken their league with them.' Others, " Boasting that they would prevail against me, they are found liars." I have little doubt that our translators give the meaning correctly, though not fully. ' They shall in many cases unwillingly submit to me, professing, though not cordially, subjection to me.' This is the meaning of the word rendered, " submit themselves," in Deut. xxx. 19. Psal. lxxx. 16; lxvi. 3. And now for the fulfilment of the prediction. The "strangers," or sons of the strangers, are, I apprehend, the pagans who were not really con-

---

[1] שמע, like ἀκούειν, signifies not only to hear, but to listen. "This applies more truly to the person of Christ, who, by means of his word, subdues the world to himself, and at the simple hearing of his name makes those obedient to him who before had been rebels against him."—CALVIN, *Anderson's Translation*. "Not so easily applicable to David, but to Christ most properly and emphatically, if the words be translated (as in the margin), 'at the hearing of the ear,'—that is, by the preaching of the Gospel."—ASSEMBLY'S ANNOTATIONS.   [2] Jarchi.

verted to the faith of Christianity, but who, in consequence of
its becoming the dominant religion of the Roman empire, pretended to be Christians, and feigned subjection to the Messiah.[1]

The 45th verse is at least as obscure as the last part of the 44th
verse. The first clause is comparatively easy, "The strangers
shall fade away"—'shall gradually wither and disappear;'[2] but
the second clause is very difficult, "They shall be afraid out of
their close places." One Jewish scholar interprets it, "They
shall fear for the prisons in which I will throw them, and keep
them confined."[3] Another,[4] "They shall tremble in their castles
to which they have betaken themselves for fear of me." Another,
"They shall surrender themselves from their fortresses." The
general meaning is plain enough. The class referred to are
represented as reduced to a state of complete helpless subjugation. As to the events referred to, if we keep to the rendering
of our translators, the meaning may be, 'The pagans, retired
now generally to villages and remote places, shall gradually
dwindle away, and fearfully anticipate the complete extinction
of their religion.' This exactly accords with history. If, with
some interpreters, we read, "the strangers shall fade away and
be afraid because of their prisons," then the meaning may be,
'that they who only feigned submission, when persecution for
the word should arise, should openly apostatize. This too would
be found consonant with facts. The first of these interpretations seems to me the more probable.[5]

The Messiah now glories in the perpetuity of his kingdom as
secured by the eternity of Jehovah. "The Lord liveth; and
blessed be my Rock; and let the God of my salvation be ex-

---

[1] Peirce prefers the sense of 'submitting, yielding obedience,'—urging as a reason,
that the first parallel employs a word which does not imply dissimulation; and he
quotes Isa. lvi. 3, 6, 7, as casting light on this passage.

[2] Psal. i. 3. The LXX. render it " ἐπαλαιώθησαν,"and are followed by the Vulgate,
"inveterati sunt."

[3] Jarchi.   [4] Abenezra.

[5] Michælis renders and paraphrases it thus:—

"Barbari autumnitate sua decidunt,
Et exeunt ex castellis suis.

"Id vero est, 'Victi, ad me cives, expugnatorum castellorum præsidia, certatim
confluunt."

"Quot folia in silvis primæ sub frigora brumæ
Lapsa fluunt, queis jam vigor et sua vita recessit."

"The sons of the stranger lose their strength,
Through alarm they quit their strongholds."—WALFORD.

alted." The first clause may either be interpreted as an assertion, 'God lives; He is not like the gods of the heathen, a
dead powerless idol,—He is the living One. All life is in him.
He is the all-powerful One;'—or, as a wish, like the second
clause, 'Let God live.' The first is the better interpretation.
When we hail an earthly monarch, it is becoming to say, 'May
the king live.' When we do homage to the King eternal and
immortal, it is more becoming to say, 'Thou livest.'[1] Because
Jehovah is the ever living God; His Messiah is the ever enduring King. He is the Messiah's Rock—his support and defence. He is the God of his salvation—his Divine deliverer;
and because He is so, it is meet that by Him and his He should
be blessed forever, and exalted in the very highest place in
the mind and heart.

In the next two verses, the Messiah particularizes some of the
benefits he had received from Jehovah as his Rock and the God
of his salvation, and on account of which he blesses and praises
Him. " It is God that avengeth me and subdueth the people
under me." The punishment of the obdurate Jews was vengeance, the execution of righteous judgment,—the execution of
the righteous judgment of God. The second clause requires a
passing remark. According as you render the word translated
"subdue," it may mean, 'He breaks in pieces the peoples on
my account;' or, 'He leads the peoples; he conducts them and
places them under me, as a flock under the care of the shepherd.' The last is the preferable meaning. " He delivereth
me from mine enemies; yea, Thou liftest me up above all that
rise against me: Thou hast delivered me from the violent man."
The "violent man" is very probably another name for him who
is called the "mighty,' the 'strong man;'[2] but whom Messiah,
" the stronger man," strong in the power of Omnipotence, bound
and spoiled of his goods. Jehovah has delivered Messiah, and
will deliver his cause and people from all evil, especially from
" the evil one."

In the next verse, the Messiah intimates the manner in which

---

[1] "Apud mortales reges acclamatur ' Vivat.' De immortali regum rege, longe
dicitur decentius, ' Vivit,' et huic voculæ correspondet altera 'benedicta.' *Vivit* in
se, *benedictus* a suis creaturis."—BURKIUS.

[2] Isa. xlix. 24. Mark, iii. 27. The Chaldee Targum paraphrases it, "From Gog
and all his armies."

he was to show his gratitude to Jehovah for his deliverance and exaltation. "Therefore will I give thanks unto Thee, O Lord, among the heathen,[1] and sing praises unto thy name." The whole of the Messiah's administration in the establishment and maintenance of his Church among the nations, is a hymn of praise to Jehovah,—a manifestation of his power, and wisdom, and faithfulness, and kindness. The apostle Paul teaches us how to understand these words, and indeed the whole psalm, in the fifteenth chapter of his epistle to the Romans. "Jesus Christ was a minister for the truth of God," "that the Gentiles might glorify God for his mercy; as it is written, For this cause I will confess Thee among the Gentiles, and sing unto thy name"[2] He is still singing this lofty song, and it well becomes us to join in it. The whole Apocalypse is an illustration of this verse.

The noble hymn concludes with an expression of gratitude and expectation. "Great deliverance"—complete deliverance—"giveth He,"—has given, is giving, will give—"to his King,"—to his Only-begotten, whom He has set as his King over his holy hill of Zion; and he "showeth mercy"—manifests special, tender, infinite love --- "to his Anointed"—his Messiah, the divinely appointed, qualified, accredited, saviour King,—"to David," the beloved one,—not the literal, but the mystical David,—"and to his seed"[3]—his Benonis, the children of his sorrow,—who are also the Benjamins, the children of his right hand; who are all beloved for his sake—"accepted in the beloved ;" the seed which he was to see and be satisfied with ; the seed that should do service to him, and be accounted to him for a generation ; the children whom God has given him throughout the

---

[1] "This the apostle applieth to Christ and his people, as a prophecy of his kingdom and of the calling of the Gentiles, Rom. xv. 9,—'*I*,' that is, Christ (but yet in the person of his faithful, and especially his ministers), 'will praise thee,' or 'confess to thee.' "—TRAPP.

[2] "From these words we conclude that this passage contains a prophecy concerning the kingdom of Christ."—CALVIN, *Anderson's Translation.* "This the apostle, Rom. xv. 9, showeth to be the speech of Christ, and a prophecy of the conversion of the Gentiles." "It is Christ who here saith, 'I will give thanks unto thee (O Lord) among the heathen, and sing praises to thy name.' "—DICKSON. "Psalmum istum ad Christum pertinere vel ex isto versiculo constat, quem Paulus, Rom. xv. 9, adducit ad vocationem gentium confirmandum."—AMYRAUT.

[3] "That is, to Christ (who was made of the seed of David according to the flesh),— Rom. i. 3; Acts, xiii. 23 ;—and to all faithful Christians, who are called Christ's seed. —Isa. liii. 10.   Psal. lxxii. 17."—TRAPP.

endless ages of eternity. Thus will He deliver and bless the Messiah and his chosen ones "for evermore"—to the latest age of time—throughout the endless ages of eternity.

I have left myself time to do little more than merely announce some of the topics of practical reflection which the subjects we have been considering naturally suggest, leaving their improvement to your private meditations.

Were the Jews so tremendously punished for their rejection of and opposition to the Messiah, how carefully should we guard against incurring their guilt; for if we do, without doubt we shall incur their responsibility. He who spared not them, will not spare us; for He is no regarder of persons. "How shall we escape, if we neglect so great salvation!"

As Christ triumphed so gloriously, through the power of his Father, over his Jewish enemies, how certainly will he, by the same power, which is infinite, triumph over all his enemies! "He must reign till all his enemies are made his footstool."

How foolish, as well as wicked—how absolutely insane—to oppose His declared designs! Let the potsherds of the earth strive with the potsherds of the earth, but let not man, whether slave or emperor, strive with his Maker. The voice of the overthrow of the Jewish polity to all kings and governments in every age is— "Be wise now therefore, O ye kings; be instructed, ye judges of the earth. Serve the Lord with fear, and rejoice with trembling.'"

If the inflictions of the Messiah's displeasure be so awful even in the world which is the theatre of the Divine forbearance, how dreadful will they be "in the day of the revelation of the righteous judgment of God." "When the great day of the wrath of God and the Lamb comes, who shall be able to stand?" "Who can abide that day of his coming? who shall stand when He appeareth?"

How pitiable the situation of men without God, without Christ, in the world. In the day of deep distress God only can help them, but they know not God; Christ only can intercede for them, but they know not Christ. They may cry on God, but if not in faith, in penitence, in dependence on Christ, they cry in vain. It is only in Christ He is the answerer of prayer. We must come to Christ, that we may be brought to God.

[1] Psal. ii. 10, 11.

What abundant encouragement have we to seek the universal Christianisation of men. Jehovah, the all-powerful, the all wise, all-faithful, has made His Son the Head of the heathen. How highly should we estimate the Gospel as the means of conversion! Not till they hear it, but as soon as they hear it—*i.e.*, with understanding and faith—will the heathen obey. The only obedience of value is the obedience of faith.

How delightful the thought, that what God is to the Messiah, He is, according to their necessities, to all His people. Every Christian may warrantably say, with an appropriating faith, 'God liveth! blessed be *my* rock, and let the God of MY salvation be exalted!'

What a high privilege, to be allowed to go along with the Saviour among the Gentile nations, giving thanks to the Lord, singing praise to His name! That honor, that delight, have all good Christian missionaries, all right-hearted supporters of Christian missions.

How encouraging to think that the new covenant embraces futurities. The Covenant God is the God of Messiah and his seed, of his people and their seed, and their seed's seed forever. "His mercy is on them that fear Him, and his righteousness unto children's children, to such as keep His covenant, and remember His commandments to do them." "As for me, this is my covenant with them, saith the Lord; My Spirit that is upon thee, and my words which I have put in thy mouth, shall not depart out of thy mouth, nor out of the mouth of thy seed, nor out of the mouth of thy seed's seed, saith the Lord, from henceforth and forever."[1]

Thus have I finished the exposition of this important and difficult portion of the book of God. The views I have been led to give, though not singular, are considerably different from those usually taken by commentators, but they are such as a careful examination of the passage has compelled me to adopt. I have laid before you not only my views, but the grounds of them. "I speak as to wise men; judge ye what I say." Exercise your own minds. "Try all things, and hold fast that which is good."

And now, arrived at the close of this sublime Divine hymn,

---

[1] Psal. ciii. 17, 18. Isa. lix. 21.

who does not feel the truth of Bishop Horne's representation?—
"Having ascended an eminence neither unfruitful nor unpleas-
ant, we have arrived at the summit, and behold, like Moses
from the top of Mount Nebo, a most lovely and extensive prospect stretching away to the bounds of the everlasting hills—valleys covered with corn, blooming gardens, and verdant meadows,
with flocks and herds feeding by rivers of waters." As from the
top of the exceeding high mountain to which the tempter carried our Saviour, we see all the kingdoms of the earth and the
glory of them, in spite of him who is called their god, subjected
to Him who, in the hour and power of darkness, seemed to fall
his helpless, hopeless victim. The kingdoms of this world are
become the kingdom of our Lord and his Christ. He is the
governor among the nations. He is Lord of all. And He shall
reign forever and ever. "Hallelujah! the Lord God Omnipotent reigneth! Hallelujah! Salvation, and glory, and honor,
and power to the Lord our God!"

Meanwhile we see these things far off. The process of subjugation, though begun, is but in progress. "We see not yet all
things put under him." It is our wisdom, each for himself, to
yield no unwilling, no mere pretended submission, but, with
deep humility and ardent gratitude, to take his place in that
sacramental host by whom it is Messiah's purpose to subdue the
world. Let us prove ourselves his "power," his army, "a willing people,"[1] a people of cheerful and abundant oblations; and
while we—a part of the redeemed church, which ere long, pure,
free, and united, shall look forth on the host of his amazed and
dismayed enemies, clear as the sun, fair as the moon, terrible as
an army with banners—move onwards to the conflict with the
powers of darkness, under the guidance of the antitype of the
mystic pillar of cloud and of fire, let this be our war-song:—

> "Gird on thy sword, victorious Prince,
>   Ride with triumphant sway;
> Thy terror shall strike through thy foes,
>   And make the world obey.
>
> "Justice and truth attend thy state,
>   And mercy leads thee on,
> Till all thine enemies shall yield
>   Obedience to thy throne."

[1] עם נדבת.   Psal. cx. 3.

NOTE

ON THE EDITION OF THIS PSALM, 2 SAMUEL, XXII

" In 2 Sam. xxii. this psalm is repeated with not a few variations. The supposition, which is now commonly received, and which has been specially defended by Lengerke[1] and Hitzig, is, that these variations have arisen from carelessness, discovering itself in both forms of the text, though principally in that of Samuel. But the following reasons may be advanced against this view :—1. If such were a correct representation of the origin of these variations, it would follow, that before the collection of the canon, the text of the books of the Old Testament had been very carelessly kept. For it is improbable that this particular psalm should have been singular in experiencing an unpropitious fate. And in that case, conjectural criticism must have a very large room assigned it. It must proceed on the expectation of finding one, or even more faults, in almost every verse. But even the rashest of our critics do not consider the text to be in such a state, and the more judicious confine conjectural criticism within very narrow limits. 2. In other places where similar variations are found, where there are texts that come in contact with each other, these variations are uniformly not the result of accident and negligence, but of design. So, for example, in Isa. ii., comp. with Mic. iv.; and in Jeremiah, comp. with the numerous passages in the older scriptures, which he has appropriated. 3. The text in each of the forms is of such a nature, that one would never have thought of regarding it as faulty in any particular place, were it not for the comparison with the corresponding place making it appear so. If negligence had here played its part, it could not have failed to produce a multitude of passages, in which the fault was discoverable at a moment's glance, and could be shown incontestably to be such. 4. A great number of the variations, nay, the greater part of them, are of such a kind, that they cannot be explained by accident. This circumstance forbids the derivation from accident, even in those cases where it might fairly be allowed to have had place, since it is improbable that the variations should have flowed from a double source. The proof of this will be found in considering the particular variations. 5. It is not difficult to discover certain principles by which the variations in the Books of Samuel are governed. That which has had the most powerful influence, is the tendency already found in Psal. liii., as comp. with xiv., to substitute for the simple, plain, and common, the far-fetched, elevated, emphatic, and rare. Besides this, there is also perceptible the desire to ex-

---

[1] Comment. de dupl. Psal. xviii., exemplo.

plain what is dark. Such pervading tendencies cannot be explained on the ground of accident.

" We derive the variations altogether from an after-polishing, accompanied by design; and as both the texts are prefaced by the superscription of David, the design must have been conceived by himself. As to the object of the after-polishing, we do not consider it to have been that of antiquating the earlier form, but for the sake of producing variations, which should be placed alongside of the original and main text. The text in the Psalms appears to us to be this original and main one, partly on the external ground, that this psalm was given up by David for public use, according to the expression, 'To the chief musician,' in the superscription; partly also on the internal ground already noticed, that in a considerable number of variations in the Books of Samuel, the design cannot be mistaken; and finally, on this account, that the text in Samuel, even apart from its being justly regarded as a variation of the other, is decidedly inferior to the text of the Psalms.

" What has been objected to this view by Lengerke, that such an artificial mode of procedure was not to be expected of David, rests upon that manner of contemplating the Psalms, which considers them as mere natural poetry, and the falseness of which has been sufficiently proved by our previous exposition; nor can it have much weight, at any rate, in a psalm like the present, which was already designated by Amyrall as *artis poeticæ luculentissimum specimen*, and by Hitzig as ' an unrivalled production of art and reflection.' "—HENGSTENBERG.

My opinion respecting these variations is brought out in the Exposition, and differs from that of the distinguished German commentator. A particular account of the variations referred to, is to be found in Rosenmüller's *Scholia*.

THE

SUFFERINGS AND GLORIES

OF

THE MESSIAH

PART II

AN EXPOSITION OF ISAIAH LII. 13—LIII. 12

"Splendet hæc prophetia instar lucis in obscuro loco. Qui in hac luce ambulat non impinget. Gloria Deo Patri, qui usque eo delexit mundum, ut filium suum unigenitum Jesum Christum ei ordinaverit mediatorem, justititiæ et vitæ æternæ causam: Gloria sit Filio Dei Domino nostro Jesu Christo quod seipsum pro nobis dederit, ut nos sanguine suo redemptos eximeret præsenti sæculo malo: Gloria spiritui sancto qui nos vera donat fide, perquam hujus redemptionis participes evadimus in spe gloriæ cœlestis. Amen."—VITRINGA.

THE

SUFFERINGS AND GLORIES

OF

THE MESSIAH

PART II

AN EXPOSITION OF ISAIAH LII. 13—LIII. 12

LECTURE I

INTRODUCTORY.—SUBJECT AND DIVISION OF THE ORACLE

My intention is, in a short series of lectures, to illustrate the prophetic oracle[1] contained in the section of the book of the prophet Isaiah, commencing at the 13th verse of the fifty-second chapter, and terminating at the end of the fifty-third : "a passage of Scripture," to use the words of one of its latest and ablest interpreters, "which in many respects may be regarded as the most important in all the writings of the Old Testament, and which is better adapted than any other to lead us to a right understanding of the whole. The partial obscurity which usually accompanies the representations of the prophets seems here to have entirely vanished. The highest operation of the Divine Spirit

---

[1] "Locus dignissimus sæpius legi atque etiam in publico carmine cantari, ut sedula inspectione quasi incorporetur nobis, ut nihil audiremus, quam intercedentem pro nobis, precantem, consolantem et ardentissime nos amantem, Christum."—LUTHER. "Hoc caput est totum de Christo, deque redemptionis nostræ per ipsum modo et ratione, atque beneficiis quæ ab eo in nos derivantur, de quibus omnibus tam aperte agit, ut non tam prophetiam, quæ solet esse obscurior, scribere, quam res gestæ simplicem et nudam narrationem instituere videatur."—LUD. CAPPELLUS.

is united with the most entire suppression of the prophet's own agency. Thus, like a pure mirror, he has imparted to us the sublime truths which he has received,—or rather, the Spirit of Christ, operating in him, employed him as an instrument to reveal the sufferings which the Messiah must undergo after his appearance in the flesh, and the glory that should follow."[1]

In common with many of the most learned and judicious interpreters, we consider the whole passage which we have now read as one prophetic oracle.

" Of whom speaketh the prophet this? of himself, or of some other man?" was the question proposed by the Ethiopian nobleman to the evangelist Philip, respecting a portion of this remarkable prediction. Let us endeavor satisfactorily to answer it.

The subject of the prophetic oracle is "the servant of Jehovah;"[2] an illustrious divine minister, who, after undergoing numerous severe and violent sufferings, was to be raised to a permanent state of the highest honor and enjoyment,—chap. lii. 13–15. This servant of Jehovah was to spring from a decayed family,—chap. liii. 2; and to grow up to manhood, a stranger to dignity and magnificence, and an object of contempt to all classes of his countrymen,—chap. liii. 2, 3. His afflictions were to be, in number, variety, and severity, so unparalleled, as to induce a general suspicion that he was, on some unknown account, the object of the peculiar judicial displeasure of the Divinity,—chap. liii. 3, 4. These afflictions, terminating in a violent death, were, however, to be in truth, not the punishment of his own sins, but the expiation of the sins of others,—chap. liii. 5, 6. He was to endure all his sufferings with patience and magnanimity, and cheerfully to lay down his life as a ransom for others,—chap. liii. 6. Though a dishonored grave among malefactors was to be intended for him, he was to be interred among the rich,—chap. liii. 9. This servant of God, though thus put to a violent death and laid in the grave, was yet, subsequently to these events, to be distinguished for a long life,—chap. liii. 10; during which he was to be raised to such a height of dignity, that even kings should stand in silent reverence—chap. lii. 15—in his presence, and vast multitudes of the most powerful of men were to become his willing followers and obedient subjects,—

---

[1] Hengstenberg.

[2] עֶבֶד יְהוָה.

chap. liii. 11, 12. And all these unparalleled honors were to be bestowed on him as the merited reward of his labors and sufferings—the recompense of the faithful and successful discharge of the high and holy work committed to him as the righteous servant of Jehovah,—chap. liii. 12. All this appears on the face of the oracle. These are the characteristics by which the subject of the prediction is to be recognised ; some of them very rare even individually,—the conjunction of them certainly to be found only in a single person.

The question then is, 'Who is this?' The more ancient Jewish interpreters, with one consent, consider this prediction as referring to the Messiah. One of them[1] thus paraphrases the first verse of the oracle:—"Behold, my servant the Messiah shall prosper ;" and remarks on the second verse, "The house of Israel has hoped for him many days." In an old Jewish commentary on the Pentateuch, we have these words in reference to this prediction :—"This is the King Messiah, who is high, and elevated, and very exalted,—more exalted than Abraham, elevated above Moses, higher than the ministering angels." In another very ancient Jewish book,[2] we have these remarkable words : "When God created his world, he extended his hand under the throne of his glory, and brought forth the soul of the Messiah. He then said to Him, Wilt thou heal my sons, and redeem them, after six thousand years? He answered, I will. God said to him, Wilt thou then suffer punishment, in order to blot out their sins ; as it is written, 'But he bore our diseases'? He said to Him, I will suffer it joyfully." Another Rabbinical writer says, "The Messiah, out of love, took upon himself all afflictions and sufferings ; as it is written, 'He was abused and oppressed.'" The strange mixture of puerile, trifling, and important truth which characterizes many of the Talmudical writings, is strikingly exemplified in the following extract :—"There was a devout man among the Jews, who, in summer, made his bed among the fleas, and, in winter, put his feet into cold water, in the freezing of which they also were frozen. When he was asked why he did this, he replied that he also must do some penance, since the Messiah bears the sins of Israel."

[1] Jonathan.   [2] Pesikta.

Even among the later Jewish interpreters, some hold by the ancient mode of explaining this prophecy. "Our old Rabbins," says one of them,[1] "have ever unanimously admitted that the language here refers to the king Messiah. Following them, we also conclude that David—*i. e.*, the Messiah—must be regarded as the subject of this prophecy, which is, indeed, evident." In a celebrated cabalistic writing,[2] there are the following statements:—"In the garden of Eden there is an apartment which is called the sick chamber. The Messiah went into this, and called all the diseases, and all the pains, and all the chastisements of Israel, that they should come upon him, and they all came upon him; and if he had not taken them away from Israel, and laid them upon himself, no man could have borne the chastisements which must have fallen upon Israel, on account of the law; as it is said, 'He took upon himself our diseases.'— "When God wishes to provide a remedy for the world, He smites one holy man among them, and for his sake grants relief and cure to the whole world. Where do we find this confirmed in the Scriptures? In Isaiah, liii. 5, where it is said, 'He was wounded for our transgressions; he was bruised for our iniquities.'" This view of the reference of the prophecy seems to have prevailed among the Jewish writers till, to rebut the arguments of Origen for the Messiahship of Jesus, they were induced to adopt another system of exposition.[3]

The modern Jews generally have deserted the interpretation of their fathers, and deny that this prophecy has any reference to the Messiah. The reasons of this change it is not difficult to discover. "Without doubt," says a great German scholar, himself no friend to evangelical truth,[4] "the later Jews abandoned the Messianic interpretation from polemic views in reference to the Christians." They found it was against them, and therefore they became against it. They are, however, by no means of one mind as to the best way of getting rid of an interpretation so fatal to their whole Messianic theory. The only thing they are

---

[1] R. Alschech.   [2] The book "Sohar."

[3] "Uni Christo etiam quæ in illo occurrunt prædicata tam aperte conveniunt ut uno omnes ore, ne Jonathane quidem aliisque Judæis antiquioribus omnino exceptis, de Messia illud sint interpretate dum tandem religionis Christianæ odium, ut ad cetera fingenda ita quoque ad excogitanda alia orationis Esaiæ subjecta, Judæorum doctores incitaverit, et præjudicatæ aliorum quorundam opiniones ad impuros istos fontes confugere eos coegerunt."—STORR.   [4] Gesenius.

agreed in is, that it must not be referred to the Messiah. They may be divided into two great classes, each including a variety of subdivisions,—those who consider the term, " the servant of Jehovah," as desciptive of a class, and those who consider it as denoting an individual. The first of these resolves itself into two subdivisions,—those who view it as descriptive of the Jewish nation, in contrast with the Gentiles,—the people, as opposed to the nations ;[1] and those who consider it as descriptive of the pious Jews, in contrast with the profane and wicked. To one or other of these classes belong the great body of the later Jewish interpreters. The second great class, consisting of those who refer the term, " servant of the Lord," to an individual, is comparatively a very small one. Some of them consider king Josiah, and others the prophet Jeremiah, as the person intended. What a striking commentary are these facts on the words of the apostle, " The rest were blinded (as it is written, ' God hath given them the spirit of slumber, eyes that they should not see, and ears that they should not hear) unto this day.' "[2]

It might have been expected that there would be no difference of opinion as to the subject of this prophetic oracle among Christian commentators, and for a long period there was not. It is, so far as I know, the undisputed and unenviable distinction of the great Dutch scholar Grotius—to whom, however, the cause of sound scripture interpretation lies under heavy obligations,—after more than sixteen hundred years of unanimity, to have introduced discrepancy of opinion on this subject among the followers of Christ.

Of the opinions of the Fathers, Augustine and Theodoret may be considered as the representatives. Augustine, after saying, what has often been repeated, that Isaiah deserved to be called rather an evangelist than a prophet, and quoting a portion of the oracle before us in proof of the assertion, adds, " Though some things need explanation, this alone is enough, which is so plain, that even our enemies, in spite of their disinclination, are compelled to understand it." " The prophet," says Theodoret, " represents his"—i. e., Christ's—" humiliation, even to the suffering of death." Similar statements abound in the writings of the Christian fathers.

---

[1] עַם, as contrasted with גוים.　　[2] Rom. xi. 7. 8.

The opinion of the Reformers may be learned from Zuinglius and Luther. " What now follows," says the reformer of Zurich, referring to the passage before us, " affords so plain a testimony concerning Christ, that I do not know whether anything more definite can be found in the Scriptures, or even whether a more explicit passage could be framed. All the perverse attempts of the Jews upon it are in vain." And the great German, in equally distinct words, states, " There is, indeed, in all the writings of the Old Testament, no plainer text nor prediction, both of the sufferings and the resurrection of Christ, than in this chapter. Therefore all Christians should be well acquainted with it, yea, even know it by heart, in order to strengthen and defend our faith, especially against the stiff-necked Jews, who deny this their only promised Saviour, merely from the offence of the cross."

For a long time—for more than a century—Grotius had very few followers; but, within the last sixty or seventy years, his opinion, that this oracle does not primarily, or indeed at all, refer to the Messiah, has become the prevailing sentiment on the continent of Europe, at least in the Protestant churches of Germany. The reason of the change, among the Christian interpreters, is substantially the same as among the Jewish interpreters. Led astray by a false philosophy, they had adopted principles to which it was impossible to reconcile this oracle, if interpreted with a reference to Christ, and *therefore* they found it requisite to discover or invent some other mode of interpretation. They had dismissed the doctrine of the atonement from their creed; and, denying the possibility of miracle, in the proper sense of the word, they, of course, could not hold the doctrine of inspiration. Indeed, this is distinctly admitted by one of themselves, who confesses that the Messianic interpretation would be very generally followed by them, were it not that they have of late come to the conclusion " that the prophets announce nothing of future events except what they might know or expect without any special Divine inspiration."

The Christian interpreters who reject the Messianic interpretation, like their Jewish brethren, are divided into two classes,— those who consider the phrase " the servant of the Lord" as descriptive of a body of men, and those who consider it as denoting an individual. Of the first class, the greater part consider the reference to be to the Jewish people ; others suppose the pious part of the Jews to be intended ; others the family of David ; others the priests ; and others the prophets. Of the second class, some refer it to king Uzziah ; others to king Hezekiah ; others to the prophet himself; others to Jeremiah. So true is it, when men abandon the truth, they "find no end in wandering mazes lost." A voyage on the sea of conjecture seldom leads to the desired haven of truth.

The only three of these conjectures to which anything approaching probability belongs, are those which refer the appellation, " servant of Jehovah," to the Israelitish people ;[1] or to the pious part of that people ;[2] or to the prophets as a body.[3]

With regard to the first, we have to remark that, although, without doubt, the Jewish people are sometimes personified, as a collective whole, and spoken of, in this view, as "the servant of Jehovah," especially by Isaiah, this personification is in no instance carried through the whole of an extended prophetic oracle. It deserves notice too, that, in the oracle before us, its subject is expressly called " a man," and a " soul"[4] is ascribed to him. Farther, it must be remarked that, when the phrase is employed in reference to the Israelitish people, as in Isaiah, xli. 8, 9 ; xliv. 1, 2, 21 ; xlv. 4; xlviii. 20, the name of Jacob or Israel is added ; and they are spoken of in the plural, as well as in the singular number, in Isaiah, xlii. 24. 25 ; xlviii. 20, 21 ; xliii. 10–13 , while, in the case before us, there is nothing of this kind. Moreover, the subject of this prediction is described as personally perfectly innocent, as suffering in the room of others, and as being a quiet, patient, unresisting, uncomplaining sufferer, not one of which statements can, with the remotest approach to truth, be made of the Israelitish people.

Most of the arguments against this first hypothesis bear also on the second, which applies the term, " servant of Jehovah," to the pious Jews ; and it may be stated in addition, that there is no reason to think that the portion of the Jews carried captive were more pious than those who were left in the land ; and that indeed, ultimately, none were left in the land,—the residue which survived the massacre of Ishmael and Jonadab having fled into Egypt.

[1] Schuster, Eichhorn, Telge, Stephani, Rosenmüller, Hitzig.
[2] Paulus, Ammon, Maurer, Thenius.　　　[3] Gesenius, De Wette.　　　[4] Isa. liii. 3, 10.

As to the third conjecture—that it is the prophets, as a body, that are referred to—we have no evidence that the prophets, as a body, ever received that appellation, though individually they were, and were called, " servants of the Lord." The " servant of the Lord" here can be no other than He who forms the subject of the parallel prophecies,[1] in which there are statements made which obviously do not admit of being applied to the prophetic order. The sufferings of the prophets were substantially just the sufferings of the people among whom they lived. They bore their share in a common calamity, and could, in no tolerable sense of the word, have been represented as standing in the room of the nation. The honors here promised are honors to which the prophetic body could never aspire; and it only shows to what extremities men will resort in support of a hypothesis to refer the death and burial to one class of the prophets—one half of the allegorical person—and the exaltation and triumph to the other half. In the inspired representation, it is plainly the same subject who suffers and who then enters into glory. Such is the evidence against the Messianic interpretation, in the shape of the evidence, or rather no-evidence, in favor of the other modes of interpretation by which it has been attempted to be supplanted.

The evidence in favor of the Messianic interpretation comes now to be considered; and that is indeed overwhelmingly power-ful. The manner in which this oracle is quoted in the New Tes-tament[2] is of itself quite sufficient to settle the question. The quotations in John, xii. 37, 38—" But though Jesus had done so many miracles before them, yet they believed not on him : that the saying of Esaias the prophet might be fulfilled, which he spake, Lord, who hath believed our report? and to whom hath the arm of the Lord been revealed ?"—and Rom. x. 16, " But they have not all obeyed the gospel : for Esaias saith, Lord, who hath believed our report?"—these quotations of themselves would scarcely be satisfactory evidence; for the phrase rendered " that it might be fulfilled,"[3] without doubt, sometimes means no more than "thus was verified:" but there is no evading the force of the argument supplied by the following quotations :—" For I say unto

---

[1] Isa. xlii., xlix.

[2] Matth. viii. 17. Mark, xv. 28. Luke, xxii. 37. John, xii. 38. Acts, viii. 30–33.
Rom. x. 16. 1 Pet. ii. 24, 25.

[3] ἵνα, or ὅπως πληρωθῇ, and τότε ἐπληρώθη. Matth. ii. 17, 23.

you, that this that is written must yet be accomplished in me, and he was reckoned among the transgressors : for the things concerning me have an end."[1] "A man of Ethiopia, an eunuch of great authority under Candace queen of the Ethiopians, who had the charge of all her treasure, and had come to Jerusalem for to worship, was returning, and sitting in his chariot, read Esaias the prophet. Then the Spirit said unto Philip, Go near, and join thyself to this chariot. And Philip ran thither to him, and heard him read the prophet Esaias, and said, Understandest thou what thou readest ? And he said, How can I, except some man should guide me ? And he desired Philip that he would come up and sit with him. The place of the Scripture which he read was this, He was led as a sheep to the slaughter; and like a lamb dumb before his shearer, so opened he not his mouth : in his humiliation his judgment was taken away ; and who shall declare his generation ? for his life is taken from the earth. And the eunuch answered Philip, and said, I pray thee, of whom speaketh the prophet this ? of himself, or of some other man ? Then Philip opened his mouth, and began at the same Scripture, and preached unto him Jesus."[2] " When the even was come, they brought unto him many that were possessed with devils ; and he cast out the spirits with his word, and healed all that were sick : that it might be fulfilled which was spoken by Esaias the prophet, saying, Himself took our infirmities, and bare our sickness." " For even hereunto were ye called : because Christ also suffered for us, leaving us an example, that we should follow his steps : who did no sin, neither was guile found in his mouth : who, when he was reviled, reviled not again ; when he suffered, he threatened not ; but committed himself to him that judgeth righteously : who his own self bare our sins in his own body on the tree "—"for ye were as sheep going astray ; but are now returned unto the Shepherd and Bishop of your souls."[3] There are, besides, numerous allusions, which prove the same thing not less satisfactorily, as, e. g. :—"It is written of the Son of man, that he must suffer many things, and be set at nought,"

---

[1] Luke xxii. 37.

[2] Acts, viii. 27-35. "Non dicit de Judæis, tacet de Jeremia, nullam Josiæ mentionem facit, de uno Jesu verba facit."—Storr. In explaining the text, he knows nothing but Christ—Christ crucified.

[3] Matth. viii. 16, 17. 1 Pet. ii. 21-25.

(where so plainly as in this oracle ?) " Jesus, who was delivered for our offences, and was raised again for our justification." " Christ died for our sins, according to the Scriptures." " For he hath made him to be sin for us, who knew no sin ; that we might be made the righteousness of God in him." " Ye know that he was manifested to take away our sins ; and in him is no sin." " The precious blood of Christ, as of a lamb without blemish and without spot."[1] From these passages it is clear that, in the minds of our Lord himself and his inspired apostles, there was no doubt that this prediction referred to him.

It is also very evident that the subject of this prophetic oracle is the same as that of the oracles recorded in the forty-second, forty-ninth, fiftieth, and sixty-first chapters of this book. Much that is said in these chapters can be referred only to the Messiah, and passages from them are, in the New Testament, explicitly referred to him.[2]

The perfect correspondence between the various predictions in the oracle and the various events in our Lord's history, is an abundant source of corroborative evidence. Try to find a similar correspondence in the case of any individual, in any age or country, who has lived since the oracle was given forth. It is also strong proof on the same side, that no other reference was, either on the part of Jewish or Christian interpreters, thought of, till the support of a favorite hypothesis made this necessary.

Against an interpretation supported by such varied and powerful direct and indirect evidence, no objection could be satisfactory. The objections which have been brought forward are feeble indeed. It has been made an objection against applying the prophecy to our Lord, that it states that kings shall bow to the servant of Jehovah ;[3] as if no monarch had embraced the Christian religion ; as if men of kingly minds and rank were not to be found among his most devoted subjects. It has been asserted, that the Messiah is never termed " the servant of the Lord," in the face of multitudes of passages in this book,[4] which

---

[1] Mark, ix. 12. Rom. iv. 25. 1 Cor. xv. 3. 2 Cor. v. 21. 1 John, iii. 5. 1 Pet. i. 19.
[2] Isa. xlii. 1, comp. with Matth. iii. 17; xvii. 17; xii. 18. Isa. xlii. 6, with Luke, ii. 32; Acts, xii. 47. Isa. l. 6, with Math. xxvi. 67; xxvii. 26. Isa. lxi. 1, with Luke, iv. 18.
[3] Isa. xlix. 7.   [4] Isa. xlii. 1; xlix. 3, 6; l. 10.

no ingenuity can explain on any other supposition, and as if there were no such passage as, " Behold I will bring forth my Servant the Branch."[1] It were a waste of time to state other objections which are even more shadowy than these. It is well observed by a learned Roman Catholic expositor,[2] "All the objections urged against this oracle as a prediction of the Messiah, are far-fetched, recondite, and artificial, and may be refuted by this one remark, that this prophecy was promulgated to the Jews, and was to be fulfilled by their instrumentality; and that if it had been clearer, it never would have been by their means fulfilled, and therefore could not, to serve its purpose, be more clearly revealed." Dr. Priestley, who is very chary in admitting references to the Messiah in the Old Testament prophets, declares it " impossible to explain this passage of any but Jesus Christ ;" and considers Grotius's application of it to Jeremiah, as " unworthy of the honor of refutation." This oracle may, indeed, as an old commentator remarks, challenge for its title " The Passion of Jesus Christ, according to Isaiah."

We consider ourselves now as fully warranted to proceed to the interpretation of this oracle, under this conviction that its subject is HE of whom Moses in the law, and the prophets, do write.[3]

By a considerable number of Christian interpreters, the last three verses of the fifty-second chapter have been entirely separated from what precedes them, and connected as a part of the same oracle and series of oracles, with what follows. In connecting these verses with what follows, I have no doubt they have done right; but I more than doubt the propriety of disjoining it so completely from what goes before. They have generally viewed the first part of the fifty-second chapter as referring entirely to

---

[1] Zech ii. 8.   [2] Jahn.

[3] " Messias clavis est totius capitis, qua non inventa clausus et obscurus procul dubio manebit intellectus horum verborum."—CRAMER. Well might Vitringa, who, after all that has been done for the interpretation of Isaiah, justly deserves the name of " ὁ ἐξηγητής," by way of eminence, after his thorough exposition, address the unbelieving Jew in these eloquent words :—" Ergo Judæe incredule, sic hic vere hæreas ut facis et ubique impingas : ingredere tandem post tot seculorum errores viam rectam : pone prejudicia inveterata : inspice et considera historiam JESU, ejusque extremorum, accurata perscriptam in Evangeliis et deprehendes ibi omnes lineas et characteres illius JUSTI Dei SERVI qui in hac prophetia pingitur : quos si deprehenderis da gloriam Deo et veritati; crede in Dominum Jesum et si toto credideris animo baptizator et viam tuam ibis cum gaudio."

the return from the Babylonian captivity. I conceive that the phraseology is borrowed from that event; but with Vitringa, who, even after the appearance of such men as Lowth, and Gesenius, and Hengstenberg, and Henderson, and Alexander, is still, *facile princeps*, the prince of the Isaian interpreters, I consider the preceding part of the chapter as a prediction of the opening of the New Dispensation, and, in particular, of the separation of the primitive church from the incredulous and impenitent Jews, and their going forth clad in heavenly armor (bearing the vessels of the Lord), under the conduct of their Divine Leader from Jerusalem, to take possession of the heritage of the nations. In the oracle, on the illustration of which we are about to enter, we have a prediction of that event on which the success of the primitive church, in her glorious enterprise to subjugate the world, depended,—the glorious exaltation of the Redeemer perfected through suffering. It is a separate oracle, but it is closely connected with—it belongs to—the same series of oracles as that which immediately precedes it.

It is a profound and just view which is given by a living interpreter of the place which this oracle has in Isaiah's prophecies. "The deliverance of God's people forms the main subject of the two parts of Isaiah's prophecy. This deliverance is twofold,—deliverance from the Babylonish exile, and deliverance from error, sin, and their consequences. The two are not kept perfectly distinct from each other; though it may be remarked in general, that the former is most prominent in the first part as far as to the forty-ninth chapter, and the latter in the second part. Each of these deliverances was to be effected by a servant and messenger of Jehovah,—the first by Cyrus, the second by Jesus Christ. The prophet had already, in a preceding part of the book, described the former with such clearness, that scarcely a single trait was left to be added. Moreover, the latter also the servant and chosen of God—him in whom his soul delights—him, too, the prophet has not forgotten. But the features which he has hitherto drawn, did not make out a complete picture. He had described Him as the Divine teacher and ambassador, who being furnished with rich gifts from God, humbled himself, and appeared in gentleness and meekness to save that which was lost. He had represented Him as a glorious King, who was to establish a kingdom of peace and righte-

ousness, to extend continually its rich blessings on all its adherents, and to punish severely the despisers of his name. But
one great feature of the picture was still wanting. The prophet
had announced that Cyrus would achieve this temporal deliverance by his military valor, and through the victories God would
grant him. But the means and manner of the spiritual deliverance had not yet been imparted to him. He had indeed spoken
of the deep humiliation of the Messiah; he had predicted in the
fiftieth chapter the severe sufferings, the scorn and contempt of
the people, which must fall on "the servant of God." But he
had not yet said that these very sufferings would be the only
efficient cause of our salvation. In this oracle he completes the
picture.

The result to which these discussions have led us cannot be
better described than in the words of another accomplished living
writer,[1]—"We turn gladly and thankfully to that interpretation which was the first ever put upon the passage, which
was the prevailing interpretation in the early Christian church,
and which has come down to us sanctioned by the infallible
authority of our Lord and his apostles. To this interpretation
there is nothing in the passage itself which offers the slightest
difficulty; on the contrary, all its statements receive upon it
a due and harmonious explanation. The sinlessness of the
suffering servant of God, his vicarious substitution for others,
his meekness and unrepining gentleness under the cruelties of
his enemies, his triumph in the salvation of those for whom he
suffered, and even the historical allusion to the circumstances of
his burial and resurrection, all find their counterpart and fulfilment in the life and work of Jesus of Nazareth, the Christ of
God. In vain has the perverse ingenuity of its enemies sought
to find these criterial qualities exemplified in any others. The
improved philology and hermeneutics of modern times have only
served more clearly to show that the earliest interpretation of
this memorable passage is not only the best, but the only one
that can stand the test of a searching and careful scrutiny."[2]

The oracle seems to me, after having considered it with all
the attention in my power, to resolve itself into the following
parts:—*First*, A revelation made in the person of Jehovah of

---

[1] Dr. W. L. Alexander.

[2] Connection and Harmony of the Old and New Testaments, pp. 365, 366.

the exaltation and glory of the Messiah as following, and rising out of, his humiliation and sufferings, chap. lii. 13–15. *Secondly*, A complaint on the part of the preachers of the good news, spoken of at chap. lii. 7, of their comparatively little success, chap. liii. 1. *Thirdly*, A statement on the part of converted Jews of the reason of this comparatively little success, introducing an account of the sufferings of Christ and the glory which has followed, and is to follow, them, chap. liii. 2–10; and, *Fourthly*, A solemn declaration from Jehovah himself, confirming the great truths contained in that statement, chap. liii. 11, 12.

The *stand point* of the prophet is between the sufferings and the exaltation of the Messiah. The former are past. The latter are future. "The prophetic spirit," says Dr. Pye Smith, "selected the point of time which the nature of the case demanded as most suitable to the intention of the whole manifestation; and this point of time is the solemn and awful pause— THE CRISIS OF HEAVEN, EARTH, AND HELL—when Jesus was lying in the arms of death. Those must be as destitute of taste as of a Christian mind who do not feel the exquisite propriety of the time as adapted to the scenery."

These introductory statements have necessarily occupied so much time, that I am prevented from entering at present on the proper exposition of the oracle. The announcement in the person of Jehovah of the exaltation and glory of the Messiah as succeeding and rising out of his humiliation and suffering, will, if it please God, form the subject of our next lecture.

Join with me, my brethren, in earnest prayer, that when you and I, at a few successive meetings, make this most important prophetic oracle the subject of consideration, the God of our Lord and Saviour Jesus Christ, who gave to his holy prophet Isaiah that spirit of inspiration by which he, at the distance of seven centuries, was enabled so graphically to describe those sufferings through which the Messiah was to enter into glory, may give to us the spirit of wisdom and revelation in the knowledge of him, the eyes of our understanding being enlightened, that we may know, as exhibited in this oracle, the depth of his wisdom and love in not sparing his Son, but delivering him up for us all, and the working of his mighty power when He raised him from the dead and set him at his own right hand in the heavenly place, "far above all principality, and power, and might, and dominion, and every name that can be named, not only in this world but in that which is to come ; and hath put all things under his feet, and given him to be head over all things to the Church, which is his body : the fulness of him who filleth all in all; that by means of this word of the truth of the gospel, Christ may dwell in our hearts by faith, and we be enabled to comprehend with all saints, what is the breadth, and length, and depth, and height of the economy of mercy, and to know the love of Christ which passeth knowledge, that we may be filled with all the fulness of God." "Now, unto Him who is able to do exceeding abundantly above all that we ask or think, according to the power that worketh in us ; unto Him be glory in the Church by Jesus Christ, throughout all ages, world without end. Amen."

LECTURE II

OPENING PROCLAMATION OF JEHOVAH

Isaiah, LII. 13–15.—" Behold, my servant shall deal prudently, he shall be exalted
and extolled, and be very high. As many were astonished at thee: (his visage was
so marred more than any man, and his form more than the sons of men ;) so shall he
sprinkle many nations ; the kings shall shut their mouths at him: for that which had
not been told them shall they see ; and that which they had not heard shall they
consider."

I proceed now to the consideration of the first of those sections into which the prophetic oracle resolves itself. A revelation made in the person of Jehovah of the exaltation and glory
of the Messiah, as following and rising out of his humiliation
and suffering.

Whether we consider the person who here speaks, or the
person spoken of, or the statement which the one makes in
reference to the other, it must be apparent that few passages of
Scripture have stronger claims on our devout attention than the
words which we have just read.

The speaker is not named, but there is no mistaking who He
is. It is the Lord Jehovah; the independent, eternal, immense,
immutable, omnipotent, omniscient Being, infinite in wisdom,
righteousness, and benignity ; the holy, holy, holy One ; the
creator, preserver, proprietor, and governor of the universe ; the
unexhausted, inexhaustible, source of being, and intelligence,
and power, and holiness, and blessedness. It is He who speaks.
His voice is full of majesty. Let all the earth be silent before
Him.

The person spoken of is not named either ; and the descriptive
appellation here given him, is one which is given in Scripture to
many individuals, and might have been given to many more.
" The servant of the Lord " is an appellation given to Moses, to
David, to Cyrus, and may, without impropriety, be bestowed on

any person employed by the Divinity as an agent in the accomplishment of his purposes. All persons, all things, all beings, all events are his servantŝ. There is no difficulty, however, in recognising the reference of the appellation here. There is but One, of all the innumerable agents who have been employed by Jehovah, to whom the statements made in this oracle can with the slightest probability be referred, and to that One every statement made is strictly applicable. "The servant of the Lord" is plainly that mysterious personage who is constantly meeting us in our perusal of the Old Testament Scriptures : "the seed of the woman," in that enigmatic oracle, delivered in Paradise after the fall of man, in which, in the bosom of a curse, was folded up the sum and substance of all the "exceeding great and precious promises;" "the seed of Abraham" in the covenant of promise; "the Shiloh" of Jacob's prophetical dying benediction; "the Angel of Jehovah," or, "the Angel Jehovah"—"the Angel of God's presence"—"the Angel in whom was the name of Jehovah" of the patriarchal and Mosaic economies; "the Captain of the Lord's hosts" of Joshua; "the King"—"the King's Son"—"Jehovah's Begotten Son," "Firstborn," "Messiah," and "Holy One," and his own "Lord" of the sweet singer of Israel; "the Rod from the stem of Jesse" —the "Emmanuel"—the "Jehovah our righteous"—"the Branch"—"the Lord of the temple"—"the Angel of the covenant" of the prophets.[1]

No well-informed Christian needs to ask, And who is this mysterious personage who bears so many names ? "The spirit of prophecy is the testimony of Jesus." It is of Him who "was in the beginning, who was with God, who was God, by whom all things were made;" "the eternal life"—living One; "who was with the Father," "the life and the light of men;" who was "made flesh and dwelt among men;" who "revealed the Father;" of Him who, while "the Man Christ Jesus," was also "over all, God blessed forever;" who was "made of the seed of David, according to the flesh;" but who at the same time was declared to be the Son of God with power, "according to the spirit of holiness, by the resurrection from the dead"[2]—it is of

[1] Gen. v. 13; xlix. 10; xlviii. 16.   Exod. xxiii. 20.   Josh. v. 14.   Psal. ii. 7; lxxii. 1; cx. 1.   Isa. xi. 1; vii. 14.   Jer. xxiii. 6.   Zech. iii. 8.   Mal. iii. 1.
[2] John, i. 1-4, 14, 18.   Rom. ix. 5; i. 4.

him that the Divine Father here speaketh. It is on him that he calls us to fix our minds in devout, attentive contemplation,— "Behold my Servant." Who dare, who can, resist such a call from such a quarter?

The statement made is one equally worthy of its author and of its subject—of Him who makes it, and of him concerning whom it is made. It is a declaration that ' this illustrious person should, through his consummate wisdom, completely succeed in the great work intrusted to him—a work involving in it the highest interests, the vindication of the claims of truth and right-eousness, the display of the glories of the Divine character, the upholding of the principles which sustain the throne of God and secure the well-being of the intelligent universe; and that, though in accomplishing it he should meet with the severest sufferings, and be exposed to the deepest degradation and shame, the variety and greatness of the blessings and honors, to which its success-ful consummation should raise him, should be proportioned, or, if that were possible, more than proportioned, to the sacrifices he had made, the labors he had performed, the privations he had submitted to, and the agonies he had endured.' Such a state-ment is surely worthy of our most considerate attention, especially if we recollect that the great work in accomplishing which "the servant of the Lord" was to be so humbled, and for accomplishing which he was to be so exalted, was a work, on the successful accom-plishment of which depended our everlasting happiness. Had he "failed, or been discouraged," where had been the hope of man ?

Let us, then, examine somewhat more minutely this most im-portant prophetic oracle. We have the great advantages of being able to look at it both in the light of New Testament revelations, and in that of partial and rapidly-extending accomplishment.

The Messiah is not termed " the servant of Jehovah " to de-signate essential inferiority. If there is a truth distinctly revealed in Scripture, it is the divinity of him who is here termed " the Servant of the Lord." The name Jehovah—a name expressive of the peculiarities of the mode of Divine being—is given him. Eternity, omnipresence, omniscience, omnipotence, are ascribed to him. He is represented as the creator, the proprietor, the preserver, the governor, the judge of the universe. In his name Divine ordinances are administered, and to him Divine homage is rendered on earth and in heaven, by men and by angels. Yet the Servant is inferior to his Lord. The inferiority in the present case is entirely official, not essential—a matter of economy or arrangement. By his own most voluntary consent, he assumed "the form of a servant."[1] In the great system of Divine dispensations, having for their object the redemption of mankind, the Father sustains the majesty of Divinity. He appoints, He commands, He requires, He sustains, He accepts, He rewards. He sends forth the Son to be the Saviour of the world, all things being "OF Him;" and the Son, "BY whom are all things," submits to the appointment, obeys the command, answers the requisitions, receives the supports, gives in his account, and receives his reward. The principle of the mediatory economy throughout is, ' The Father is greater than the Son.'

The work referred to here is plainly the work of man's salvation—the manifestation of the combined glories of the Divine holiness and benignity in the deliverance of an innumerable multitude of the ruined race of man from guilt, and ignorance, and error, and depravity, and wretchedness, and the making them good, and wise, and happy, like God, the infinitely good, and wise, and happy one, to the utmost limits of their capacity, during the whole eternity of their being. The execution of this great work includes in it both the doing of what is necessary to make the ultimate happiness of such beings as fallen men consistent with the perfections of the Divine character and the principles of the Divine government, and the actually making them happy, by an agency suited to their constitution, and to the nature of the blessings to be conferred on them. These two things comprehend the whole of our Lord's saving work on earth and in heaven.

Now, in executing this work, Jehovah declares that his Servant " shall deal prudently,"[2] as our translators render it. The word no doubt has this signification, but it also signifies to prosper.[3] This is its meaning in Deut. xxix. 9; 2 Kings, xviii. 7; Josh. i. 8; Prov. xvii. 10. If it be used in this sense, the verse before is quite parallel to the passage in Jer. xxiii. 5, " Behold, the days come, saith the Lord, that I will raise unto David a righteous Branch, and a King shall reign and *prosper*."[4] In

---

[1] λαβὼν. Phil. ii. 7.   [2] ישׂכיל.

[3] This is the view given by the Chaldee Pharaphrast, and by the Rabbinical commentators generally.

[4] Vitringa prefers this sense, and says, very justly, " In consequenti contextu, non *intelligentia* Messiæ, sed *gloria* ejus commendatur."

agreement with one of the most learned interpreters of the passage,[1] I am disposed to consider the word as expressive both of prudence in management and success in accomplishment. The idea seems to be, ' The Messiah shall wisely conduct to a prosperous issue the work committed to him.'

In both departments of that work a high degree of wisdom was necessary. for numerous and powerful obstacles lay in the way of gaining the object in view. With consummate wisdom did the Messiah conduct the work of making expiation for sin ; and of furnishing, in a plain and well-accredited revelation of that work which involves in it a manifestation of the Divine character, fitted, if understood and believed, to make men holy and happy ; and of securing the all-powerful, all-persuasive influences of the good Spirit to make this revelation effectual for its purpose : and with equal, that is, with infinite wisdom does he guide all those arrangements in reference to external event and inward influence, which are necessary to the salvation of individuals, to the diffusion of his gospel, and the establishment of his kingdom. He desisted not from the work of obtaining redemption till he could say, "It is finished ;" and in bestowing the blessings he has promised, " he shall not fail nor be discouraged, till he bring forth judgment unto truth, till he set judgment in the earth," and make "the isles wait for his law," till "the glory of the Lord be revealed, and all flesh see it together." "He has girt his sword on his thigh : and he will, with his glory and majesty, ride forth prosperously, because of truth, and meekness, and righteousness; and his right hand shall teach him terrible things. His arrows shall be sharp in the hearts of the king's enemies, and the people shall fall under him : and his throne shall be forever and ever." [2]

The words which follow, " He shall be exalted and extolled, and be very high," [3] refer to a state of very high dignity to which the servant of Jehovah is to be raised, in consequence of having successfully performed the first part of his saving work, and in order to his successful accomplishment of the second part of that work. We are not, I apprehend, to seek a particular distinct meaning in each of these expressions. It is ingenious trifling,

---

[1] Hengstenberg.

[2] John, xix. 30.   Isa. xlii. 3, 4 ; xl. 5.   Psal. xlv. 4, 5.   [3] ‏.ירום ונשא וגבה מאד‏

[4] " In verbis bis tribus non est argutandum neque quærendum quomodo singula inter se differant."—ROSENMULLER.

not satisfactory exposition, to say the first word refers to the
Messiah's being exalted to the right hand of the Father, the
second to his being extolled in the destruction of all who oppose
him, and the third to his being very high when placed on the
tribunal of universal judgment.   This mode of interpretation is
much on a level with that of the Jewish Rabbins, who paraphrase the words, "This is the King Messiah.   He shall be
'exalted' above Abraham, 'extolled' above Moses, 'made very
high' above the angels of ministry."   The prophet, as Kimchi
remarks, uses all the terms which the Hebrew language contains expressive of elevation, heaping word on word to convey
the idea of the highest degree of possible exaltation.[1]   The
meaning is, 'The Messiah shall be raised to the highest degree
of honor, shall receive the largest measure of blessedness.'

The best way of illustrating such a statement is by parallel
passages.   Take the following as a specimen from the Old Testament writers :—" The king shall joy in thy strength, O Lord ;
and in thy salvation how greatly shall he rejoice !   Thou hast
given him his heart's desire, and hast not withholden the request
of his lips.   For Thou preventest him with the blessings of goodness : Thou settest a crown of pure gold on his head.   He asked
life of Thee, and Thou gavest it him, even length of days forever and ever.   His glory is great in Thy salvation : honor and
majesty hast Thou laid upon him.   For Thou hast made him
most blessed forever: Thou hast made him exceeding glad with
thy countenance."   "The Lord said unto my Lord, Sit thou at
my right hand, until I make thine enemies thy footstool.   The
Lord shall send the rod of thy strength out of Zion : rule thou
in the midst of thine enemies."   " The Lord hath sworn, and
will not repent, Thou art a priest forever after the order of Melchizedek.   The Lord at thy right hand shall strike through
kings in the day of his wrath.   He shall judge among the heathen, He shall fill the places with the dead bodies; He shall
wound the heads over many countries."   "I have set my king
upon my holy hill of Zion.   Thou art my Son; this day have I
begotten thee.   I shall give thee the heathen for thine inheritance, and the uttermost parts of the earth for thy possession.

[1] " לְפִי סמעלתו תחיה מעלה יתרה."—KIMCHI.   ὑπερύψωσε is the apostle's word, Phil.
ii. 9.

Thou shalt break them with a rod of iron; thou shalt dash them in pieces like a potter's vessel."[1]

Take the following as a specimen of the statements of the New Testament writers respecting the exaltation of "the servant of Jehovah." "God also hath highly exalted him, and given him a name which is above every name; that at the name of Jesus every knee should bow, of things in heaven, and things in earth, and things under the earth; and that every tongue should confess that Jesus Christ is Lord, to the glory of God the Father." God "raised him from the dead, and set him at his own right hand in the heavenly places, far above all principality, and power, and might, and dominion, and every name that is named, not only in this world, but also in that which is to come; and hath put all things under his feet, and gave him to be the head over all things to the church, which is his body, the fulness of Him that filleth all in all." He is "gone into heaven, and is on the right hand of God; angels, and authorities, and powers, being made subject unto him."[2]

The 14th and 15th verses form a long complicated antithetical sentence, the object of which seems to be twofold; to illustrate the manner in which "the servant of Jehovah" was to obtain this state of transcendent dignity and ineffable blessedness, and to bring out the glories of that state by contrasting them with the degradation and suffering which preceded and prepared for it. "As many were astonied at thee; (his[3] visage was so marred more than any man, and his form more than the sons of men;) so shall he sprinkle many nations; the kings shall shut their mouths at him: for that which had not been told them shall they see; and that which they had not heard shall they consider."[4] The last clause in the 14th verse is to be considered as parenthetical, and as explanatory of what is stated in the first clause. The antithesis is between the first clause of the 14th and the first clause of the 15th verse. "As many were astonied at thee;" "So shall he sprinkle many nations." The change

[1] Psal. xxi. 1–6; cx. 1, 2, 4–6; ii. 6–9.   [2] Phil. ii. 9–11. Eph. i. 20–23. 1 Pet. iii. 22.

[3] " Τὸ εἶδος σου καὶ ἡ δόξα σου."—*Sept.*

[4] " Lyke as the multitude shal wondre upon him; because his face shall be so deformed, and not as a man's face, and his beutie lyke no man: Even so shall the multitude of the Gentiles loke unto him, and the kynges shal shut their mouthes before him; for they that have not bene tolde of him shall se him, and they that herde nothinge of hym shall beholde him."—COVERDALE, 1550.

of person in the two clauses sounds strange to an English ear.
Such translations are not, however, uncommon in oriental poetry.   You have instances of it, Isa. i. 29 ; xlix. 25, 26 ; Deut.
xxxii. 15, 17, 18 ; Micah ii. 3.   It might have been quite faithfully translated according to the English idiom, " As many were
astonied at him ; so shall he sprinkle many nations."

Many are said to have been astonied at " the servant of Jehovah."   The obsolete word, astonied, seems more than its modern
substitute, astonished, to convey the idea of what is shocking, as
well as amazing.   The original word expresses astonishment
often with the accompaniment of aversion and derision.   "Every
one that passeth thereby shall be astonished, and wag his head."
" I will make this city desolate, and an hissing ; every one that
passeth thereby shall be astonished and hiss."[1]   The reason of
this astonishment is stated in the parenthetical clause,[2]—" His
visage was so marred more than any man, and his form more
than the sons of men."   These words admit of two modes of
interpretation, bringing out substantially the same meaning.
According to the one, the sentiment is, ' His countenance and
form were more disfigured than those of any other man.   His
face, and figure, and demeanor, and whole external appearance,
exhibited tokens of a state of more complete destitution and
wretchedness than had ever been witnessed in any human
being.'   In this case, the word rendered " man "[3] probably signifies, as it signifies elsewhere, a man of rank, such as a prince
or a prophet ; the term rendered " sons of men,"[4] persons of the
humbler order ; and the one clause rises above the other.[5]   According to the other mode of interpretation, the sentiment is
still stronger.   ' His countenance was so marred as to be no
more that of a man ; his form so as no longer to have the appearance of a human form.'   In either case, it strikingly expresses the privation and suffering, the shame and contempt, to
which " the servant of Jehovah " was to be subjected, while
finishing the work which had been given him to do.   It would
be wrong to confine the reference to the Messiah's countenance
and form literally, though there can be no doubt both bore dis-

---

[1] Jer. xviii. 16 ; xix. 8.

[2] Dathé's supposition of an ellipsis of לֵאמֹר, though ingenious and plausible, seems
unnecessary.

[3] אִישׁ.   [4] אָדָם.   [5] Psal. xlix. 2.   Isa. ii. 9.

tinct traces of those sufferings, so unparalleled for number, variety, severity, and continuance, which he endured.[1] Bodily pain and mental anguish write "strange defeatures" in the human face divine, and bend to the earth the most manly figure; and the words must have been verified to the letter, when, hanging on the cross, his face was livid with blows, besmeared with blood, yet pale with exhaustion, and every limb of his body quivering with agony. The words are, however, principally intended to direct our thoughts to that, of which all this was but a partial manifestation,—the degradation and suffering to which he submitted in doing the will of God. "He was despised and rejected of men; a man of sorrows, and acquainted with grief; stricken, smitten of God, and afflicted; as a worm, and no man; a reproach of men, and despised of the people."

Such being the external circumstances of "the servant of Jehovah," he did not attract the admiring gaze of mankind. He did arrest attention; he did excite wonder; but it was not the wonder of admiration. A few, whose eyes God had opened, saw, indeed, in some measure, the real grandeur there was amid all this apparent meanness. They "beheld his glory—the glory as of the Only-begotten of the Father,"—a glory that bedimmed all created lustre. But the great body of those who behold him were "astonied" at him. His external appearance, especially when contrasted with his claims to Messiahship, shocked them. The Galilean peasant—the Nazarene carpenter—the son of Joseph, claiming God for his own Father—declaring himself "the bread of life," and "the light of the world," and asserting that the destinies of eternity hung on the reception or rejection of him and his message,—all this excited a mingled emotion of amazement and indignation, scorn, and horror, in the bosom of the great majority of his countrymen. He was "a wonder,"[2] a prodigy to many. A mixture of pity and contempt, disgust and wonder, seems to have stirred the stern bosom of the Roman governor, when he brought him out wearing the robe of mock royalty and the torturing crown, and exclaimed, "Behold the man." Even his friends were confounded, though their aston ishment bore a different character. The closing scene, notwith-

---

[1] Jerome says well, "Non qua formæ significat fœditatem, sed qua in humilitate venerit et paupertate."

[2] Psal. lxxi. 7.

standing what appear to us very plain forewarnings, appears to
have come on them like a thunderbolt. They were overwhelmed
with amazement, as well as with sorrow. What blank astonishment sat on their countenances when he made the announcement, "Verily I say unto you, One of you shall betray me,"—
"All ye shall be offended because of me this night!"[1] How
must their amazement have risen at the successive scenes of
Gethsemane, and the hall of the high priest, and the court of
Pilate, till at last they saw him, in whom they trusted that he
should redeem Israel, nailed to a cross like a felonious slave,
—execrated by men, and deserted of God! Then their
amazement reached its consummation: they were "astonied at
him."

But that cross was the way to the crown—to many crowns;
and the depth of his debasement is to be the measure of the
height of his exaltation. "As many were astonied at him,"
"so shall he sprinkle many nations; the kings shall shut their
mouths at him: for that which had not been told them shall
they see; and that which they had not heard shall they consider."

"The servant of Jehovah" was to "sprinkle many nations."
This is one of the most difficult passages in the Old Testament
Scriptures. The difficulties lie in the word rendered "sprinkle,"[2] and these difficulties are various. While there can be no
doubt that in every place where the word occurs in the Old Testament, it signifies 'to sprinkle;' yet its construction here is
remarkable. In all other cases the word "sprinkle" is followed
by a term expressing the substance sprinkled, as water or
blood. It is the usage of the language to say, not sprinkle a
person or thing with blood or water, but sprinkle blood or water
on a person or thing. Besides this grammatical difficulty, it is
difficult to see how "sprinkling many nations," whatever it
may mean, can be a contrast to, "many were astonied at
thee." Some disregarding the first difficulty, have supposed
that the "sprinkling many nations" refers to the diffusion of
the Messiah's doctrine among many nations,—referring to such
passages as, "My doctrine shall drop as the rain, my speech
shall distil as the dew;" or, "He shall come down like rain

---

[1] Matth. xxvi. 21, 31.   [2] יַזֶּה, from נָזָה.

upon the mown grass; as showers that water the earth."[1]
Others have supposed the reference to be to the lustratory purifying influence of the Messiah's atonement or spirit. He shall,
by the sprinkling of his atoning blood, or, of the cleansing influence of his spirit, justify and sanctify multitudes of men. There
can be no doubt the Messiah has shed abroad his doctrine and
the influence of his sacrifice and spirit; but it is not easy to see
how these ideas at all contrast with, "many were astonied at
thee." Where is the contrast between, "*As* many were shocked
at him, *so* will he" teach, or make reconciliation for, or purify,
or consecrate, "many nations."[2]

I feel constrained to go along with the great body of the more
learned recent interpreters,[3] who consider the word rendered
"sprinkle," used here in a way different from that in which it
is used in any other part of the Old Testament, but in a way warranted by the manner in which a similar word in some of the cog-
nate languages is employed. "So shall he make to leap many
nations."[4] As he in his humiliation excited the contemptuous
wonder of many individuals, so shall he in his exalted state excite
the joyful admiration of many nations; there being a contrast
both between the kind of emotion called forth and those among
whom the emotions were called forth. As he excited astonishment of one kind, he shall excite astonishment of another kind; as
he excited the former emotion in many individuals, he will excite
the latter in many nations.[5] The astonishment he will produce,
will be that of admiration; the wonder, that of delight. There
is, indeed, a period approaching when he shall excite amazement
in another way. "Behold, he cometh in clouds; and every eye
shall see him; and they also which pierced him; and all the
kindreds of the earth shall wail because of him." Then will
be astonishment. "Who may abide the day of his coming?

---

[1] Deut. xxxii. ii.   Psal. lxxii. 6.   Muntzer.

[2] Spanheim's exegesis,—"So shall he disperse many nations," as drops are dispersed when a fluid is sprinkled,—is quite fanciful.

[3] Genesius, Rosenmüller, Martini.

[4] The LXX. translate the clause, "οὔτω θαυμάσονται ἔθνη πολλὰ ἐπ' αὐτώ." "Quid
legerent," says Musculus, "non video." Whatever they read, they seem to have
lighted on the prophet's thought.

[5] Grotius' notion of astonishment, produced by his sprinkling, shedding his rays on
them, as the Sun of Righteousness,—and Bishop Chandler, of astonishment such as
persons feel when water is suddenly sprinkled on them,—are both far-fetched.

and who shall stand when he appeareth?"[1] Here, however, it
is plain that the astonishment is of a joyful description; corresponding with the reverent demeanor of those who hold the
highest place in society.

The contrast is striking. It is not only between the astonishment of contempt and the astonishment of admiration, but between the astonishment of individuals and the astonishment of
nations.   Many Jews were shocked at his appearance, wondered
at his poverty and wretchedness; "but a multitude that no
man can number, out of every kindred, and people, and tongue,
and nation," shall, on being made to know the truth respecting
the servant of Jehovah and his work, be filled with delighted
astonishment at the unsearchable depth of his wisdom, the im-
measurable extent of his power; the length and breadth, the
height and depth of his love, and of the salvation which has
resulted from it,—both passing knowledge, yet the first being
infinitely greater than the second.

"Kings shall shut their mouths at him," *i. e.*, shall own him
their superior, and show their awe of him. The force of the expression "shut their mouths at him," may be illustrated by the
two following passages of Scripture:—"O that I were as in
months past, as in the days when God preserved me; when his
candle shined upon my head, and when by his light I walked
through darkness;" "when I went out to the gate through the
city; when I prepared my seat in the street! the young men
saw me, and hid themselves; and the aged arose and stood up.
The princes refrained from talking, and laid their hands on their
mouths.   The nobles held their peace, and their tongue cleaved
to the roof of their mouth." "The nations shall see, and be
confounded at all their might; they shall lay their hand upon their
mouth; their ears shall be deaf."[2] Some learned expositors
have more ingeniously than soundly interpreted these words of
" the repeal of persecuting edicts against Christianity by Gentile
kings." That is a proof of awe and submission; but it were
fanciful to confine the text to such comparatively rare occurrences. The general idea is, 'The highest and proudest of the
sons of men shall be obliged to give him tokens of the most
reverent submission." The prediction is nearly parallel to that

---

[1] Rev. i. 7. Mal. iii. 2.   [2] Job, xxix. 2–10. Mic. vii. 16.

in chap. xlix. 7,—"Thus saith the Lord, the Redeemer of Israel, and his Holy One, to him whom man despiseth, to him whom the nation abhorreth, to a servant of rulers, kings shall see and arise, princes also shall worship, because of the Lord that is faithful, and the Holy One of Israel, and he shall choose thee."

This astonishment is not to be ignorant astonishment; this submission is not to be constrained submission. The kings are intelligently to admire and willingly to submit. Both the astonishment and submission are to spring from their knowing and believing the truth respecting "the servant of the Lord" and the mighty work he has accomplished, and is accomplishing. "For that which hath not been told them shall they see; and that which they have not heard shall they consider."

This passage is expressly applied by the apostle Paul to the conversion of the Gentiles by his ministry. "I have strived to preach the gospel, not where Christ was named:" "but, as it is written, To whom he was not spoken of, they shall see: and they that have not heard shall understand."[1] The Gentiles were to have the mystery which had been kept secret from former ages and generations made known to them. Christ the Messiah was to be among them the hope of glory. The gospel was to be preached and believed; and the result was to be, the Saviour was to be admired and obeyed. The prediction has been accomplished, is accomplishing, and shall yet be more illustriously accomplished.[2] Every knee must bow to him. Every tongue confess that he is Lord, "to the glory of God the Father." The kingdoms of this world must become "the kingdom of our God and of his Christ, and he shall reign forever and ever." In the beautiful words of the Christian poet,—

> "Arabia's desert ranger
>   To him shall bow the knee;
> The Ethiopian stranger
>   His glory come to see.

> "With offerings of devotion,
>   Ships from the isles shall meet,
> To pour the wealth of ocean
>   In tribute at his feet.

[1] Rom. xv. 20, 21.

[2] "Viget adhuc evangelii vis, et porro vigebit. Unde plures subinde gentes et cum his reges etiam adorabunt Jesum, quem vix natum venerati jam sunt gentium magnates, quem sine dubio principum etiam haud pauci recte adhuc coluerunt, plures vero. ut speramus in posterum venerabuntur."—STORR.

" Kings shall fall down before Him,
And gold and incense bring;
All nations shall adore Him,
His praise all people sing.

" For He shall have dominion
O'er river, sea, and shore;
Far as the eagle's pinion,
Or dove's light wing can soar.

" For Him shall prayer unceasing,
And daily vows ascend;
His kingdom still increasing,
A kingdom without end.

" The mountain dews shall flourish,
A seed in weakness sown;
Whose fruit shall spread and nourish,
And shake like Lebanon.

" O'er ev'ry foe victorious,
He on his throne shall rest;
From age to age more glorious,
All blessing and all bless'd.

" The tide of time shall never
His covenant remove;
His name shall stand forever:
That name to us is love."[1]

And the grand means of accomplishing this glorious consummation, is to be the declaration to them, and the belief by them, of what is news, good news,—the truth about " the servant of Jehovah," and his wise and prosperous administration of the great enterprise committed to him.   " As soon as they shall hear of him, they shall obey him."   " The mystery which was kept secret from former ages and generations, but is now made manifest by the Scriptures of the prophets according to the commandment of the everlasting God made known to all nations."   And " all the ends of the world shall remember, and turn unto the Lord; and all the kindreds of the nations shall worship before thee.   For the kingdom is the Lord's; and he is the governor among the nations.   All they that be fat upon earth shall eat and worship: all they that go down to the dust shall bow before Him; and none can keep alive his own soul.   A seed shall serve Him; it shall be accounted to the Lord for a generation.   They shall come, and shall declare his righteousness unto a people that shall

[1] Montgomery.

be born, that He hath done this.'"[1]   Or, in the words of the old Paraphrast,—

> "All who behold the sun's uprise
>   Shall Him profess and serve alone,
> And all the heathen families
>   Shall cast themselves before his throne;
>   Because the kingdom is his own,
> And over all his empire lies.

> "A sanctified posterity
>   Shall ever celebrate his name—
> Adopted sons of the Most High,
>   They shall his righteousness proclaim,
>   And works of everlasting fame,
> To their believing progeny."[2]

Thus have I endeavored to set before you "the Servant of Jehovah" as wisely and prosperously accomplishing the great work given him by the Father to do, on earth and in heaven,— the salvation of men; and as enjoying that state of perfect blessedness, supreme dignity, and boundless authority, to which he has been raised as the reward of accomplishing that part of this work which was to be done by him on earth, and as the means of enabling him to accomplish that part of this work which is yet to be done by him in heaven; and have placed in contrast the degradation and contempt to which he was exposed when accomplishing the first, with the homage and honor that are to be done him while accomplishing the others.

And now, what remains as the appropriate practical improve-ment of this discourse?   What but to comply with the command from the throne of heaven,—"Behold my Servant" suffering and reigning.   Assuredly HE is well worth contemplating. Turn away your minds, then, from every other object.   Look to Jesus.   Behold him; behold him; and in him behold God reconciling the world to himself, and blessing men with all heavenly and spiritual blessings.   Look at him as the Lamb on the altar giving himself for you to bring you to God, bearing and bearing away the sins of the world.   Look at him as the Lamb in the midst of the throne unsealing the book of the Father's counsels; having " all power in heaven and in earth;" " able to save you to the uttermost coming to God by him."

---

[1] Psal. xxii. 27–31.   [2] Sandys.

Behold him with firm faith, devout reverence, adoring amazement, entire dependence, ardent love, lively gratitude, and humble cheerful submission.   And thus looking to him, gird yourselves for the high and holy work to which you have devoted yourselves, and in which, if in any, you are "workers together with Christ."[1]   "Lay aside every weight, and the sin which doth so easily beset you, and run with patience the race set before you;" considering him the Apostle and High Priest of our profession, "the Author and Finisher of our faith; who, for the joy that was set before him, endured the cross, despising the shame, and is set down at the right hand of the throne of God."

[1] συνεργοί Χριστοῦ.

LECTURE III

THE COMPLAINT OF THE PRIMITIVE EVANGELISTS

ISAIAH, LIII. 1.—"Who hath believed our report? and to whom is the arm of the
Lord revealed?"

IT is a remarkable circumstance, which must have struck
every considerate student of the history of Christianity, that
frequently what was meant, and what seemed fitted, to injure or
destroy that religion, has contributed to its establishment and
extension.   Objections against its evidence have, on examination, often been found to be corroborations; and occurrences which
threatened to retard or arrest its progress have generally, in the
event, accelerated it.   "The bonds" of the apostle Paul are but
a type of a numerous class of apparently ruinous events which
"have fallen out rather to the furtherance of the Gospel."

Perhaps no event at first sight appears to wear a more sinister
aspect towards the evidence and progress of Christianity, than
the general rejection of the Gospel by the Jews, when it was first
preached to them; yet it was the means of evolving proofs of its
Divine origin which otherwise it could not have possessed; of
preventing plausible objections to which otherwise it would have
been exposed; and of opening the way for its more speedy and
extensive dissemination among the Gentiles, than, in other circumstances, could have taken place.[1]

The Messiah is represented in the prophetic scriptures, as a
sufferer—a sufferer from his own countrymen; and therefore no
conclusion can be more clear and direct than this; Had Jesus
not suffered—suffered from his countrymen—whoever, whatever
he might have been, he could not have been the predicted Mes-

[1] See "Discourses and Sayings of our Lord Jesus Christ, Illustrated."   Vol. ii.
p. 299–301.

siah of the Old Testament. Thus, what at first view to superficial minds seems a strong objection against Christianity, on
close examination not only loses all its power as an objection, but
assumes the form of a conclusive argument in its favor. The
accuser's witness disproves the accusation. When the heathens,
in the first ages of Christianity, urged, as they probably did, the
unbelief of the Jews as an objection against the truth of that
religion, its primitive teachers had but to point them to the writings of the Old Testament prophets and say, "Thus it was
written that the Messiah should suffer," and had Jesus not suffered, had he not thus suffered, we should have had one argument
fewer that he was indeed "the Christ;" nay, we should have
wanted the means of giving symmetry and completeness to our
moral demonstration, that in Jesus "we have found him of whom
Moses in the law, and the prophets did write." The answer would
have been a satisfactory one; and the reply is not less appropriate
to the modern sceptic or infidel, than to the ancient heathen.

It may well appear strange and lamentable, that when the
Messiah came to his own territories, his own people did not receive him, and that his wonderful and gracious miracles made so
little impression on them; but the more unlikely an event is in
itself, the more surprising is it that it should have been predicted;
and the exact fulfilment of such strange predictions, just in proportion to their strangeness, tends to remove every suspicion of
imposture from a considerate mind. What a striking thought,
that in their very rejection of Jesus Christ as the Messiah, his
unbelieving countrymen were unconsciously furnishing evidence
of the strongest kind that he was indeed the person they denied
him to be, and that every token of their contempt and abhorrence
but more distinctly marked him as that righteous servant of Jehovah, whom, though despised by men, and abhorred by the nation, "kings should see and arise, princes also should worship!"[1]

No prophetic oracle is better fitted for presenting this argument
in a clear and impressive form, than that contained in the last
verses of the fifty-second and the whole of the fifty-third chapter
of Isaiah, on the illustration of which we lately entered. You
will recollect that, after a preliminary discourse establishing the
Messianic reference of the oracle, I remarked to you that it

[1] Isa. xlix. 7

resolves itself into four parts :—First, a revelation made, in the person of Jehovah, of the exaltation and glory of the Messiah, as following and rising out of his humiliation and sufferings,—chap. lii. 13–15 ; second, a complaint of the first preachers of the Gospel—the good news spoken of, chap. lii. 7, and substantially contained in Jehovah's declaration concerning his righteous servant—of their comparatively little success,—chap. liii. 1 ; third, a statement on the part of the converted Jews, of the reason of this comparatively little success,—introducing a farther and more circumstantial account of the sufferings of the Messiah, and the glory which was to follow them,—chap. liii. 2–10; and fourth, a solemn declaration on the part of Jehovah, confirming the great truths contained in this statement,—chap. liii. 11, 12.

Our last discourse was occupied with the illustration of the first of these divisions. We proceed now to the consideration of the second : The complaint of the first preachers of the glad tidings of the complicated expiatory sufferings of the Messiah, and their following glories, of the comparatively little success of their ministry. This is contained in these words,[1]—" Who hath believed our report ? and to whom is the arm of the Lord revealed ?"[2]

The first question here is, Who speaks ? It is obviously not He who has just spoken ; and it is almost as obviously not the prophet, in his own person. It is not *one*, but a number, from whom the complaint comes. And who can they be but the apostles and primitive preachers of the Gospel, so picturesquely described at the 7th verse of the preceding chapter ? We need nothing more than the words of the apostle Paul to identify those spoken of at the 7th verse of the fifty-second chapter, with those speaking in the 1st verse of the fifty-third chapter,—and both with the Christian apostles and evangelists : " How shall they call on him in whom they have not believed ? and how

---

[1] In all the copies of the LXX. Κύριε is prefixed; and it is so, too, in the citations in John, xii. 38, and Rom. x. 16. The omission is remarkable. Dr. Kennicott supposes the word יהוה might in ancient MSS. have been written י, or ײ, and so, *per incuriam*, left out. His remarks, Diss. Gen. § 25, are ingenious.

[2] " Quod alibi sæpe (*e. g.*, Heb. xi., Gal. iv., Rom. viii., 2 Cor. iii.) hic quoque contigit ut perperam et incommode capita dividerentur. Qui sibi dederunt id negotii, quos pios homines nihil dubito, non raro videntur parum hoc agere ut capitum divisio sensum adjuvet non abrumpat."—MORUS. Hæc capitis distinctio aut potius divulsio omittenda est: nam initium potius a versu 13 superioris capitis fieri oportebat."—CALVIN.

shall they believe in him of whom they have not heard? and how shall they hear without a preacher? and how shall they preach except they be sent? as it is written, How beautiful are the feet of them that preach the Gospel of peace, and bring glad tidings of good things! But they" to whom these good news are brought " have not all obeyed the Gospel: for Esaias saith,"—*i. e.* plainly, says of them,—"Lord, who hath believed our report?"[1]

Having thus satisfactorily established who are to be considered as the speakers here, I shall proceed to consider the import of the complaint they utter, after making a few remarks expository of the language in which that complaint is expressed.

The word "report"[2] properly signifies something that has been heard, or something that is spoken in order to be heard. The reference in the passage before us is in no degree doubtful. The words just quoted from the tenth chapter of the Epistle to the Romans, identify " the report" here with " the Gospel" preached by the apostles. This is a strikingly descriptive designation of the gospel revelation. It is not the creature of human reason or fancy; it is no curiously-constructed theory; it is no " cunningly-devised fable;" it is not a human invention; it is not a human discovery. It is a report made to their fellow-men of what they had heard of God—what had been communicated to them by Divine revelation.

The following apostolic declarations are the best illustrations of the import of the word " report," as applied to the Gospel:— " We speak the wisdom of God in a mystery, even the hidden wisdom, which God ordained before the world unto our glory; which none of the princes of this world knew: for had they known it, they would not have crucified the Lord of glory. But, as it is written, Eye hath not seen, nor ear heard, neither have entered into the heart of man, the things which God hath prepared for them that love him. But God hath revealed them unto us by his Spirit: for the Spirit searcheth all things, yea, the deep things of God. For what man knoweth the things of a man, save the spirit of man which is in him? even so the things of God knoweth no man, but the Spirit of God. Now we have received, not the spirit of the world, but the Spirit which

---

[1] Rom. x. 14–16.

[2] שמועה is properly a feminine participle used as a noun: ἀκοή. Isa. xxviii. 9, 19. Jer. li. 46. 1 Kings, x. 7.

is of God ; that we might know the things that are freely given to us of God. Which things also we speak, not in the words which man's wisdom teacheth, but which the Holy Ghost teacheth ; comparing spiritual things with spiritual." " I declare unto you the Gospel which I preached unto you."—" I delivered unto you that which I also received." " That which was from the beginning, which we have heard, which we have seen with our eyes, which we have looked upon, and our hands have handled, of the Word of life ; (for the life was manifested, and we have seen it,"—*i. e.*, the Word, who was " in the beginning," " which was with God, which was God"—the " light" and the " life"—" the Only-begotten, who was in the bosom of the Father," he revealed him—revealed him to us,—" and bear witness, and show unto you that eternal life which was with the Father, and was manifested unto us ;) that which we have seen and heard declare we unto you, that ye also may have fellowship with us : and truly our fellowship is with the Father, and with his Son Jesus Christ."[1] The gospel is thus God's report to the apostles—their report to us ;—his testimony to them respecting his Son—their testimony to us embodying his testimony to them.

To " believe" a report, is to count it true, to reckon it a faithful saying and worthy of all acceptation, understanding the meaning of the report, and apprehending its evidence, especially that originating in the character of the reporter as well-informed and faithful, and perceiving its force. " Who hath believed our report," is, then, just equivalent to, ' Who has received as true that message we have received from Jehovah respecting his righteous Servant—these good tidings publishing peace and salvation, which, according to his command, we have proclaimed to our countrymen.'

According to the well-known usage in Hebrew poetry, commonly termed parallelism—a usage singularly conducive to the perspicuity as well as the beauty and impressiveness of Scripture—what is said literally in the first clause, is substantially repeated in figurative language in the second clause. " And to whom is the arm of the Lord revealed ?"[2] The arm, as the seat or instru-

---

[1] 1 Cor. ii. 7–13 ; xv. 1, 3. 1 John, i. 1–3.

[2] " The arm of the Lord is not to be understood *properly* but *figuratively*. By it we understand, *generally*, the power of God,—Psal. cxviii. 15 ; xviii. 1 ;—and more *particularly*, that power put forth in the work of saving grace,—Rom. i. 16 ; 1 Cor. i. 23, 24."—DURHAM.

ment of active energy, is often used as expressive of power or strength. An "arm of flesh," is human power, which is but feeble. The "mighty man" is called, The man of arm.[1] For a person to "trust in man," and to "make flesh his *arm*," is the same thing.[2] In this sense, the arm of Jehovah is his omnipotence. In this way the phrase often occurs in Scripture. "His arm," is said to bring salvation to him.[3] He works his people's deliverance by his omnipotence. He brought out his people from Egypt by a "stretched out arm."[4] In this way the phrase before us may be considered as equivalent to, 'Who perceives the glorious display made of the Divine power in the great work of human salvation through the humiliation and glory of Jehovah's righteous servant?' He to whom a person's arm is revealed, is he who sees him working, and perceives the true character of his work. The inquiry in this case is, 'Who is aware that "this is the doing of the Lord"? Who is so impressed with the magnitude and importance of what has taken place, and of which we have made the report, as to be constrained to say, not only with the Egyptian magicians, "This is the finger of God," but "This is the arm," the strong arm, "of Jehovah;" this cometh forth from the Lord of Hosts, who is "wonderful in counsel and excellent in working."' This brings out a true, an important, and an appropriate sense, and I should have been inclined to rest in it, had the words not stood in parallelism with, "Who hath believed our report?" and therefore may be expected to express the same sense, though modified in some way.

Some, perceiving the force of this remark, have supposed that "the arm of the Lord" is here a descriptive appellation of the Messiah.[5] All things are of God by his Son. He is, as it were, his Father's arm. By him "God made the worlds."

---

[1] Job, xxii. 8.   [2] Jer. xvii. 5.   [3] Isa. lix. 16.   [4] Deut. iv. 34; v. 15; xxvi. 8.

[5] דרדע יהוה. "*Brachium Domini* Athanasius et Hieronymus Christum ipsum intelligunt non temere profecto. si modo Christus accipiatur, ut sæpe alibi pro doctrina Christi. Solet enim Scriptura Christum, et Christi doctrinam seu evangelium iisdem nominibus vocare. *Verbi, sapientiæ, salutis, lucis, gloriæ. Christus* dicitur *verbum*, John, i. 1, etc. Evangelium itidem *passim.* Christus *verbum vitæ*, 1 John, i. 4; et evangelium *verbum vitæ*, Phil. ii. 16. Christus *Dei Sapientia* et evangelium pariter ibidem, 1 Cor. ii. 6, 7. Christus *salus*, Luc. i. 69, 77; et evangelium, Heb. ii. 2, 3; Acts, xiii. 46; xxviii. 28. Ille *Dominus gloriæ*, 1 Cor. ii. 8. Hoc *evangelium gloriæ* 1 Tim. i. 11. Christus *Lux*, John, i. 9; et similiter evangelium, John, iii. 19–21; Acts, xxvi. 23; Eph. v. 13. Christus *Judex*, John, v. 27; et evangelium, John, xii. 48; Heb. iv. 12. Denique Christus *potentia Dei*, 1 Cor. i. 24; et evangelium, 1 Thes. i. 5;

" All things were made by him ; and without him was not anything made that was made." He is the great agent of Divinity in creation, providence, and grace. A prime minister may be called his prince's right arm. It has been supposed that this is the reference of the expressions, " His arm shall rule for him ;" " Awake, awake, O arm of the Lord ;" " The Lord hath made bare his holy arm in the eyes of all the nations."[1] In this case, the inquiry is, " Who has seen the servant of the Lord to be what he is, the omnipotent agent of the Divine purposes ?" This is ingenious, but not satisfactory.

I have no doubt at all that the words before us look back to those which I have just quoted. The prophet had said, " The Lord" in the good news which he hath sent forth messengers to proclaim, has made bare his arm—has made an illustrious display of his power. And these messengers finding comparatively few understanding and believing these messages, complain. ' The arm of the Lord is made bare, but it is among the blind ;— bare as it is, To whom is it revealed ?' Keeping to the general meaning of " the arm of the Lord," that in which he displays —by which He exerts—his strength, I am strongly disposed to consider the term as just a figurative expression for what is literally described as the " report" in the first clause of the verse. The Gospel is a revelation of the most wonderful display of divine power, as well as divine wisdom and grace, God ever made to the universe ; it was originally accompanied with mighty supernatural works as its evidence ;[2] and it is the powerful instrument by which He effects all the moral miracles of the

---

[1] Cor. ii. 4 ; vi. 20 ; Rom. i. 16. Sive igitur *evangelium Christi* sive *Christus evangelizatus* intelligatur eodem res volvitur."—MORUS. " Credere Christo et credere evangelio idem reapse est."—CAPELLUS. AUGUSTINE, interpreting " the arm of the Lord," of Christ, derives an argument from it, more ingenious than solid, for the consubstantiality of the Father and the Son : " Brachium ejusdem est substantiæ cum pectore unde procedit ; nec ab eo separatur cum porrigitur : sic nec Filius missus in mundum a Patre separatur, cui est consubstantialis." It is treason against truth to defend it with arguments like these.

[1] John, i. 3. Isa. xl. 10 ; li. 9 ; lii. 10.

[2] It was attended with the Holy Ghost—" the power of the Highest"—sent down from heaven. The manner in which the words are quoted, John, xii. 37, 38, supports this view. But the unbelieving Jews, instead of recognising in these miraculous accompaniments a revelation of " the arm of the Lord," considered them as " the working of Satan, with all power, and signs, and lying wonders :"—" He casteth out devils by Beelzebub, the prince of the devils."—Luke, xi. 18.

new creation. The gospel is "the power of God unto salvation to every one that believeth." It is the effectual means of God's saving men, which is an exertion of "the exceeding greatness of his power —according to the working of the might of his power."[1] The preaching of Christ crucified, the very report referred to, though men count it a foolish and a weak thing, is really the power of God and the wisdom of God. But "it is hid to them who are lost, whose eyes are blinded by the god of this world." In this sense, which I apprehend is the true one, to have "the arm of the Lord revealed," is just substantially the same thing as to "believe the report." If the reference be to the power that the gospel reveals in the purchase of redemption, then the meaning is, 'Who so understands, believes, the gospel as to see in it the manifestation of saving omnipotence?' If the reference be to the power which the gospel exerts under the influence of the Spirit in the application of redemption, then the meaning is, 'Who, through the belief of the Gospel which works effectually only in them who believe, has experienced its power as the arm of God in producing a new creation, in pulling down strongholds, and bringing down every high thought to the obedience of Christ?' The whole inquiry seems equivalent to,—'Who by truly believing, experiences the saving power of the Gospel of the grace of God? Who apprehends the meaning and evidence of the gospel revelation, and thus becomes sensible of the efficacy of the Divine power which it at once reveals and exerts?' The *words* are now, we trust, sufficiently explained.

It remains that we inquire into the import of the complaint which they embody. "Who hath believed our report?" and to[2] whom is the arm of the Lord revealed?" The reference is plainly to the effects of the first preaching of the Gospel. Now we know the appointed order was "To the Jew first." We are not to interpret the words as to make them contain a prophecy of complete want of success, as if no Jews were to become converts to the faith of the deeply humbled—gloriously exalted— servant of Jehovah. The event proves that this cannot be its

---

[1] "Τὸ ὑπερβάλλον μέγεθος τῆς δυνάμεως αὐτοῦ—κατὰ τὴν ἐνέργειαν τοῦ κράτος τῆς ἰσχύος αὐτοῦ."—Eph. i. 19.

[2] Hengstenberg thinks that the use of the particle עַל, instead of אֶל, or לְ, intimates that the revelation is from above. Hitzig supposes an allusion to the elevation of the arm itself.

import. Three thousand believed the report when first published by Peter; and to them "the arm of the Lord was revealed." They felt its power; and though formerly enemies, they bowed to the resistless might of mercy;[1] and ere long we find in Jerusalem tens of thousands[2] bearing the name of Christ. The phraseology does not necessarily suggest any such idea. No doubt interrogations are often equivalent to strong negations, as, "Who may abide the day of his coming? and who shall stand when he appeareth?" "Who shall abide with the devouring fire? Who shall dwell with everlasting burnings."[3] The answer there is plainly, 'None.' The questions are stronger than any negative. 'None may abide; none can stand; none can dwell.' But such interrogations are by no means uniformly equivalent to absolute negations. When Solomon says, "A faithful man who can find?"[4] he certainly intends to intimate not the impossibility, but only the difficulty, of meeting with such a person: not that there are none, but that there were few such to be found. He meant to say, 'Such men form a small class;'—not, 'No such class exists.' In like manner, when the prophet presents the apostles and evangelists engaged in the opening of the New Dispensation to the Jews, as saying, "Who hath believed our report? and to whom is the arm of the Lord revealed?" he intimates not that they should have no converts among their countrymen, but that they should have few.[5]

And even this explication must be taken with limitations. *Absolutely* considered, the converts among the Jews when the Gospel was first preached to them, were not *few*. Read the Acts of the Apostles, and you will find that the Christian Church was composed of many thousands before Peter was commissioned to execute the second part of his honorable commission —to use the keys of the kingdom of heaven to open its gates to the Gentiles. But there were *comparatively* few converts among the Jews.

There were few in comparison of what, from the clearness of the evidence for the Messiahship of Jesus Christ, there should have been. Had justice been done to that evidence, all, without exception, to whom it became known, would have been converts.

---

[1] Acts, ii. 41.   [2] "Πόσαι μυριάδες Ἰουδαίων τῶν πεπιστευκότων.—Acts, xxi. 20.
[3] Mal. iii. 2. Isa. xxiii. 14.   [4] Prov. xx. 6.
[5] " *Quis?* quasi dicat quam pauci."—*Glossa Ordin.*

There were few, in comparison of those who rejected the Gospel, continuing in unbelief. "The election obtained; but the rest," forming by far the greater body of the nation, "were blinded." The oracle of Esaias was verified—"Though the number of the children of Israel was as the sand of the sea, a remnant only was saved." [1] They did not *all* believe the Gospel. The great body of them were "a disobedient and gainsaying people."

They were few in comparison of what the apostles wished and expected. Their heart's desire and prayer to God was, that Israel, that all Israel, might be saved; and they thought that the evidence which had convinced themselves must convince all others to whom it was presented. The same number appears great or small, according to circumstances. "All men come to him," said John's disciples. "No man," says John, "receiveth his testimony." [2] Thus far the import of the plaintive inquiry seems satisfactorily ascertained. It is a prediction that comparatively few of the Jews, to whom the Gospel was to be first preached, should believe it, and, by believing it, experience its Divine power to save, and that this should excite a feeling of mingled wonder and regret on the part of its primitive preachers.

It is not impossible that the words may be intended to express another thought. The interrogative "who" [3] has been considered as referring not merely to number, but to quality. The apostles, like the rest of their countrymen, originally expected that when the Messiah came, the great, the wealthy, the wise, and the learned, should be found in the foremost ranks of his followers. They were astonished at what our Lord said as to the difficulty of a rich man being saved. They exclaimed, "Who then can be saved?" [4] The words may suggest the thought, "Have any of the Scribes and Pharisees, the chief priests and the rulers, believed on him?" What kind of persons have believed our report? to what kind of persons hath the arm of the Lord been revealed? Not only are many called while few are chosen; but even among the chosen, comparatively few belong to the better classes. When the apostle has stated that the preaching of Christ crucified—that is, the report—though to the Jews a stumbling-block and to the Greeks foolishness, was to all who were called, both Jew and Greek, the power of God and the wisdom of God,

---

[1] Rom. ix. 27.   [2] John, iii. 26, 32.   [3] מִי.   [4] Matth. xix. 25.

because the foolishness of God is wiser than men, and the weakness of God stronger than men, he adds, " Ye see your calling, brethren, how that not many wise men after the flesh, not many mighty, not many noble, are called ; but God hath chosen the foolish things of the world to confound the wise ; and God hath chosen the weak things of the world to confound the things which are mighty ; and base things of the world, and things which are despised, hath God chosen, yea, and things which are not, to bring to naught things that are." The arm of the Lord was " hid from the wise and prudent, and revealed to babes." [1] There is the greater probability that this thought was intended to be insinuated, if not expressed, from the fact that the reasons assigned in the following verses for the rejection of the Gospel message and the Saviour it reveals, while applicable to the Jews generally, were peculiarly so to the higher classes among them.

Before passing from this part of the oracle, I may remark the strange shifts to which the most learned and judicious of the anti-Messianic interpreters are reduced, in bringing anything like meaning out of the words which we have found so replete with important truth. One of them, who considers the heathens as speaking after Jehovah had manifested his favor to Israel, subsequently to a long period of degradation—" Had we merely heard, and not seen, Jehovah's kindness to his people, we could not have believed it. To whom was there ever made such a manifestation of Jehovah as to us, in this wonderful change in the circumstances of his chosen nation ?" If this is to interpret, the Bible is a book of riddles, and you may extract any meaning you please out of any combination of words you may find in it. [2]

We should now proceed to the consideration of the third and principal division of the oracle, consisting of a statement on the part of the Jewish converts—those who had believed the report, and to whom the arm of the Lord had been revealed—of the reasons why so few of the Jewish people had received the Gospel and embraced the Saviour it reveals, introducing an account of the sufferings of the Messiah as violent, severe, penal, vicarious, expiatory, and saving, and of the glory that was to follow them. It is obvious we have no time to proceed with this

---

[1] 1 Cor. i. 23–28.   Matth. xi. 25.

[2] " Si id est interpretari, ex quocunque loco, quæ placent extundi poterunt."— JAHN.

part of the subject at present; but it may serve a good purpose to indicate the leading subdivision and train of thought in this part of the oracle, which reaches from the beginning of the 2d verse to the end of the 10th. In the 2d and 3d verses, they state the general rejection of the Messiah by their countrymen—a rejection in which they for a season joined—and its causes in the meanness of his origin, the abjectness of his external condition, and his severe, multiplied, and judgment-like sufferings. In the 4th verse, they state that his unexampled tenderness of sympathy and gracious miracles should have induced them to receive him, but that, so strong were their prejudices, that they imputed his remarkable sufferings to remarkable though unknown sins, considering him as a signal monument of the Divine indignation—"the man who saw affliction by the rod of God's wrath." In the 5th verse, they give the true account of his unparalleled sufferings—they were penal, vicarious, expiatory, and saving. In the 6th, 7th, 8th, and 9th verses, they give, as it were, a history of our Lord's sufferings, from their origin to their close. God constituted him the victim for human transgressions. Exaction was made, and he became answerable. He endured his sufferings with uncomplaining patience. He was most unjustly, though under the cloak of legal forms, brought to a violent death, through the instrumentality of the Jewish people; and in his being honorably interred among the rich, while a grave had been destined him among malefactors, an intimation of his innocence was given, even when he had been put to death under the charge of blasphemy and treason. In the 10th verse, they state that, amid all his sufferings, he was the object of the complacent approbation of Jehovah, and that this was to be proved, on his having finished his offering for the expiation of human guilt, by his seeing his seed, prolonging his days, and having the pleasure of Jehovah prospering in his hand. So closely connected and consecutive is that passage, which, to a superficial reader, seems so disjointed and immethodical. Turn these hints in your mind, and you will be the better fitted for accompanying us in that more close investigation of the meaning of this paragraph, on which, if it please God, we will enter in our next discourse.

In conclusion, I would press on your consideration and my own, the fact that the Divine report here referred to has reached our ears, and is urged on our belief, and that the arm of the Lord is still bare in the sight of the nations, and the momentous bearings which this fact has on our duty and on our destiny. The apostles have long ago fallen asleep. They rest from their labors, and their works do follow them. But in their inspired writings they still go, and will continue to go, unto all the world, preaching the Gospel to every creature, till the end come, and the mystery of God be finished. And have we not heard their report? "Yea, verily, their sound went unto all the earth, and their words to the ends of the world." "To us hath the word of this salvation come." And this report is still the arm of the Lord, exhibiting saving power, exerting saving power. It is the everlasting Gospel, powerful still through God. His arm is not shortened that it cannot save. Miracles of mercy are still done by this arm of the Lord. But still, it is true, "*all* have not obeyed the Gospel." Still it is true, all have not felt its transforming power. The great majority, even in those countries where the Gospel is best known, are deaf to the report, blind to the arm of the Lord. Still, is there abundant reason, on the part of the heralds of mercy, to complain, "Who hath believed our report? and to whom is the arm of the Lord revealed?"

This should lead the minister of the Gospel often to ask, Am I proclaiming the report as I ought, without extenuation, without exaggeration—the pure, free, full Gospel of God's grace? Do I give forth no uncertain sound? Do I throw no unhallowed covering—it may be under the pretext of an ornament—over the bared arm of the Lord? How is it that our ministry is in so limited a degree successful?

And it should lead the hearer of the Gospel often to ask, Have I believed the report? Has the arm of the Lord been revealed *to* me, *in* me? You have the blessedness of those who hear,—have you the blessedness of those who "*know*, the joyful sound?" The first is a privilege, but it is the last that is true secure blessedness. Have you understood the Gospel? Alas, how many do not! Have you believed the Gospel? Alas, how few do! You have received this grace of God. We beseech you that you receive it not in vain. Has it come to you not in word only, but in power, with the Holy Ghost, and much assurance? Remember, the report is not believed if the arm of the Lord is not revealed. The Gospel "works effectually," both in making holy and happy, wherever it is believed, and only when it is believed. If you have believed the report, hold it fast: beware of the evil heart of unbelief; beware of the power of this present evil world. Keep the truth and its evidence constantly before your minds, and let your habitual prayer be, " Lord, increase my faith." Has the arm of the Lord been revealed to you? Have you experienced his power, put forth by its instrumentality, quieting the jealousies of guilt, calming the tumult of passion, overmastering every opposing influence, which would keep you secular, and impure, and miserable.   Oh, how little of the power of the Gospel to sanctify and bless have the holiest and the happiest of us yet experienced! Let us seek to be thoroughly " transformed " by that " renewing of the mind" which the faith of the Gospel produces, that we may " prove the good, and perfect, and acceptable will of the Lord."

What a mercy the arm of the Lord is bared for salvation, not for destruction! Think of this ye who have not yet believed the report—to whom the arm of the Lord has not yet been revealed. That report will not always be proclaimed to you. Pass the boundary which divides time from eternity, unbelieving and disobedient, and to you it will come no more forever. You will then know that it is indeed a true report; but to you it never can become the vehicle of salvation.   He called — oh, how often, how urgently!—and ye refused; He stretched out his hands, but ye would not regard.   Then He " will laugh at your calamity, and mock when your fear cometh ; when your fear cometh as desolation, and your destruction cometh as a whirlwind ; when distress and anguish cometh upon you."   The arm now bared for salvation will one day be bared for vengeance. If, while favor is showed to you, ye will not learn righteousness ; if, in the land of uprightness, ye will do unjustly; if ye will not behold the majesty of the Lord ; if, when his hand is lifted up, ye will not see, be assured that time is coming when ye shall see, and when the fire of his enemies shall devour you. Oh, listen to his salutary threatenings, and let them shake your inmost soul with a healthful commotion.   "See now that I, even I, am He, and there is no God with me. I kill, and I make alive ; I wound, and I heal ; neither is there any that can deliver out of my hand. For I lift up my hand to heaven, and say, I live forever. If I whet my glittering sword, and mine hand take hold on judgment, I will render vengeance to my enemies, and will reward them that hate me. I will make mine arrows drunk with blood, and my sword shall devour flesh, with the blood of the slain and of the captives, from the beginning of revenges on the enemy." Blessed be God it is not come to this yet with any of us. It is still, "Rejoice, O ye nations, with his people. Look unto me, all ye ends of the earth, and be ye saved, for I am God and not man." "To-day, if ye will hear my voice." We again proclaim the report; we again point to the arm bared for deliverance; we again perform the ministry of reconciliation. "God is in Christ reconciling the world to himself, not imputing to men their trespasses, seeing He hath made him who knew no sin to be sin for us, that we might be made the righteousness of God in him." "We beseech you that ye receive not *this* grace of God in vain. For He saith, I have heard thee in a time accepted, and in the day of salvation have I succored thee. Behold, *now* is the accepted time; behold, *now* is the day of salvation." The next hour may be too late. Turn at *his* reproof. "Turn ye, turn ye, why will ye die?" "He that, being often reproved, hardeneth his neck, shall suddenly be destroyed, and that without remedy."

LECTURE IV

Isaiah, liii. 2-4.—" For he shall grow up before him as a tender plant, and as a root out of a dry ground : he hath no form nor comeliness; and when we shall see him, there is no beauty that we should desire him. He is despised and rejected of men ; a man of sorrows, and acquainted with grief ; and we hid as it were our faces from him : he was despised, and we esteemed him not. Surely he hath borne our griefs, and carried our sorrows : yet we did esteem him stricken, smitten of God, and afflicted."

THE prophetic oracle, contained in the three concluding verses of the lii. and the whole of the liii. chapter of the Prophecies of Isaiah, in the illustration of which we are engaged, resolves itself, as I have repeatedly had occasion to observe, into four sections. First, a revelation made, in the person of Jehovah, of the exaltation and glory of the Messiah, as following and rising out of his humiliation and sufferings, chap. lii. 13–15; second, a complaint of little success on the part of the first preachers of the Gospel—the "good news" spoken of, chap. lii. 7, and substantially contained in Jehovah's declaration concerning his righteous servant, chap. liii. 1; third, a statement, on the part of the converted Jews, of the causes of this comparatively little success—introducing a farther and more circumstantial account of the sufferings of the Messiah, and of the glory which was to follow them, chap. liii. 2–10; and, fourth, a solemn declaration, on the part of Jehovah, confirming the great truths contained in this statement, chap. liii. 11, 12.

We have considered the first two of these sections, and are now about to enter on the consideration of the third,—a statement, on the part of the converted Jews, of the causes of this comparatively little success of the first preachers of the Gospel —introducing a farther and more circumstantial account of th

sufferings of the Messiah, and of the glory which was to follow
them.

There can be no reasonable doubt that the words, verses 2–10,
are spoken as by converted Jews, in reply to the complaint
of the first preachers of the Gospel.[1] They are plainly the
words of *converts*—persons who had rejected, but who now had
cordially received "the servant of the Lord;" who had altogether misconceived his true character, verses 2, 3, but had
"repented"—changed their mind—verses 5–10; and they are
as plainly the words of *Jewish* converts, for they claim a peculiar relation to that nation, by whose wickedness he had been
brought to a violent and untimely death, verse 8. The character of the speakers in this section is very strikingly described
by the apostle Peter: "By whose stripes ye are healed. For
ye were as sheep going astray; but are now returned unto the
Shepherd and Bishop of your souls."[2]

This reply of the converted Jews naturally divides itself into
five parts: first, a statement of the reasons of the rejection of
the Messiah by the great body of their countrymen, verses 2, 3;
second, a statement of what ought to have induced them to receive him, but did not, verse 4; third, an account of the true
nature, cause, and design of the Messiah's sufferings, verse 5;
fourth, a brief history of these sufferings from their origin to
their close, verses 6–9; and, fifth, a statement of the glorious
result of the sufferings of the Messiah as a proof of his being,
notwithstanding these sufferings—on account of these sufferings—the object of the peculiarly complacent regard of Jehovah, verse 10.

The substance of the whole may be thus expressed:—'The
causes why so few of the Jews receive apostolic message are to
be found in their misapprehension of his true character. He
was not the kind of Messiah they desired and expected. When
they looked at his mean origin, abject condition, and severe and
multiplied sufferings, they could not recognize in him the promised deliverer of their nation. Though there was much about
him which should have led them to a different conclusion—
especially his unexampled sympathy and gracious miracles,—

---

[1] "Alios nunc loquentes inducit propheta—Judæos nempe cum servo Dei viven-
tes."—STORR.

[2] 1 Pet. ii. 24, 25.

yet, so strong was their prejudices, that they considered him as, in a remarkable degree, the object of the Divine displeasure, on account of great though unknown crimes. Such was the general state of the mind of the Jewish people respecting the Messiah,—such had been the state of their own minds. But they now knew that he had suffered in the room of men to obtain their salvation. He had been divinely constituted the victim for the sins of men, and had, with meek submission, answered all the requisitions of the Divine law on those in whose place he stood. By a shocking combination of the forms of law with the grossest injustice, indicating the extreme depravity of those among whom, and by whom, such a mockery of justice could be perpetrated, he had been brought to an untimely, violent, disgraceful death. His grave had been appointed for him along with the malefactors ; but while in the state of the dead, he lay in a rich man's sepulchre. In undergoing the whole of these divinely-appointed and divinely-inflicted sufferings, he was the object of the complacent approbation of Jehovah, who manifested his approbation of him and his work, by restoring him to an undying life, and giving him a numerous spiritual seed, and making him the prosperous administrator of the great divine economy of mercy.' Such is, I am persuaded, the substance of the section, on the illustration of which we are about to enter ; and it will be my object to make it plain to you that the words do indeed convey these sentiments.

Let us, then, with all the attention in our power, consider the statement made by the converted Jews, of the causes why the Messiah was so generally rejected by his countrymen, and why so few comparatively believed the report of the primitive preachers of the Gospel, or recognized and felt that Divine power, of which that report is at once the record and the instrument. " For he shall grow up before Him as a tender plant, and as a root out of a dry ground : he hath no form nor comeliness ; and when we shall see him, there is no beauty that we should desire him. He is despised and rejected of men ; a man of sorrows, and acquainted with grief; and we hid as it were our faces from him : he was despised, and we esteemed him not." The confusion of tenses in these words, arising from translating very literally out of one language into another of very different idiom, throws obscurity over the passage to an English reader. The meaning would be plainer if the whole statement, referring, as it does, to past events, had been expressed in the past tense. 'For he grew up;" 'he had no form;' 'he was despised:' as well as, 'He was despised, and we esteemed him not;' 'he hath borne;' 'we did esteem,' etc.

In the answer of the converted Jews, there is a plain refer- ence to the question-form in which the primitive preachers utter their complaint. The connective particle "for" is equivalent to, 'The reason why few comparatively believe your report—why the arm of the Lord is revealed to comparatively few, is, that the servant of the Lord, the great subject of that report, "grew up before Him as a tender plant, and as a root out of a dry ground: he had no form nor comeliness; and when we saw him, there was no beauty that we should desire him. He was despised and rejected of men; a man of sorrows, and acquaint- ed with grief; and we hid as it were our faces from him: he was despised, and we esteemed him not."' I will endeavor, first, to explain what may appear difficult in these words, and then attempt to unfold their import, as a statement of the rea- sons why the Messiah was so generally rejected by his country- men while among them, and why the apostles' report concern- ing him was so generally discredited.

"He grew up before Him as a tender plant." The word ren- dered "tender plant"[1] properly signifies "a suckling;" and, after some of the most ancient versions, some very learned in- terpreters have thus understood it in the passage before us. They render it, 'he came forth an infant;'[2] and seek the literal fulfilment of the prediction in the facts so beautifully narrated in the beginning of the second chapter of Luke's gospel. The first exhibition of the Messiah was to the shepherds,—a new-born "babe wrapped in swaddling-clothes, lying in a manger." The word is, however, often applied to vegetables, just making their way out of the earth—sprouts; and the parallel word, rendered "root,"[3] undoubtedly means a shoot springing forth from a root; and as "out of a dry ground" seems to refer to both expressions, there can be but little doubt of its meaning. The image before

---

[1] יונק.

[2] "Succrevit servus Deei cui tantam majestatem tribuisti (lii. 13), uti alius quisque infans succrescat in conspectu ejus."—STORR.

[3] שרש.

the prophet's mind is a tender plant, or a slender shoot from
the root of a decayed tree, springing up in an arid, barren soil.[1]

There is some difficulty as to the *meaning* of the phrase, " before him," rising chiefly from the uncertainty of its reference.
Who is the person before whom "the servant of Jehovah" grows
up, or comes forth, like a tender plant—a shoot from a root in
a desert? Some refer it to Jehovah. " He grew up before
Him"—under his eye,—the object, to Him, of deep interest and
entire complacency. 'The grace of God was on him.'[2] Others,
rendering the words " in their sight," refer it to the Jewish
people, and suppose the meaning to be, 'He, in their estimation,
was as a tender plant, and a shoot from the root of a decayed
tree in a desert place,'—*i. e.*, they considered him as the fit object of contempt. Had the Jewish people been mentioned in the
previous context, I should have thought this a very probable
interpretation ; but, as they are not, it seems to me inadmissible.
Others consider the phrase as referring to the Messiah himself,
rendering it, ' He grew up, " as to his appearance," as a tender
plant—a shoot from the root of a decayed tree.' Upon the
whole, I prefer the first mode of interpretation. The word rendered " before" sometimes conveys the idea of benignant influence ; as, "He is green before the sun."[3] With his eye set on
him, Jehovah had him always before Him.

" He had no form nor comeliness ; and, when we saw him"—
looked on him, considered him,—" there was no beauty that we
should desire him."[4] The words have been more literally rendered, 'He had neither form nor splendor that we should regard him, nor appearance that we should desire him.' There

---

[1] יונק is generic,—שׁרשׁ is specific, as either springing from the root of a decayed
or cut down tree. " Supervacaneum hic existimamus anquirere quid per terram
sitientem intelligi debeat. Marias Bethlehem an gens Judaica. Non est immorandum
in ascensu, aut terra silienti, sed in scopo prophetæ ac proportione terminorum :
sicut nihil tristius est agricolis, quam surculus oriens ex terra sitiente nihil erit in
oculis hominum calamitosius abjectiusque Christo."—Morus.

[2] " Παρὰ Θεῷ,"—Luke, ii. 52. " Deo ei favente," is Le Clerc's exposition. " *Coram
eo* opponitur sensibus humanis."—Calvin. " Deo presente, providente, ac probante,
natus est ; Deo presente ac providente crevit puer et adolevit. Ab hominibus de-
spectus ; Deo carus."—Vitringa.—Eccles. ii 26. 1 Pet. iii. 4, comp. Prov. viii. 30.
" Quo modo tenella planta coram agricola, qui eam plantavit dicitur crescere—qua-
tenus ejus curam singularem habet."—Spanheim.   [3] Job, viii. 16.

[4] " ' Form' is here put for ' beautiful or handsome form,' as, 1 Sam. xvi. 18, David
is called ' a man of form.' "—Alexander.

was nothing about him fitted to attract our notice, to fix our regard, to awaken our admiration.[1]

The words that follow, "He was despised and rejected of men,"[2] expressing, in a positive form, what had been negatively stated in the preceding words, need no particular explication. They are equivalent to, 'He was an object of general contempt.'[3]

"A man of sorrows" is, according to the Hebrew idiom, an emphatic expression for a very sorrowful or afflicted man,—just as a man of war is a warlike man; a man of understanding a very intelligent man; a man of iniquity a very bad man; a man of words[4] an eloquent man; a man of chastisements or reproofs[5] a man who is frequently chastised or reproved.

The expression rendered "acquainted with griefs," has been considered by some as equivalent to, distinguished by, known for, suffering or disease—sickness—as the word literally signifies. The rendering of our translators, 'Acquainted with grief or sickness, familiar with it as an intimate associate,' is far more appropriate, and better adapted to the parallelism.[6] It is very well given in our metrical paraphrase, "Grief was his close companion still."

The words rendered, "And we hid as it were our faces from him," have been variously rendered and explained. Some connect the clause with what follows, in this way, 'Like a thing from which men turn away the face, so we proudly contemned

---

[1] "From this text, and chap. lii. 14, Justin Martyr, Clemens, Alexandrinus, Tertullian, and others of the ancient fathers, concluded our Saviour's person to have been deformed,—an opinion, in my judgment, not at all probable. In the fourth and fifth centuries a quite contrary notion was advanced, that he was a person of extraordinary comeliness, Psal. xlv. 3. From these two contrary opinions, we may conclude that the making or setting up the image or picture of Christ was no part of religious worship in the very early ages of Christianity."—LOWTH. Calmet has a dissertation, "Sur la Beauté de Jesus Christ." "Utique mihi persuadeo, Messiæ nostro quod ad speciem corporis et compositionem membrorum formam constitisse honestissimam: sed de ea, hic plane non agitur."—VITRINGA. It is his form as Messiah that is referred to, and that viewed with the prejudiced eye of a Jew. "The want of form and comeliness is not to be understood of any personal defect in our Lord's human nature, but in respect of the tract of his life, that it was low and mean, —without that external grandeur, pomp, and splendor, which the world esteem to be comeliness and beauty."—DURHAM.

[2] "אישים is a rare plural, instead of אנשים,—occurring only besides in Psal. cxli. 4; Prov. viii. 4."—HENDERSON.

[3] Symmachus' rendering is—"ἐλάχιστος, ἀνδρῶν," for חדל אישים.

[4] Exod. iv. 10.   [5] Prov. xxix. 1.

[6] Symmachus' rendering, "γνωστός νόσω," is preferable to that of the LXX.—"εἰδὼς φέρειν μαλακίαν."

him.' It is doubtful whether the hiding of the face refers to the
servant of the Lord, or to his countrymen. Some render it,
' He was like one hiding the face from us,'—with allusion to
the veiling of the face by the lepers ; as the Psalmist says, " I
have borne reproach ; shame hath covered my face."[1] No doubt
the Jews looked on Jesus with more horror than they did on
any leper ; yet, as he was unconscious of crime, and as it is said
expressly, " he hid not his face from shame and spitting," upon
the whole, we prefer the rendering, ' He was as one before
whom a man covers his face. His appearance was to us disgust-
ing ; we covered our faces that we might not see him.'[2]

"He was despised," may with equal propriety be rendered,
' we despised him ;' and " we esteemed him not," ' we esteemed
him as nothing.' This is an instance of what is very common
in Hebrew composition—the stating a sentiment first positively,
and then negatively, to make the statement more emphatic.
' We despised him ; we did not esteem him.'

Having thus explained the words, let us now consider what
is their import, as an answer to the complaining question of the
primitive evangelists, " Who hath believed our report? and to
whom is the arm of the Lord revealed ?" They assign the
reason for this. The words indicate this general truth. The
report is not believed ; and he whom it proclaims to be the promised deliverer is generally rejected, because he is not at all such
a person as the Jewish people expected and desired as the Messiah. The emblem under which they delighted to think of the
promised deliverer, was " a tree in the midst of the earth, the
height of which was great, reaching to heaven, and the sight
thereof to all the earth : the leaves whereof were fair, and the
fruit thereof much ; the hills covered with its shadow, and the
boughs thereof, like the goodly cedars, sending out its boughs to
the sea, and its branches to the river." But, instead of this,
nothing met their view but an insignificant and puny plant,—a

[1] Psal. lxix. 7.

[2] " Alii, qui ad damnatos, respexere Romanos ritu juxta prætoris formulam, ' I
lictor, collega manus, caput obnubito, infelici arbori suspendito,' eo tueri se possunt
quod olim antequam nomen Romanum notum esset, constat hunc morem Persis non
ignotum fuisse ex historia Estheræ et Amani ut patet ex iis quæ commentantur
Hebræi, quos vide ad Esther vii. ubi postquam ira regis in Amanum exarsit additus:
' Et statim operuerunt faciem ejus:' Et de Sedechia, cum cantivus ductus est,
Ezech. xii. 12, ' Facies ejus operietur.' Morem illum obnubendi capita damnatorum
apud orientales viguisse patet ex Job, ix. 24 ; xl. 8."—Morus.

sickly shoot sprung from the root of a decayed tree in the midst of the wilderness. That this should be " the Plant of Renown," seemed to them inconceivable.

But the words not only suggest this general truth, but they assign the three causes which chiefly led to the rejection of the Saviour, and the disbelief of his Gospel, among his countrymen ; the meanness of his origin ; the abjectness of his external appearance ; and his severe and multiplied sufferings.

The first cause assigned for the rejection of the Messiah, and the disbelief of his Gospel, was the meanness of his origin. No figure could have more graphically represented the facts of the case than that employed in the prophetic oracle. In the midst of wide-extended wastes, a sickly plant raises its head above the arid sand, which seem to have no juices to nourish it; a slender shoot springs from the root, buried in the earth, of a tree which the blast of the desert has laid low, or the wasting power of time withered up. The family of David, from which our Saviour sprung, was the most illustrious of all royal houses, in the estimation of the Jews; but its ancient honors had long been lost and forgotten, like a mighty tree, whose root alone remains, and sends forth only a few shoots, indicating little more than that the power of vegetation is not altogether extinguished. The lineal descendant of David was a Nazarene carpenter; and Jesus was supposed to be his son. The circumstances of our Lord's origin were all fitted to produce strong prejudice against him in the Jewish mind. Born in a stable—cradled in a manger—bred in Galilee, in Nazareth of Galilee—his supposed father a carpenter, and himself his assistant in his humble toils,—can this be the king whom Jehovah is to set on his holy hill of Zion, and to whom he is to give the heathen as his inheritance, and the uttermost ends of the earth as his possession? Is this he of whom the prophet so loftily sings, " Unto us a child is born, unto us a son is given ; and the government shall be upon his shoulder; and his name shall be called Wonderful, Counsellor, The mighty God, The everlasting Father, The Prince of Peace. Of the increase of his government and peace there shall be no end." ?[1] The prediction was verified. The general sentiment of our Lord's contemporaries is expressed in such expressions as these,

[1] Isa. ix. 6, 7.

—"Can any good thing come out of Nazareth?"   "Is not this the carpenter's son? is not his mother called Mary? and his brethren, James, and Joses, and Simon, and Judas? And his sisters, are they not all with us?"[1] Thus were they offended, stumbled at him, as "the tender plant," the "root out of the dry ground."

A second cause assigned by the converted Jews for the general rejection of the Messiah, and disbelief of the Gospel, by their countrymen, is the abjectness of his external condition. "He had no form nor comeliness" that they should regard him; "no beauty that they should desire him." He was, in truth, all fair; there was no spot in him; he was "the chief among ten thousand, and altogether lovely." The glory of God was in his countenance; he had a glory, "the glory of the Only-begotten of the Father." He was all-glorious, but it was within; and they had no eyes to behold such glories. He had none of the qualities they looked for in their deliverer. He had no treasures, no armies. "The foxes had holes, the birds of the air nests; he had not where to lay his head." He had to work a miracle to enable him to pay the temple tax. His most intimate friends belonged to the humbler classes of society—fishermen and publicans. There does not appear to be any reference in the words, "He had no form nor comeliness," "no beauty," to the form of his body, or to the lineaments of his countenance. The idea intended to be conveyed is, the whole that was visible to the carnal Jews, about the servant of the Lord, was of a kind not to excite their respect, but to draw forth their contempt and indignation, when found in one who seemed to be laying claim to the honors of Messiahship.

Few things went farther in hardening the great body of the Jews against the natural influence of the proofs brought forward by our Lord for his Messiahship, than his general rejection by the classes most distinguished for their rank and learning. "He was despised and rejected of men." They expected that to Shiloh should be the gathering of the people, and that their rulers should be among the foremost to do him homage. The Pharisees, the most influential of the Jewish sects, called him a Samaritan and a demoniac. Herod and his men of war set him at nought. The

[1] Matth. xiii. 55, 56.

rulers of the Jews handed him over to the Roman governor, that he might be crucified, as if unworthy even of dying any death appointed by Jewish law or usage for the punishment of a Jewish criminal. The people preferred Barabbas, a convicted sentenced robber and murderer, to him; and he was nailed to the middle cross, as deserving of greater infamy than either of his companions in suffering. All these things had a plain tendency to induce, and no doubt did exert a powerful influence in inducing, the body of the Jewish people, notwithstanding the miracles of Jesus and his apostles, to reject him as the Messiah, and them as divinely-appointed messengers.

The third reason assigned by the Jewish converts for the general rejection of Christ and his Gospel by their countrymen, is his numerous and severe sufferings. "He was a man of sorrows, and acquainted with griefs; and therefore they hid as it were their faces from him : he was despised, and they esteemed him not." The Jews expected a prosperous and happy prince for their Messiah. But the Messiah, when he came, was distinguished by the unparalleled number, variety, and severity of his sufferings, both bodily and mental. He was, above all other men, " the Man who knew affliction by the rod of God's wrath." "There never was sorrow like unto the sorrow wherewith the Lord afflicted him in the day of his fierce anger." "He was poured out like water, and all his bones were out of joint; his heart was melted like wax in the midst of his bowels; his strength was dried like a potsherd; his tongue cleaved to his jaws, and he was brought to the dust of death." He was apprehended as a criminal, condemned as a blasphemer and traitor, and executed like a felonious slave. His sufferings, while they fixed attention, excited disgust and horror. Men wished to have nothing to do with such an ill-fated man. He was " as a worm, and no man—a reproach of men, and despised of the people. All that saw him laughed him to scorn." These sufferings, in a great variety of ways, acted as obstacles in the way of men becoming his disciples. The cross was the master stumbling-block to the Jew. It is so still.

The Jewish converts, having thus assigned the reasons why they for a season rejected the Messiah, and why the great body of their countrymen reject him still, proceed to show what ought to have induced them to receive him, though it did not. This is the second part of their reply to the complaint of the primitive preachers,[1] verse 4, "Surely[2] he hath borne our griefs, and carried our sorrows: yet we did esteem him stricken, smitten of God, and afflicted."

The great body of orthodox expositors have considered the first part of this verse as the first enunciation of the doctrine of the vicarious character of our Lord's sufferings, which is more fully illustrated in the succeeding verses. The reasons of their taking this view of the passage seem to be, that the Greek version commonly in use in the times of the apostles renders the word *sins* which our translators render *griefs*—that they supposed that the apostle Peter, in his first Epistle,[3] when asserting the vicarious nature of our Lord's sufferings, quotes this passage—and that they were afraid of giving any handle to the enemies of this doctrine by adopting another mode of interpretation, though the original text admits, and perhaps requires it. But though great deference is due to ancient versions of Scripture, there is no reasonable doubt that the word is rightly rendered griefs, or rather infirmities or bodily diseases. It seems plain, too, that the apostle does not refer to this passage, but to the 11th and 12th verses, as he uses the very words of the Greek translation there; and as to the last, which does not seem to have been the least, reason, it is certainly a very bad one. We are not to speak deceitfully, even for God. It is treason against truth to support it by falsehood. It is mortifying to know, that an indisposition to adopt a reading or an interpretation because it has been adopted by men holding erroneous views, has been a considerable source both of false criticism and false exposition of the sacred writings.

The true meaning of the passage may be learned from an infallible commentator, the evangelist Matthew: "When the even was come, they brought unto him many that were possessed with devils; and he cast out the spirits with his word, and healed

---

[1] Storr considers the next three verses as an answer by the prophet to the Jews; but this does not seem at all a probable supposition.

[2] אכן is often just the adversative particle, equivalent to *verum ast*, etc.; but the LXX. render it " ὄντως,"—for οὕτως, the ordinary reading, seems plainly a mistake of a transcriber. The Vulgate has "*vere*," and the Syriac a corresponding word. Symmachus has "ὄντως." 'Profecto, certe, sane,' seems the meaning: 'It is true,—yet.'

[3] 1 Pet. ii. 24.

all that were sick: that it might be fulfilled wnicn was spoken by Esaias the prophet, saying, Himself took our infirmities, and bare our sicknesses."[1] Those who consider the prophet as referring to the vicarious sufferings of Christ have been much perplexed with this explicatory note of the evangelist; some contending that Matthew has applied the passage only by accommodation, in which case he supplies no authority as to the precise meaning of the prophet; while others maintain that the expressions have so comprehensive a meaning as that both bodily and spiritual diseases may be referred to; and that the prediction consequently received a twofold fulfilment. Neither of these modes of explication is at all satisfactory.

How utterly unsatisfactory they are, will appear from the statements of two of the ablest of those expositors who take this view. Calvin, so justly famed for his felicitous expositions, says —"Matthew cites this prophecy, after declaring that Christ had cured certain diseases; though it is certain it was not the object of his mission to heal the body, but rather the mind. For the prophet has in view spiritual maladies. But in the miracles which Jesus wrought for the cure of the body, he gave us, as it were, a specimen of that salvation which he brings to our souls, and therefore Matthew transferred to the symbol that which was in accordance with the reality itself." Another living expositor, worthy of being named along with Calvin, Hengstenberg, says— " Matthew is certainly far from intending to take away the principal reference by his specific one. Christ was sent with the general design of removing, by the sacrifice of himself, the evil which sin had introduced into our world. This he accomplished, in the first place, when he removed corporeal diseases. In this he pointed also to his principal aim, which was, with the same power to take away spiritual evil from men, through the vicarious satisfaction." A very learned interpreter[2] considers Matthew as merely saying that Christ's miracles prove him to be the person who is to fulfil Isaiah's prediction in all the extent of its meaning; but, first, our Lord's miracles do not directly prove that he was to expiate human guilt; and, secondly, this is not a meaning which can be brought out of the evangelist's words.

What Matthew says is plainly, ' What Isaiah says about bear-

---

[1] Matth. viii. 16, 17.   [2] Capellus.

ing our griefs and carrying our sorrows, was fulfilled in what
Christ did on the occasion referred to.' That is what his words
mean—all that his words mean. There cannot, then, be the
least doubt, if we may trust the evangelist as the interpreter of
the prophet, that this prediction was fulfilled by our Lord miraculously removing diseases, and laboring even to fatigue in order
to make his countrymen happy.

The word translated here "griefs," properly signifies diseases
or bodily maladies;[1] and the word rendered "bear" signifies to
carry away,[2] except when it is connected with sin, iniquity, or
some such word, in which case it uniformly signifies to bear the
punishment of sin, or to forgive sin. On the other hand, the
word rendered "sorrows" generally has a reference to mental
distresses;[3] and the word rendered "carried" uniformly signifies
to bear as a burden is borne.[4] The expression, then, "He bore
away our infirmities," refers to our Lord miraculously removing
the diseases of his countrymen; and the other phrase, "He carried our sorrows," refers to that deep sympathy with the sufferings of the afflicted, which induced him to labor even to fatigue
in order to relieve them.[5] This seems plainly the sense which
the prophet's words, and the inspired commentary on them, con-
cur in obliging us to adopt; and it will clearly appear in the
course of our explication of the remaining part of the oracle,
that, by doing so, no injury is done to the argument furnished
by it for the vicarious nature of our Lord's sufferings.[6]

But, it may be asked, How does our exposition correspond with

---

[1] Deut. vii. 15; xxviii. 61.   Isa. i. 5.

[2] 1 Sam. xvii. 37.   Hos. v. 14.   Judges, xvi. 31.

[3] Psal. xxxii. 10; xxxviii. 17; lxix. 29.   Eccles. i. 18.   Isa. lxv. 14.   Jer. xxx. 15.

[4] 2 Chron. ii. 18; xxxiv. 13.

[5] The force of βαστάζω, the word the evangelist used for סבל, may be learned from
Matth. xx. 12; Luke xiv. 27; John, xvi. 12; Acts, xv. 10; Gal. vi. 2; Rom. xv. 1.

[6] Forerius' note is good: "Ego aliam hujus loci interpretationem non afferam quam
Matthæi qui, cap. viii., cum infinitam multitudinem ægrotantium et male habentium
a Christo Domino sanatam narasset addit, ' Ut impleretur quod dictum est per
Jesaiam prophetam dicentem, "Ipse infirmitates nostras accepit et ægrotationes
nostras portavit."' Est enim juxta Hebraismum *levare* interdum idem quod auferre
ut Job, vii. 21, et multis aliis locis.   Quare ut ex verbis evangelistæ aparet verbum
ελαβε non pro *super se suscipere* accipiendum est, sed quasi manu apprehendere
ut ab eo qui habebat auferret.   Quo modo verbum *nasa* Hebræis non raro accipitur."
Archbishop Magee's long note, in the first volume of his work on "Atonement and
Sacrifice," deserves to be read,—No. XLII.   See also Campbell's Four Gospels, *ad loc*

the object of the passage, viewed as expressive of the sentiments and feelings of the Jewish converts? This question is not difficult to answer; and the answer will furnish us with a new argument, if it were necessary, for the mode of explication which, after the evangelist, we have adopted. Having stated, in the preceding verses, the causes why they did not immediately embrace the Messiah, they here state, that in his miraculous cures and wonderful sympathy and kindness, there was much that should have led them to take a different view of his character from that which they did take; yet so strong was the force of prejudice, that, after all, they viewed him as a person peculiarly obnoxious to the Divine displeasure. 'It is true,' say they, 'that he did bear away our diseases, he did bear our sorrows. He took more than half of them, so deep was his sympathy. This supernatural energy, this superhuman kindness, should have opened our eyes to his true character; yet it did not produce this effect; still "we did esteem him stricken,[1] smitten of God, and afflicted."' The word rendered "stricken"[2] includes in itself the idea of *Divine* infliction. The meaning is, they considered him as a person remarkably guilty, and marked by singular judgments from God; as a notorious criminal, an impostor, a false prophet, a blasphemer; and strangely traced his benignant miracles to the influence of malignant spiritual agents. They viewed his sufferings as the immediate effect of Divine displeasure at him, on account of his supposed crimes. They could not but perceive that he was, in a very uncommon degree, a sufferer; and, not aware of the true cause, they, with a malignity that is not peculiar to their nation and age, though very common among them, from a misapprehension of the theocratic doctrine of visible retribution, concluded that so uncommon a sufferer must have been equally an uncommon sinner.

The words of the evangelist are a striking commentary on this verse,—" But though he had done so many miracles before them, yet they believed not on him: that the saying of Esaias the

---

[1] Jerome interprets this "*leprosus*," for leprosy was reckoned a stroke directly from the divine hand; but this is to be unwarrantably minute. Theodotion gives the meaning—μεμαστιγομένος. Some Roman Catholic interpreters strangely render the words—"*a stricken God*," and find here a proof of the divinity of Christ. What must the state of exegesis have been in that church, when such interpretations were sanctioned by such men as Bellarmine and Galatinus?

[2] נָגוּעַ.

prophet might be fulfilled," or, 'so that the saying of Esaias the prophet was fulfilled,' "which he spake, Lord, who hath believed our report? and to whom hath the arm of the Lord been revealed? Therefore they could not believe, because that Esaias said again, He hath blinded their eyes, and hardened their heart; that they should not see with their eyes, nor understand with their heart, and be converted, and I should heal them. These things said Esaias, when he saw his glory, and spake of him."[1]

But though notwithstanding the evidence suggested by his miracles and benevolence, the Jewish converts had long, under the influence of national prejudice, as well as the depravity common to the race, considered the sufferings of Jehovah's servant as the effects of the Divine displeasure against him for enormous though unknown sins, they had now a very different view of the subject. They had been led to "consider that" mysterious "poor man," and the consideration had led to "repentance"—a change of mind; and in that change, they were, as the Psalmist says all who rightly consider him are, "blessed."[2] And they declare in the words that follow, that they now admire what they once despised; and glory above all things in that which, above all things, they had formerly accounted infamous. 'Such were our views; but now we know and are sure that "He was wounded for our transgressions, he was bruised for our iniquities: the chastisement of our peace was upon him; and with his stripes we are healed."' This is the third great topic of the statement of the converted Jews—the true origin, nature, and design of the sufferings of the servant of the Lord. To the illustration of this we will, if it please God, proceed in our next discourse.

The Saviour is still rejected by the majority of those to whom his claims are presented. The Gospel is still discredited by the majority of those who hear it; and the reasons for this are substantially the same in the nineteenth that they were in the first century. "The natural man receiveth not the things of God." Christ is not the kind of Saviour men merely born of the flesh wish for. The blessings of his salvation are not objects of their desire. Truth and holiness have no charms to their mind. It is therefore that they reject him and disregard his Gospel. The

---

[1] John, xiii. 37–41.   [2] Psal. xli. 1.

offence of the Cross has not ceased. It is still, though not quite in the same way as in the primitive age, to one class a stumbling-block, to another foolishness.. The real objections against Christ and his Gospel when fairly unfolded and carefully examined, resolve themselves into the leading principles of the depraved, unchanged human mind and heart, of which the Jewish habits of thought and feeling were merely a variety, rising out of the circumstances in which that nation had been placed.

It were well for those who are yielding to the force of these principles, if they would but seriously inquire, whether, in the miraculous evidence and in the moral character of Christianity, there be not what will leave them utterly inexcusable if they persist in neglecting or resisting its claims ; and consider whether most of their difficulties, like those of the Jews, do not result from their continuing wilfully ignorant of, or unbelieving respecting, well-established facts which, if understood and believed, would make what seems foolishness and weakness, appear to be what it is—" the power of God, and the wisdom of God."

The undoubted fact, that the disbelief of the Gospel originates chiefly in moral causes—causes which ratiocination alone cannot remove (and none are more convinced of this than those who have been delivered from a state of disbelief), should lead all real believers to be frequent and fervent in prayer to Him who alone can change the heart, that the statement of Christian truth may be accompanied with the shedding forth of the influence which alone can bring that truth and the alienated mind so into contact, as that cordial belief and thorough transformation shall be the results. When we look at the nature of the chief obstacles in the way of men becoming Christians—internal obstacles—we cannot but feel that the *prayers* of the church are fully as necessary as the *labors* of the church for christianising the world. They must go together. The Gospel must be carried to all nations by the labors of the church ; and the Holy Ghost must be sent down from heaven in answer to the prayers of the church ; and then— not till then—will there cease to be reason for the complaint, " Who hath believed our report? and to whom is the arm of the Lord revealed?" Then the tender plant—the sickly shoot—will appear to be the plant of renown, the branch of Jehovah ; then the rejected and despised One, will be acknowledged and felt to be the chief among ten thousand, altogether

lovely, the desire of all nations.   The power of truth—the
beauties of holiness—will be discerned and owned ; the doctrine
of the Cross, instead of the greatest objection against Christianity, will be perceived to be its highest recommendation ; and the
exclamation of the apostle, which sounds like madness in every
unregenerate ear, will burst from millions of renewed hearts :—
" God forbid that I should glory save in the cross of our Lord
Jesus Christ, whereby the world is crucified to me, and I to the
world."

LECTURE V

STATEMENT AND PROFESSION OF THE JEWISH CONVERTS
CONTINUED

Isaiah, liii. 5.—"But he was wounded for our transgressions, he was bruised for our iniquities : the chastisement of our peace was upon him; and with his stripes we are healed."

None of the numerous arguments which establish the claims of Christianity to a Divine origin, is better fitted to produce entire conviction in an unprejudiced mind than that which is by a short and easy process deducible from the fulfilment of Old Testament prophecy. The argument may be stated in a few sentences.

In books satisfactorily proved to have been written before, some of them many centuries before, the appearance of Jesus of Nazareth, we find numerous minute descriptions of the leading traits in the character and incidents in the life of an illustrious personage who was to arise among the Jews at a distinctly defined period. To all these descriptions—descriptions of a kind not very likely to suit any *one* individual—we find an exact correspondence in the character and history of Jesus Christ, the time of whose birth answers to the day fixed in the ancient oracles, while it is impossible to find in the records of the past any individual, either before or since that period, to whom the prophetic declarations can with the slightest appearance of probability be referred. The agreement between the Old Testament prediction and New Testament history, is a great deal too minute and extensive to be the result of accident ; and the circumstances of the case obviously exclude the operation of human contrivance. The only rational account of these easily demonstrable facts is that which involves in it the admission equally of the inspiration of the prophets and the Messiahship of Jesus.[1] No un-

---

[1] "Apply these prophecies to any hero, warrior, statesman, king, sage, or philosopher, that history, sacred or profane, makes mention of: if one particular suits, a second does not, a third renders it evident that not one of them is the man designed.

prejudiced person, even moderately acquainted with the writings of the Old Testament, can attentively peruse the writings of the New Testament without being conducted to Philip's conclusion,—"We have found him of whom Moses in the law and the prophets did write."[1]

It is, however, not in this way only that "the spirit of prophecy is the testimony of Jesus." It is not in this way only that the ancient oracles accredit the religion which bears his name. We find in the Old Testament Scriptures not only evidence of the Divine mission of Jesus Christ, and of course, of the truth of all the doctrines which he has taught; but also striking and satisfactory proof of many, if not all, of the leading characteristic principles of the Christian revelation. In the harmony which exists between the doctrines of the Gospel, as those are stated by Jesus Christ and his apostles in the New Testament, and the doctrines which, according to the ancient prophets, the Messiah as the great Prophet was to promulgate, we have, along with the proof of his Messiahship, an additional proof of the truth of these doctrines. The doctrine of the Old Testament and the New, in its great principles, is not only consistent but co-incident. What the prophets indicated figuratively and obscurely as to be taught by the Messiah, was by Jesus and his disciples declared in simple and plain language. "The Gospel," in its great principles, "was promised afore by the prophets in the Holy Scriptures." "The righteousness of God," which is revealed in the gospel, and the revelation of which makes the gospel what it is, "glad tidings of great joy to all people," is "witnessed by the law and the prophets."[2]

The oracles of none of the Old Testament prophets bear a more extensive and distinct testimony to Jesus Christ personally, and to the fundamental doctrines of his religion, than those of Isaiah. They are characterized by an unambiguousness and a minuteness well fitted to excite in the friends of Christianity a mingled emotion of astonishment and delight, and to overwhelm its enemies, whether Jewish or infidel, with perplexity and con-

Apply them to Christ,—apply all the hundred, or more: an astonishing correspondence appears; every one fits him; there is not a single prediction that is discordant. He that will call this chance, and ascribe the agreement merely to fortuitous circumstances, is not fit to be argued with, and must not say that Christians alone are credulous."—BOGUE.

[1] John, i. 45.   [2] Rom. i. 2; iii. 21.

fusion. They have been peculiarly useful in bearing evidence to the principle that vicarious expiation is the ground of pardon and salvation to men, which forms as it were the key-stone of the arch of Christian doctrine. They make it very manifest that, though the enemies of this doctrine were to succeed in the attempt on which they have wasted so much learning and genius, time and labor, of explaining away all those texts in the New Testament which in their obvious meaning teach it, the conclusion fairly deducible from their success would not be that this doctrine is not true, but that Jesus Christ is not the Messiah; for in this case his doctrine, as these men explain it, and the doctrine of the Messiah as the prophets exhibit it, are not only not coincident, but not consistent. Whatever Jesus Christ and his apostles taught, it is clear to a demonstration, that Isaiah taught vicarious expiation by the Messiah's sufferings as the procuring cause of salvation; and if Jesus and his apostles did not teach this doctrine, what conclusion can we arrive at, but that whatever he and they may have been, he is not the Messiah of whom Isaiah speaks, and they are not the messengers whom that prophet represents as bringing "good tidings of good," publishing peace and salvation, and saying unto Zion, "Thy God reigneth."[1] So long as the oracle, in the illustration of which we are at present engaged, is admitted to be an inspired prediction, the only alternatives presented to a reflecting mind are, the admission of the doctrine of vicarious atonement, or the denial of the Messiahship of Jesus Christ. This is peculiarly evident from that part of the oracle at the illustration of which, in the course of these expositions, we are now arrived.

You are aware that we consider the oracle which begins at the 13th verse of the preceding chapter, and terminates with the close of this, as dividing itself into four sections. *First*, A revelation made in the person of Jehovah of the exaltation and glory of the Messiah, as following and rising out of his sufferings. *Second*, A complaint of little success on the part of the first preachers of the gospel. *Third*, A statement on the part of the converted Jews of the causes of this comparatively little success, introducing a farther and more circumstantial account of the sufferings of the Messiah and of the glory which should follow

---

[1] Isa. lii. 7.

them; and, *Fourth,* A solemn declaration on the part of Jehovah, confirming the great truths contained in this statement.

On entering on the consideration of the third of these sections
in my last lecture, after showing you that it is to be considered
as containing a statement on the part of converted Jews, I remarked that it resolves itself into five parts, each of which
naturally rises out of that which precedes it. They first state
the reasons of the rejection of the Messiah by the great body of
his countrymen; then advert to what ought to have induced
them to receive him, but did not; then unfold shortly the true
origin, nature, and design, of his sufferings; then detail more
particularly these sufferings from their commencement to their
close; and then, finally, declare the glorious results of these sufferings both to himself and to his people. The greater part of
my last discourse was occupied in the illustration of the first
two of these parts. (1.) The statement of the reasons why so
few of the Messiah's countrymen received him,—he was not the
kind of deliverer they desired and expected. His obscure origin, his abject appearance, his severe sufferings, did violence to
their national prejudices, and incapacitated them from judging
rightly of his claims. (2.) The statement of what ought to have
induced them to receive him, but did not,—his miraculous cure
of their diseases, and superhuman sympathy with their sufferings.

I proceed now to consider the third part of the statement of
the converted Jews, which consists of an account of the true
nature, origin, and design, of those sufferings of the Messiah,—
misconception with regard to which had been the principal cause
of his rejection by his countrymen. "But he was wounded for
our transgressions, he was bruised for our iniquities: the chastisement of our peace was upon him; and by his stripes we are
healed."

There is not much in the *words* which require explanation.
The connective particle "but," is very expressive. 'We
thought him "stricken, smitten of God, and afflicted. *But*"
we were egregiously mistaken—we were utterly wrong. We
thought him a victim—a doomed one,—a sufferer for his own
enormous though unknown crime. He was indeed a victim—a
doomed one,—a sufferer for sins; but they were not his own
sins. They were ours. In these sufferings, he stood in our

place: he met with our desert; and thus he accomplished our deliverance.'[1]

The term "wounded," properly signifies, 'to perforate, transfix, or pierce.' It is the word used for severe and mortal wounds, and is applied usually to persons slain by violence, and especially in battle. The ancient Syriac version, in perfect consistency with Hebrew usage, renders it "killed," or put to death.

The term rendered "bruised," signifies, 'pressed hard, crushed;' indicating one of the ways in which excruciating pain may be inflicted on the human frame.

"Chastisement" is a word which often means correction by words—instruction and reproof; but here there can be no doubt it is correction by strokes, for the effect of this chastisement is *stripes*, or rather weals—the inflamed swollen marks of stripes, which are said to be effectual to our healing.

The "chastisement[2] of our peace,"[3] is the suffering, by the endurance of which our reconciliation or happiness was secured. The words rendered "transgressions," and "iniquities," are nearly synonymous, and describe sins, violations of the Divine law.

This verse is a wonderfully complete representation of the sufferings of Jehovah's righteous servant. It represents them as violent, severe, fatal, numerous, diversified, penal, vicarious, expiatory, saving, and reconciling. The great truth contained in it may be thus stated: The numerous, varied, violent, severe, fatal sufferings of the righteous servant of the Lord, were the endurance of those evils in which God expresses his displeasure at sin, in the room of those who had merited them; and were intended, and have been found effectual, for the expiation of guilt and the obtaining of salvation. Let us endeavor to illustrate this principle; and, for this purpose, let us shortly show how plainly all these qualities are here ascribed to the Messiah's

---

[1] "Multos spectaculum crucis abalienat a Christo, dum ea quæ oculis objiciuntur considerant, nec finem rei attendunt. Omnis vero tollitur offensio, dum hac morte expiata esse nostra peccata et partam nobis salutem intelligimus."—CALVIN.

[2] The force of the word מוסר may be learned by consulting Lev. xxvi. 18, 23, 28; Deut. xi. 2; xxi. 18; xxii. 18; 1 Kings, xii. 11, 14; 2 Chron. x. 11, 14; Psal. vi. 1; xxxviii. 1; xxxix. 11; cxviii. 18; Prov. iii. 11; xiii. 24; xix. 8; xxii. 15; Isa. xxvi. 16; Jer. ii. 19, 30; v. 3; x. 24; xxx. 11, 14; xxxi. 18; xlvi. 28; Ezek. v. 15; xxiii. 48; Wisd. iii. 5; Hos. vii. 12.

[3] "The stripes that wounded and killed him, cured us."—DURHAM.

sufferings, and how wonderfully they actually met in the sufferings of Jesus Christ,—those sufferings which, in a solemn religious rite, we have acknowledged as the ransom of our souls, the ground of our hope, the subject of our gloriation.[1]

The Messiah's sufferings were to be violent sufferings—sufferings not coming on him in the ordinary course of things, but inflicted on him. All the words used are expressive of this kind of suffering,—"wounded," "bruised," "chastised," "scourged." Neither in the body nor in the soul of the righteous servant of Jehovah were there, as is the case with every other man, any seeds of suffering, which needed only time and occasion to germinate and bring forth bitter fruits. It is remakable that we never read of our Lord being affected with disease of any kind. He did not die of disease or natural decay; he was taken by wicked hands, crucified, and slain. All his sufferings were from causes external to himself.

They were not only to be violent in this sense, but they were to be severe. All the terms employed express severe as well as violent suffering: "Wounded," or pierced; "bruised," pressed down, so as to be crushed by an intolerable burden or irresistible force; "chastened," scourged, not slightly, but so as to leave behind the proofs of the severity of the infliction in inflamed contusions and swellings. There can scarcely be a doubt that there is a reference here to the pierced hands, and feet, and side of Jesus,—to the weight which prostrated him on the earth in Gethsemane, and forced the ensanguined sweat from every pore in his body,—and to the scourging by the Roman soldiers, which we know was a fearfully severe punishment; but it would be wrong to limit the reference to these. The general truth is, plainly, the sufferings of the servant of Jehovah were to be intensely severe. His poverty was deep poverty; his reproach, foul reproach; his anguish, bitter anguish; his bodily pain was all that human nature can bear. "He was poured out like water, and all his bones were out of joint: his heart was like wax; it was melted in the midst of his bowels."[2] His mental suffering was ineffable, inconceivable; the temptations he was exposed to were all that satanic ingenuity could make them, to harass and shock his holy mind. "The deeps environed him;

---

[1] This discourse was delivered after the celebration of the Lord's Supper.
[2] Psal. xxii. 14.

the waters came into his soul : all God's waves and billows
passed over him." He was indeed the man who saw affliction
by the rod of God's wrath. Never was there sorrow like his
sorrow. All human sufferings, compared with his, scarcely
deserves the name. The violent death inflicted on him was a
peculiarly agonizing one ; and when we reflect on his patience
and fortitude, what an idea do these words give of the intensity
of his agony !—"Now is my soul troubled ; and what shall I
say ?" "My soul is exceeding sorrowful, even unto death."
"O my Father, if it be possible, let this cup pass from me."
"My God, my God, why hast Thou forsaken me ?"[1]

The sufferings of the Messiah were not only to be violent and
severe, but fatal. That is more distinctly stated in a following
verse, when it is said, "He was cut off out of the land of the
living ;" but it is also intimated in the word "wounded," which,
as I have already remarked, is usually equivalent to 'fatally
wounded—killed.' Our Lord became "obedient to death ;" he
was "put to death in the flesh." His sufferings did not terminate till "he bowed the head, and gave up the ghost."

The number of the sufferings of the Messiah is indicated in the
description. Six different figures are employed to express his
sufferings. "Many were the afflictions of that Righteous One."

And they are represented not only as numerous, but diversified. He suffered from being pierced, bruised, beaten with rods.
He suffered in every way in which an innocent man could suffer.
Sufferings came on him from every quarter they could come.
Not only did the same calamity often recur : there was to be an
unparalleled combination of calamities—bodily pain and mental
anguish, poverty and contempt, neglect and reproach. He suffered from his countrymen and from foreigners, from his friends
and from his foes, from men and from devils, from creatures and
from the Creator. Every sensibility of pain was touched, every
capacity of suffering filled to an overflow.

These violent, severe, fatal, numerous, diversified sufferings of
the Messiah were to be penal. They were to be sufferings for
sins, for iniquities. They were not disciplinary sufferings. The
righteous servant of Jehovah needed no discipline to perfect his
character. They were not primarily intended even to attest his

---

[1] John, xii. 27. Matth. xxvi. 38, 39 ; xxvii. 46.

mission. For this purpose they were not necessary. They were
well fitted to teach others to suffer, but this was not their leading
object either. They were the endurance of what sin deserves.
They were the very evils which, by Divine appointment, are the
result of the violation of his holy, just, and good law. This was
strikingly marked. In the kind and degree of his sufferings,
there was something which, even to his unreflecting countrymen,
seemed to point him out as a doomed person, "stricken of God;"
and this was especially strongly indicated in the manner of his
death. In the Mosaic law, it was provided that the bodies of all
who should be put to death, by whatever means, for crime, should
be exposed on a gibbet: "Cursed is every one that hangeth on
a tree."[1] Every one whose body was hung on a tree, was thus
publicly declared to have paid his life as a forfeit to justice.
On the cross another inscription besides that which Pilate ordered to be inscribed there, strikes the enlightened eye—"The
victim for guilt—the wages of sin."

But how could this be? He never contracted guilt; he never
committed sin; he was the Just One, God's righteous servant.
The reply to these questions is to be found in the next property
that, in this wondrous oracle, is ascribed to the sufferings of the
Messiah. These sufferings were to be vicarious sufferings. He
was wounded for iniquities—but they were our iniquities; he
was bruised for transgressions—but they were our transgressions.
The plain meaning of these words certainly is, that our sins were
the procuring cause of his sufferings. No doubt, taken by themselves, the words may mean, that through means of men's wickedness the righteous servant of Jehovah suffered. Their sinfulness was the occasion of his being such a sufferer. But taken in
connection with what follows, where the idea of substitution is
clearly brought out, there can be no reasonable doubt that the
sentiment they were meant to express was, that our Lord's sufferings were endured in the room of those he came to save—that
he stood in their place, and underwent their desert.[2] The Messiah

---

[1] Deut. xxi. 23.

[2] " Minima vox difficultatem hic maximam parit, imo litera unica מ quæ pro præ-
positione מין posita vel *ab* vel *ob* reddi possit. Judæi, et cum iis Sociniani, reddunt,
' Vulneratus est *ab* iniquitatibus nostris.' Nos autem rectius et verius ' *ob* iniquitates
nostras.' Nihil est autem certius quam utroque modo reddi posse. Neque Christum
loco nostro passum esse recte conficias ex illis formulis *pro, propter*, quæ sensu alio
atque alio usurpantur. Neque nos argumentamur ex mera illa vocula מ, quod esset

was "cut off, but not for himself." He suffered the punishment of sin, but it was "the just in the room of the unjust." This is the only principle which can harmonize the sufferings and death of the immaculately innocent, the absolutely perfect, incarnate Son of God, with the Divine wisdom, righteousness, and benignity. It converts what appears the most unaccountable of all things—a piece of folly, injustice, and cruelty, on the part of the all-wise, the infinitely holy, the infinitely benignant Jehovah—into the most glorious of all displays of his unsearchable wisdom, his eternal righteousness, and his exceedingly rich grace. This is the great doctrine, to prepare for the full revelation of which was one great design of the appointment of the sacrificial services before and under the law, especially of those rites which marked the sacrificial victim as the substitute of the guilty offerer. Christ died for the ungodly in the same sense in which one man dies for another sentenced to death, that he may be delivered from death. "He bare our sins in his own body to the tree." If the vicarious nature of our Lord's sufferings is not stated in such words as those in the text before us, and in the other passages we have quoted in illustration of it, we may, I believe, very safely say it is impossible that it should be revealed; for language furnishes no terms more clear and unequivocal to express this idea, than those which have been already employed. If God had intended to convey the idea, he could not have used words better calculated for this purpose. No ingenuity can ever torture them into the natural expression of any other meaning.

Still farther, the words before us intimate that the sufferings of God's righteous servant were to be expiatory. That follows from their being penal and vicarious. If HIS sufferings are penal and vicarious, they must have been expiatory in their design—they must be expiatory in their virtue. They must have been intended to expiate sin—they must be effectual in expiating sin. The chastisement of our peace was on him. The chastisement of our peace is the punishment, the infliction of which is necessary to our reconciliation. We had lost the Divine favor. We deserved chastisement, "stripes and a dungeon"—chastisement,

argutari. Sed cum perspicuum sit eam interdum ita sumi necessario, ut causam significet meritoriam, non efficientem, hoc loco ita esse accipiendam non tantum dicimus sed probamus (1) ex totius orationis complexu; (2) ex circumstantiis loci; (3) ex ipsius natura rei."—MORUS.

the infliction of which on us could never have ended in our peace
—stripes, which would have inflicted incurable wounds—a dungeon, the door of which would never have been opened. We
never could have fully endured the punishment we deserved,
and its effect on our unchanged nature would not have been to
make us more fit objects of the Divine approbation, but more fit
objects of his disapprobation. Inflicted on us, it would have
sunk us deeper and deeper in the abyss of guilt and depravity,
removed us farther and farther from the friendship and complacency of God. That chastisement must be endured by another, or we are undone forever; and, as endured by him in our
room, it serves the purpose. It expiates sin. It propitiates the
offended law. It appeases Divine wrath. It makes the pardon
of our sins and the salvation of our souls consistent with, gloriously illustrative of, all the perfections of the Divine character
and all the principles of the Divine government.

The sufferings of our Lord were expiatory in design. When
Messiah was to be cut off, it was to "finish transgression and
make an end of sin, and bring in an everlasting righteousness."
When the incarnate Son became the Lamb of God, it was that
he might "take away the sins of the world." When he laid
himself on the Divine altar, it was that he might "give himself
a ransom for many." When he came in the end of the age, it
was to "put away sin by the sacrifice of himself." When God
made him who knew no sin to be sin for us, it was "that we
might be made the righteousness of God in him."[1] Indeed, it
may well be asked, What could be the object of *his* penal, vicarious sufferings, but expiation?

And as these sufferings were expiatory in their design, they
have been so in their effect. We are reconciled through the
body of his flesh by death. We who were afar off are brought
nigh. The enmity is abolished and taken out of the way. God
is in Christ, reconciling the world to himself. He is well pleased
for his righteousness' sake. His anger is turned away. He is
pacified toward us, for all the iniquities we have done. "God
is just, and the justifier of him that believeth in Jesus. The
blood of Jesus Christ, God's Son, cleanseth us from all sin." We
are redeemed by this price, so "much more precious than silver

---

[1] Dan. ix. 24.   John, i. 29.   Matth. xx. 28.   Heb. ix. 26.   1 Cor. v. 21.

and gold." "In him we have redemption through his blood, the forgiveness of sins." "He is set forth a propitiation for our sins, through faith in his blood." "He is the propitiation for our sins; and not for ours only, but also for the sins of the whole world."[1] There is no condemnation to those in him. Who shall condemn them? Christ has died; and the faith which unites them to him makes his death their death.

The only other statement contained in this wonderful passage respecting the sufferings of Christ is, that they are saving. "By his stripes[2] we are healed."[3] I have illustrated this remarkable statement elsewhere,[4] and may be permitted, in a somewhat abridged form, to repeat the illustration.

"Sin" is often, in the Scripture, represented as a disease. The representation is a very instructive one. Sin makes men miserable in themselves—useless sometimes, loathsome, often dangerous to others; and its natural and certain termination, if it be allowed to run its course, is death—the second death—eternal death. Various, endlessly various, methods have been invented by men for curing this disease. The best of them are mere palliatives. The only effectual cure is that mentioned by the prophet—the "stripes" of the righteous servant of God. This is a cure which it never could have entered into the heart of man to conceive; and even when made known, it seems foolishness to the wisdom of this world,—the disease of one man healed by the stripes of another—the death of Jesus Christ on a cross the means of making men holy and happy. Yet so it is: "The foolishness of God is wiser than men; and the weakness of God stronger than men." Man's disease is a deep-rooted one. It arises out of the circumstances in which he is placed. It has affected the inmost springs of life, and it discovers itself by an endless variety of external symptoms. The stripes of the Great Physician are a remedy which answers all these peculiarities. The expiatory sufferings of Christ, when the sinner believes, changes his state. They take him out of the pestilential region of the Divine curse, and translate him into the health-breathing region of the Divine favor. In the Divine influences, for

---

[1] Col. i. 21, 22.   Eph. ii. 13.   1 Cor. v. 19.   Ezek. xvi. 63.   Rom. iii. 26.   1 John, i. 7.   1 Pet. i. 18.   Eph. i. 7.   Rom. iii. 25.   1 John, ii. 2.

[2] 'Bruises, wounds, weals.'—Gen. iv. 23.   Exod. xxi. 24.   Isa. i. 6.   Psal. xxxviii. 5.

[3] Literally, "it is healed to us," == 'healing is to us,' = 'we are healed.'

[4] Expository Discourses on the First Epistle of Peter, Vol. i. p. 459–461.

which they open the way, is given a powerful principle of health, which penetrates into the very first springs of thought, and feeling, and action; and, in the views which these sufferings give us of the holy benignant character of God, the malignity of sin, the vanity of the world, the importance of eternity, there are furnished, as it were, remedies fitted to meet and remove all the various external symptoms of this worst of diseases.

The Jewish converts speak from their own experience. They knew, when they made these statements, that they had been re-conciled through the blood of the Cross; that they had peace with God through him, by whom they had received the atonement. They knew they were once guilty, depraved, and miserable; they knew that they were now pardoned, and accepted; and truly, though only imperfectly, holy and happy; and they knew that the change had taken place through the violent, severe, fatal, numerous, diversified, penal, vicarious, expiatory saving sufferings of the righteous servant of God; and therefore they testify what they knew from experience when they say, "But he was wounded for our transgressions, he was bruised for our iniquities: the chastisement of our peace was upon him, and by his stripes we are healed."

Having thus stated generally the true character of the sufferings of "the servant of the Lord," which were such a stumbling-block to the great body of their countrymen, and prevented them from receiving and acknowledging him as the Messiah, they proceed to give a statement more in detail—a brief history, as it were—of the Messiah: 'We all,' they say, 'like a strayed flock have wandered; we were a guilty, depraved, self-ruined race, each of us choosing his own way, but all the ways chosen being ways from God—paths all leading downward to endless ruin. The race were lost, hopelessly lost. But God, who is rich in mercy, interposed to prevent universal, irretrievable destruction. He constituted his righteous servant the representative—the high priest, the sacrifice—of lost men. He made to meet on him the iniquities of us all. This is no legal fiction; it is a glorious fact; and most important results have flowed from it. Exaction was made for the debt which man owed to Divine justice, and he answered the exaction. He presented himself a willing sponsor, and cheerfully did and suffered all that was necessary for man's salvation. By a most shocking combination of law and injustice, which could have taken place only in an age of extreme degeneracy, among men of extreme depravity, he was brought to an untimely and violent death, which was intended to be followed by a disgraceful burial; but, as a token of his innocence, in the deepest stage of his humiliation, he, while in the state of the dead, lay in the sepulchre of a rich man. Yet, even while Jehovah afflicted him, he was the object of his most entire complacency; and now that he has accomplished his work, in bearing and bearing away the sins of men, by presenting himself as a sacrifice for sin, that complacency shall be manifested in giving him an undying life, and a numerous posterity; while the prosperous administration of the great Divine saving economy shall be placed entirely under his guidance and superintendence.'

Such is, if I mistake not, the substance of the statement contained in the five succeeding verses. The illustration of that statement will be proceeded with in our next lecture. Meanwhile, we conclude with a few reflections from what has been said.

How inconceivably malignant is sin, that made such an expiation necessary in order to the salvation of men! How infinite must be the love of God and his Son to man, who, rather than man should perish, have appointed and effected such an expiation! How powerful are the obligations under which those saved through this expiation are laid to love and serve Him who gave his Son to be a propitiation for their sins, and to live entirely devoted to him, who died entirely devoted for them! How utterly hopeless the condition of those who neglect and despise the servant of Jehovah as the only expiator of human guilt! A word or two in illustration of each of these reflections.

How inconceivably malignant must sin be! Fools make a mock at it: only fools can do so. The cross of Christ teaches that it is no trifle. Had anything less than the blood of the incarnate Son of God been an adequate atonement for human transgression, assuredly that blood had not been shed. God would have spared his Son, and not delivered him up for us all. The value of the blood of Christ is the measure of the demerit of sin. Can man or angel, then, compute it? Think of what Christ suffered; think who he was who suffered; think who He was who inflicted these sufferings, and then say what must be the malignity of that demerit, in order to the expiation of which, such sufferings must be inflicted by such a Father on such a Son,—sustained by such a Son from such a Father.

How infinite must be the love of God and of his Son! Yes, "herein is love, not that we loved God, but God hath loved us, and given his Son to be the propitiation for our sins." He "commended his love to us, in that, while we were yet sinners, Christ died for us." "Greater love hath no man than this, that a man lay down his life for his friends." But Christ not only died for us, he became a curse for us, that we might be redeemed from the curse; he became sin for us, that we might be made the righteousness of God in him; and he did all this for us when we were not friends but enemies. Surely such love has a height and a depth, a length and a breadth, that pass knowledge!

How powerful are the obligations under which those saved through this expiation are laid to serve Him who gave his Son to be a propitiation for their sins—to devote themselves entirely to him who devoted himself entirely for them! "Ye are not your own, ye are bought with a price; therefore glorify him" who bought you "with your bodies and with your spirits, which are his." Forasmuch as ye have been redeemed, not by corruptible things, such as silver and gold, but by blood—not the blood of bulls and of goats, but the blood of Christ, as of a lamb without blemish and without spot,—taught by the grace, the free sovereign love of God, thus displayed, in perfect accordance with His holiness and justice, bringing salvation to all, through the finished and accepted sacrifice of His Son,—"deny ungodliness and worldly lusts, and live soberly, righteously, and godly in this present world; looking for the blessed hope, and the glorious appearing of the great God, your Saviour, Jesus Christ, who gave himself for you, that he might redeem you from all iniquity, and purify unto himself a peculiar people, zealous of good works."

Finally, how absolutely hopeless is the condition of those who neglect or despise the great expiation, the only expiation of human guilt! "If these things were done in the green tree, what will be done in the dry?" There is no pardon for unexpiated sin; there is no expiation of sin but in the cross of Christ; and no saving virtue can come forth from that cross to the unbeliever. "There remaineth no more sacrifice for sin;" and he who rejects Christ's sacrifice must answer for his own sin. God marks his iniquity; He will make exaction for it; and who can stand where the incarnate Son stood? who can bear what he bore? Be warned ere it be too late. You can neither merit the Divine favor, nor bear the Divine wrath. Oh, let my counsel be acceptable to you, and seek what may now be found,— union to Him who has done both. "It is a fearful thing"—this is a loud and bitter cry coming from the Cross, and reverberated from the dark caverns of hopeless misery,—"It is a fearful thing to fall into the hands of the living God."

LECTURE VI

Isaiah, liii. 6.—"All we, like sheep, have gone astray; we have turned every one to
his own way; and the Lord hath laid on him the iniquity of us all."

The existence of suffering, and, still more, the wide prevalence
of severe suffering, in a world which owes its origin and continued subsistence to a Being of infinite power, wisdom, and benignity, seems at first view utterly unaccountable. On reflection, however, we find an adequate cause for this strange effect
in the existence and wide prevalence of sin in that world. Under the government of a holy, just, and good God, physical evil
is the natural result of moral evil. Where there is sin, there
must be suffering—where there is much sin, there must be much
suffering—where all are sinners, all must be sufferers. We may,
we do, find it difficult to account for sin finding its way into
God's world; but when it has once entered, we do not wonder
that death should have followed it, nor that death should have
passed upon all men, since all men sinned. The wonder is, not
that in a world so full of sin there is much misery, but that
there is not more. It is not wonderful that man the sinner
should be of few days and full of trouble—that he should flee as
a shadow and have no continuance. Anything short of the severest suffering the sinner can sustain, is mercy. "Why should
a living man complain—a man for the punishment of his sin?"
"It is of the Lord's mercies that *we* are not *consumed*, and because his compassions fail not."

There is, however, one instance of severe suffering in the history of our race, for which this principle, so widely applicable,
affords no satisfactory account. In one instance, the highest
excellence and the deepest suffering of which human nature

capable, met in the same individual, in strange and apparently unaccountable union. I need scarcely say I refer to the perfect man Christ Jesus. "In him was no sin." "He knew no sin."[1] He was equally free from hereditary and personal liability to suffering on account of sin—equally a stranger to natural and acquired dispositions to evil. Every holy principle dwelt in his heart—every active, every suffering, virtue adorned his conduct. None could convict him of sin. The human judge who condemned him declared that he had found no fault in him; and the supreme, infallible Judge declared, in the most solemn manner, that He was well pleased *with* him, *in* him. Yet this spotlessly innocent, this absolutely perfect man, instead of enjoying that supreme happiness to which he was entitled, or even that freedom from suffering which it might seem injustice to withhold, was pre-eminent in suffering as in excellence. He was "the Man who saw affliction," "the Man of sorrows and acquainted with grief." Never was there privation, pain, anxiety, sorrow like his. "His visage was more marred than any man's, and his form more than the sons of men." He was "wounded, and crushed, and smitten with a deadly stroke." Men hated him, devils tormented him, God forsook him. He lived a houseless wanderer; he died, like a felonious slave, on a cross.

This is, viewed by itself, an inscrutable enigma—the mystery of mysteries—the deepest and darkest of the ways of God; and the strangeness of these events is indefinitely increased, when we consider that this real man was not a mere man, but an incarnation of the Divinity—"the Word who was with God, who was God, made flesh."[2] In the evidence which was thus yielded to the perfection of his character, the divinity of his mission, and the truth of his doctrine, in the advantages secured to mankind by so perfect an example of virtue, and so powerful a motive to obedience, and in the high dignities and ineffable enjoyments to which he has been raised, as the merited rewards of his voluntary humiliation to promote the cause of truth, and holiness, and benignity, the glory of God and the salvation of man,—in these has been sought an explanation of this strangest of all anomalies in the administration of God. But none of these considerations—no, not all of them taken together—furnish anything like a satisfac-

---

[1] 1 John, iii. 5.   2 Cor. v. 21.   [2] John, i. 1, 14.

tory solution of the problem, How the sufferings of Jesus Christ
are to be reconciled with the perfections of the Divine character
and the principles of the Divine government. The only satisfactory account—the only account which dissipates the dark
shadows which they seem to cast almost equally on the wisdom,
and righteousness, and benignity of Jehovah—is that given us
in the great Christian doctrine of atonement by vicarious sacrifice, so clearly taught by our Lord and his apostles, so abundantly witnessed by the law and the prophets.

This is the account given of the unparalleled sufferings of
"the servant of Jehovah" in that wonderful oracle, in the illustration of which we have for some time been engaged. The converted Jews, in reply to the complaint of the first preachers of
the Gospel, of the comparative fewness of those who received the
report they had heard of God, respecting the sufferings and the
glory of the Messiah, in stating the causes of the event which
the primitive preachers deplored, place great stress on the unparalleled sufferings of the servant of the Lord. They could not
think such a sufferer could be the servant of Jehovah—nay, mis-
applying a true principle, they thought that such sufferings indicated that he who endured them must be an object of the
peculiar judicial displeasure of God, and sought for their cause
in some great though undiscovered—undiscoverable—violation
of the Divine law. He seemed to them, by way of eminence,
"the stricken of God;" and how could he be so, if he had not
deserved such strokes? They admit that his supernatural works
and superhuman kindness should have prevented their coming to
this conclusion, and should have convinced them that this was
not the right way of accounting for his sufferings; and they then
proceed to unfold the truth which they had been taught by being
led to understand and believe the report, and having the arm of
the Lord revealed to them. These numerous, varied, violent, severe, fatal sufferings, so utterly unparalleled, were the endurance,
in the room of those who deserved them, of those evils in which
God expresses his displeasure at sin; and were intended, and
fitted, and found effectual, for the expiation of guilt, and the procuring of salvation for those who otherwise must have continued
forever unforgiven and lost. "He was wounded for our transgressions, he was bruised for our iniquities: the chastisement
of our peace was upon him; and with his stripes we are healed."

They then proceed, in the paragraph of which our subject of
lecture forms the commencement, to give a somewhat more detailed account of this wondrous Divine economy of salvation, in
a brief connected statement of the sufferings of the servant of
the Lord, and of the glories which were to follow them. That
detailed account is introduced by a statement of the circumstances which, on the supposition that man was to be saved,
rendered those sufferings necessary, and of the Divine arrangement and agency in which these sufferings originated.[1] We
will consider these in their order.

The statement of the condition of man in his fallen state, is
contained in the first part of the 6th verse,—"All we, like sheep,
have (rather, had) gone astray; we have (rather, had) turned
every one to his own way." The Jewish converts describe their
own natural condition, and the natural condition of the race they
belonged to, under the figure of a strayed flock of sheep. The
word rendered "sheep," though in the singular, properly signifies a flock—generally a flock of sheep. 'We are all like a
strayed flock.'[2] The leading thoughts are these:—The state of
man by nature since his fall, is a state of error; a state of sin;
a state of helpless misery and danger; a state of alienation from
God and from one another.

The holy, just, and good law of God, and the security and
happiness which are to be obtained—obtained only in conforming to it, is that fold or enclosed pasture-ground from which the
human flock have strayed. And false views of God and themselves, of happiness and the way of attaining it, lead them to
wander—that is, to violate the Divine law. All sin involves in
it the grossest error—the most deplorable delusion. Sin is reasonable only on the supposition that man is wiser and stronger than
God,—that he knows better than God what can make him happy,
—that he can make himself happy in spite of God.

[1] " Ut melius infigat animis hominum beneficium mortis Christi, ostendit, quam
necessaria sit ista sanatio cujus prius mentionem fecit. Est hic elegans antithesis.
Nam in nobis dissipati sumus, in Christo collecti; aberramus natura atque in exitium
præcipites agimur, in Christo viam reperimus, qua ad salutis portam ducamur;
obruunt nos scelera nostra at transferuntur in Christum a quo exoneramur."—
CALVIN.

[2] "אָן significat animalia minuta, sed plura non unum, gregem non singula, deque
capris aut ovibus potissimum dicitur. At שֶׂה quod postmodum de Messia usurpatur
de unica etiam ove."—MORUS.

In wandering, they have done wrong. They have violated obligation; they have contracted guilt; they *ought* to have remained in the fold. And by thus, under the influence of error, itself guilty because self-chosen, having rendered themselves more and more guilty by ever departing more and more in heart and life from the holy commandment delivered to them, they have brought themselves into a state of misery and danger. The welfare and safety of the sheep are connected with being in the fold, or at any rate under the eye and care of the shepherd. When they wander, they suffer from hunger and thirst, and are ever in hazard of being starved to death or devoured by wild beasts. Men have by their sin lost all true happiness, exposed themselves to suffering in endless forms; and—continuing in the state into which sin has brought them—before them, as the certain consequence of unsubdued depravity, unremitted guilt, is not only death, but everlasting destruction.

This state of misery and danger is, so far as they themselves are concerned, a hopeless one. The strayed flock never returns to the fold if it is not brought back. Sinful men, left to themselves, will never find their way back to God. They will sink deeper and deeper in delusion, and error, and guilt, and depravity, and misery—retiring farther and farther from God and happiness forever and ever.

The idea of alienation from God is strongly indicated by this figurative description. Jehovah is the great shepherd. Men are the sheep of his pasture. When they wander from his fold, they abandon Him. They cannot indeed do what they often wish they could do, " flee from his presence," so as to escape the notice of his eye, and get beyond the reach of his arm; but they abandon his fellowship. They thus go far from Him. They become every day more the objects of his judicial displeasure and moral dislike. They do not like to retain Him in their knowledge. They forget Him; and spend sometimes the whole of life without ever once realizing the idea of his existence, or the relation in which they stand to Him.

This is the state, the deplorable state of all mankind. All are thus wanderers. "There is none righteous, no, not one : there is none that understandeth, there is none that seeketh after God. They are all gone out of the way." " All have sinned, and come

short of the glory of God."[1]   All are in a state of error, sin,
misery, danger, helplessness, and alienation from God.

To the declaration, " All we, like sheep, have gone astray," is
added, " we have turned every one to his own way."   All had
wandered, but each in his own path.   They had not kept together; they were no longer a united body, but a crowd of
stragglers.   This may be intended to indicate that, while all err
and sin, and involve themselves in danger and misery, every one
has his own errors, and sins, and miseries, and dangers.   That
vast variety of circumstances which form what is called individual
character, gives a peculiar direction to the principles of depravity
common to the race in different men.   All are wanderers—none
go in the right direction; but all do not wander in the same
direction and to the same extent.   All are idolaters—none worship the only living and true God; but they do not all worship
the same idol, nor are they equally mad on these idols.

The words, " we turned every one to his own way," naturally
enough suggest another true and important sentiment as to the
condition of fallen man.   They are not only alienated from God,
but from one another.   Had men kept together in God's fold,
they not only would have had intimate blissful relation to, and
communion with, Him, but they would have been connected together by the bands of an affectionate brotherhood, and would
have made themselves happy in promoting each other's happiness
—the individual finding happiness in promoting the happiness of
the community.   They would have all been engaged in common
pursuits.   There would have been no uncomfortable jarrings and
collisions.   Wars and fightings would never have been known.
All loving God and loving each other, they would have been of
one heart and mind.   Both this union of affection and pursuit is
broken up.   " As a lonely wanderer pursues his way in sadness
and exposed to many dangers, so men are proceeding, as it were,
through the wilderness of life, neither led by God nor united
with brethren by his love."[2]   Selfishness, in some of its forms,
is the leading principle of unchanged men.   They live for themselves—not for a common cause.   They have not the spirit which
would unite all mankind in one holy, happy, brotherhood.   It is
common union to God that alone can properly unite us to one

---

[1] Rom. iii. 10–12, 23.   [2] Hengstenberg.

another: without this, there is nothing but self-will, caprice, and discord. Instead of being disposed to unite, men differ and quarrel about everything. And when they do unite, how often is the bond of union less love to each other, than abhorrence of some object of common dislike; or, at best, a common object of pursuit, which self-love leads them to seek together, as the surest way of attaining it. "Hateful, hating one another," is the natural development of the human character in a state of estrangement from God. So full of important humbling truth is the figurative view given us of the state of fallen man in the words before us,—"We all, like sheep, have gone astray; we have turned every one to his own way."

This was not man's original state. It was a superinduced condition—a condition superinduced by man's own voluntary choice. Men were not driven from the fold or the pasture-ground of God; they, following the bent of their own inclination, abandoned them. It is this which gives the darkest shade to the picture. They are the objects not so much of pity, though they are to be pitied, as of blame. When sheep wander they can never, in the proper sense of the word, be the objects of blame. Their shepherd is often, usually, to be blamed. It is his business to keep them from wandering. When they wander, they but follow the irresistible instinct of their nature. It is otherwise with man. His errors are wilful errors. He might have avoided them. His transgressions are wilful transgressions. He did what he knew he ought not to have done. He did not do what he knew he ought to have done. He did what he knew was wrong. He neglected to do what he knew to be right. His miseries are self-incurred—often self-inflicted. It is on this peculiarity of man's condition as a moral wanderer that our attention is fixed in the passage before us, for it is this which lies at the foundation of the necessity and the suitableness of the sufferings of the servant of Jehovah as the means of deliverance from this condition. Man's wandering has brought "iniquity,"[1] ill-desert, on him. He is guilty,—i. e., liable to, doomed to, punishment.

"Iniquity"[2] often signifies the act of violation of the Divine

---

[1] עָוֺן.

[2] "As for the word *iniquity,* by it is meant sometimes *sin formally taken,* Psal. li. 3; xxxviii. 4,—and sometimes for the effect which sin procureth—punishment, Gen.

law—that which makes the man guilty ; but it also often signifies
the guilt or exposure to punishment thus contracted, and also the
punishment to which guilt binds over the sinner.   To " bear sin"
and to " die" seem the same thing, Exod. xxviii. 43.   In Gen. xix.
15, " the iniquity of Sodom" seems to be the punishment of that
city.[1]   And " sin,"[2] in the writings of the apostle Paul, is often
equivalent to guilt, exposure to punishment on account of sin.

When men violate God's law, they often seem to think, if
nothing like punishment immediately follow, that there will be
no more of it.   It is as if it had never been.   Fatal mistake !
As our Lord says, " Their sin *remaineth*."[3]   The act may be
momentary, but the effects are lasting.   By that act—so lightly
committed, so soon forgotten—they have touched a spring which,
if the order of things God has established goes forward, has put
in operation a train of causes and effects which will assuredly
end in their everlasting perdition.   They have violated a Divine
law, which is sanctioned by a tremendous penalty ; and the
power, and wisdom, and faithfulness of the supreme Governor
are guarantee sufficient that the sanction shall be duly honored.
Every sin draws down on the sinner the Divine disapprobation,
displeasure, wrath ; and as these are not capricious, but founded
on the deepest truth and reason, this wrath abideth on him on
whom it once rests, if it is not removed by something which does,
at least as well as the execution of the threatened penalty, answer
the purposes of God's holy, righteous, benignant government.
The guilty race, then, on whom iniquity rested for their wilful
wandering from God, were in a state of tremendous danger.
The united wisdom of all created intelligence would probably
have pronounced their condition utterly hopeless ; and, even
though informed that it was not so, could never have conjectured
from what quarter the light of hope was to dawn on its darkness.
Iniquity, guilt—the iniquity; the guilt, of a world of sinful men
—must be dealt with in a way which will satisfy the demands
of the holy, just, good law of Jehovah, if man, the sinner, is to
be pardoned and saved.   How is this to be done ?

iv. 14. It is not here to be taken for sin formally, but for sin in the punishment of
it, as appears from the scope of the passage, which is to show how it came to pass
that Christ suffered, from verse 8,—and from other parallel passages of Scripture,
Gal. iii. 13 ; 2 Cor. v. 21."—DURHAM.

[1] See, also, 1 Sam. xxviii. 10 ; Lam. iv. 6.   [2] ἁμαρτία.   [3] John, ix. 41.

The answer is to be found in the words of the apostle, "God hath made him, who knew no sin, to be sin for us, that we might be made the righteousness of God in him,"[1]—words which are but the translation into New Testament language of the concluding statement of the verse now under consideration, "The Lord laid upon him"—his righteous servant—"the iniquity"—the liability to punishment—"of us all." We have the same thoughts brought into the same connection in the third chapter of the Epistle to the Romans,—"All have sinned, and come short of the glory of God." "God hath set forth"—*i. e.*, either pre-appointed, or exhibited—"Christ Jesus a propitiation in his blood."

This brings us to the second great topic in this prefatory statement,—the Divine arrangement and agency, in which these sufferings of "the servant of the Lord" originated—sufferings which the condition of man rendered necessary, on the supposition of his salvation. The general idea intended to be conveyed is very obvious. "The iniquity of us all,"—that is, the iniquity which belonged to us in consequence of our all having, like a flock, gone astray, "every one in his own way,"—is, by Jehovah, so transferred to his righteous servant, as that he suffers what we deserved to suffer, and we are saved from suffering what we deserved to suffer. However we may explain it, this is clearly the sentiment which the words convey.

It is plain, then, that "iniquity" must be something that can be transferred from one being to another. The act of sin cannot. My act can never become another man's act. If I have sinned, it will continue to all eternity true that *I* have sinned ; and it never can become true that what I did was done by any one else. Transference of iniquity, in this sense, is an utter impossibility. Sin, in the sense of blameworthiness, cannot be transferred to another. If I have been blameworthy for a particular action, I must continue to be so, and no person can relieve me from this burden. No person can deserve blame for what I, not he, did. In neither of these senses could our iniquity be transferred to "the servant of the Lord." But "iniquity," in the strict, legal sense of "guilt"—that is, liability to punishment, and in the sense of "punishment,"—may be transferred

---

[1] 2 Cor. v. 21.

to another. 'I am liable to the evil which was the appointed
punishment of the first man—death ; and I must submit to it.
But I did not do what Adam did, and I cannot be justly blamed
for doing what he did ; but I may be—I am—liable to the evils
which are the punishment of that sin ;' and he must be a bold
rather than a wise man who would question the justice of that
arrangement, so obviously rising out of a Divine appointment.
In like manner, the righteous servant of Jehovah did not do
what all men did, when they, like sheep, went astray, and is in
no degree involved in their blameworthiness ; but he is, by a
Divine appointment, made liable to those evils which are the
punishment of their sins ; and he undergoes these evils as the
punishment of their sins, for the purpose of delivering them
from that punishment. Such, looking at the passage in its connection, is undoubtedly its general meaning. It has been very
justly remarked, that " if vicarious suffering can be described
in words, it is so described in these verses ; and the amount of
ingenuity that has been expended in attempting to bring some
other sentiment out of the words, only shows how artificial and
devoid of solid foundation are the hypotheses which require to
be thus supported."[1]

It is not quite so easy to define the precise image under which
this sentiment is presented to the mind in the passage before us.
The clause has been variously translated. In the margin of our
version it is rendered, " The Lord hath made to meet on him
the iniquities of us all." The strictly literal rendering, approved
by many of the best scholars, is, " The Lord hath made to fall
on him the iniquity of us all." Either is a preferable rendering
to that in the text of our version, " The Lord laid upon him the
iniquity of us all." Supposing the marginal rendering the just
one, the reference would be to the sacrificial rite of emblematic-
ally transferring to the victim the sins of the offerer, by the imposition of his hands, or the hands of the high-priest. Thus

---

[1] Alexander. "Nec illud otiosum est, quod quemadmodum omnes communiter
transgressionibus et iniquitatibus subjicit: ita omnibus etiam transgressionum et
iniquitatum remissionem in Christo promittit, dicens non simpliciter Dominus impinget illi nostram iniquitatem, sed notanter ut præcedenti correspondeat, Dominus
impinget illi omnium nostrum iniquitatem. Quorum omnium nostrum? Errantium
videlicet. Quare excipitur hic nemo nisi qui seipsi de numero errantium et deli-
quentium eximunt, quibus in ore est non propriæ corruptionis confessio, sed alienæ
reprehensio: et propriæ justitiæ, quam non habent, fiducia et gloriatio."—MUSCULUS.

Aaron is said to lay the sins of the congregation on the head of the scape-goat. In this case the meaning would be, that Jehovah appointed his righteous servant to be a vicarious sacrifice for the sins of men, and treated him as their representative. There are objections of considerable force to this way of viewing the passage. It does not seem very congruous to attribute to Jehovah what is always represented as done either by the offerer in his own person, or by the high-priest as his representative ; it seems strange to connect together two figurative representations, so totally incapable of forming parts of one picture, as those of a wandering flock exposed to danger and ruin by wandering, and the sacerdotal rite of imposition of hands, on a third party, as the means of preventing that ruin ; and, finally, the original word does not properly signify either to lay on, or to make to meet.

To arrive at a satisfactory result as to the precise form in which these words present to us the great leading truth of the Christian system, which we have already stated, the safest course will be to inquire, first, what is the meaning of the original term rendered " laid on," and then whether, in conformity with that meaning, it be possible to find in the text a coherent figurative representation of the truth which, there can be no doubt, lies in it. There is no difficulty of fixing the meaning of the word. It is used to describe the hostile assault of the avenger of blood, when he slays the murderer.[1] When Samson's unworthy compatriots came to bind him, and deliver him into the hands of the Philistines, " Swear unto me," said he, generously allowing himself to be bound—" Swear unto me that ye will not fall upon me yourselves."[2] When Solomon dispatched Benaiah, the son of Jehoiada, to slay Adonijah, it is said " he fell upon him, so that he died."[3] When Jehovah, by the prophet, declares the judgments with which He was about to visit Babylon, He says, " I will take vengeance on thee ; I will not meet thee ;"—literally, ' I will not fall on thee as a man.'[4]

It is plain, then, that the word is expressive of fierce hostile attack. Jehovah is represented as making the iniquity of man to fall on—to make a hostile assault on—his righteous servant. " Iniquity"—guilt—armed with the Divine curse, is a powerful thing—powerful to destroy. " The strength of sin is the law."

---

[1] Num. xxxv. 19, 21.   [2] Judges, xv. 12.   [3] 1 Kings, ii 25.   [4] Isa. xlvii. 3.

Now, this power, in the ordinary course of things, guilt exercises against the sinner. But here God is represented as making it to fall on his righteous servant, as a ruthless executioner,—making him sin for sinners—a curse for the accursed,—*i. e.*, by a Divine ordination, constituting him the victim for the sins of men, and treating him accordingly.[1]

The metaphor may appear to our occidental imaginations a bold one; but I confess myself inclined to go along with those interpreters who consider the last clause of this verse as a following out of the figure in the first clause. The strayed flock, by wandering, has exposed itself to the wild beasts of the wilderness, who are ready to devour it,—striking emblem of the dangers to which we have exposed ourselves by our sins, the guilt of which, like a band of ravening wolves, stands ready to devour us. But Jehovah, instead of allowing us to be devoured, does not spare his Son, but delivers him up for us all—appoints him to come between us and our destroyers, and to meet the attack which would have been ruinous to us.[2] It is the same sentiment as in that striking oracle, quoted by our Lord himself, "Awake, O sword, against my Shepherd, and against the man that is my fellow, saith the Lord of hosts; smite the Shepherd, and the sheep shall be scattered."[3] It is difficult not to suppose that our Lord had in his mind this passage, when he said, "I am the good Shepherd: the good Shepherd giveth his life for the sheep."[4] He places himself between them and the wild beasts seeking their destruction. By his death he saves them from death, and lays a foundation for gathering them, when he again takes the life which he had power to lay down, and power to take up again, according to the commandment received of the

---

[1] "When we say iniquity is laid on Christ, we mean, not only that our Lord Jesus is made liable to our debt, but that he is really made to satisfy it. In short, we have done the wrong, but he makes the amends, as if he had done the wrong himself."— DURHAM.

[2] Rosenmüller, though strangely applying the words to the Jewish people, gives the meaning very well:—"Verba ad literam ita vertenda erunt: 'incursare feræ instar—seu hostiliter in eum irruere jussit crimina nostrum omnium,' *i. e.*, poenas nostræ impietati debitas illum unico preferre jussit Jova." His *scholion* on the paragraph, 4–6, is, "Quem nos ob sua crimina atrocissimis malis a Deo affectum existimavimus, illum eos dolores sustinuisse nunc intelligimus, qui nobis pro peccatis subeundi fuerunt."

[3] Zech. xiii. 7.   [4] John, x. 11.

Father. The words seem to refer both to the eternal Divine appointment, that Jehovah's righteous servant should be the victim for human guilt, and to the execution of the appointment, when "God sent forth his Son, made under the law"—made sin, made a curse,—when He "delivered him for our offences."[1]

The other Old Testament predictions well accord with this mode of interpretation. I will content myself with a single specimen. There can be no reasonable doubt that the fortieth psalm is one of the psalms in which it is written of the Messiah. There we find him, when Jehovah actually made the iniquity of men to fall on him—to make a hostile attack on him—saying, "innumerable evils have compassed me about; *mine iniquities*," —*i. e.*, the liabilities to punishment which I sustain,—the sins of men, which were his sins, in the only sense in which any sins can be his,—" Mine iniquities have taken hold upon me, so that I am not able to look up : they are more than the hairs of mine head; therefore my heart faileth me." Yet he did not fail, neither was he discouraged, till he had completed the great work of expiation, and could say, "It is finished," ere he "bowed his head, and gave up the ghost."

Thus have I completed the illustration of what may be considered as the introduction to the statement of the converted Jews respecting the sufferings of the Messiah, and the consequent glories. It brings before our mind the circumstances in the condition of man, which, on the supposition of his salvation, made the sufferings of the servant of Jehovah necessary, and the Divine appointment and agency, which gave to those sufferings that character without which they could not have served their purpose.

The remaining part of the statement contains, first, a general account of Messiah's sufferings, and the manner in which he bore them ; then an account of his violent, unjust death, under the forms of law, and brought about by the extreme wickedness of his countrymen ; then an account of his intended disgraceful, and really honorable interment ; and, lastly, of the glorious results of all this, in his unending life and prosperous reign. These, however, will form the subject of future discourse.

---

[1] The LXX. render the clause, " Καὶ Κύριος παρέδωκεν αὐτὸν ταῖς ἁμαρτίαις ἡμῶν,' —' The Lord delivered him up to our sins.'

How intimately connected are the various doctrines of revelation ! They can be but imperfectly apprehended when viewed
separately.   The doctrine of the atonement is incredible—it is
scarcely intelligible—apart from the doctrine of human guilt
and depravity.   No man will, for himself, seek to Him on whom
God has made to fall the iniquity of us all, till he see and feel
that, like a strayed sheep, he has wandered, and exposed himself to hazards, from which there is but one way of escape.
Low and limited views of the nature and extent of man's miseries
and dangers as a sinner, arising out of low and limited views of
the moral perfections of God, and the consequent requirements
of his law, lie at the foundation of the difficulties which so many
feel in the way of acceding to the doctrine of vicarious expiation
through the sufferings and death of an incarnation of Divinity.
The more clearly we apprehend the truth regarding our own
helpless state of guilt and depravity, the more readily shall we
be disposed to cling to him who " was wounded for our transgressions—bruised for our iniquities,"—on whom the chastisement of our peace was laid, and by whose stripes alone we can
be healed.   We must have low thoughts of ourselves, if we
would have high thoughts of the Saviour.

How deep are our obligations to Him who made all our iniquities fall on his righteous servant!   We can never think too
highly of our obligations to him who willingly stood in our place,
and sustained the attack from " our iniquity," which, if made
on ourselves, must have destroyed us ; but we are in danger of
not thinking highly enough of the kindness of Him, " of whom
are all things," in the economy of salvation,—of Him who
" spared not his Son, but delivered him up for us all ;" who
" so loved the world, that He gave his only-begotten Son," to be
" lifted up as Moses lifted up the serpent in the wilderness, that
whosoever believeth in him might not perish, but have everlasting life."   " Herein is love, not that we loved God, but that
God hath loved us, and sent his Son to be the propitiation for
our sins."   " God commendeth his love to us, in that while we
were yet sinners Christ died for us."   Surely we should love
Him who has thus loved us, and prove, by our conduct, that we
understand and believe the apostle's doctrine, "This is the love
of God, that we keep his commandments."

What will become of those who, by obstinately refusing to

accept, in the faith of the Gospel, the personal benefit which
every believer receives, from the iniquity of us all being made to
fall on Jehovah's righteous servant, madly persist in a course
which must end in their being fallen on by their own iniquity!
Their sin—their guilt—shall assuredly find them out, and come
on them—it may be when they are least expecting it—like a wild
beast or an armed man. Those who put away from themselves
the all-perfect satisfaction given to the law and justice of God,
by him who is the propitiation for the sins of men, must take the
consequences; and these will be found to be more dreadful than
it has ever entered into the heart of man to conceive. The law
must seek vindication, where it never can find full satisfaction,
in the execution of the penalty on them, so far as they are capable
of enduring it; and, as they cannot endure it in a limited period,
the infliction must be eternal. What, suppose ye, is the punishment of which he will be thought worthy, who has thus "trodden
under foot the Son of God—counted the blood of the covenant,
by which he was sanctified, an unholy thing, and done despite
to the Spirit of grace?" There is but one efficacious sacrifice
for sin, and he has rejected it. Henceforth he must himself lie
as an ever-burning, unconsumed, unaccepted sacrifice on the
altar of Divine justice, amid the fire that is unquenchable. God
forbid, my friends, that this awful doom should be yours or
mine! Oh, while it is called to-day, after so long a time, let us
flee for refuge, and lay hold on the hope set before us in the
Gospel,—" the just One who suffered in the room of the unjust;"
who "was made sin for us, that we might be made the righteousness of God in him;" and in whom "God is reconciling the
world to himself, not imputing to men their trespasses." Then
will it be said of us, "Ye were as sheep going astray, but ye are
now returned to the Shepherd and Bishop of souls." He has
settled accounts with "our iniquity;" he has finished transgression, and made an end of sin; he has made peace through
the blood of his cross; his righteousness has obtained peace;
and, to us who are righteous—righteousness in him—united to
him,—its effect will be "quietness and assurance forever."

LECTURE VII

STATEMENT AND PROFESSION OF THE JEWISH CONVERTS—CONTINUED

ISAIAH, LIII. 7.—" He was oppressed, and he was afflicted; yet he opened not his mouth: he is brought as a lamb to the slaughter, and as a sheep before her shearers is dumb, so he openeth not his mouth."

To the satisfactory interpretation of a prophetic oracle, clear apprehensions in reference to its subject and to its form are of the last importance,—What is treated of? and, How is it treated? Happily there is no great difficulty in ascertaining either of these points with regard to that prophetic oracle in the illustration of which we have for some time been engaged. The subject of the oracle is, as we have seen by abundant evidence, external and internal, demonstrated to be " the suffering of the Messiah and the glory which was to follow them." The form of the oracle is not that of direct prediction, or continuous narrative, by the prophet. It resolves itself into four parts; and though not, strictly speaking, a dialogue, these parts are plainly to be viewed as proceeding from different speakers. The prophet is, as it were, but the recorder of the statements uttered in his hearing. First, Jehovah himself, from the most excellent glory, calls the attention of men to his righteous servant wisely and prosperously executing the great work intrusted to him; who, for a season, was reduced to a state of the deepest humiliation and suffering, but is now raised to a state of the highest dignity and enjoyment,—chap. lii. 13–15. Then Jehovah's messengers, who had been proclaiming this truth with regard to his righteous servant, utter a complaint, that few comparatively believe the Divine testimony which they had been appointed to announce, or recognise the Divine power which that testimony reveals, and by which, too, that testimony is confirmed,—chap. liii. 1. This is followed by a statement on the part of those who had discredited, but now believed, the Divine report,—who had disregarded, but now clearly discovered, "the arm of the Lord," of the causes of that comparative want of success of which the divine heralds complain, introducing a declaration of their present convictions respecting the origin, nature, and results of Messiah's sufferings,—chap. liii. 2–10; a declaration confirmed by Jehovah again breaking silence, and proclaiming how well pleased He is for his servant's righteousness' sake, and how secure and glorious are the high and holy rewards with which He has crowned him,—chap. liii. 11, 12. This is plainly what may be termed the form of the oracle.

We are at present engaged in the illustration of the third, by much the longest, of the parts into which it resolves itself. The Jewish converts, for they, as we have endeavored to show, are the speakers from the beginning of the 2d to the end of the 10th verse, begin by stating that few believed the apostolic report, because the Messiah it proclaimed was not at all the Messiah the Jewish nation desired and expected. The meanness of his origin, the abjectness of his external appearance, and the number and severity of his sufferings, which they could not help tracing to peculiar Divine judicial infliction, prevented them from recognising in him the Great Deliverer promised to the fathers. They admit that there was much in his miraculous works and superhuman kindness that should have led to a conclusion different from that at which they arrived,—that he was a sufferer for enormous though unknown sins. They declare that, now having believed the report, they account for these sufferings on a very different principle,—that as the divinely-appointed substitute of men, he sustained those evils which are the expression of the Divine displeasure against their sins, thus expiating guilt and procuring salvation. They then go on to state the circumstances in man's condition as fallen, which, on the supposition of his salvation, made such sufferings necessary on the part of their Deliverer, and the Divine ordination and agency in reference to these sufferings which were requisite to give to them that peculiar character without which they could not have answered their purpose. Thus far we have endeavored to bring out the meaning of this most important statement.

In the words now before us, the attention is directed to two important topics,—first, to those penal substitutionary expiatory sufferings of the Messiah rising out of the sinfulness of man and the righteous merciful ordination of God; and, secondly, to the disposition in which he sustained them. "He was oppressed, and he was afflicted; yet he opened not his mouth : he is brought as a lamb to the slaughter, and as a sheep before her shearers is dumb, so he opened not his mouth."

The general sentiment contained in these words, viewed in their connection with what goes before, undoubtedly is,—' In consequence of this Divine appointment by which "the iniquity of us all" was made to fall on the righteous servant of Jehovah, he was exposed to severe suffering, which he bore with entire resignation and uncomplaining patience.' As to the manner in which this sentiment is to be brought out of the original words, there is considerable variety of opinion among the best interpreters, owing to the somewhat doubtful grammatical construction of the first division of the verse rendered by our translators, "He was oppressed, and he was afflicted." They obviously considered both these clauses as statements made in reference to the servant of Jehovah, when He had made to fall "on him the iniquity of us all." In this view, the two clauses are just equivalent to ' He was most severely afflicted. He was exposed to extreme suffering in consequence of " the iniquity of us all " being made to fall on him.' We know it was so—we have already, in the course of these illustrations, had occasion to lay before you abundant evidence of the intensity of the Messiah's sufferings ; and we cannot help seeing from the nature of the case that it must have been so. When a man's iniquity falls on him, when conscience is awakened, and when the natural effects of his sin to produce suffering are allowed to develop themselves, how fearful is the extent of suffering produced even here ! Such a man has often been made a *magor-missabib*,[1] a terror to himself and to all around him ; and if he is not delivered out of its hand, it will make his eternity an eternity of unmingled, ever-increasing misery. What, then, must have been the oppression and affliction of him on whom Jehovah made " the iniquities of us all " to fall !²

[1] Jer. xx. 3.

² Mr. Dodson, in his work on Isaiah, mentions that, in conversation, Dr. Kennicott had suggested as a translation of this clause, " He was brought forth, and, being questioned, he opened not his mouth." But, for sufficient reasons, no scholar has seconded the suggestion.

It is proper to observe, that the expression rendered, " He **was** afflicted," admits of being rendered, and probably should have been rendered, ' He submitted himself;' or, to use the apostle's phrase, " he became obedient." [1] He made no objection to the Divine ordination, that " the iniquity of us all " should fall on him.   The language of his heart was " Lo, I come ;" " I de-light to do thy will." [2]   And when the Divine ordination was carried into effect, he made no resistance, he showed no reluct-ance.   " The Lord God," says he in the ancient oracle, " hath opened mine ear, and I was not rebellious, neither turned away back.   I gave my back to the smiters, and my cheeks to them that plucked off the hair: I hid not my face from shame and spitting." [3] He never employed his miraculous powers to pre-vent, to mitigate, to remove, his own sufferings. He did not even use means in his power to escape from impending danger. And when suffering came in its most terrific forms, amid the natural shrinkings from pain of a sensitive nature, there was an entire readiness to submit to whatever might be the results of the Divine ordination, that the sins of us all should fall on him,— that his sufferings were to be the expiation of human guilt. Still, still does he say, " the cup which my Father hath given me, shall I not drink it?"   Even when his soul is troubled and he knows not what to say, this is his language,—not, " Father, save me from this hour;" but, mindful of the cause for which he had come unto that hour, " Father, glorify thy name."   When his soul was " sorrowful even unto death," and he prayed that if it was possible that cup of which he was then drinking might pass from him, the bitterness of which threatened to produce immediate death, he added, " not as I will, but as Thou wilt." [4] When he was oppressed " he submitted himself."

The sense brought out of the words in this mode of interpre-tation, is in itself true and important, and every way suitable to the context.   At the same time it must be stated, that there is a peculiarity in the construction of the original text, not very easy to make intelligible to a person unacquainted with the Hebrew tongue, which throws difficulties in the way of adopting it, and which seems to admit, perhaps to require, a somewhat different rendering and exposition.   The nature of the difficulty will,

---

[1] Phil. ii. 8.   [2] Psal. xl. 7.   [3] Isa. l. 5, 6.
[4] John, xviii. 11 ; xii. 27.   Matth. xxvi. 38, 39.

however, be apparent, even to an English reader, when I remark
that, had our translators been as exact as they usually are in
marking supplements, *He* in the beginning of this verse would
have been so distinguished.[1] The words rendered, "He was
oppressed," may be literally rendered, 'It was exacted,' or,
'Exaction was made.' The reference seems to be to "the
iniquity of us all"—our liability to punishment, or the punishment to which we were liable. 'That was exacted—exacted of
him.'[2] The word is the same as that employed, chap. lviii. 3,
"Ye exact all your labors."[3] That is the true account of
Messiah's sufferings. The punishment due to us all was exacted
of him, as having been most voluntarily appointed to be our representative, our Goel, our Kinsman-redeemer, our daysman. Man's
salvation is not amnesty, but redemption. The throne of grace
does not rest on the ruins of the throne of righteousness. The
sinner is saved, not by the penalty being dispensed with, but
endured in his room. Exaction was made ; judgment was done ;
the law magnified and made honorable ; and "grace reigns
through righteousness unto eternal life," when sinners are "justified freely by God's grace," not without, but "through the
redemption that is in Christ Jesus ; whom God hath set forth
to be a propitiation through faith in his blood, to declare his
righteousness for the remission of sins that are past, through the
forbearance of God ; to declare" "his righteousness ; that he
might be just, and the justifier of him which believeth in Jesus ;"
"for he hath made him who knew no sin, to be sin in our room,
that we might be made the righteousness of God in him."[4]

These are pregnant words, "Exaction was made"—indicating the origin, nature, and results of the suffering of our divine
Substitute. Exaction must be made,—if not on him, on us ; and
if on *us*, we are undone forever. But in the eternal counsels of
infinite wisdom, righteousness, and love, the guilt had been laid

---

[1] "*Exigebatur*, scil. *pravitas nostrum omnium, h. e.*, pœna pro eo debita sanctitati
et legi Dei."—COCCEIUS.

[2] See 2 Kings, xxiii. 33 ; Deut. xv. 2 ; Exod. i. 11.

[3] To warrant the authorised rendering, either the pronoun should have been in-
serted before the first verb, or omitted before the second. The rendering, "Exaction was made," is supported by Jarchi among the Jews, by Cyril among the fathers,
and by Sanctius, Tremellius, Hensler, Dathe, Kuinoel, Jahn, Lowth, Crusius, Möller,
Green, Boothroyd, and others, among the moderns.

[4] Rom. iii. 24–26 ; v. 21.

on one able and willing to bear it. The Lord laid on him the iniquity of us all. And what took place when exaction was made of him? He must, at the appointed period in the fulness of time, lay aside "the form of God," in which he had hitherto appeared. He must take on him the nature of a man, the form of a servant, the likeness of a sinner. Found by the law in the likeness of a man, he must do what man ought to do, but will not—suffer what man deserves to suffer, but cannot. He must eat his bread in the sweat of his brow; he must be of few days, and these full of trouble; he must endure, so far as a perfectly innocent man can do, all the evils in which God manifests his displeasure at the sins of man; he must become obedient to death, even the death of the cross; he must become a curse; he must die the death of a felonious slave, deserted by his friends, insulted by his enemies, forsaken of his God; he must descend into the grave—the lonely, loathsome dwelling sin has prepared for the noblest of all God's material works. All this—and who can tell how much more than all this?—is implied in "Exaction was made." When he was delivered for our offences, delivered up for us all, God spared him not, though his own Son, neither spared him from suffering, nor spared him in suffering. He was required to do all and suffer all that infinite wisdom and righteousness saw to be necessary and sufficient for rendering the salvation of sinners perfectly consistent with, gloriously illustrative of, all the perfections of the Divine character, all the principles of the Divine government. So much for the import of that one word with which the verse opens, and the most adequate rendering of which into our language seems to be, "It was exacted," or, "Exaction was made."

The parallel clause, rendered by our translators so tautologically, "*He* was afflicted," and which we have stated may be rendered "He submitted himself," has generally, by those who render the first clause "Exaction was made," been translated, "And he became responsible," or, "He answered the exaction made." He yielded all the satisfaction demanded. He fully paid the debt—life for life. He gave cheerfully—gave till the law said, 'I can demend no more.' Then—not before—he said "It is finished." This is truth, very precious truth; but, I am disposed to think, truth rather put into than fairly drawn out of these words. The word which these interpreters would render "became responsible," or "answered the exaction," seems never employed in the sense of legal or moral responsibility. I prefer taking the word in the sense already explained, " He submitted himself." When the punishment due to the iniquity of us all was exacted of him, he, the righteous servant of the Lord, submitted himself to it. He did not say, 'I never committed those sins. I never incurred such liabilities by personal violation of the Divine law.' He meekly took man's place, and readily met man's responsibilities. The sufferings were very severe—the burden very heavy. He had in no degree deserved to bear them. But they were the manifestation of the righteous displeasure of God for sin, and it was the will of his Father that he should bear them, and, by bearing them, bear them away, and therefore he chose to suffer and to die. " It was his meat to do the will of the Father, and to finish his work."[1]

This gave his sufferings a character which fitted them for serving their purpose. Their being cheerfully submitted to by him was as necessary for this purpose as their being appointed of Jehovah. It would have been injustice to inflict such sufferings on him against his will, without his good-will. And it was not mere suffering which could expiate the sin of man. The eternal sufferings of the wicked in hell will never satisfy justice—never make atonement for one sin. It must be suffering readily submitted to, as a token of entire approval of that law which man had violated, both in its precept and its sanction. And it was thus Messiah suffered. He had "a baptism to be baptised with, and how was he straitened till it was accomplished." He " stedfastly set his face to go to Jerusalem," where these sufferings were to be consummated. He was " obedient unto death, even the death of the cross."[2] Thus, in the parallelism in the beginning of the verse—' Exaction was made,' and ' He submitted himself'—we have a striking picture of the sufferings of the Messiah, as originating in that divine appointment which was necessary to give them the character by which alone they could answer their purpose, and of the disposition in which they were borne by him, equally necessary with the Divine appointment to render them fit for serving their end.

The second part of the verse seems to us to be another parallelism, bringing out substantially, though with slight modifica-

[1] John, iv. 34.   [2] Luke, xii. 50; ix. 51. Phil. ii. 8

tion, the same great sentiment respecting the Messiah's sufferings, and the disposition with which he was to sustain them. "And he opened not his mouth, as a lamb led to the slaughter :[1] and as a sheep before her shearers is dumb, so he opened not his mouth."[2] Here, if I mistake not, we have a figurative view of the Messiah's sufferings. He was led as a lamb to the slaughter. He was as a sheep in the presence of her shearers. And we have also a representation of the temper in which he bore them. He was like the uncomplaining lamb, the dumb sheep—he opened not his mouth.

"He was as a lamb led to the slaughter." This indicates both his situation and disposition.[3] There can be little doubt that the slaughter here referred to is slaughter on the altar as a victim; and that John the Baptist referred to this passage when he said, "Behold the Lamb of God, which taketh away the sin of the world!" and Peter when he said, "Ye were not redeemed with corruptible things, as silver and gold, but with the precious blood of Christ, as of a Lamb without blemish and without spot."[4] This is a picture of the whole life of our Lord—a lamb led to the altar thus to be sacrificed. In one point of view, the whole of our Lord's humbled state may be considered as his sacrifice.

---

[1] Calvin says cautiously, "In voce 'pecudis' *forte* allusio est ad legales victimas : quo sensu alibi vocatur agnus Dei." I think the "*forte*" might have been omitted.

[2] This is one of the passages in which Grotius finds support to his hypothesis, that the oracle has Jeremiah for its subject. He refers to Jer. xi. 19:—"I was like a lamb or an ox that is brought to the slaughter ;" but the parallelism is merely verbal. The idea in Jeremiah is not patience, but unconsciousness (" I knew not that they devised devices against me"), and perhaps helplessness.

[3] "Cæteras autem circumstantias hujus similitudinis omittimus non imprudentes. Novimus enim recte monitum illud ' In omni similitudine scopus, non circumstantiæ.' Quo minus ferendum est, quod hic tam sæpe profertur etiam in publico de agnino vel hircino sanguine quo solo frangi dicunt adamantem, ut corda nostra lapidea et adamantina solo sanguine Christi. Sed primo Plinius dixit *hircino*, et quidem addidit *fædissino animalium*. Deinde tantum non clamat experientia quotidie frangi adamantem a seipso, nec agnino nec hircino sanguine frangi posse. Audivimus alias coram Magno Principe concionatorem inclytum, qui se profitebatur in præloquio nihil Theologicæ rei aut altioris indaginis quidquam allaturum, quoniam adesset Princeps cum conjuge ac aula cetera, sed tantum in gratiam celsitudinum illarum 'cette bellissime historie cavate del Plinio.' Quod cordata Principi probatum non est. Exulent a sanctoribus pulpitis illæ næniæ quæ tametsi veritatem continerent, præ similitudinibus evangelicis plane frigerent. At ubi fictæ sint et ab experientia refutantur, fiunt intolerabiles. Nimis vero multi, quod ait Seneca, ' Instar ovium, eunt quo itur, non quo eundum est.' "—MORUS.

[4] John, i. 29. 1 Pet. i. 18, 19.

What he offered was himself—his whole self—the man Christ Jesus, with all his thoughts, and feelings, and actions, every one of them in perfect accordance with the Divine law.   But in another point of view—one more commonly taken—the sacrifice may be considered as presented in his last passion, and all his previous life may be viewed as a preparation for it, a leading of him towards the altar.   He was born that he might suffer and die.   Every step in his life was a step towards the cross.   Everything was so ordered as to secure the great intended result—the doing what "God's hand and counsel had before determined to be done."   The events of every year, every day, conducted him so much nearer the high altar, before which he was to bleed, on which he was to be consumed as the victim for the sins of men.   And he knew all this. He was perfectly aware where his lonely path—for it was a lonely one—was to terminate.   He sacrificed his own human will.   He did not go where it would have led him.   It would have led him away from the cross.   He sunk his own will in the will of his Father.   He was led, and, though he knew whither that path led, he never showed the least reluctance to follow it.   "I came not to do my own will, but the will of Him who sent me."[1]   He did not need to be dragged—he did not need to be driven.   He was led.

How affecting is this view of the Saviour's sufferings !   We, with good reason, thank God for covering the future with a veil, and concealing from us the coming trials of life and agonies of death.   But the servant of the Lord was all his life, and knew all his life that he was, a lamb led to the slaughter.   Gethsemane and Calvary seem seldom to have been out of view.   And how beautiful the picture of his disposition !   Like a meek lamb, he makes no resistance, discovers no reluctance.   He follows his leader.   The objects in the nearer distance—the agonies of Gethsemane, the traitor's kiss, the disciples' desertion, the impious insolence of the Jewish rulers, the brutality of the Jewish populace and Roman soldiery, the cross, and the sepulchre—were all revolting enough ; but he had entire confidence in Him who led him, and, in the far-off distance, such objects as sin expiated, man redeemed, Satan dethroned, death abolished, God glorified to the uttermost, made him go steadily forward, for, like his great type, the deliverer of Israel, "he had respect to the recompense of reward."

[1] John, vi. 38.

This figure seems to look at Christ's sufferings as they proceeded from God. It was He who led him as the lamb to sacrifice. The other kindred figure leads us to think of his sufferings as they proceeded from men and devils. He was "as a sheep before her shearers is dumb." This, too, seems the picture of his life. He spent his whole life among those who had no friendly regard towards him, who were waiting for the opportunity most favorable for themselves of taking from him whatever was most valuable to him—liberty, reputation, and life. He knew that they would take from him everythng that could be taken from him, and leave him only himself. He knew that they would strip him of all human rights, of which their disrobing of him was but an emblem. What a dreadful thing would it be to live among men, the great body of whom, we knew, were just waiting for the fitting season to spoil us of all that is most precious to us! What a striking picture of his demeanor amidst his enemies! He is like the sheep who is dumb before her shearers. He makes no attempt to prevent their injuring him. He makes no effort to escape out of their hands. He acts as if their way of treating him was much more their concern than his. All he has to do is to submit to be shorn by them. Their wanton rudeness and cruelty provoke no threat, nor lead to any attempt to mitigate their ferocity. "They that sought after his life laid snares for him; and they that sought his hurt spake mischievous things, and imagined deceits all the day. But he, as a deaf man, heard not; and he was as a dumb man, that openeth not his mouth. Thus was he as a man that heareth not, and in whose mouth are no reproofs."[1]

The temper, however, in which our Lord bore his sufferings, both from the hand of his Father and from the hands of his enemies, is more distinctly indicated in the expression, "He opened not his mouth," which is connected with both parts of the parallels,—beginning the first, closing the second. "He opened not his mouth, as a lamb who is led to the slaughter: and as a sheep who is dumb before her shearers, he opened not his mouth."

There is a sense in which our Lord did "open his mouth." He opened his mouth to his Father frequently in those devotional

---

[1] Psal. xxxviii. 12–14.

exercises in which we find him so often engaged. In the very midst of the sufferings here predicted, he "cried to God in the day time, and in the night he was not silent." "With strong crying and tears, in supplication and prayers, he lifted up his voice to Him that was able to save him from death." "O my Father, if it be possible, let this cup pass from me." "My God, my God, why hast thou forsaken me?"[1] And as he spoke to, so he spoke about, his Father to his fellow-men. He had a message to deliver, and he was faithful to Him who had appointed him. He taught in their synagogues ; and on the mountain brow "he opened his mouth," and poured out floods of heavenly truth and wisdom. In him the ancient oracle found ample fulfilment : "I have preached righteousness in the great congregation : lo, I have not refrained my lips, O Lord, Thou knowest. I have not hid thy righteousness within my heart ; I have declared thy faithfulness and thy salvation : I have not concealed thy loving-kindness and thy truth from the great congregation."[2] Before Pontius Pilate he witnessed a good confession : "My kingdom is not of this world." "Art thou a king then?" said the Roman governor. He confessed, and denied not, "I am. To this end was I born, and for this cause came I into the world, that I should bear witness unto the truth. Every one that is of the truth heareth my voice.[3]

But still, the words before us have an important meaning, and it is not far to seek. He submitted in silent patience to his sufferings, as coming from the hand of God,—he did not complain of their undue severity or long continuance ; and as to the insults and injuries that he sustained at the hands of men, not only were they submitted to without reproach, but generally received in silence. It has been well said, "If he did complain, it was not of the violence of the Jews, but of their unbelief ; not of their treatment of his person, but of their rejection of his message ; not of the injury done to him, but to themselves." The unjust sentence of his judges, and the contumelies of the attendants, he bore with a meekness which astonished his enemies. Whenever his speaking might have prevented or mitigated suffering, he is silent; he then answered not a word. When he did speak, it was in vindication of truth ; and what he did say

[1] Psal. xxii. 2.   Heb. v. 7.   Matth. xxvi. 39 ; xxvii. 46.
[2] Psal. xl. 9, 10.   [3] John, xviii. 37.

was fitted rather to precipitate than to arrest his impending doom. He opened his mouth, but it was to declare the truth, the annunciation of which he knew would seal his condemnation. But he opened not his mouth in complaints or reproaches, in petitions to his enemies for mercy, or to God for the vengeance due to their injustice and cruelty. From them he asked for nothing—for them he supplicated forgiveness.[1] Thus did "he endure the contradiction of sinners against himself;" thus, though he had done no sin, and though no guile was found in his mouth, "when he was reviled, he reviled not again; when he suffered, he threatened not; but committed himself to Him that judgeth righteously."[2]

The repetition of the expression, "he opened not his mouth," is striking. It may only be a way of strongly marking emphasis; but it deserves notice that there were three very remarkable separate cases of silence on the part of our Lord, when we might have expected him to speak,—before the Sanhedrim, before Pontius Pilate, and before Herod. Of the first we have an account, Matth. xxvi. 63, 64. After the false witnesses had given their testimony, the high priest arose and said to him, "Answerest thou nothing? what is it which these witness against thee? But Jesus held his peace. And the high priest answered and said unto him, I adjure thee by the living God, that thou tell us whether thou be the Christ, the Son of God." Jesus now opened his mouth. "Jesus saith unto him, Thou hast said,"—*i. e.*, 'It is as thou hast said:' "nevertheless I say unto you, Hereafter shall ye see the Son of man sitting on the right hand of power, and coming in the clouds of heaven." Of another remarkable instance of silence, we have an account, Matth. xxvii. 11–14. When "Jesus stood before the governor, and was accused of the chief priests and elders, he answered nothing. Then saith Pilate unto him, Hearest thou not how many things they witness against thee? And he answered him to never a word; insomuch that the governor marvelled greatly." The third instance is recorded, Luke, xxiii. 9. "Then Herod questioned with him in many words; but he answered him nothing." Who can read these narratives without saying, "Then was fulfilled the saying of the

---

[1] "*Sic* os aperire quemadmodum Christus aperuit, cum pro persecutoribus, oraret, quam non aperire benignius et, ut sic loquor, magis *agninum* est."—MORUS.

[2] 1 Pet. ii. 22, 23.

prophet Isaiah, He opened not his mouth"? Like a lamb brought to the slaughter, like a sheep who, before her shearers, is dumb, "he opened not his mouth."[1]

The converted Jews now proceed to state the truth, first with regard to our Lord's violent death, and his intentionally disgraceful, but really honorable burial; and then with regard to his immortal life, and glorious reign, when he had finished the work given him to do on the earth. On these statements, however, we do not at present enter, but must conclude with a few reflections.

What a mercy is it that, when the inflexible justice of the Divine law made exaction for the iniquity of us all, there was found one able and willing to take our place, and sustain our responsibilities,—to bear, and bear away, our sins! Had it not been so, the fate of men must have been the same as that of the sinning angels. They must have borne their own iniquity, and its weight would have pressed them down into the abyss of hopeless ruin. All had sinned, and all must have perished. The divine dignity of him who bore our sins on his own body to the tree, gives infinite value to his atoning sacrifice. There is a sufficiency of merit in his one offering for the salvation of a world —of a universe—of sinners.

But that merit, by the constitution of the scheme of mercy, becomes effectual, in the communication of pardon, and holiness, and eternal life, only in the case of those who, through the faith of the Gospel, become united to the Saviour. To them there is

---

[1] The observations of Lardner on our Lord's silence, though defective from the influence of his creed, are judicious: "The silence of our Lord," when the false witnesses gave their testimony before the Sanhedrim, "was highly becoming a person of distinguished character and well-known innocence; especially when men sitting in judgment as magistrates show themselves destitute of a regard to justice and equity, and betray a malicious design to put a man to death though they have no evidence against him, and the witnesses that appear, at their procurement, are inconsistent, and do not agree with one another." Before Herod "he says not a word by way of apology for himself,—his innocence being conspicuous, and all the accusations brought against him false and groundless. Our Lord's behavior was admirable. If he had not been a person of consummate wisdom, and had not now had the full command of himself, he might have been induced to exert his power in performing some work of an extraordinary kind, or to say something strongly in his own behalf; but his silence and inaction are more becoming."—It was not for *him* to seek Herod's interposition in his favor. The repetition, "he opened not his mouth," is emphatic. Such emphatic repetitions are common in the Old Testament Scriptures —Psal. lxvii. 4, 6; cxxi. 3. 4; cxxx. 6.

not—there never will be—there never can be—any condemnation. "Who shall lay anything to the charge of God's elect?
It is God that justifieth; who is he that condemneth? It is
Christ that died, yea rather, that is risen again, who sitteth at
the right hand of God, who also maketh intercession for us."
He is in them, and they are in him. What he did, he did for
them; what he merited, is secured to them.

To all who continue in unbelief and impenitence, apart from
Christ, it is as if exaction had not been made from him of the
punishment of human iniquity; with this difference, that, where
the finished work of atonement is exhibited and disregarded,
there is incurred a heavier guilt, in the contempt of God's grace,
than could have been merely by the violation of his law. To
the unbeliever who rejects the sacrifice of Christ, there remains
no more sacrifice for sin, but "a certain fearful looking for of
vengeance," to destroy him as an adversary of God. It is an
inappreciably valuable privilege to hear of a full and a free salvation to the guiltiest of the children of men, through judgment
executed, and justice satisfied, in the righteous servant of Jehovah submitting himself, when exaction was made for the iniquity of men; but if that salvation is not gladly and gratefully
received, in the faith of the plain, well-accredited testimony of
God, they who have heard, but not believed, will have cause
throughout eternity to regret that they ever heard it, and to
envy those who could not contract their guilt, because they did
not enjoy their privilege.

Beware, careless, unbelieving hearer of the Gospel—beware.
Whatever you may think now, if you come not to a better mind,
ere long you will find that it is no light matter to trample under
foot the Son of God—to count the blood of the covenant, by
which alone there is sanctification, a common thing, and to do
despite to the Spirit of grace.

How rich in persuasive example and powerful motive, as well
as in atoning efficacy, are the sufferings of Christ! When he
suffered for us, he "left us an example, that we should follow
his steps." Why should the followers of a suffering Saviour
think it strange that they should suffer? How unbecoming is
it in them to be in any degree fretful and impatient under the
afflictive dispensations of Divine providence? This is not to
have in them the mind which was in Christ Jesus,—this is not

to be in the world as he was in the world.   This is not to tread in the steps of the example he has left us.   Uncomplaining, cheerful suffering of wrong from the hand of men, and of chastisement from the hand of God, is one of the least ambiguous proofs of a genuine Christianity.   Well may we " count them happy," as the apostle James says, who thus " endure."   For, as his beloved brother Paul says, " It is a faithful saying, If we suffer with him "—suffer as he suffered,—" we shall also reign with him "—reign as he reigns.

" Wherefore," as the apostle Peter says, " let them who," like their Lord, " suffer according to the will of God," like him, " commit the keeping of their souls to God in well-doing, as unto a faithful Creator."   Let them rejoice that their sufferings are not punishments—are not exaction of the penalty of the law. That has been paid for them; and the penal sufferings of their representative have converted their sufferings from penal inflictions to disciplinary chastisements—secured that *all* things shall work together for their good; and that their " light afflictions " —light in comparison of his,—" which are but for a moment, shall work out for them a far more exceeding, even an eternal weight of glory."   Brethren, " consider what has been said, and the Lord give you understanding in all things."

LECTURE VIII

STATEMENT AND PROFESSION OF THE JEWISH CONVERTS—
CONTINUED

IsAIAH, LIII. 8, 9.—" He was taken from prison and from judgment: and who shall declare his generation? for he was cut off out of the land of the living: for the transgression of my people was he stricken. And he made his grave with the wicked, and with the rich in his death; because he had done no violence, neither was any deceit in his mouth."

To perceive the full amount, to feel the full force, of the evidence furnished by the argument from prophecy for the Messiahship of Jesus Christ, for the divinity of Christianity, and generally for the truth and authority of the scriptural revelation, it is necessary that we keep steadily in view those distinguishing characters of the Old Testament predictions, which clearly place them in a different category, on the one hand, from the sagacious conjectures of men who have, in the constitution, and circumstances, and past history of man, studied the principles on which the progress of society and the development of civilization depend; and, on the other, from those unconnected, improbable—generally ambiguous—oracular announcements of which, in the course of ages, there sometimes has been found in events a startling realization.

One of the most striking of these characters of the Old Testament predictions is the circumstantiality of their details, especially when taken in connection with the perspicuous language in which these are expressed. Had all the prophecies respecting the Messiah been couched in figurative language and in general terms; or had they been merely eloquent descriptions in which, notwithstanding all the ornaments and amplifications of oriental poetry, little more was said than that he should suffer severely, and that afterwards he should reign gloriously; and especially had no particular period been fixed for his appearance, it might have been urged, with much appearance of reason, that there was no difficulty in finding at different times, in different nations, individuals to whom such predictions might be referred; and that, as there was nothing superhuman in the prophecy, there was nothing strange in its fulfilment.

But the Old Testament predictions are circumstantial in a degree scarcely suspected by the careless reader of the Bible. Of the Messiah, we are not only told that he was to be at once a prophet, a priest, and a king—no common union of official functions,—and that he should pass through the deepest degradation to the highest dignity; but a great variety of minute circumstances respecting his origin, the time of his appearance, his character, his actions, his sufferings, and his glory, are clearly foretold. We are informed that he was to be a descendant of Abraham, Isaac, and Jacob; that he was to be of the tribe of Judah and of the family of David; that he was to be born of a virgin mother in Bethlehem, when his family had sunk into obscurity and the sceptre was departing from his tribe; that he should begin his public labors in Galilee; that he should have a distinguished prophet for his herald; that he should work numerous and beneficent miracles; that he should enter Jerusalem in triumph riding upon an ass; that he should be rejected by the great body of his countrymen; that he should be betrayed by a familiar friend; that he should be sold for thirty pieces of silver, and that these should be given for a piece of ground called the potter's field; that he should be stripped of his garments, and that for his vesture they should cast lots; that his hands and his feet should be pierced; that none of his bones should be broken; that he should be buried in a rich man's tomb; that he should not see corruption; that he should ascend to heaven, and that his religion should, in the course of a short period, be widely diffused and established among mankind.

That all these circumstances were to meet in the character and history of one individual, was in the highest degree improbable, and was obviously equally beyond the power of human foresight to conjecture, and of human contrivance to secure. Yet in Jesus of Nazareth we find every one of these predictions fulfilled to the letter; while, in the case of no other individual, either before or since his age, can there be found anything that even approximates to their fulfilment.[1] I scarcely know any one oracle in which this character of circumstantiality is more clearly marked than that in the illustration of which we have for some time been engaged. You are aware of the general view I take of its subject and structure.

The subject of the oracle is " the sufferings of the Messiah and the glory which was to follow them." The form of the oracle is not that of direct prediction or continuous narrative by the prophet himself. It resolves itself into four parts ; and though not, strictly speaking, a dialogue, these parts are plainly to be viewed as proceeding from different speakers. First, Jehovah himself, from the most excellent glory, calls the attention of mankind to his righteous servant wisely and prosperously executing the great work entrusted to him, who for a season was reduced to a state of the deepest humiliation and suffering, but is now raised to a state of the highest dignity and enjoyment. Then Jehovah's messengers who had been proclaiming this truth with respect to his righteous servant, utter a complaint, that few comparatively believe the Divine testimony or recognise the Divine power which it reveals and by which it is confirmed. This is followed by a statement on the part of those who had once discredited, but now believed, the Divine report,—who had once disregarded, but now clearly discerned, "the arm of the Lord," of the causes of that comparative want of success of which the Divine heralds complain, introducing a declaration of their present convictions respecting the origin, nature, and results of Messiah's sufferings; a declaration confirmed by Jehovah again breaking silence, and worthily closing the solemn oracle, by proclaiming how well pleased He is for his righteous servant's sake, and how secure and glorious are the high and holy rewards with which He has crowned him. We are at present engaged in the illustration of the third, by much the longest, of these four parts into which the oracle divides itself. The Jewish converts—for they, as we have endeavored to show, are the speakers from the beginning of the 2d to the end of the 10th verse—begin by stating, that but few among their countrymen believed the apostolic report,

[1] Bishop Burnet, in his admirable account of the conversion of the notorious Earl of Rochester, mentions that this was one of the circumstances which made a very deep impression on the Earl's mind, when led to examine the evidence of the Divine origin of the scripture revelation.

because the Messiah it proclaimed was not at all the Messiah they expected and desired. The meanness of his origin, the abjectness of his external appearance and his diversified and severe sufferings, which they could not help tracing to direct Divine judicial infliction, prevented them from recognising in him the Great Deliverer promised to the fathers. They admit that there was much in his miraculous works and superhuman kindness that should have led to a conclusion very different from that at which they arrived, that he was a sufferer for his own enormous, though to them, unknown crimes. They declare that, now having believed the report, they account for these sufferings on a very different principle, that as the divinely-appointed Substitute for men, he sustained those evils which are the expression of the Divine displeasure at their sins, thus expiating guilt and procuring salvation. They then go on to state the circumstances in man's condition as fallen, which, on the supposition of his salvation, made such sufferings necessary on the part of their Deliverer, and the Divine ordination and agency in reference to these sufferings which were necessary to give them that peculiar character which was requisite to their answering their purpose. They then describe those sufferings as the exactions of penal justice on him, the sacrificial victim for the sins of men, and the cheerful submission and uncomplaining patience with which he endured those sufferings. So far we have proceeded in the illustration of the statement of the Jewish converts.

In the two verses which are to form the subject of this discourse, they complete their account of the sufferings of the Messiah by a description of his death and burial. His violent death, as occasioned by the wickedness of his countrymen, is described in the 8th verse; and his burial, which was intended to be a disgraceful, but was indeed an honorable one, is described in the 9th verse. Let us attend to them in their order.

" He was taken from prison and from judgment: and who shall declare his generation ? for he was cut out of the land of the living : for the transgression of my people was he stricken." Many interpreters consider the first clause in this verse as descriptive of the deliverance of the Servant of the Lord from the penal sufferings to which he was exposed, in consequence of the iniquity of us all being made to fall on him, and exaction being

made ; and from the manner in which our translators have rendered the words, it is obvious that this was the view entertained
by them of their meaning and reference. " He was taken"—
delivered—" from prison"—oppression, pressure, from that state
of confinement and suffering into which his vicarious character
had brought him—" and from judgment"—from that state of
judicial exposure to suffering in which, till the expiation of sin
was completed, the Divine appointment had placed him. This
is the very truth most sure, and these words, taken by themselves, might be fairly enough considered as expressing this truth.

With the great body of the more learned modern interpreters,
from the time of Tremellius, we, however, feel ourselves constrained to take a different view of their meaning and reference,
and to consider them, not as a statement of Messiah's deliverance
from suffering, but as a continuation of the description of his
sufferings. It seems strangely to break the continuity of discourse to suppose these words to refer to our Lord's deliverance
when imediately there follows a declaration that he was cut off
out of the land of the living, and laid in the grave.

Without doing any violence to the words, they admit of a
different rendering. They may be literally translated, " By oppression and by judgment he was violently taken away."

The word rendered "taken" is that used in reference to the
preternatural removal of Enoch and Elijah out of the world.[1]
Jacob uses it when he says, " Me have ye bereaved of my
children : will ye take Benjamin away also ?"[2] Jeremiah, when
pleading to be preserved from a violent death says, "Take me
not away."[3] It is used of the sudden death of Ezekiel's wife—
" Son of man, behold, I take away from thee the desire of thine
eyes with a stroke."[4]

The word rendered " prison" means restraint or oppression.[5]

The word translated " judgment" means judicial decision,
sometimes sentence to punishment.[6]

The expression, " By oppression and by judgment" he was

---

[1] Gen. v. 24. 2 Kings, ii. 11. [2] Gen. xlii. 36. [3] Jer. xv. 15.
[4] Ezek. xxiv. 16. "Sublatus," in Latin, often means ' taken off,' in the sense of a
violent death. " *Take* ye and crucify him," were Pilate's words to the Jews. " Ye
have *taken* Jesus of Nazareth," says Peter, " and with wicked hands crucified and
slain him."
[5] Psal. cvii. 39. [6] Jer. i. 16. 2 Kings, xxv. 6.

violently taken away, seems to us a remarkable one.   And well it might be, for the transaction referred to was an unexampled one.   The words may indicate that the violent taking away of the Servant of Jehovah was at once the result of oppression, injustice, and of a judicial sentence ; or, by a Hebrew idiom—of which we have specimens in the use of "silence and a voice" for "a still small voice,"[1] and "futurity and hope" for "a hopeful future,"[2]—the expression may be considered as equivalent to, ' By an oppressive judgment he was taken away.'

How exactly this describes what took place with regard to the Messiah, is well known to all familiar with the evangelical histories.   The forms of justice were to a certain extent observed, while the grossest oppression was committed.   There is an accusation and an examination of witnesses, and the pronouncing of a sentence by the Sanhedrim ; but he is allowed no means of self-defence, and condemnation goes forth while crime is unproven.   A multitude with swords and staves, from the chief priests and elders of the people, come out against him as a thief, to take him.   Having thus laid hold of him, they take him to Caiphas the high-priest, where the scribes and the elders were assembled.   They seek false witnesses, but they find none whose testimony could warrant the sentence they were already determined to pronounce. They declared him deserving of death for asserting, when questioned on oath, what he had proved by unnumbered miracles. They then took counsel to put him to death. They bound him, and took him away to the Roman governor. They urged him to condemn him, but he declared that he could find in him no fault—no proven crime deserving of punishment. They terrified the unprincipled Roman judge to give sentence that it should be as they required, and then they led our Lord away to be crucified.[3]   Can we in spirit witness this without saying, By oppression and by judgment he is taken away ? " Taken away" may refer either to his being taken to punishment, or to his being taken out of the world.   It does not matter much which interpretation is preferred, though it seems to preserve the order of the narrative better to adopt the first, as to death— the being " taken out of the land of the living," is mentioned in

---

[1] 1 Kings, xix. 12.   [2] Jer. xxix. 11.

[3] Matth. xxvi. 57–75 ; xxvii. 1–27. Mark, xv. 1–26. Luke, xxii. 66–71   xxiii. 1–26. John, xviii. 13–40; xix. 1–17.

the following part of the verse. The same meaning substantially
is brought out of the words by rendering them, as they will bear,
' Without restraint and without judicial sentence he was taken
away.'[1] In this case we must seek the fulfilment of the prediction in the conduct of the Roman judge, who should have
been his protector, not restraining the Jews from carrying into
effect their murderous purpose, and, without pronouncing a
judicial condemnation (which neither the forms of the Roman
law nor the dictates of his conscience allowed him to do), merely
deciding that it should be as the Jews required.

The words under consideration are cited in the book of the
Acts of the Apostles as translated in the ancient Greek translation, which the Ethiopian eunuch was reading, and which still
exists—" In this humiliation his judgment was taken away."[2] It
is difficult, or rather impossible, to bring such a version out of
the Hebrew text. The meaning is, however, abundantly plain,
and is quite accordant with what we have attempted to show is
the sense of the Hebrew text, ' In his humiliation—when he was
humbled, oppressed—his judgment, his right—was taken from
him—he was deprived of common justice.' We are under no
obligation to hold that this version is the true meaning of the
Hebrew text; for all that Luke says is, that these were the words
which the Ethiopian eunuch found in the copy of the Septuagint
he was reading,—and there they are to be found to this day.

The clause that follows—" And who shall declare his generation ?"—has been very variously interpreted.[3] Some have understood it as indicating the incomprehensibility of the origin
of that relation in the Godhead, by which the second person is
the Son of the first, and of which the ancient oracle speaks, " I
will declare the decree : the Lord hath said unto me, Thou art
my son ; this day have I begotten thee ;" or of that new thing
in the earth, when the Holy Ghost came on the virgin of Nazareth, and the power of the Highest overshadowed her, and she
conceived and brought forth a son, a holy thing, the Son of
God. This is to introduce a thought which has no connection
either with what goes before or follows it, and to give to the word

---

[1] Zwingle, Vatable, Coverdale, Henderson, Luzzatto.

[2] " Ἐν τῇ ταπεινώσει αὐτοῦ ἡ κρισίς αὐτοῦ ἤρθη."—Acts, viii. 33.

[3] It is parenthetical. " Hæc verba," says Le Clerc, " parenthesi claudenda censui-
mus quod nexum orationis interpellent ut lectio ipsa verborum ostendit."

translated " generation" a meaning altogether alien from its proper sense.

Others, referring the previous clause to our Lord's exaltation, have considered it as equivalent to ' Who can describe his posterity,' their number, and their blessedness ?' or ' Who can tell his age ? Who can number the years of his immortality ?'[2] But both these interpretations not only go on what, we are persuaded, is a mistaken opinion as to the meaning of the previous clause, but give to the principal word in the clause a meaning which cannot be satisfactorily established.

It has been supposed by some ingenious interpreters, that the meaning of the question is, ' The manner of his life, who shall declare ?'[3] and that the reference is to a custom said to have existed among the Jews, of proclamation being made before any one was punished for a capital crime, that if any man knew of his innocence, he should come and declare it. In the notes of the Babylonian Talmud, where this custom is noticed, it is stated, undoubtedly without any foundation in fact, " that before the death of Jesus this proclamation was made for forty days, but no defence could be found." It has been supposed that the omission of this ordinary form was an additional injustice done to our Lord, and that to this he refers when he says, " Why askest thou me? ask them who heard me, what I have said unto them: behold, they know what I said."[4] But not only is there no evidence that any such custom existed, but there is no reason to think that the word rendered " generation" ever signifies " manner of life."

The proper meaning of that word is " men living at the same time,"[5] as Noah is said to have been " perfect in his generations" —to have lived an upright life, both along with the race with whom he lived before the flood, and the race with whom he lived after the flood. The Messiah's generation is just another word for his contemporaries—the men of his age; and the whole contemporary race who had offended Jehovah in the desert is termed " all that generation."[6] The word rendered " declare"

---

[1] Kimchi and Hengstenberg.   [2] Luther, Calvin, Vitringa.
[3] Kennicott and Lowth.   [4] John, xviii. 20, 21.
[5] Gen. vii. 1. Deut. ii. 14. Num. xxxii. 13. Eccles. i. 4. Judges, ii. 10. Psal. lxxviii. 9. Prov. xxx. 11. Psal. xii. 8 ; xxiv. 6.
[6] בל הדור.—Num. xxxii 13.

signifies to conceive in the mind, and then to give utterance to such conceptions. The words are a striking declaration of the extreme wickedness of that race. ' Who can conceive—who can describe—his contemporaries ?'[1] It is not improbable that this passage was in our Lord's mind when he said, " Whereunto shall I liken the men of this generation ? and to what are they like ?"

That the Jews of our Lord's times were a very depraved people, is abundantly evident from the facts recorded in the New Testament. They deserved the character our Lord gives them, when he calls them emphatically, " This wicked generation ;"[2] and that which Paul gives them, when he says, " They pleased not God, and were contrary to all men." The following is the account given of them by their own historian, Josephus :— " I cannot say it without regret, yet I must declare it is my opinion, that if the Romans had delayed to come against these wretches, the city would have been swallowed up by an earthquake, or overwhelmed by a deluge, or else been consumed by fire from heaven as Sodom was ; for it bore a generation of men more wicked than those which suffered such things."[3] And in another place he says, " To reckon up all their villanies is impossible ; and, in a word, never did any city suffer so great calamities, nor was there ever, from the beginning of the world, a generation more prolific in wickedness."[4]

The evidence of the inconceivable, indescribable wickedness, of the men of the Messiah's age, is given in the words that follow, " For he was cut off"—i. e., by them—" out of the land of the living."[5] "The land of the living" is just this world, as

[1] Gill.

[2] Matth. xii. 45. The word דּוֹר, in Isa. xxxviii. 12, is translated "γενεὰ μου" by Aquila and Theodotion, and by the Vulgate ; "generatio mea" certainly means ' the men of my age.'—Vide Harmer's Obs. iv. 451, etc. Dr. Whitby, in his " Stricturæ Patrum," and Dr. Gill, take this view of the passage.

[3] Jos. Wars of the Jews, v. 13, 6.

[4] Ibid. x. 5. There is little doubt that it is to this passage the rabbins refer in the following citations, for which we are indebted to Wetstein. " In generatione in qua filius Davidis veniet, synagoga erit lupanar, Galilæa destruetur, et Gablæa desolabitur. R. Levi dixit : Filius Davidis non veniet nisi in generatione in qua facies erunt impudentes, et dignæ excidio. R. Jannai dixit : Cum videris generationem post generationem convitiantem et blasphemantem ; tunc expecta pedes regis Messiæ"

[5] " Who can describe that generation ?" is a parenthetical clause thrown in. It puts us in mind of the Latin poet's—" Quis cladem illius noctis, quis funera fando explicet ?" " Exclamatio in pravos Judæos, qui Christi tempore vixerunt et eum ad mortem traxerunt." —VATABLUS.

contrasted with the land of the dead,[1] the grave, or the separate
state ;[2] and to "cut a man off out of the land of the living," is
just to bring him to an untimely and violent death. It is the
same word which Daniel uses, when he says, "Messiah shall be
cut off, but not for himself."[3] What sort of a people must they
have been, who "killed the Lord of Life,"—who, when the great
Proprietor's Son came, said, "Come, let us kill him, that the
inheritance may be ours" ?

The same sentiment, according to the usage of Hebrew poetry,
is repeated in the second branch of the parallelism, "For the
transgression of my people was he stricken."[4] The expression,
" *my* people," is remarkable. It is plain that these are the words
of the converted Jews. We should have expected ' *our* people.'
But they may be considered as represented by the one who
speaks, and such a change of number is not unprecedented in
Scripture.[5] Had it been ' *his* people,' we should have thought it
very appropriate, and found the New Testament correspondence
in—"He came unto his own, and his own received him not."[6]
The particle rendered "*for*,"[7] ' on account of,' may with equal
propriety be rendered ' *by*,' ' through means of.' It is common to
suppose that the great doctrine taught so plainly in verses 5 and
6, and again verses 10–12—the doctrine of vicarious suffering—
is here asserted ; but it seems far more natural to understand the

---

[1] A German expositor, Hendewech, explains "the land of the living," of the Holy
Land, and renders the whole passage, "By a Divine judgment was the people taken
away, and yet who can declare its future increase ? It was cut off out of its own
land; for the transgression of the fathers were the children smitten." This is to
make, not *find*, a sense.

[2] ᾅδης. Psal. xxvii. 23 ; cxvi. 9 ; cxlii. 6. Job, xxviii. 13. Isa. xxxviii. 11. Ezek.
xxxii. 23. Jer. xi. 19.

[3] Dan. ix. 26.

[4] "The stroke was on him,"—לָמוֹ, the poetic form of לֹּ. Jahn remarks that the
poetic suffix is compounded of the plural, מ, and the singular, וֹ, so that it is used for
both numbers.—Isa. xliv. 15. Hab. iii. 4. Comp. Deut. xxxiii. 2. The Septuagint had
read לָמוּת ; but there is no reason to think this the true reading. לָמוֹ might readily be
changed to לָמוּת, as furnishing an easier meaning, but the reverse change was not likely
to take place. Dr. Pye Smith considers לָמוֹ as plural, and renders the whole clause,
"From the transgression of my people, the stroke is on them,"—*i. e.*, ' The Jewish
people are punished on account of their transgression in so maltreating the servant
of Jehovah.' But this sadly disturbs the succession of thoughts in the passage.

[5] 1 Sam. v. 10. Zech. viii. 21. 　　　　　　　　　　　　　　　[6] John, i. 11.

[7] מ may be rendered, according to the exigence of the context, either *propter* or *per*.
The LXX. give " ἀπὸ τῶν ἀνομιῶν,"—Tertullian and Lactantius, "a facinoribus," etc.

words as meaning, 'By the wickedness of that generation he was smitten.' Their wickedness brought him to his untimely grave. The Romans were but the executioners of the Jews. "They took him, and by wicked hands"—lawless hands, the hands of the Roman soldiery—" crucified and slew him;--"they killed the Lord Jesus."

This seems to me a much more natural mode of explanation than that which has been adopted by a very learned interpreter,[1] who considers the second part of the verse as one sentence, and reads it thus, " Who of his contemporaries considered that he was taken away from the land of the living? that the stroke was on him for the iniquity of my people?"[2] This destroys the obvious parallelism,—" He was cut off," " he was taken away," " he was smitten;" and altogether the construction has very little of the appearance of idiomatical Hebrew.

The meaning of the whole verse seems to be,—' By injustice under the forms of law he was brought to a violent and untimely death by the wickedness of his contemporaries; a race, the depth of whose guilt and depravity, especially as indicated in his sufferings, cannot be described—cannot be conceived.' This, then, is the account of the death of the Servant of Jehovah.

The following verse gives an account of the circumstances of his burial,—" And he made his grave with the wicked, and with the rich in his death; because he had done no violence, neither was any deceit in his mouth." These words in our translation are obviously elliptical, and require something to be supplied to make them express a distinct meaning. " He made his grave with the wicked," and he was with " the rich in his death." The natural signification of this statement is, " He was buried with the wicked, and was with the rich in dying.'

Those interpreters who deny the reference of this oracle to the Messiah, have been reduced to the greatest difficulties in their attempts to extract anything like a coherent meaning out of these clauses. It would serve no good purpose to detail their absurdities. One specimen, not worse than many others, will

---

[1] De Wette.

[2] Hengstenberg translates נגע למו, "on whom"—i. e., my people—"the stroke should have fallen." In this case, אשר must be supplied, and למו viewed as plural, referring to עמו.

suffice. "They, *i. e.*, my people, treated him, *i. e.*, my servant, as a wealthy tyrant."[1]

But even those interpreters who hold the Messianic reference of the oracle, have had some difficulty in satisfactorily explaining the passage. It seems strange that the burial should apparently be put before the death, and there is no correspondence with the facts of the evangelical history. He whom we acknowledge as the Messiah, was not buried among the wicked, nor was he associated with the rich in his death.

Various methods have been adopted to meet the difficulty. Some have supposed that the words, "the wicked" and "the rich," have been transposed, and that the prophet wrote, 'He made his grave with the rich, and was with the wicked in his death;' and that the clauses, too, have been transposed,—'He was with the wicked in his death, and made his grave with the rich.' This is to use a very unwarrantable freedom with the sacred text. Others have supposed that the word rendered "in his death," means his sepulchre;[2] so that the two clauses are strict parallels,—'His grave was given him among the wicked, but his sepulchre was with the rich;' but there is no reason to suppose that the word has any such meaning.

By the application of the principles of a cautious interpretation, a sense has been brought out of the words as they stand in entire correspondence with the facts of the case. The word "wicked" is in the plural. It designates very wicked men— "malefactors." The word "rich" is in the singular, and signifies 'a rich man.' The word rendered "he *made*," literally signifies, 'he gave;' or, 'it was given.'[3] The word "*in*," in the

---

[1] Hoffmann. "Et dedit impios pro sepultura."—Hieronym.—What that means is not very clear. Houbigant's interpretation is far from satisfactory: "Significat propheta, impios sua morte ac pernicie necem Messiæ expiaturos; quasi dicat impios fore pro eo victimam vicariam." Abundant information respecting the interpretations which have been given to this clause may be found in Geier's dissertation, "De Messiæ morte, sepultura et resurrectione," Opera, Tom. ii.; and in Clingius' dissertation, "De Ossilegio circa sepulchrum Christi ad Esai. liii. 9," in the first volume of the "Thesaurus Theologico Philologicus."

[2] Lowth, following Abenezra, Forerius, Œcolampadius, Zwingle, Schindler, Drusius, A. Morus, and Kennicott, supposes ב, radical in במותיו, במה signifies 'a high place,' but nowhere does במית signify 'a tomb;' it signifies the high places where idols were worshipped.

[3] It is used in the sense of appointing, Isa. lv. 4; Gen. xv. 18; Jer. i. 4; Psal. lxxii 15; Eccles. ii. 21.

phrase, "in his death," sometimes signifies '*after;*' as, *e. g.*, Isa. xvi. 14, "In three years," 'after three years.' And "death" signifies not merely 'the act of dying,' but, 'the state of the dead.' In Lev. xi. 31, "Whosoever doth touch them, when they be dead," means, 'Every one who touches them when dead.' And in Psal. vi. 5, "In death there is no remembrance of thee," is, 'In the state of the dead there is no remembrance of thee.'

Taking along with us these well-established facts, the following meaning comes clearly out of the original words as they stand :—' My people, by whose wickedness he was " cut off out of the land of the living," gave'—*i. e.*, appointed, assigned— 'his grave with the malefactors;' or, impersonally, 'his grave was appointed with the malefactors; but he was with a rich man after his death,' or, 'in the state of the dead.'

We have no express record of the intention of the Jews to give our Lord an ignominious funeral. But there can be no reasonable doubt of the fact. The injunctions of their law prevented them from adopting the Roman custom, which otherwise their cruelty would have preferred, of allowing the body to hang on the cross till wasted by the elements or devoured by dogs; but there can be no doubt that they meant that he should be interred, probably in a common grave,[1] with the malefactors along with whom he had suffered. In following this course, they would only have done what was usual. "Let him," says Josephus, "who blasphemes God be stoned, and then hanged for a day (a reference to the custom mentioned by the apostle, Gal. iii. 13), and let him have a disgraceful and obscure burial."[2] Maimonides remarks, "Those who are condemned to death by a judicial tribunal, are not interred in the sepulchres of their ancestors, but two places of burial are appointed by the court,— one for those stoned and burned, another for those beheaded and strangled." The place where the crucifixion took place was called Golgotha, not improbably because the place of execution was also the place of interment. It is indeed highly probable that as the bodies could not, without a violation of the Mosaic law, hang on the cross all night, the common grave was already dug. His grave was prepared for him among the malefactors.

But the malignant purpose of those who, having murdered him, wished to heap posthumous infamy on him, was disappointed.

---

[1] πολυάνδριος τάφος.   [2] Jos. Antiq. iv. 8, 6.

Our Lord died sooner than was usual in such cases—died before the time fixed for taking the bodies down and burying them; and this gave opportunity for an application being made and granted, while it fulfilled the latter part of the prediction,—'But he was with a rich man after his death,' or, 'in his dead state.'

The wonderfully exact fulfilment of this prediction cannot be so well represented in any other way than by quoting the evangelical narrative, "And now, when the even was come, Joseph of Arithmathea, a rich man, an honorable counsellor, who had not consented to the counsel and deed of them, which also waited for the kingdom of God, who also himself was Jesus' disciple, but secretly for fear of the Jews; this man came and went in boldly unto Pilate and craved the body of Jesus. And Pilate marvelled if he were already dead: and calling unto him the centurion, he asked him whether he had been any while dead. And when he knew it of the centurion, he commanded the body to be delivered, and he took it down; and there came also Nicodemus, which, at the first, came to Jesus by night, bringing a mixture of myrrh and aloes, about an hundred pound weight; and these two rich men took the body of Jesus, and wrapped it in clean linen clothes with the spices, as the manner of Jews," of the higher order, "is to bury. Now, in the place where he was crucified, there was a garden, and in the garden was a sepulchre wherein was never man yet laid. That sepulchre was Joseph's own new tomb which he had hewn out of the rock. *There* laid they Jesus."[1] Is not this "He of whom the prophet did write"?'

It deserves notice, before we conclude the exposition of this clause, that the word in the phrase, "in his death"—'after his death'—is plural,—'after his deaths.' It is probably emphatic. We find the violent death of the king of Tyre expressed in this way,—"Thou shalt die the death"—literally, "the deaths"—"of the uncircumcised by the hands of strangers."[2] Our Lord's death, as it were, included many deaths—all kinds of death. It thus very forcibly expresses the awful nature of that death to which our Lord submitted.[3]

---

[1] Mark, xv. 42–47. John, xix. 39–41. Matth. xxvii. 57. Luke, xxiii. 51.

[2] Ezek. xxviii. 10.

[3] The interpretation of HILLER is worth quoting, if but for its strangeness: "Et posuit milites Romanos (improbos) ad sepulchrum ejus, ac ditatum mortibus ejus, *i. e.,*

There is little difficulty in the words of the clause which follows,—"*because* he had done no violence, neither was any deceit in his mouth;" but there is some doubt as to its connection, which to a certain extent modifies its meaning.

Some have connected it with the next verse; thus, "Although"[1]—for the particle "because" not unfrequently has this force—"he had done no violence, neither was guile found in his mouth, yet it pleased the Lord to bruise him." There is no sufficient ground for this change; and, if we mistake not, the next verse, when rightly interpreted, does not admit of this connection.

The words have been viewed as connected solely with the last clause,—'he was with a rich man after his death,' or, 'in his dead state;' and have been considered as indicating, that this very remarkable occurrence was intended to be a declaration of our Lord's innocence, even when he had undergone the punishment of a felon. It was because he had done no violence, and that no guile had been found in his mouth, that Pilate gave his body to Joseph, with the distinct understanding, that he meant to give an interment suited to his own rank. Pilate would not have done this, if he had supposed Jesus the "malefactor" the Jews said he was.[2]

The words may, however, be considered as hanging from the first clause (the words, "but he was with the rich in the state of the dead"), like the words in the previous verse ("who shall declare his generation?") being a parenthetic interjection; and indeed connected, as to meaning, with the whole statement, from the beginning of the 7th verse. 'Exaction was made, and he submitted himself. "He opened not his mouth. "As a lamb led to the slaughter—as a sheep before her shearers is dumb—he opened not his mouth." By an oppressive judgment

---

reticentia resurrectionis Dominiciæ fictaque corporis ablati fama."—*Inst. L. S,* p. 557. It were easy to add other interpretations, but I choose to say, with Vitringa, "Alia non recenseo; neque enim finis est. Sunt in mundo homines, qui liquida turbant; et quæ certiora ante occulos sunt, incertis et dubiis postponunt."

[1] Job, xvi. 17; x. 7; xxxiv. 6. Jer. ii. 34, 35.

[2] Morus' note is,—"Voluerunt ipsi dare sepulchrum cum impiis: Deus autem noluit: quamobrem? Scilicet minime decebat eum post mortem conjungi cum impiis, quem pia mors et vita tam innocenter acta, tam longo ab impiis intervallo separabat. Itaque divitem illum suscitavit Deus, cujus in monumento minime vulgari honorifice conderetur."

he was taken away (who can describe the men of his age ?) " he was cut off out of the land of the living ;" by the wickedness of my people was he smitten ; and they assigned him his grave with the malefactors (though their malignant intention was frustrated). He endured all this, " although he had done no violence, neither was guile found in his mouth." '

In these words we have a description of the faultless excellence of the character of the servant of Jehovah. I can scarcely persuade myself that there is not, in these two clauses, a reference to the twofold charge brought against our Lord as a mover of sedition, and as a blasphemer and impostor. Before Pilate he was accused of treason against the Roman government, pretending to be a king, and stirring up sedition. That accusation was unproved, and was groundless. Neither his conduct nor his doctrine was revolutionary. He was no demagogue. He did "not strive, nor cry ; neither did any man hear his voice in the streets."[1] So far from thus doing violence, he checked every tendency in his audience towards tumult—refused to be their leader—withdrew when they would by force have made him a king—and commanded to " render unto Cesar the things which were Cesar's."[2] He was charged before the Sanhedrim with making false pretensions to Messiahship,—with being a blasphemer, an impostor, a deceiver of the people.[3] This accusation was equally unfounded. " There was no guile found in his mouth " when he said he was the Son of God ; he but spoke the truth—the truth confirmed by abundant evidence. There would have been guile in his mouth had he denied this.

These are striking correspondences ; but we ought to consider the words as also an assertion of the spotless innocence—the absolute perfection—of the character of the servant of the Lord. If his inveterate enemies were unable to prove any guilt against him, what could be the cause but that there was no guilt to be proven ? They were wise enough to fix on the most plausible charges. They failed in substantiating any one of them. The declaration is indeed equivalent to, ' He knew no sin ; in him was no sin. He was equally free from hereditary and personal guilt—original and acquired depravity. His life was perfect holiness, his doctrine pure truth. Instead of doing violence, his life was a constant tenor of acts of beneficence. He went about

---

[1] Matth. xii. 19.   [2] Matth. xxii. 21,   [3] ὁ πλάνος.—Matth. xxvii. 63.

doing good.   Instead of guile being in his mouth, as the sent and sealed of the Father, he spoke the words of eternal verity. Not violence and guile, but grace and truth, were the leading features both of his character and his doctrine.'

Yet, notwithstanding all this, exaction was made.   He was as the lamb led to the altar.   By an oppressive judgment he was taken away; by the transgression of his people " he was cut off out of the land of the living," and they assigned him a grave among the malefactors.   All this is plainly intended to bring out more forcibly the evidence of the statement made in the 5th verse—the only satisfactory account that can be given of these deepest and darkest of all the Divine dispensations,—" He was wounded for our transgressions, he was bruised for our iniquities: the chastisement of our peace was upon him; and by his stripes we are healed."

This closes the statement of the Jewish converts respecting the sufferings of the Messiah.   Their statement respecting the glory which was to follow them is contained in the next verse. On its illustration we do not now enter.

We conclude with a few reflections.   How strangely may the most opposite characters be apparently combined in the same action!   Real oppression and ostensible judgment were equally the characters of the course of action by which the servant of Jehovah was taken away.   How often has the appearance of devotion been conjoined with the reality of irreligion!   What strange disclosures will that day make, when everything and every person will appear what they really are!

When religious and moral advantages are not improved, the probable result will be, that they who enjoy them will become worse than they who never possessed them.   The worst men in the world, at the time of our Lord, were probably his countrymen the Jews.   Who can describe the men of his age?   Let us take care how we use our advantages.   If their right use does make us among the best, their abuse is likely to make us among the worst, of our race.

How obviously are the events which, so far as man is concerned, are contingent and accidental, under the direction of the Divine providence?

How easily can, and how strangely often does, God disappoint the designs of the enemies of Christ and his people? They appointed him his grave with the malefactors, but he was laid in a rich and honorable man's tomb.

Let us beware of judging rashly or harshly of men's characters, on the ground of the number and severity of their trials. Had it been just thus to judge, the Jews would have been right in their judgment of our Lord, that he was guilty of enormous though unknown sins, and an object of the peculiar displeasure of the Almighty. Singular adversity is no more a proof of God's peculiar displeasure, than singular prosperity of his peculiar complacency.

Let all the followers of Christ count on suffering from the world, which, in its substantial character, is still what it ever was. Entire freedom from chastisement would prove—what no severity of chastisement would—bastardy, not sonship. The most afflicted man the world ever saw was God's *dear* Son; and it is still true, "whom the Lord loveth He chasteneth, and scourgeth every son whom He receiveth."

Let them take care that their sufferings from the world be, like his, undeserved sufferings. Let them be in the world as he was in the world. Let them do no violence, and let no guile be found in their mouth.

I conclude, as I began, with pressing on your consideration the evidence for the truth of Christianity, from the minute fulfilment of Old Testament prophecy. Who can reflect on such a circumstantial prophecy as that we have been considering, uttered and recorded more than seven hundred years before Jesus Christ was born, being fulfilled in its minutest details, without feeling that the spirit of prophecy is indeed the testimony of Jesus, and that, in acknowledging him as a Divine messenger and the promised Saviour, we but "set to our seal that God is true," and do homage to Him who seeth the end from the beginning, and who worketh all things according to the counsel of his own will,—whose counsel stands, and who "will do all his pleasure"?

LECTURE IX

STATEMENT AND PROFESSION OF THE CONVERTED JEWS—
CONCLUDED

Isaiah, liii. 10.—"Yet it pleased the Lord to bruise him; He hath put him to grief: when thou shalt make his soul an offering for sin, he shall see his seed, he shall prolong his days, and the pleasure of the Lord shall prosper in his hand."

The path of error, like that of vice, which lies so near it, and from which and into which it has so many openings, is a downward one; and it is equally true of both, that he "who leaves the paths of uprightness, to walk in the ways of darkness,"[1] is likely to descend to a depth, and, in his ultimate progress, with a rapidity, which, had he been forewarned of it, would have excited in him a mingled feeling of scepticism and horror. The declivity may seem gentle at first, but it gradually increases— the descent becomes steeper and steeper; and by the time he has reached the precipice of infidelity and profligacy, which was not at all in his view when he left the table-land of truth and virtue, he is sure, unless held back by a power superior to his own, to take the desperate leap. He has got an impetus he cannot resist. To change the figure: The angle at which he leaves the straight onward path is so acute, that for some time he is scarcely aware that he has abandoned it; but he has changed the direction, and the terminating points of the two paths in eternity are wide as heaven and hell. Every step leads him farther and farther from the right road, till the divergence becomes distinctly evident to himself and every one else, and he finds himself, not without something like alarm, where he never meant he should come—where he never dreamed he could come.

---

[1] Prov. ii. 13.

These remarks have, if we mistake not, often been verified to a most melancholy extent in the experience of those who have been led to deviate, as they thought, only in a slight degree, from any one of the great principles of evangelical truth. These are not, as many seem to suppose, unconnected facts or principles; they form part of one great, closely linked together system; and if a man is determined to be consistent, he will find that he must either hold them all, or let them all go.

The following history is, I am afraid, not an uncommon one. A young man has been instructed in the letter of the doctrines of the Christian faith. Man can instruct man in nothing more. He thinks he believes them all. He is quite sure he has never doubted as to any of them. But he has not—he never has had—true seriousness. His faith lies on the surface, or, if it have at all penetrated into the mind, there does not lie at the root that deep sense of the reality and power of "things unseen and eternal"—that realization in the mind of the existence, and character, and government of God, and of his own relation to God as a creature and a sinner, without which men may speculate, but can never believe in religion, and without which, indeed, speculation about religion, however ingenious, or even accurate, is likely to do more harm than good. He meets, in some of the sceptical publications of the day—wearing, it may be, the form of an attempt to purify the prevailing notions of Christian doctrine or evidence —or in the intercourse of society, with certain suggestions which lead him to suspect that the doctrine of redemption through the vicarious suffering and death of the Son of God, which he has been accustomed to hold as the very key-stone of the arch of Christianity—though he never felt his own need of it as a guilt-stricken, conscience-condemned sinner—is not reconcilable with the fundamental principles of reason and justice; and, trusting to his own understanding, he renounces a doctrine which he perhaps had long zealously maintained, but had never rightly understood nor really believed. He has made one change, and, likely, has no wish to proceed any farther. He is not aware of the many alterations of sentiment to which, if he is a reflecting man, this one change must lead, should he wish to preserve anything like conscious consistency in his religious opinions. It will probably not be long before he discover that, as he has renounced the atonement, he cannot hold the divinity of the Saviour. With his new creed, he will find it difficult to assign a reason why a divine person should become incarnate to do all that which his new system gives Jesus Christ to do. Something far inferior to Deity might have answered the purpose. The divinity of Christ is certainly not less mysterious than his atonement, and it is not wonderful that any man's reason should recoil at the incongruity that an incarnation of Divinity should suffer and die, merely to attest the truth of doctrines, however important, or exhibit an example of virtue, however perfect. The Saviour is now degraded, in his mind, to the rank of creatures, though he still occupies the highest place in that rank. He thinks of him as the incarnation of some super-angelic and perfectly holy nature. But a little reflection must convince him that even still his system wants coherence and consistency. For how, upon any principle his system allows him to assign, does it consist with the leading attributes of the Divine character—how is it reconcilable with the benevolence, or even the equity of God, to inflict, or allow to be inflicted, on a creature so dignified and excellent, such sufferings and such a death as Jesus Christ did undergo? To get rid of this difficulty, in opposition to the plainest declarations of Scripture, the Saviour is brought down to the level of humanity, and Jesus Christ is now with him a mere man—with this distinction, that he was free from and incapable of moral guilt or depravity. But there is no secure standing even here. The last movement has not materially lessened his difficulties. A perfect, impeccable man suffering and dying, seems as incongruous with the Divine justice and benignity, as the sufferings and death of the highest created being clothed in human nature ; and, revolting as the thought would once have been to him, he begins to question whether the freedom from sin, ascribed to Jesus Christ in Scripture, can reasonably be supposed to extend farther than exemption from mistake or fault in his public conduct as a divinely-commissioned teacher, and ends with holding that, like other men, he was liable to sin, and with thinking his personal guilt, to a certain degree, a possible and probable thing, as being that which alone, on the principles adopted, can reconcile his sufferings and death with the perfections of the Divine character, and the principles of the Divine government. Dismal as is this depth of error—more deplorable, indeed, in some points of view, than an entire renunciation of the Christian faith—I do not wonder so much that some who began with doubting or denying the doctrine of atonement have reached it, as that any considerate person who gives up with that doctrine, can stop short of this or of open infidelity. Indeed, the denial that the Scriptures are a Divine revelation is the more reasonable course ; for there are doctrines contained in them, stated in terms as explicit as language can furnish, which nothing but the admission of the doctrine of the atonement can prevent from appearing utterly contradictory. How, but on this principle, can we reconcile the equally clear statements respecting the justice and benignity of God, the moral perfection of Jesus Christ, and the Divine agency in his sufferings and death, and the bestowment of the highest blessings on persons deservedly doomed to punishment ?' These truths, which nothing but the doctrine of vicarious atonement can harmonize, are very explicitly brought forward in that portion of this very remarkable prophetic oracle which yet remains for consideration.

In the eight expository discourses which I have already delivered to you on this subject, after laying before you the evidence that the sufferings of the Messiah and the glory that should follow them is the subject of the oracle, I remarked that it naturally divides itself into four parts : (1). A call on the part of Jehovah, to make the sufferings and the glories of his righteous servant, prosperously executing the great work He had committed to him, the object of considerate thought ; (2). A complaint on the part of His messengers, pressing this subject on the attention of men, that few believed their message, or recognized the Divine power which it revealed, and by which it was confirmed ; (3). A statement on the part of the Jewish con-

---

¹ These are striking words of Mr. Douglas, in his " Errors regarding Religion :"— " Thus one step of error leads to another, nor is there any rest to those who depart from the faith. Those who deny the absolute Deity of Christ, have only to be consistent in their opposition, and they will proceed without delay or cessation from Arianism to Socinianism. Nor does the downward path of error end here. They may, indeed, find more difficulty in giving up the name of Christianity than its truths, but the same impulse which before pressed them forward, still urges them on. The regions of darkness lie open and interminable before them : they have only to continue admitting nothing contrary to their reason, and the Divine government and the Divine existence will appear to them encumbered with still greater absurdities than the revealed religion which they have left far behind ; and they will arrive at the ultimate bourne to which their philosophic strength of mind is conducting them—a grave without a resurrection, and a world without a God."—*Errors regarding Religion*, p. 199.

verts, of the false views of the nature and design of the Messiah's mission which prevented so many—had long prevented themselves—believing the Gospel, and of the just views on this subject which, from the reception of the apostolic report, they now entertained ; and (4). A declaration, on the part of Jehovah, of the absolute certainty of those glorious results, in which the labors and sufferings of his righteous servant were to terminate. The words which come before us to-day for exposition, are the conclusion of the third division of the oracle.

In that portion of it which we have considered, the Jewish converts have traced the paucity of converts among their countrymen to the fact—manifested by the meanness of his origin, the abjectness of his external appearance, and the number and severity of his sufferings—that the servant of Jehovah was not at all the kind of Messiah they desired and expected ; intimated that his beneficent miracles and unexampled sympathy ought to have led them to a very different conclusion as to the cause of his sufferings than that at which they did arrive—that he was, for great though unknown sins of his own, the object of the peculiar displeasure of God ; declared that the true cause of these sufferings is to be found in his being the victim for the sins of men ; stated the condition of men, which, on the supposition of their salvation, rendered such sufferings, on the part of their Saviour, necessary, and the Divine arrangements giving to these sufferings the character which was requisite to their serving their purpose ; and narrated some of the most remarkable circumstances respecting his sufferings, death, and burial. In the verse now before us, they state that, amid all these sufferings, the servant of Jehovah was the object of the most complacent regard on the part of Him who had appointed him, and that that complacency should be remarkably displayed on his completing the sacrifice of himself for the sins of men, by Jehovah's bestowing upon him rich and appropriate rewards, indicated in the figurative expression of his " seeing his seed, prolonging his days, and the pleasure of the Lord prospering in his hand."

The words, as they stand in our version, are—" Yet it pleased the Lord to bruise him ; He hath put him to grief : when thou shalt make his soul an offering for sin, he shall see his seed, he shall prolong his days, and the pleasure of the Lord shall prosper in his hand."

These words have been variously explained.[1] Some, among whom seem to have been the authors of our version, consider them as a farther and very powerful illustration of the severity of the sufferings of the servant of the Lord. The sufferings came directly from the hand of God. Not only did men despise and reject him,—not only did *they* wound, and bruise, and scourge him,—not only did *they* cut him off out of the land of the living,—but the hand of the Lord was on him directly. He was "the Man who knew affliction from the rod of God's wrath." Men reckoned him as "stricken, smitten of God, and afflicted." And they were right in the fact, though wrong as to its cause. God did bruise him; He did put him to grief, or reduced him to extreme weakness. And in this strange work, He seemed to do what He did with his whole heart. "It pleased the Lord to bruise him." When men's iniquities were made to fall on him, he not only fell into the hands of men and devils, but he fell into the hands of the living God, as the vindicator of the honor of his law, broken by those in whose room his righteous servant stood. He found that this was indeed a fearful thing. It was this which bruised him, crushed him down to the earth in Gethsemane. This that made him sick at heart, sorrowful even to death, sore amazed, and very heavy. This made him exclaim, "Now is my soul troubled, and what shall I say?" "My soul is exceeding sorrowful, even unto death." "My God, my God, why hast Thou forsaken me?"

That this was the bitterest ingredient in our Lord's sufferings—that they were the expression of the displeasure of God against the sin of those with whom he was, as it were, identified—that this was the greatest of all those aggravations, there can be no reasonable doubt. These sufferings of his soul were the soul of his sufferings. But there are two very strong reasons against adopting this mode of exposition of the words before us. First, there is something unnatural in reverting again to a description of our Lord's sufferings, after, in the previous verses, the con-

---

[1] Perhaps the most extravagant interpretation ever given of the words is that of Cocceius :—"Et Dominus, cupientem ipsum, *i. e.*, servum Jehovæ conterere, *h. e.*, Satanam, ad impotentiam redegit."—*Anecdota*. It is a strong proof of the *prestige* of Cocceius' genius and fame, that all that Vitringa can bring himself to say of this strange παρερμηνεία is, " Est sane altæ speculationis meditatio quam rectius in medio relinquo, quam refello ; nec potui tamen a judicio meo impetrare, ut eam mihi vindicarem."

summation of these sufferings has been described in his being " cut off out of the land of the living," and laid in the grave ; and what seems to me a still stronger reason, the word rendered " pleased," is descriptive of complacential delight.   It is the word that is employed when it is said, that the " delight" of the good man is " in the law of the Lord."   When the Messiah is introduced as saying, " I delight to do thy will."[1]   Now, though this is just the word, because the strongest the language furnishes to express Jehovah's entire satisfaction in the sufferer and in his sufferings, as the necessary means of a most desirable end, it does seem very harsh to say that Jehovah had pleasure—" delight"—in inflicting suffering on his righteous servant, who was his " beloved Son."   These sufferings were undoubtedly the result of his appointment and agency ; and as the best, probably the only, means of accomplishing the end of his glory in man's salvation, and as the manifestation, on the part of the sufferer, of the very highest degree of moral excellence and loveliness, were regarded by Him with entire approbation and complacency.   But assuredly He who " does not afflict willingly," could have no satisfaction in inflicting such sufferings on one so infinitely and deservedly dear to Him.   Abstractly considered, it could not be pleasing to Jehovah to bruise, to put to grief, his righteous servant.

This difficulty has been felt, and it has been attempted to get rid of it by representing the words as an expression of this sentiment,—'These sufferings were the result of the Divine appointment—the execution of the Divine counsel and will.'   Men rejected him, and " cut him off out of the land of the living ;" but in doing so, they only did " what God's hand and counsel had aforetime determined to be done."[2]   All this suffering is sent from God, and will in due time answer its purpose, which is the glorious exaltation of the meek and magnanimous sufferer. But the words do not naturally express this undoubtedly true and important sentiment.   The leading idea in the word "pleased," is, without doubt, not sovereign will, but complacency.

I go along with a small but learned section of interpreters in considering the words as expressive of the complacent approbation of Jehovah towards his righteous servant amidst all his

---

[1] Psal. i. 2; xl. 8.   [2] Acts, iv. 28.

sufferings, which showed itself even while he was under them, and was gloriously manifested in delivering him from them, and crowning him with appropriate honors and blessings; and would render the words,—'Therefore[1] Jehovah was pleased with his bruised One,[2] whom He had put to grief.'

The righteous servant of Jehovah was HIS bruised One. This intimates near relation to, peculiar property in. Christ is God's. He stood in a most intimate relation to Him—His Servant; his Son; his elect, and sent, and sealed One; his holy One; his fellow; his delight; so *his* as that, though all in heaven and earth are his, nothing was *his* like him, except his Spirit, for he was *one* with Him. It intimates, too, that the sufferings of the bruised One came from Jehovah. He was *his* bruised One. HE put him to grief. His sufferings, though many of them directly inflicted by men or devils, were the result of Divine ordination and agency. The cup of trembling put into his hand, was the cup his Father gave him to drink.

Now Jehovah was pleased *with* his bruised One,—pleased *in* him—entirely satisfied with the manner in which he bore these sufferings—entirely satisfied with these sufferings as a vindication of His law and as the ransom of a doomed race. The words seem to me to look back to all that has been said from the 7th verse. In consequence of the Lord making to fall on him "the iniquities of us all," exaction was made, and he submitted himself, and opening not his mouth, was led like a lamb to the altar, taken away by an oppressive judgment, "cut off out of the land of the living," and laid in the grave, although he had done no violence, "neither was guile found in his mouth." Therefore Jehovah was well pleased *with* his bruised One—well pleased *in* his bruised One.

He was well pleased *with* him; and well He might, for the eye

---

[1] This is no uncommon meaning of the particle ו.—Gen. iii. 23. Num. xxii. 27. Deut. xxviii. 48. 1 Sam. xxvi. 2. Jer. xiv. 22. Job, v. 17.—Especially, Ezek. xviii. 32.

[2] "דכא masc. *contritus.* Hoc nomen puto illud ipsum esse quod reperitur, Esa. liii. 10, cum affixo, דכאו *contritum suum,* per Scheva loco Kametz. Non deest exemplum Schevæ pro Kametz positio in simili casu, Num. xviii. 19."—GUSSETII Comm. Ling. Eb., *in voc.* "*Et Dominus delectatus est contrito suo, quem infirmum reddidit.* Maluimus cum Gusselio דכא pro nomine habere cujus Kametz in incremento mutatum sit in Scheva. Num. xviii. 19; 1 Sam. xiii. 15; xix. 20."—STORR, Com. Exeg. Es. lii. 18-liii. 12. "Luzzatto (a learned Jew) makes דכאו an adjective used as a noun, 'his crushed or afflicted one'—*contritus suus.*"—ALEXANDER. The great body of interpreters consider דכאו as a verb inf. pih.

of Omniscience could see nothing in the outward or the inward man of the sufferer on which the eye of perfect holiness and rectitude could not rest with the most entire approbation : not a thought, not a feeling, that was not in perfect accordance with the Divine will. His delight was to do his Father's will, and his Father's delight was to see him do it.

He was well pleased *in* him,—propitiated—satisfied—with the sacrifice he offered ; and well He might, for in it more honor was done his law than could have been done by the perfect obedience of a whole world of innocent creatures, or by the eternal sufferings of a whole world of sinning creatures. The ancient sacrifices could not satisfy Him. It would have been strange if they could. They could not take away sin,—could not purge the conscience. In *them* He had no *pleasure*[1]—He delighted not in them. But He was pleased with his bruised One's sacrifice of righteousness when "he made his soul an offering for sin." *It* was "a sacrifice of a sweet-smelling savor to God."[2] "Sacrifice and offering He would not ;" but when in the " body prepared for him," his righteous servant fulfilled all righteousness, then, by the offering of his body, " once for all," the good pleasure of Deity in the salvation of men was drawn forth to the uttermost. "God was in Christ reconciling the world to himself, not imputing to men their trespasses ;" seeing "He made him who knew no sin, to be sin in our room, that we might be made the righteousness of God in him."[3]

Thus, and thus far, was Jehovah pleased with his bruised One. Men contemned him, but He regarded him with supreme approbation. " He was disallowed of men, but chosen of God and precious."[4] Men thought that HE was displeased at his righteous servant ; but He was pleased, thoroughly pleased, with him. " The grace"—the favor—" of God was ever upon him,"[5] as well as in his childhood. He was daily Jehovah's "delight" in his humbled as well as in his pre-existent state.[6] And Jehovah gave evidence of this. He habitually testified it to the mind of the sufferer. He knew that he was doing his Father's will, and this enabled him to rejoice in spirit even amid suffering, and to say, " I lay down my life for the sheep ; there-

---

[1] Psal. li. 16.   [2] Eph. v. 2.   [3] Heb. x. 8–10. 2 Cor. v. 21.
[4] ἐκλεκτὸν, ἔντιμον.—1 Pet. ii. 4.
[5] " Τὸ δὲ παιδίον ηὔξανε—καὶ χάρις Θεοῦ ἦν ἐπ' αὐτό."—Luke, ii. 40.   [6] Prov. viii. 30.

fore doth my Father love me.'"[1] And again, and again, by sending his angels to minister to him, He showed his approbation;
and again, and again, and again, by a voice from the most excellent glory, He proclaimed in explicit words his entire complacency, "This is my beloved Son, in whom I am well pleased.'"[2]

And when his work was finished, this complacency in his
bruised One was still more remarkably manifested. Then He
showed that He was the God of peace—the propitiated Divinity.
To this the concluding part of the verse refers,—"When Thou
shalt make his soul an offering for sin,[3] he shall see his seed, he
shall prolong his days, and the pleasure of the Lord shall prosper in his hand."

Our translators have made the first member of this concluding
clause an apostrophe—a direct address to Jehovah. The words
admit this, but do not require it. It seems harsh and unaccountable, especially as the direct form of composition is resumed in
the concluding member,—not *thy* pleasure, but " the pleasure
of the Lord shall prosper in his hand." It is better to adopt
another version, which does no violence to the words or construction,—" When his soul shall make an offering for sin,[4] he shall
see his seed, he shall prolong his days, and the pleasure of the
Lord shall prosper in his hand." The particle rendered " when"[5]
may, with at least equal propriety, be rendered *if*, or *since;* and
there can be little doubt the inspired writer meant to indicate,
not merely that the events mentioned in the second member of
the sentence should follow that mentioned in the first, but should
be its results,—not only that it should precede them, but that it
should produce them.

The " soul" of the righteous servant of Jehovah was to make
—*i. e.*, to make itself—an offering for sin; that is, he should,
with his whole soul, with all his heart, most voluntarily lay down
his life—offer his whole living self on the altar of Divine justice,
to secure pardon and salvation for sinners. Translate the de-

---

[1] John, x. 17.   [2] Matth. iii. 17; xvii. 5.

[3] אשם—properly 'sin, guilt,' then ' sin-offering.'—Lev. v. 5–7; xv. 24; 2 Kings, xii.
17. Between this word and חטאת, Dr. Henderson says, " there is no further difference
than that the latter relates to the sinful act, considered simply in itself; the former,
to its guilt, as affecting the individual in the way of exposing him to punishment."

[4] In this case, נפשו is the nominative of תשים, the third pers. fem., which our translators consider as the second pers. masculine.

[5] אם.—Num. xxii. 20. Jer. xxiii. 38. Ezek. xxxv. 6.

claration into New Testament language, and you have the words of our Lord, " The Son of man came to give his life a ransom for many." " The good Shepherd giveth his life for the sheep." Or of his apostle, " Christ hath in love given himself for us an offering and a sacrifice to God for a sweet-smelling savor." The offering which is here said to be of his soul is, in other places of Scripture, represented as the offering of his body. He is represented as reconciling us—making reconciliation for us by a sacrifice for sin—by "the body of his flesh, through death;" and we are said, in accordance to the will of God, to be sanctified " by the offering of the body of Jesus Christ once for all."[1] The idea in both cases is substantially the same. He, in dying, offered *himself*—his whole man—soul, body, and spirit—all that he had thought, and felt, and willed, and done, and suffered, in human nature, to God, as what might harmonize the exercise of mercy with the rights of justice. This was what the servant of Jehovah did when his soul offered a sacrifice for sin.

The *consequence* of this self-sacrifice, both in the sense of what followed it, and what was effected by it, is described in the close of the verse, " He shall see his seed, he shall prolong his days, and the pleasure of the Lord shall prosper in his hand." These words do not contain an explicit prediction of a resurrection of the servant of the Lord; but they obviously imply his restoration to life.[2] He has been " cut off out of the land of the living;" he has been in the state of the dead. His soul has made " an offering for sin;" and, after all this, he is to " see his seed, he is to prolong his days, and the pleasure of the Lord is to prosper in his hand." This certainly proceeds on the supposition of the fulfilment of the prediction, made in another place, in reference to the same glorious person,—" My heart is glad, and my glory rejoiceth; my flesh also shall rest in hope: for thou wilt not leave my soul in hell; neither wilt Thou suffer thine Holy One to see corruption. Thou wilt show me the path of life: in thy presence is fulness of joy; at thy right hand there are pleasures for evermore."[3]

In this state of restored and higher life, " the servant of the Lord" is to "see his seed, and to prolong his days." Some interpreters, following the ancient Greek and Latin versions, con-

---

[1] Matth. xx. 28.   John, x. 11.   Eph. v. 2.   Col. i. 22.   Heb. x. 10.
[2] Mede—Works, 51.   [3] Psal. xvi. 9–11.

nect these two clauses, so as to form one promise,—" He shall
see a seed which shall prolong their days." But the construction
is simpler, and the sense is richer, by considering them as two
separate promises.

" He shall see his seed." ' He shall have a spiritual posterity.'
According to another oracle respecting the sufferings of the Messiah, " A seed shall serve him." Those who were to enjoy the
blessings of Messiah's reign are most frequently spoken of as the
children of God—the younger brethren of his first-born Son, the
Messiah, " the first-born among many brethren." Yet, in one
passage, we find the Messiah represented as " the Father of the
coming age,"[1] and saying, in reference to his followers, "Behold
I and the children which God hath given me ;" and they are
represented as " born again by his word."[2] The disciples of the
prophets were called their sons. In the East, " the family of
Christ" is to this day a common appellation for Christians.
When " he was cut off out of the land of the living," and laid
in the land of the dead, it seemed as if he would have no posterity. His enemies, no doubt, count on its being so. But the
enigmatic declaration was to be fulfilled, " Except a corn of
wheat fall into the ground and die"—falling into the ground, be
dead,—" it abideth alone ; but if it die, it bringeth forth much
fruit." His followers are his seed—his children : produced by
his energy—bearing his image, It seems also implied in the
words, that his spiritual posterity should be numerous. They
are plainly " the many" whose sins he bore. According to
another prediction, his " youth"—the same as his seed here—
shall be as the drops of dew " from the womb of the morning,"
beautiful and numberless.[3] He shall not only have a numerous
posterity—he shall see them. They shall grow up under his eye,
and he shall have all the delight of an affectionate father behold-
ing a numerous and prosperous family. To him the promise
will be fulfilled, " Thou shalt see the good of Jerusalem all the
days of thy life. Yea, thou shalt see thy children's children,
and peace upon Israel." And, " when he seeth his children,"
he " shall not be ashamed, neither shall his face wax pale,"
" for they are the seed of the blessed of the Lord, and their offspring with them ;" and " race unto race shall praise him," and

---

[1] Isa. ix. 6. אבי עד.   [2] Psal. xxii. 30. Heb. ii. 13. 1 Pet. i. 23.
[3] John, xii. 24. Psal. cx. 3.

" instead of the fathers he will take the children, and make them mighty princes in all the earth.'"

" He shall prolong his days." His new life will be an unending one. " God will prolong the king's life, and his years as many generations. He shall abide before God for ever." " Yea, he shall live." " He asked life, and Jehovah gave it him, even length of days for ever and ever." " He died for sin once," but, and therefore, " he lives for ever by the power of God,"—" ever lives to make intercession for them for whom he died."²

With a numerous happy posterity, living forever, "the pleasure of the Lord shall prosper in his hand." "The pleasure of Jehovah," is that in which Jehovah finds pleasure—that in which He delights. And what is that? The best answer I can find to that question is in the book of the prophet Jeremiah : " I am the Lord which exercise loving-kindness, judgment, and righteousness, in the earth : for in these things I *delight*, saith the Lord."³ The exercise of infinite benignity, wisdom, and justice,—the manifestation of the Divine glory, in so administering the government of the world as that the great interests of truth and righteousness are promoted, and intelligent beings rendered holy and happy, according to their capacities for holiness and happiness,— this is Jehovah's delight.⁴ Now, this most glorious of all enterprises is to be put into the hand of the righteous servant of Jehovah. He is to be " set as God's King, on his holy hill of Sion." In the language of the New Testament, which records the fulfilment of the prophecy, " all judgment"—all government —" is committed to him,"—" power over all flesh,"—" all power in heaven and in earth." And, in conducting this enterprise, he was not to "fail or be discouraged"—" the pleasure of the Lord" was to " prosper in his hand."⁵ " He was to "set judgment in the earth, and the isles were to wait for his law." Since, in his sacrifice, " mercy and truth had met together, righteousness

---

¹ Psal. cxxviii. 5, 6. Isa. xxix. 22 ; lxv. 23. Psal. xlv. 16.

² Psal. xxi. 1–7. 2 Cor. xiii, 4. Heb. vii. 25.   ³ Jer. ix. 24.

⁴ " Voluntas Dei benevola, bene placitum Dei, sive decretum quod ante jacta mundi fundamenta fecit de reconciliatione mundi secum instauranda per Christum, et de collectione Ecclesiæ ex omni natione sub cœlo, ejusdem gubernatione, uno verbo quicquid placuerit Deo de nostra salute id omne per Christum prospere ac unice expedietur."—GEIER.

⁵ " Latet hic tacita oppositio Mosis *per cujus manum* lex data, Lev. viii. 36 ; Num. xxxvi. 13 ; Acts, vii. 53 ; Gal. iii. 19 ; Ebr. ii. 2 ; et CHRISTI per quem gratia et veritas facta, Joh. i. 17."—GEIER.

and peace had kissed each other,"—under his administration, "truth shall spring out of the earth, and righteousness shall look down from heaven. Yea, the Lord shall give that which is good ; and our land"—our world—" shall yield her increase. Righteousness shall go before him, and shall set men in the way of his steps." He will " create new heavens, and a new earth," wherein nothing but righteousness shall dwell; and Jehovah will pronounce them very good, and " rejoice in all his works."[1]

This is to follow, and to follow as an effect of, the servant of Jehovah's " making his soul"—himself—" a sin-offering." You see the connection in the Saviour's prayer : " Father, the hour is come ; glorify thy Son, that thy Son also may glorify Thee : as Thou hast given him power over all flesh, that he should give eternal life to as many as Thou hast given him. And this is life eternal, that they might know Thee the only true God, and Jesus Christ, whom Thou hast sent. I have glorified Thee on the earth : I have finished the work which Thou gavest me to do. And now, O Father, glorify Thou me with thine own self with the glory which I had with Thee before the world was." You see this connection in the statement of the apostle Paul : He who was " in the form of God, thought it not robbery to be equal with God, made himself of no reputation, and took upon him the form of a servant, and was made in the likeness of men : and being found in fashion as a man, humbled himself, and became obedient unto death, even the death of the cross : *therefore* God also hath highly exalted him, and given him a name which is above every name : that at the name of Jesus every knee should bow, of things in heaven, and things in earth, and things under the earth ; and that every tongue should confess that Jesus Christ is Lord, to the glory of God the Father." You see this connection in the statement of the apostle Peter : " Christ hath once suffered for sins, the just for the unjust, that he might bring us to God, being put to death in the flesh, but quickened by the Spirit ;" and " is gone into heaven, and is on the right hand of God ; angels, and authorities, and powers, being made subject unto him." You see this connection, in fine, in the symbolical representation of the Apocalypse : "I beheld, and, lo, in the midst of the throne and of the four beasts, and in the

---

[1] Isa. xlii 4. Psal. lxxxv. 10–13. Isa. lxv. 17.

midst of the elders, stood a Lamb as it had been slain." " And
he came and took the book," which no man in heaven, nor on
earth, neither under the earth, was able to open, neither to look
thereon, "out of the right hand of Him that sat upon the throne.
And when he had taken the book, the four beasts and four-and-
twenty elders fell down before the Lamb, having every one of
them harps, and golden vials full of odors, which are the prayers
of saints. And they sung a new song, saying, Thou art worthy
to take the book, and to open the seals thereof : for thou wast
slain, and has redeemed us to God by thy blood."

Such is the connection which, according to the oracle, was to
exist between the sacrifice of his soul for sin and the high exaltation of the servant of Jehovah. The one was not only to precede, but to be the procuring cause of, the other.

What was prophecy when these words were uttered, more
than twenty-five centuries ago, has long ago become history ;
and yet much of it continues prophecy still. The prediction has
been fulfilled, is fulfilling, shall be yet more illustriously fulfilled.
One part of it has been finally accomplished : "it is finished ;"
"there is no more sacrifice for sin," for there needs not. But
not only has the servant of Jehovah, for more than eighteen
hundred years, been "seeing his seed, prolonging his days, while
the pleasure of the Lord has been prospering in his hand ;" but
"he shall see his seed, he shall prolong his days, and the pleasure
of the Lord shall prosper in his hand," till the latest hour of
time, ay, during the endless ages of eternity. "Jehovah's
counsel shall stand, and He will do all his pleasure."

This closes the third of the four sections into which the Divine
oracle naturally resolves itself. In it, in reply to the complaint
of the first preachers of the Gospel of comparatively little success, the converted Jews make substantially the following statement—'He whom you proclaim as the sent of God and the Saviour of man, was not at all the kind of deliverer we expected
and desired. His obscure origin, his abject appearance, his unparalleled sufferings, forbade us to think him the Messiah, and
even led us to consider him as an object of the peculiar displeasure of God. His beneficent miracles and superhuman sympathy
should, indeed, have conducted us to a different conclusion ; but,

¹ John, xvii. 1–5.   Phil. ii. 6–11.   1 Pet. iii. 18, 22.   Rev. v. 6–9.

so strong were our prejudices, they did not. We now know how to account for these sufferings, which so stumbled us. They were endured in our room, for our salvation. We had all violated the Divine law, and exposed ourselves to the Divine vengeance. Jehovah appointed him to occupy our place, and to meet our liabilities, and this appointment was carried into effect. Standing in our place, he was charged with our responsibilities, and met our deserts. Exaction was made; and he patiently, cheerfully, submitted to be led to the altar of Divine justice, as the victim for our sins. By an oppressive judgment he was brought to an untimely and violent death; and, though the malignant intention was frustrated, it was the intention of his enemies to crown their indignities by laying him in a dishonored grave,—and all this though he was entirely innocent, absolutely perfect. In thus enduring these divinely-appointed and divinely-inflicted sufferings, he was the object of the most complacent regard of Jehovah; and when his sacrifice of himself for sin is completed—in a countless host of saved men, in an immortality of blessedness, and in the prosperous administration of the government of the universe, in which he will effectually gain the great objects of Divine wisdom, holiness, and love—he shall enjoy the adequate and dearly won rewards of his toils and sufferings.' Such are the sentiments brought out of, we trust, not put into, the inspired words.

The oracle closes, as it opened, with a voice from the most excellent glory, saying in effect, what it uttered many centuries afterwards, "This is my beloved Son, in whom I am well pleased." "He shall see of the travail of his soul, and shall be satisfied: by his knowledge shall my righteous servant justify many; for he shall bear their iniquities. Therefore will I divide him a portion with the great, and he shall divide the spoil with the strong; because he hath poured out his soul unto death: and he was numbered with the transgressors; and he bare the sin of many, and made intercession for the transgressors."

On the illustration of these words we do not at present enter. They shall form the subject of a concluding lecture on this most fruitful passage of Scripture.

Practical reflections crowd on us. Was Jehovah well pleased with his bruised One? should not *we* be well pleased with

him too? Is it not monstrous to set our judgment in opposition to the judgment of Him who alone hath wisdom? And
yet, alas! to what an extent is he whom the great King—the
Lord of hosts—delights to honor, still despised and rejected of
men!

Is Jehovah well pleased *in* his bruised One,—well pleased
with *us*, if we are of but one mind with Him about his bruised
One? Surely we should be reconciled to Him! He had good
reason to be displeased at us; we never had any cause to be displeased at Him; and now, surely, we have cause to love Him.
How hardened are our hearts, if the disinterested kindness of
God, manifested in his not sparing his Son, but delivering him
up for us all, will not melt them! If that will not, nothing can.

Has HIS soul made an "offering for sin"? how foolish—how
wicked—to seek for pardon in any way but through this sacrifice! How unreasonable to doubt that, through this sacrifice,
we shall obtain pardon!

If HE so willingly devoted himself entirely for us, should we
not willingly devote ourselves entirely to him? If he made himself "an offering for sin," should we not, influenced by the
mercies of God, present ourselves "living sacrifices, holy and
acceptable"?

Shall HE "see his seed"? Is it certain that he shall have a
numerous spiritual posterity? What an encouragement to missionary exertion, especially when we consider that it is by the
belief of the word of the Lord, which liveth and abideth forever
—to diffuse which is the great object of missionary enterprise,
—that the children of the wicked one become his children!

Shall HE "prolong his days"? What a comfort to his friends,
—"Fear not; I am the first, and the last, and the living One.
I was dead, but am now alive, and live for evermore." "Because
I live, ye shall live also."

Shall "the pleasure of Jehovah prosper in HIS hand"? Let
us not, then, be discouraged, whatever obstacles seem to lie
in the way of the progress of holiness and happiness in God's
world. He will work, and who can let it? His counsel shall
stand; He will do all his pleasure. That is "the pleasure of the
Lord." It is in the Messiah's hand, and it shall prosper there.
"He must reign, till all his enemies are made his footstool."

In the full assurance of this truth, let us pray and labor—

labor and pray—for our own salvation, and the salvation of our fellow-men. Let us make God's pleasure our pleasure, as the Messiah does. Let us seek for the kingdom, which is "righteousness, peace, joy in the Holy Ghost;" its establishment within us—its extension around us. In this way let "our fellow-ship truly be with the Father, and with his Son Jesus Christ." "Our Father who art in heaven, hallowed be thy name. Thy kingdom come, thy will be done on earth as it is done in heaven." Our Saviour and King in heaven, at the right hand of thy Father and our Father, send forth the rod of thy strength—rule in the midst of thine enemies. Thou blessed, bruised One, fairer than the fairest, mightier than the mightiest, "gird thy sword on thy thigh, and with thy glory, and with thy majesty, and in thy majesty, ride prosperously, because of truth, and meekness, and righteousness." "O come forth from thy royal chamber, Prince of the kings of the earth. Put on the visible robes of thy imperial majesty. Take up that unlimited sceptre which thy almighty Father hath bequeathed thee; for now the voice of thy bride calleth thee, and all thy creatures sigh to be renewed."[1]

May all the good pleasure of the Divine goodness to our lost race be thus soon accomplished, in a transformed world. "Drop down, ye heavens, from above, and let the skies pour down righteousness: let the earth open, and let them bring forth salvation; and let righteousness spring up together." Let us rejoice that, while "the pleasure of the Lord is in his hand," He is pleased to employ our hands in effecting it; and let our constant prayer to Him be, "Let thy work on earth—in heaven —appear to thy servants, and thy glory to their children"—a portion of thy seed—the race that shall serve Thee,—and be "counted to Thee for a generation." "And let the beauty of the Lord our God be upon us: and establish Thou the work of our hands upon us; yea, the work of our hands establish Thou it."

[1] Milton.

LECTURE X

CLOSING PROCLAMATION OF JEHOVAH

ISAIAH, LIII. 11, 12.—"He shall see of the travail of his soul, and shall be satisfied: by his knowledge shall my righteous servant justify many; for he shall bear their iniquities. Therefore will I divide him a portion with the great, and he shall divide the spoil with the strong; because he hath poured out his soul unto death: and he was numbered with the transgressors; and he bare the sin of many, and made intercession for the transgressors."

"THE spirit of prophecy is the testimony of Jesus."[1] "In the Psalms it is written of *him;*" and "to him all the prophets bear witness." "The Spirit of Christ which was in them did testify of the sufferings of Christ, and of the glory that should follow them."[2]

"Ought not Christ"—the Messiah,—said our Lord himself, when he drew near to the two disciples on the way to Emmaus, sadly conversing of their blasted hopes, and showed how groundless were their doubts of the Messiahship of their Master, arising from his sufferings and death,—"Ought not" the Messiah "to have suffered these things, and to enter into his glory? And"—in illustration of this principle—"beginning at Moses and all the prophets, he expounded unto them in all the Scriptures the things concerning himself."[3]

We have much more of that "Scripture, given by inspiration of God," than we make a good use of. Alas! how much in our Bibles is, by the best informed among us, but half understood, if understood at all; and it is doubtless a much wiser and more dutiful part to improve to the utmost what we have of Divine revelation, than to complain that we have not more, especially when we reflect that what has been granted is at once an unmerited gift, and sufficient for every valuable purpose,—able to

---

[1] Rev. xix. 10,—"Ἡ μαρτυρία τοῦ Ἰησοῦ ἐστὶ τὸ πνεῦμα τῆς προφητείας." This seems a convertible proposition.

[2] 1 Pet. i. 11.   [3] Luke, xxiv. 26, 27.

make all "wise to salvation ;" and "to make the man of God perfect, thoroughly furnished to all good works ;" and that what has been withheld has been withheld in wisdom and kindness, as well as righteousness.

But though all this is obviously true, I believe that few Christians have ever considerately read the passage of gospel history just referred to, without indulging an ardent, though but a passing, wish, that they had heard that conversation, or, at any rate, that our Lord's commentary on the ancient prophetic oracles respecting himself had been committed to writing, and preserved for the edification of believers, and the confutation of gainsayers. This has not seemed meet to infinite wisdom and kindness ; and to this, as to all the determinations of God, we ought, with entire acquiescence, to submit, though we were utterly incapable of perceiving the grounds on which it proceeds.

It is easy, however, to see that at least one good and important end has been served by the omission, which we are so naturally apt to regret. We are thus furnished with a powerful additional motive to the study of the Old Testament prophecies. Had there been embodied in the New Testament a complete collection of all the predictions in reference to Christ, and an infallible exposition of their meaning, it is to be feared that the prophetic writings—that necessarily comparatively obscure portion of the volume of revelation—so replete, however, both with religious and moral instruction—would have been entirely neglected, since, even in the present state of things, when a careful search is acknowledged to be necessary to find in them what makes them peculiarly valuable to us—the evidence that Jesus is "he of whom Moses in the law, and the prophets did write,"— the great body of professed believers in revelation devote so little attention to them. We cannot but perceive that the arrangement adopted is much better fitted to secure our searching these prophetic Scriptures, which testify of Christ. Prophetic passages, in sufficient number and variety, are quoted and applied by our Lord and the apostles, to serve as a key to the whole prophetic writings ; and it is left for us to apply this key, so as to unlock the hidden treasures of doctrine and evidence which they contain, and discover what are the portions which, in the writings of Moses and all the prophets, refer to the Messiah, as suffering and as reigning.

With a moderate degree of care, there is no difficulty in discovering the predictions which refer to the Messiah, and with
regard to which it can be clearly shown that they refer to the
same person, and admit of no other reference.   There are very
many which speak of his sufferings, and very many, too, which
speak of his glory; and there are not a few in which, in the
same oracle, the sufferings and the glories of the Messiah are
both spoken of; and the connection subsisting between these is
pointed out.   The first promise, of which all future predictions
of the Messiah is but a development, is of this character.   The
heel of the Conqueror of the old dragon is wounded in crush-
ing the monster's head.   The twenty-second psalm begins with
showing us Messiah suffering, and ends with showing him reigning.   He—and there can be no doubt the Messiah is the speaker
—who, in the sixty-ninth psalm, begins, "Save me, O God, for
the waters are come in unto my soul," ends it, "I will praise
the name of God with a song, and will magnify Him with
thanksgiving."

In no instance, perhaps, did the Holy Spirit signify to the
holy men, who spake as they were moved by him, more distinctly and graphically the sufferings of the Messiah, and the
glory that should follow, than to the prophet Isaiah, in that very
remarkable oracle, in the illustration of which we have been for
some time engaged.   There can be no reasonable doubt of its
reference; and there is little difficulty of ascertaining the meaning of its various parts.   Many of the other prophets "opened
their mouth on this subject in parables;" but Isaiah "speaks
plainly, and speaks no proverb."   They "uttered these dark sayings on the harp," but he "writes the vision, and makes it plain
on tables, so that he may run who readeth" it.[1]

You are aware that I consider the whole passage, from the
13th verse of the fifty-second chapter, to the end of the fifty-
third, as one oracle, and that it divides itself into four parts.   The
first section, which is contained in the three concluding verses of
the fifty-second chapter, consists of a call, by Jehovah, to mankind to contemplate his righteous servant wisely and prosperously
executing the great work committed to him.   The second sec
tion, contained in the 1st verse of the fifty-third chapter, is oc-

---

[1] "Si a Paulo post Christum glorificatum esset scriptum, nihil planius dici potuis
set."—MELANCTHON.

cupied with the complaint of Jehovah's messengers, that their report respecting his righteous servant found but few believing recipients. The third and longest section is contained from verse 2d to verse 10th of the chapter, and consists of a statement, by the Jewish converts, of the causes why so few among their countrymen believed the apostolic message, and of the views which, from the belief of that message, they had been led to take of the nature, design, and results of the Messiah's sufferings. The fourth section occupies the two concluding verses of the chapter, and contains a declaration, by Jehovah, respecting the honors and enjoyments in which his righteous servant was to find the merited reward of his labors and sufferings.

In the nine previous discourses, I have endeavored to illustrate the first three of these sections. The last of them is intended to form the subject of the present discourse.

That the words contained in the two verses I have read are spoken by Jehovah, is obvious. "My righteous servant"—"I will divide him a portion." These words become only one Being in the universe. They form a fittingly solemn close to this sublimest of all oracles. The primitive Jewish converts, a small and despised handful, have declared their faith in the atoning efficacy of Messiah's sufferings, and in the glorious results which were certainly to flow from them. His soul shall make " an offering for sin ;" and, because of this, "he shall see his seed, he shall prolong his days, and the pleasure of the Lord shall prosper in his hand." Anything more improbable than this could not be conceived at the point of time when the oracle must be considered as spoken,—"the solemn awful pause," to borrow Dr. Pye Smith's words,—"the crisis of heaven, earth, and hell, —when Jesus was lying in the arms of death." But "the Lord of hosts hath purposed it, and who shall disannul it? his hand is stretched out, and who shall turn it back?" "The Lord of hosts hath sworn, saying, Surely as I have thought, so shall it come to pass ; and as I have purposed, so shall it stand."[1] Who can read these verses without seeming to hear the solemn words pealing from the opening heaven, amid the splendor of the excellent glory, and saying in his heart, 'It is the voice of Jehovah ? "The voice of the Lord is powerful ; the voice of the

---

[1] Isa. xiv. 24.

Lord is full of majesty." "He shall see of the travail of his
soul, and shall be satisfied : by his knowledge shall my righteous
servant justify many ; for he shall bear their iniquities.   Therefore will I divide him a portion with the great, and he shall
divide the spoil with the strong ; because he hath poured out his
soul unto death : and he was numbered with the trangressors ;
and he bare the sin of many, and made intercession for the transgressors." ' Let us proceed to examine these words more closely.

The first clause of the 11th verse, in our version, seems elliptical.   Something seems to require to be supplied to bring out
the sense.   ' He shall see the *fruit* ¹—the *product*—of the travail
of his soul, and shall be satisfied.'   The idea these words bring
before the mind is, ' Glorious results shall immediately proceed
from the agonizing toils and sufferings of the righteous servant
of Jehovah—results which He shall contemplate, and the contemplation of which shall produce entire satisfaction.'   And this
idea *seems* presented under the striking figure of the pangs of
travail issuing in the birth of a strong and beautiful child, which
the mother gazes on with unspeakable delight, and finds in the
sight a recompense for her multiplied sorrows.   It calls up to
the recollection the striking words of our Lord, respecting the
very events here foretold, though they refer not to him, but to
his disciples,—"A woman when she is in travail hath sorrow,
because her hour is come : but as soon as she is delivered of the
child, she remembereth no more the anguish, for joy that a man
is born into the world."²

This is substantially the thought, but it is not in this way it
is brought before the mind.   The word rendered "travail" has
not the peculiarity of meaning which, in later times, belongs to
that English word.   It has no reference to childbirth.³   It signifies, as "travail" did at the time our version was made, severe
labor—painful exertion ; and refers to the whole toils and sorrows of the servant of the Lord, which were included in that
offering of his soul for sin, which was consummated when "he
was cut off out of the land of the living."

¹ This supplement is made by Bishop Lowth, and it appears in the Bible of 1574.
² John, xvi. 21.
³ The allusion to the pains of parturition, which some English writers find, has no
foundation in the Hebrew text.   The meaning of the word will appear by consulting
Exod. xviii. 8 ; Psal. lxxiii. 5 ; Job, vii. 3 ; xi. 16 ; Num. xxiii. 21, 22.

It may be doubted if our translators have been happy in placing and rendering the phrase, " Of the travail of his soul." It stands in the original, in the beginning of the clause, " Of the travail of his soul he shall see ;" and the only meaning which these words, as rendered in our version, can fairly be made to bear, is, ' He shall see a part of the travail, or of the results of the travail, of his soul.'[1] The particle translated "of," is one which admits of different renderings. It is variously rendered in this very oracle. It is the same particle which, in the 5th verse, is rendered "*for*"—on account of. " He was wounded for our transgressions, he was bruised for our iniquities,"—which, in the beginning of the 8th verse, is rendered "*from*." " He was taken from prison and from judgment,"—where we consider it equivalent to ' by,' ' by means of.' " By an oppressive judgment he was taken away ;" and, in the end of that verse, it is rendered "*for*,"—" for the transgression of my people was he stricken,"—generally interpreted ' on account of,' ' because of,' but which we consider as meaning ' by,' ' by means of,'—' by the wickedness of my people was he stricken.' Some would here render it "*from*," or " without,"[2]—*i. e.*, ' Delivered from the travail of his soul, he shall see,'—*i. e.*, " his seed," spoken of in the preceding verse. Others, " *after*"[3] the travail of his soul " he shall see his seed." It seems to me much better to adopt one of the most common of the meanings of the particle—that which it certainly has in the 5th verse,—' on account of,' ' because of.'[4] ' Because of the travail of his soul, he shall see, and shall be satisfied.'[5]

The figure of a husbandman lies at the foundation of the representation. At the cost of much painful labor he prepares the soil, and casts into it the seed. His hard labor is not lost : yet a little while, and he sees with pleasure the unsightly bare brown surface covered with the beautiful green of spring, ere long to be exchanged for the rich yellow of autumn. He contemplates with delight his ripening crops ; and now the months of harvest come, and the stately corn bows to the stroke of the joyous reaper's sickle ; and he that went forth weeping, bearing

---

[1] " The English version makes מיק partitive ; but this detracts from the force of the expression."—ALEXANDER.

[2] Knobel.   [3] Rosenmüller, Gesenius, Hitzig, Maurer, Henderson.

[4] Vulgate.   [5] Le Clerc, Hengstenberg, Vitringa, Dathe.

precious seed, comes again rejoicing, bringing his sheaves with him ; and yet a little longer, and he and his household are found seated around a well-furnished table, laden with the produce of his toil, and they eat and are satisfied, and praise the name of the Lord, who thus blesses the labors of the husbandman, and crowns the year with His goodness.

"Because of his travail, he sees and he is satisfied." The labors and sorrows of the Messiah shall be productive of important salutary visible effects, which he shall contemplate, and in which he shall find satisfaction. That is the thought; let us look at its various parts.

The servant of the Lord had had travail—travail of soul—in "making his soul an offering for sin." What a life of toilsome labor—of varied severe suffering—had the servant of the Lord ! His powers of exertion and of suffering were tasked to the uttermost. His labor was soul-labor : he threw his whole heart into his work. His suffering was soul-suffering : the wounded spirit none can bear, was never felt by any as by him. While the expression is applicable to the whole of our Lord's active and suffering life, it has peculiar significance in reference to those mental struggles, of which, towards the close of his mortal course, he was peculiarly the subject,—that found utterance in such words as these : "Now is my soul troubled ; and what shall I say ?" "Father, if it be possible, let this cup pass from me." "My God, my God why hast Thou forsaken me ?"—and were more impressively indicated still, by his groaning in spirit— "groanings which could not be uttered ;" and by his sweat, like "great drops of blood falling down to the ground." These were what the ancient Greek church, in her litany, calls our Lord's "unknown agonies."

Now, none of this was to be lost labor. No ; whatever appearances might say, he did "not labor in vain—he did not spend his strength for nought and in vain." His judgment was with the Lord—his work was with his God ; and this is His declaration, " Because of the travail of his soul, he shall see and be satisfied." " He shall see "—see what ? "his seed," spoken of in the former verse ?[1] Doubtless he will see *them*—they are included ; but the natural answer is, ' He will see what the travail of his soul has produced.'

---

[1] Jerome, who has many followers.

And what has the travail of the soul of the righteous servant of the Lord produced? What will it yet produce? We must go to heaven and remain there forever to get that question answered. In his own words, "Now is the judgment of this world : now is the prince of this world cast out. And I, if I be lifted up from the earth, will draw all men unto me." "Now is the Son of man glorified, and God is glorified in him. If God be glorified in him, God shall also glorify him in himself, and shall straightway glorify him."[1] God is glorified to the highest. Justice is satisfied, and "grace reigns through righteousness unto eternal life." The works of the devil shall be destroyed. Satan shall fall like lightning from heaven. "The kingdom of righteousness, and peace, and joy in the Holy Ghost, shall be established among men." "An innumerable multitude" of immortal beings who must otherwise have sunk in the hopeless abyss of ever-growing depravity and misery, shall be made holy and happy to the utmost limits of their capacity during the whole eternity of their being. By that travail of soul, he has removed the obstacles—obstacles otherwise insuperable—in the way of mercy finding vent to the uttermost to lost men, in consistency with righteousness. He has secured the effusion of the influences of the Holy Ghost necessary and sufficient to transform a fallen world. He has obtained for himself the throne of the universe, from which he is to guide all the events by which the great ends "of the travail of his soul" are to be wrought out. Every event bearing on the glorifying of God in the highest in the salvation of his innumerable family of redeemed men, is the result of that travail of soul.

Now, all this he was to see. It was to take place under his eye. He was to be thoroughly cognisant of every one of the salutary results of his toils and sufferings, and to see how every one had been the fruit "of the travail of his soul." He was to see in the primitive age the Spirit poured out from on high ; thousands converted in one day, many of them his murderers ; the Gospel preached throughout the world ; churches everywhere established, and multitudes turned to the Lord ;—and wherever the Gospel has been planted or received, wherever sinners have been converted and saints edified, wherever a brand has been

---

[1] John, xii. 31, 32; xiii. 31, 32.

plucked as from the burning, or a Christian compassed with infirmity transformed into one of the "spirits of the just made perfect," he has marked the event. He was to see the kingdom of this world become his kingdom; infidelity, superstition, Paganism, Mohammedism, anti-Christianity, vanishing from the earth; polygamy, caste, slavery, anarchy, misgovernment, put down forever. He was to see all his enemies made his footstool; he was to see every one of his sheep safely housed in the fold of heaven; he was to see his church fully collected together, not one wanting,— a glorious church, "without spot, or wrinkle, or any such thing;" he was to see the graves emptied by a resurrection of which he is the Author, and death, the last enemy, destroyed; he was to see all nations stand before him in judgment; he was to see new heavens and a new earth, "wherein dwelleth righteousness," of which he is the Creator; he was to behold every creature in heaven, and on the earth, and under the earth, and such as are in the sea, and all that are in them, bowing before the throne of his Father and himself, and hear them saying, "Blessing, and honor, and glory, and power, be unto Him that sitteth upon the throne, and to the Lamb for ever and ever." And all this is "because of the travail of his soul." But for "the travail of his soul," it could not have been thus. All this is because "he was slain, and has redeemed men to God by his blood."

Need we wonder that it should be added, "He shall be satisfied"?[1] His soul shall feed on the varied holy happiness he perceives he is diffusing all around him. It was his *meat* to do the Father's will, even when that will was "the travail of his soul." How much more when his whole employment through endless ages is, as the grand reservoir of Divine benefits, to diffuse ever-growing holiness and happiness throughout innumerable millions of angels who never were lost, and of men who have been redeemed! Yes he is, he must be, "most blessed for ever—exceeding glad in the light of his Father's countenance."

What an exalted view does this representation give of the glory of that state of things which is to be the final result of the Messiah's travail of soul! It is to be sufficient to satisfy his great soul, to meet all the requirements of his mighty mind, to gratify all the benevolence that is in his large heart. And what

---

[1] "Satisfied,—*i. e.*, 'filled, abundantly supplied.'"—ALEXANDER.

a view does it also give us of the benevolence of that heart! He is entirely satisfied: Bethlehem, Gethsemane, Calvary, have left no regrets.. He does not grudge the price of what he has purchased. If it were to do, he would do it over again. He is satisfied. "Looking back on all he has endured, and forward to all that it is to accomplish, he is contented—he is satiated—with the sight."[1]

Let us now look at the second clause of the verse,—"By his knowledge shall my righteous servant justify many; for he shall bear their iniquities." "By his knowledge" is, by some interpreters, connected with the preceding clause.[2] 'Because "of the travail of his soul," he shall see and be satisfied in his knowledge,—in his being known or acknowledged to be the Author of salvation by all his followers.' The Masoretic accentuation, which, though not a part of the inspired record, is not lightly to be disregarded, connects it with the second clause, and this brings out a richer, while at the same time a quite natural and appropriate, sense. 'My righteous servant shall justify many by his knowledge.'

The phrase, "my righteous servant," is literally, 'the righteous One my servant;' or, 'my servant as righteous, being righteous. The Messiah is the righteous One,—not only immaculately innocent and absolutely perfect, personally considered, but the righteous One as Jehovah's servant, having fulfilled all righteousness in his official character as the Redeemer of men, having fully answered the demands of the law when exaction was made, "having learned," experimentally become acquainted with, "obedience" to the law of the Representative-man "by the things which he suffered." In his public character, "he so loved righteousness and hated iniquity," as to magnify the law and make it honorable, by fully obeying its precept and enduring its penalty in the place of his people, "the just in the room of the unjust," thus bringing in an everlasting righteousness.

This righteous One, because he is thus righteous, Jehovah declares, shall "justify many." Some consider "justify" here as equivalent to 'convert to the true religion,' or, 'to sanctify—turn from sin to righteousness.' No doubt the word here used is the same as that employed in Dan. xii. 3, where it is said, "they that turn many to righteousness shall shine as stars in the

[1] Bishop Wilson.   [2] Jahn, Martini.

firmament for ever and ever." But the whole subject of this chapter is expiation and pardon, not instruction or influence and transformation ; and then the reason assigned for the righteous One, Jehovah's servant, justifying many, is one that holds directly with regard to justification, properly so-called, and only mediately with regard to sanctification.[1] It is true, indeed, that justification, as a judicial act changing the relation of those justified, properly belongs to the Supreme Judge, Jehovah, God the Father, the sustainer of the majesty of Divinity in the economy of human salvation ; but it is equally true, that as by the righteousness and obedience of the Messiah are sinners justified. Christ is the cause of the sinner's justification. We are " made the righteousness of God in him"—united to him. It is "in him we have redemption through his blood, the forgiveness of sins." We are "accepted in the Beloved." "In the righteous One we have righteousness." He brings men into a state of enjoyment of the Divine favor, as if they had in their own persons fully answered all the demands of the law on them ; so that it may be said, "Who can lay anything to their charge?" Who can condemn them ? Translated into New Testament language, the passage before us would run thus :—"We have an advocate with the Father, Jesus Christ the righteous : and he is the propitiation for our sins; and not for ours only, but also for the sins of the whole world." "By the offence of one, many are made"—constituted—"righteous," i. e., are justified.[2]

It is said the righteous One, the servant of Jehovah, shall thus by his knowledge "justify *many.*" What the relative proportion of the justified to the finally condemned may be, we cannot tell. Hitherto the proportion of mature men, of whom we can rationally hope that they are among the justified, is very small. But when we think what reason we have to hope that all who die in infancy are " justified freely by God's grace, through the redemption which is in Christ Jesus,"—when we think how widely and how long the Gospel is to be diffused in the millennial ages, we have reason to hope that the justified will be by far the majority of the race. But whatever may be truth as to the relative number of the justified, their absolute number shall most

---

[1] "The context abundantly shows that הצדיק is used in the forensic sense, and not in that of moral improvement."—HENDERSON.

[2] Eph. i. 6, 7. Rom. viii. 33, 34. 1 John, ii. 1, 2. Rom. iii. 10.

assuredly be great. The Captain of salvation is conducting *many* sons to glory; and the company to stand before the Throne and the Lamb, is "a multitude that no man can number."[1] This is secured by the promise of Him that cannot lie. "The righteous One, my servant, shall justify many."

If many is to be opposed to *few*, it must be opposed also to *all*. His righteousness is of infinite value; it lays a foundation for an offer of pardon and salvation to all. But, alas, alas, all will not accept the offer; and refusing the righteousness of the righteous One, they continue condemned, and must die in their sins.

The righteous one, the servant of the Lord, justifies many "by his knowledge," *i. e.*, not, as some have supposed, in the exercise of his wisdom—that is the truth; but it is not the meaning of the words; but, "by the knowledge of himself,"—by bringing those whom he justifies to know and believe the truth respecting himself.[2] It is through the faith of the truth respecting the servant of the Lord as the Righteous One, that men are justified by him. In New Testament language, the statement runs thus, "The righteousness of God, which is by faith of Jesus Christ," manifested "unto all," is "upon all them that believe:" "being justified freely by his grace, through the redemption that is in Christ Jesus." "He that believeth on him is not condemned." "And by him all that believe are justified from all things, from which ye could not have been justified by the law of Moses."[3]

How he comes to be the cause of justification to many, is stated in the close of the verse, "for he shall bear their iniquities."[4] There is some slight difficulty from the word "bear their iniquities," being in the future tense. The declaration of Jehovah is given after his righteous servant has been "wounded for our transgressions and bruised for our iniquities;" after he has been "cut off out of the land of the living; after he has "made his soul"—himself—"an offering for sin," and expiation as the ground of justification goes before it. Some have ex-

[1] Heb. ii. 10.   Rev. vii. 9.

[2] "Per scientiam sui, non qua ipse cognoscit, sed qua vera fide et fiducia ipse—tanquam propitiator cognoscitur."—MICHAELIS.

[3] Rom. iii. 22, 24.   John, iii. 18.   Acts, xiii. 39.

[4] The force of the phrase, "bear iniquity," is well illustrated by Lam. v. 7,—"Our fathers have sinned, and are not; and we have borne their iniquities,"—*i. e.*, 'suffered their evils, which are the pure results of their sins.'

plained the peculiarity of the phrase on the undoubtedly true
principle, that though our Lord made a perfect atonement for
sin, the guilt of the individual remains on himself, till by faith
he is united to him who is the propitiation; and no man can say,
'Christ has so carried my sins as that I am relieved from
their penal consequences,' but the believer in Jesus ; but while
this is truth, most important truth, it does not accord with
scriptural representation to say Christ takes men's sins on him
when they believe.

Upon the whole, we agree with those[1] who hold that the scope
of the passage compels us to translate, "because[2] he has borne,"
or, "bears their iniquity."[3] He justifies many, all who believe,
all who know him, because "God hath set him forth a propitiation in his blood." He was "delivered for our offences, and was
raised again for our justification." "*Therefore*, being justified
by faith we have peace with God." It is in consequence of
"him who knew no sin" being made sin in our room, "that we
are made the righteousness of God in him."[4] Had he not, as
the Lamb of God, borne the sins of the world, he never could
have justified many—he never could have justified any. The
peculiar propriety of noticing the number of the justified appears from the consideration that the multitude of them forms
a most important part of the reward which has been conferred
on him for his labors and sufferings. It is on *his* account that
God justifies any, and on his account he is ready to justify *all*,
if they will but believe in him.

We have another view of the exaltation of the servant of the
Lord given us in the next verse; and here, as in the case we
have been considering, that exaltation is represented as based
on his vicarious obedience and sufferings. "Therefore will I
divide him a portion with the great, and he shall divide the
spoil with the strong ; because he hath poured out his soul
unto death : and he was numbered with the transgressors ;

[1] Rosenmüller.

[2] The ו is casual. It is strange to find Hengstenberg saying that "he shall justify," and "he shall bear their iniquities," are synonymous expressions. Expiation
and justification are not the same thing : they stand in the relation of means and
end, cause and effect.

[3] "Egregia nimirum est permutatio. Christus justificat homines dando ipsis jus-
titiam suam, et vicissim in se suscipit peccata ipsorum, ut ea expiet."—CALVIN.

[4] Rom. iii. 25 ; iv. 25 ; v. 1.

and he bare the sin of many, and made intercession for the transgressors."

The sentiment which these English words naturally convey—indeed, the only sentiment they can convey—is, that in assigning portions to a class of persons called "the great," Jehovah would give *one*—no doubt a large one, probably the largest—to his righteous servant; and that, along with either this class or another called "the strong," he should divide the prey.[1] It is difficult, or rather impossible, to find anything either in the prophetic or the historical accounts of the results of our Lord's sufferings, that corresponds to such a description. The word rendered "great"[2] usually signifies many, and is indeed just the word thus rendered in chap. lii. 14, 15, and in the end both of this and of the preceding verse. The question naturally occurs, Who are these great—or rather these many—and those strong or mighty, among whom, as one of whom, the servant of Jehovah receives his portion? Our Lord had no coadjutor in his labors and sorrows, and he has no compeers in his reward. To what man but to "the Man of his right hand"—to what angel but to "the Angel of his presence, the Angel of the covenant"—did He ever say, "Sit on my right hand, until I make thine enemies thy footstool"? "His name is *above* every name." He is put, not among, but above, all that are greatest and mightiest in human or angelic nature. He is "made so much better than the angels, as he hath by inheritance obtained a more excellent name than they."[3]

Without doing violence to the received text, or to the usages of the original language, some of the best interpreters[4] thus

---

[1] The exegesis of Grotius, who applies the whole passage to Jeremiah, is absolutely ridiculous: "*Dabo ei partem in multis,—i. e.,* multos servabant Chaldæi in ipsius gratiam : *Et fortium dividet spolia,—i. e.,* Nebuzadam magister militum capta urbe de præda ipsi dona mittet,—Jer. xl. 5. Oblatum etiam ipsi a Chaldæis terræ quantum vellet." Well may Seiler say, "To him who rejects the true doctrine concerning the prophecies and their fulfilment, everything seems askance and crooked; and he transforms the prophets themselves into visionaries."

[2] Hengstenberg prefers the sense of 'great,' or 'mighty;' but the reason he assigns for it is not satisfactory. Parallels are not necessarily synonymous: we rather expect, in such a parallel as that before us, epithets no doubt suited to the same class, but expressing different qualities.   [3] Heb. i. 4, 13. Phil. ii. 9.

[4] This is the interpretation given to the passage both in the LXX. and in the Vulgate, by many of the fathers, and, among the moderns, by Hensler, Lowth, Martini, Dathe, Boothroyd, Hengstenberg, Reiske, Jones. Rosenmüller, after

translate the words, 'Therefore will I assign to him his portion in multitudes'—*i. e.*, assign multitudes to him as his portion—' and he shall have the strong, or the mighty, as his prey.'[1]

The first part of the Divine declaration seems parallel to such passages as the following :—" I shall give thee the heathen for thine inheritance, and the uttermost parts of the earth for thy possession." " Thou hast made me the head of the heathen"— the nations. " Men shall be blessed in him : all nations shall call him blessed." " Behold, I have given him for a witness to the people, a leader and commander to the people :"[2] And the second to such as the following:—" Thou shalt break them with a rod of iron ; thou shalt dash them in pieces like a potter's vessel. Be wise now, therefore, O ye kings ; be instructed, ye judges of the earth." " Thou hast given me the necks of mine enemies." " All they that are fat on earth shall worship : all that go down to the dust shall bow to him." " The kings of Tarshish and of the isles shall bring presents : the kings of Sheba and Seba shall offer gifts. Yea, all kings shall fall down before him ; all nations shall serve him." " The Lord at thy right hand shall strike through kings in the day of his wrath. He shall judge among the heathen, he shall fill the places with the dead bodies ; he shall wound the heads over many countries." " I will make him my first-born, higher than the kings of the earth." " Thus saith the Lord, the Redeemer of Israel, and his Holy One, to him whom man despiseth, to him whom the nation abhorreth, to a servant of rulers, kings shall see and arise, princes also shall worship, because of the Lord that is faithful, and the Holy one of Israel, and he shall choose thee." " I saw in the night-visions, and, behold, one like to the Son of Man came with the clouds of heaven, and came to the Ancient of days, and they brought him near before Him. And there was given him dominion, and glory, and a kingdom, that all people, nations, and languages, should serve him: his dominion is an everlasting dominion,

quoting Job, xxxix. 17, in proof that הלק may be so construed, adds, " Quasi dicas: partem alicui assignare *in* re aliqua." Spanheim's exegesis—making " the many" the whole body of the saved, who are " co-heirs with Christ," and " the strong" the apostles, " mighty through God" in subjugating the nations—is no better than a " pia hallucinatio," *they* share in HIS inheritance, not *he* in *theirs*.

[1] " Verbum הלק non significat modo distribuere dare, sed consequi etiam occupare, —Isa. xxxiii. 23 ; Job, xxvii. 17 ; Gen. xlix. 27 ; Prov. xvii. 2."—STORR.

[2] Psal. ii. 8 ; xviii. 43 ; lxxii. 17.   Isa. lv. 4.

which shall not pass away, and his kindom that which shall not be destroyed.'"[1]

As to the fulfilment of the prediction, there is little difficulty. When our Lord was " lifted up, he drew all men unto him." He received " power over all flesh," " all power in heaven and in earth," " all judgment was committed to him." He has obtained " a name above every name." To him has been, is, and will be, the gathering of the nations. " All that the Father has given him shall come to him."[2] He has many for his portion ; and that portion given him, assigned him, put into his possession, by Jehovah. *He* " brings his truly First-begotten into the world," puts him in possession of it, as He brought in Israel, his typical first-born, into the inheritance of the Gentiles.

And he treats the strong, the mighty, as his prey. They must either submit *to* him, or be destroyed *by* him. All principalities and powers, human or angelic, are subject to him. The strong, the mighty, have usually opposed him, but he controls their exertions, rendering them conducive to his own purpose ; and, at his own time, he completely triumphs over them, and shows the universe how entirely they are his.

See how he treated the great as his prey at the dissolution of the pagan Roman empire. " The kings of the earth, and the great men, and the rich men, and the chief captains, and the mighty men, and every bond man, and every free man, hid themselves in the dens, and in the rocks of the mountains ; and said to the mountains and rocks, Fall on us, and hide us from the face of Him that sitteth on the throne, and from the wrath of the Lamb : for the great day of his wrath is come ; and who shall be able to stand ?"[3]

See the result of the struggles of the kings of the Latin earth against him—" These shall make war with the Lamb, and the Lamb shall overcome them : for he is Lord of lords, and King of kings."[4]

Contemplate his triumph hastening onwards over his anti-Christian foes, strong and mighty as they are :—" I saw heaven opened, and behold a white horse ; and he that sat upon him was

---

[1] Psal. ii. 9, 10; xviii. 40; lxxii. 10, 11; cx. 5, 6; lxxxix. 27. Isa. xlix. 7. Dan. vii. 13, 14.

[2] John, xii. 32; xvii. 2. Matth. xxviii. 18. Phil. ii. 9. John, vi. 37.

[3] Rev. vi. 15-17.   [4] Rev. xvii. 14.

called Faithful and True ; and in righteousness he doth judge and make war. His eyes were as a flame of fire, and on his head were many crowns ; and he had a name written, that no man knew but he himself : and he was clothed with a vesture dipped in blood : and his name is called The Word of God. And the armies which were in heaven followed him upon white horses, clothed in fine linen, white and clean. And out of his mouth goeth a sharp sword, that with it he should smite the nations ; and he shall rule them with a rod of iron : and he treadeth the wine-press of the fierceness and wrath of Almighty God. And he hath on his vesture and on his thigh a name written, KING OF KINGS, AND LORD OF LORDS. And I saw an angel standing in the sun ; and he cried with a loud voice, saying to all the fowls that fly in the midst of heaven, Come and gather yourselves together unto the supper of the great God ; that ye may eat the flesh of kings, and the flesh of captains, and the flesh of mighty men, and the flesh of horses, and of them that sit on them, and the flesh of all men, both free and bond, both small and great. And I saw the beast, and the kings of the earth, and their armies, gathered together to make war against him that sat on the horse, and against his army. And the beast was taken, and with him the false prophet that wrought miracles before him, with which he deceived them that had received the mark of the beast, and them that worshipped his image. These both were cast alive into a lake of fire burning with brimstone. And the remnant were slain with the sword of him that sat upon the horse, which sword proceeded out of his mouth : and all the fowls were filled with their flesh.''[1] Who shall live when God doeth this ?

One more remarkable fulfilment of the prediction remains yet to be noticed. Before this great white throne, on which he sits as universal judge, must be gathered all nations—the whole race of man ; and he will treat them all as his property, disposing of them according to his most righteous and benignant will, proclaimed from the judgment-seat. At the expression of his will, the wicked—the strongest and mightiest of them, and the most outrageous and obstinate in their opposition to him—helplessly, now unthinking of resistance, go away into everlasting punish-

---

[1] Rev. xix. 11–21.

ment ; and the *many* righteous—the nations of the saved, his purchased possession—go along with him into life eternal[1] Such is the reward with which Jehovah crowns the travail of the soul of his righteous servant.

That it is a *reward* is marked by the introductory *therefore*, and still more by the following *because*,[2] which might justly be rendered ' in room of,' or ' as the reward of.' ' I will assign him multitudes as his possession, and he shall have the mighty as his prey, in exchange for—as the reward of—his pouring out his soul unto death, and being numbered with the transgressors.' Psalm, xxii. 29, seems parallel—" All they that be fat on earth shall worship ; all they that go down to the earth shall bow to him : *because he hath not preserved in life his own soul.*"[3] Instead of preserving in life, as he might have done (for " no man taketh," says he—that is, can take—" my life[4] from me"), he " poured out his soul unto death, therefore shall he have the multitude for his inheritance." There is an appropriateness in the reward. He gave his soul as a sacrifice, and he receives souls as his hire. By giving his own self as a price, he purchased innumerable men.

" He poured out his soul unto death." " He emptied himself," as the apostle has it.[5] He threw his whole heart into the work of obedience and sufferings, and he continued to do so till all that could be exacted of him, as the representative-man, was fully paid in his death. He was obedient unto death, even the death of the cross. He was not a victim dragged to the altar. He " had a baptism to be baptized with ;" and " how was he straitened till it was accomplished?" " With desire he desired to eat the passover," which was immediately to precede his passion.

" And he was numbered among the transgressors." The best interpreters consider these words as equivalent to—' He suffered himself, or submitted, to be numbered among transgressors.' He took on him the likeness of sinful flesh. In external appearance he was just like one of our sinful race. And he was made sin —constituted liable to suffer the manifestation of the Divine displeasure against sin. It was not the mere fact of his being numbered among transgressors that was the ground of his glorification, but his voluntarily suffering himself to be numbered

---

[1] Matth. xxv. 31, 34, 41, 46.   [2] תחת אשד.   [3] Weisse.

[4] ψυχή μου. John, x. 17, 18.   [5] ἑαυτόν ἐκένωσεν. Phil. ii. 7.

among them that they might be numbered among the righteous.'
The evangelist marks the striking versification of these words, in
our Lord's being fastened to the cross between two thieves;[1]
but the words refer to a much more general fact—his being
found among sinners, and treated as if he were one of them.

There are some minor difficulties connected with the interpretation of the last parallel, rendered " And he bare the sins of
many, and made intercession for the transgressors." The construction shows clearly enough that these words do not hang
from the *because* which precedes.[2] The first clause is in the past
or indefinite tense, and is rightly rendered, ' He bare'—or ' he bears
—the sins of many;' but the second clause is in the future tense,
and strictly signifies, ' He shall make intercession for the transgressors.' It is doubtful whether the words refer to our Lord's
humbled or to his exalted state. If they refer to his humbled
state, then the first clause refers to his bearing the punishment of
the sins of men on the cross; and the second clause, which in
this case must be rendered as in the past tense, was most exactly
fulfilled in his dying prayer for his murderers, " Father, forgive
them; for they know not what they do."[3] It is against this
mode of interpretation, not only that it obliges us to change the
tense of the word " shall make intercession," but that *this* intercession for our Lord's murderers should naturally be noticed before his bearing the sins of many in his death. The words may,
without any violence, be translated so as to refer to his employment in his exalted state. The expression " bare the sins," here,
is altogether a different one from that employed in the last verse,[4]
" bear their iniquities," which, as the ground of justification,
must be expiatory sacrifice, vicarious suffering. A very common
meaning of the phrase is, ' to forgive sins—to lift up and take
away sin by forgiving it.'[5] In this case the oracle closes with
stating that the servant of Jehovah, in his exalted state, prose-
cutes the same benignant purposes for which he labored, and
suffered, and died. He takes away the sins of men by securing

---

[1] Mark, xv. 28.

[2] " The word וזרא indicates that we are not to regard the last two members as
depending on אשר תחת."—HENGSTENBERG.

[3] Luke, xxiii. 34.

[4] " Whiche neverthelesse shall take awaye the sin of the multitude."—COVERDALE.
" Whiche neverthelesse hath taken away the sinnes of the multitude."—BIBLE, 1574.

[5] Gen. l. 17.   Exod. x. 17; xxxii. 32.   Psal. xxxiv. 7; lxxxv. 3.   Job, vii. 21.

their forgiveness, as a Prince and a Saviour, giving repentance and the remission of sins, " in whom we have redemption through his blood, the forgiveness of sins."[1] And he is permanently our advocate with the Father, ever living to make intercession (a word more extensive in its meaning than ' pray for,' though including that meaning ; ' interpose favorably in behalf of,' is the idea) for transgressors who come to God by Him, and therefore able to save men to the uttermost. His high exaltation has not altered his object—the salvation of men. Though he has the whole universe of creatures for his possession, yet still this is his work. He takes away that sin by forgiveness which he took away in expiation, and he continues to intercede for those for whom he died. " His blood cleanseth us from all sin, and he ever lives to make intercession."

Thus we have finished our exposition of this remarkable prophetic oracle. The result of the whole, to borrow the words of a learned expositor,[2] is obviously this—"that the righteous servant of Jehovah, having no sin himself, was to submit to be treated as the vilest of sinners ; and, having the burden of our sins laid on him, to suffer on account of them ; and, by offering up his life a propitiatory sacrifice, to procure for us a release from the punishment which was due for our offences ; and that, as the reward of this, he was to be raised to an endless life, and an unlimited dominion." And we cannot but recognise a plain reference to this oracle, when we are told, in the words of our Lord, that " the Son of man came to give his life a ransom for many ;" and, in the words of his apostles, that " he gave himself a ransom for all"—that "he was offered to bear the sin of many"—that " God made him who knew no sin to be sin for us"—that " Christ has redeemed us from the curse of the law, being made a curse for us"—that " he suffered for sins, the just for the unjust"— that "he died for the ungodly"—that " he gave himself for us" —that " he was delivered for our offences"—that " he gave himself for us, a sacrifice and an offering to God"—that " we are reconciled to God by the death of his Son"—that " his blood was shed for many, for the remission of sins"—that " he is an

---

[1] Calvin refers the words to expiation, and has the strong expression, " Totius mundi reatus illi impositus est, multos enim pro omnibus interdum accipi cum ex aliis locis tum ex quinto ad Romanos capite liquet."

[2] Archbishop Magee.

advocate for us with the Father, and ever liveth to make intercession for us "—that " because he humbled himself, God has highly exalted him, giving him power over all flesh," " all power in heaven and earth," " setting him at his own right hand, and putting all things under his feet."

The leading practical reflections rising out of the oracle have already come before our minds. We shall only farther urge on your attention the following :—

What a searching test are we here presented with for trying our character! " He who has not the spirit of Christ is none of his." His spirit was an *earnest* spirit: his soul was in his work. It was a *self-sacrificing* spirit: it was "the travail of the soul" for the glory of God in the salvation of man. And he found support in his work, however laborious, in the assurance that it would serve his purpose,—and abundant reward for it, in seeing that it had served its purpose. He is no Christian who is not willing to surrender his own ease, and submit to privation and suffering, to serve the purposes for which Christ labored, and suffered, and died. Such persons could have no sympathy with Christ in the satisfaction he has in seeing "the travail of his soul."

How infinite is the importance of that salvation of the human soul, to procure which the Saviour suffered, and to bestow which the Saviour reigns! What a solemnizing consideration, '*I* have an interest to look after, to secure which there has been so wondrous an expenditure of wisdom, and energy, and suffering by incarnate Divinity! Can I think lightly of that soul, which he so highly valued that " he made his soul a sacrifice for sin"— " poured out his soul unto death"—that that soul should not taste eternal death, but enjoy eternal life? What must be the depth of misery from which nothing could save me but such exertions and sufferings on the part of the incarnate Saviour? and what must be the height of happiness to which these can raise those who are interested in their saving power? And shall I act as if both the misery and the happiness were mere creatures of the imagination, and as if the Son of God had "died as a fool dieth"? Shall I treat as worthless what he showed he thought invaluable? Oh! what must be the amount of madness implied in my conduct, if, after all things, by such miracles of mercy, are ready for the salvation of my soul, I shut myself out from the only means of obtaining eternal happiness, or even of escaping everlasting misery, by counting that blood by which alone expiation can be made a common thing?'

How earnestly should we seek that in us and in others the Saviour may "see of the travail of his soul, and be satisfied!" Can we be satisfied without having reason to think he is *satisfied* as to the end of his travail being gained in us? And who would not desire to be the occasion—ay, the cause—of gladness to him who for us "was sorrowful," "sorrowful even unto death"?

Finally, how should we rejoice in the unlimited, never-ending honors and enjoyments of him who "died for us, the just in the room of the unjust!" how should we exult in the extent of his dominion, the stability of his throne, the progress of his conquests, and the triumphs of his grace! and with what earnestness of desire should we pray for the full accomplishment of the Father's promise to him!

Let, then, this be the habitual breathing of our heart, manifesting itself in our habitual conduct:—

> "O come, and added to thy many crowns,
> Receive yet one, the crown of all the earth,
> Thou who alone art worthy.   It was thine
> By ancient covenant ere nature's birth;
> And thou hast made it thine by purchase since,
> And overpaid its value in thy blood."[1]

[1] Cowper.

APPENDIX

RECENT TRANSLATIONS OF THE PROPHETIC ORACLE, WHICH IS THE
SUBJECT OF THE SECOND EXPOSITION

ISAIAH, LII. 13—LIII. 12

IT is a just remark of the late venerable Dr. Pye Smith, that "the comparison of translations, whether the ancient versions, or those made at the
period of the Reformation, or those which have been produced by the learning and piety of more recent biblical scholars," is of great use in scripture
researches. Following his example, and availing ourselves of his help, in
the "Supplementary Notes" to his "Four Discourses on the Sacrifice and
Priesthood of Jesus Christ," we present our readers with six translations of
the prophetic oracle, in parallel columns, by scholars of distinguished eminence,—Lowth, Gesenius, Rosenmüller, Hitzig, Pye Smith, and Henderson.
The second, third, and fourth of these are but translations of translations;
but the accurate scholarship and unimpeachable integrity of Dr. Pye Smith,
who rendered them from the Latin or German, give the highest security
that could be desired in reference to their having lost or gained as little as
possible in their conversion into English.

[13] Behold, my servant shall prosper;

He shall be raised aloft, and magnified, and very highly exalted.

[14] As many were astonished at him;

(To such a degree was his countenance disfigured, more than that of man; And his form, more than the sons of men;)

[15] So shall he sprinkle many nations:

Before him shall kings shut their mouths;

For what was not before declared to them, they shall see,

And what they had not heard, they shall attentively consider.

[1] Who hath believed our report;

And to whom 'hath the arm of Jehovah been manifested?

[2] For he groweth up in their sight like a tender sucker;

And like a root from a thirsty soil:

He hath no form, nor any beauty, that we should regard him;

Nor is his countenance such, that we should desire him.

[3] Despised, nor accounted in the number of men;

A man of sorrows, and acquainted with grief;

As one that hideth his face from us:

He was despised, and we esteemed him not.

[4] Surely our infirmities he hath borne;

---

[13] Behold! my servant shall be prosperous; high and exalted and greatly honored.

[14] As now many are astonished before him (—so disfigured in his aspect before men, and his figure before the children of men,—)

[15] so shall many nations exult in him; kings shall close their mouths before him: for what had not been related to them, shall they see; and understand what they had never heard.

[1] Who trusts our message? The arm of Jehovah, to whom is it made known?

[2] He grew up, like a sprig before him; as a root-shoot out of dry land. Appearance he had none, nor beauty, that we should feel joy in him; no aspect, that we should have pleasure in him.

[3] Disdained was he, and deserted by men; sorrow-laden and marked with disease: as one before whom men conceal their countenances, we disdained him and gave him no esteem.

[4] But he was bearing our disease; with our sorrows

---

[13] Behold! my servant shall act prosperously: he shall be illustrious and exalted and very high.

[14] As many were astonished at thee, (so deformed was his aspect more than that of any one, and his appearance more than that of any child of man,)

[15] so he shall rouse up many nations before him kings shall shut their mouths; for things untold them they shall see, things unheard they shall understand.

[1] Who hath believed what we have understood by hearing? Who perceives what the arm of Jehovah is preparing?

[2] He hath grown up as a twig before him, as a shoot out of dry ground. He had no form nor beauty. We looked at him, but there was no fair appearance that we should be desirous of him.

[3] The most despised and rejected of men, he was; a man afflicted with sorrows, eminently marked with disease: as an object from which men turn away their faces, he was so despised that we regarded him as nothing.

[4] Truly, he hath borne our sicknesses

HITZIG.	PYE SMITH.	HENDERSON.
¹³ See! well proceeds my servant, mounts on high, raises up himself, and is very greatly exalted.	¹³ Behold, my servant shall be successful: he shall be exalted, and extolled, and be very high.	¹³ Behold! my Servant shall prosper; He shall be raised, and extolled, and highly exalted.
¹⁴ As many were terrified before him, —so disfigured, not human, was his look, and his form not that of men's children,	¹⁴ Though many are struck with astonishment at thee; his appearance is disfigured more than that of any man, and his form more than that of any of the children of men:	¹⁴ As many were shocked at thee, (Such was the disfiguration of his appearance more than that of man, And of his form more than that of the sons of men:)
—¹⁵ So will he make many nations to leap [for joy;] before him kings will close their mouth; for what had not been told them, they see, and what they had not heard, they descry.	¹⁵ yet shall he consecrate many nations: kings shall keep silence before him; for what had not been related to them they shall see, and what they had not heard they shall understand.——	¹⁵ So shall he sprinkle many nations; Kings shall shut their mouths on account of him; For what had not been told them, they shall see; And what they had not heard, they shall perceive.
¹ Who hath believed our announcement; and, the arm of Jehovah,—to whom is it manifested?	¹ (—Who believeth our declaration? And to whom is the arm of Jehovah revealed?—)	¹ Who hath believed our report? And to whom hath the arm of Jehovah been revealed?
² And he grew up as a sprig before him, as a shoot out of dry ground, no form hath he, nor beauty, that we should look at him [with admiration;] and no look [of attraction,] that we should long for him.	² Yet he shall spring up as a tender shoot before them; [i. e., the Jewish people], and as a root out of dry ground: he has no form nor beauty, that we should gaze at him; no appearance, that we should be delighted with him:	² For he grew up like a sucker before them, And like a root out of dry ground: He had neither form nor splendor, that we should regard him; Nor appearance, that we should desire him.
³ Despised and abandoned by men, a man of sorrows, and well knowing disease, and as one before whom men covered their faces; despised, and we esteemed him not.	³ despised and neglected by men, a man of sorrows and familiar with sufferings, and like one who hideth his face from us [to bury his griefs in seclusion;] disdained; and we gave him no attention.	³ He was despised and contemned by men, A man of sorrows, and familiar with grief, So that men hid their face from him; He was despised, and we regarded him not.
⁴ But our diseases—he bore them,	⁴ Surely, our sufferings he beareth, and our pains he	⁴ But it was our griefs he bare,

LOWTH.	GESENIUS.	ROSENMULLER.
And our sorrows, he hath carried them: Yet we thought him judicially stricken; Smitten of God, and afflicted.	he charged himself: and we esteemed him punished by God, smitten and distressed by God.	and carried our sorrows: but we reckoned him to be ruin-stricken, smitten by God, and afflicted.
5 But he was wounded for our transgressions; Was smitten for our iniquities: The chastisement, by which our peace is effected, was laid upon him; And by his bruises we are healed.	5 He was wounded for our sins, smitten down for our transgressions; for our welfare the punishment fell upon him; by his wounds we are healed.	5 But he was wounded for our crimes, bruised on account of our sins: the chastisement which causes our welfare was inflicted upon him, and by his wheals we have got healing.
6 We all of us like sheep have strayed; We have turned aside, every one to his own way; And Jehovah hath made to light upon him the iniquity of us all.	6 We all, like sheep, were wide-wandering; each went his own way; but Jehovah threw all our punishment on him.	6 We all like sheep have wandered; each one has looked to his own way: but Jehovah commanded to fall on him alone, the punishment which we should all have endured.
7 It was exacted, and he was made answerable; and he opened not his mouth: As a lamb that is led to the slaughter, And as a sheep before her shearers, Is dumb; so he opened not his mouth.	7 Ill-treated was he, the only-distressed, yet he opened not his mouth; as a lamb which is led to the slaughter-bench, and as a sheep which is dumb before its shearers and openeth not its mouth.	7 He was cruelly treated and afflicted; but he opened not his mouth, as a sheep which is led away to the slaughter; and as a lamb which is dumb before its shearers, he opened not his mouth.
8 By an oppressive judgment he was taken off; And his manner of life who would declare? For he was cut off from the land of the living; For the transgression of my people he was smitten to death.	8 From the oppression and judicial sentence he was taken away: and who, of his contemporaries, reflected that he was taken away out of the land of the living; that for the sin of my people the punishment befell him?	8 He was snatched away from oppression and judicial punishment: but who was there among the men of his age, that reflected that he was cut off out of the land of the living? [Who was there that would say within himself,] for the crimes of my people this suffering has been inflicted upon him?
9 And his grave was appointed with the wicked;	9 His grave was assigned with the evil-doers, with	9 When he died, he yielded himself up to the impi-

HITZIG.	PYE SMITH.	HENDERSON.
and our sorrows he took upon himself; and we regarded him smitten, stricken by God and tortured.	supporteth. But we deemed him stricken, smitten by God, and devoted to affliction.	It was our sorrows he carried. We, indeed, accounted him smitten, Stricken by God, and afflicted;
⁵ And he was wounded on account of our sins, crushed on account of our transgressions; the punishment, which was our benefit, lay upon him; and through his stripe-wheals is healing brought to us.	⁵ Yet he is pierced for our transgressions, crushed for our iniquities: the chastisement of our reconciliation is upon him, and by his bloody stripes we have healing.	⁵ But he was wounded on account of our transgressions; He was bruised on account of our iniquities: The punishment with a view to our peace was upon him, That by his stripes we might be healed.
⁶ We all as sheep were wandering, we took each to his own way; but Jehovah threw upon him the guilt of us all.	⁶ All we like sheep have gone astray, each to his own way have we turned, and Jehovah causeth to fall upon him the iniquity of us all.	⁶ All we, like sheep, have gone astray; We have turned each to his own way; But Jehovah hath inflicted upon him the punishment of us all.
⁷ Cruelly treated was he; and though tortured yet he opened not his mouth: as a lamb which is led to the slaughter-bench, as a sheep before its shearers silent; and he opened not his mouth.	⁷ It is exacted, and he answereth to it and openeth not his mouth [in any complaint, i. e., he entirely acquiesces in being held responsible]; he is led forth as a lamb to slaughter, and, as a sheep before her shearers is silent, so he openeth not his mouth.	⁷ He was severely afflicted, yet he submitted himself, And openeth not his mouth; As a lamb that is led to the slaughter, Or as a sheep before her shearers is dumb, So he opened not his mouth.
⁸ By oppression and judicial punishment he is snatched away; and his fate, who minds it? that he was torn out of the land of the living, [that] for the sin of my people a stroke hit him?	⁸ From custody and from sentence he is taken away: but who of his generation attendeth to it? Since he is cut off out of the land of the living; from the transgression of my people, the stroke is upon them, [i. e., the divine judgment upon his persecutors and murderers.]	⁸ Without restraint, and without a sentence he was taken away; And who can describe his generation? For he was cut off from the land of the living; On account of the transgression of my people he was smitten.
⁹ And with wicked men his grave was made, and with the malefactor in his	⁹ A grave is assigned him with the wicked; but his tomb is a rich man's: for	⁹ They had also assigned him his grave with the wicked,

APPENDIX

LOWTH.	GESENIUS.	ROSENMULLER.

LOWTH.

But with the rich man was his tomb.

Although he had done no wrong,

Neither was there any guile in his mouth ;

[10] Yet it pleased Jehovah to crush him with affliction.

If his soul shall make a propitiatory sacrifice,

He shall see a seed, which shall prolong their days,

And the gracious purpose of Jehovah shall prosper in his hands.

[11] Of the travail of his soul he shall see [the fruit], and be satisfied :

By the knowledge of him shall my servant justify many ;

For the punishment of their iniquities he shall bear.

[12] Therefore will I distribute to him the many for his portion ;

And the mighty people shall he share for his spoil :

Because he poured out his soul unto death ;

And was numbered with the transgressors :

And he bare the sin of many ;

And made intercession for the transgressors.

GESENIUS.

the godless in his death ; though he had done no injustice, and no deceit was in his mouth.

[10] It pleased Jehovah deeply to wound him. But, because he hath given up himself to be a trespass-offering, he beholds his posterity, and lives yet long, and the work of Jehovah prospers by his hand.

[11] His soul, free from sufferings, is satisfied with the prospect. By his wisdom my righteous servant leads many to righteousness, and he lightens the burden of their sins.

[12] Therefore I give him his lot among the mighty ; with heroes he shall share the booty : because he gave up his life unto death, and was numbered with the transgressors ; because he bare the guilt of many, and prayed for the criminals.

ROSENMULLER.

ous and haughty, to be buried ; although he had done no violence, nor was deceit in his mouth.

[10] Yet it pleased Jehovah to smite him with a death-wound. But, since he hath interposed himself as an atoning sacrifice, he shall see his posterity, he shall prolong his life, and he shall successfully execute the mandates of Jehovah.

[11] After the sorrows which he hath endured, he shall obtain that which will satisfy him : by his knowledge shall my godly servant bring many to godliness, having made atonement for their crimes.

[12] Therefore I will distribute to him many [nations], and he shall obtain the mighty for his spoil ; because he poured out his life unto death, and was numbered with the wicked, and bare the sins of many, and interceded for the guilty.

HITZIG.	PYE SMITH.	HENDERSON.
death; though he no wrong had done, and no fraud [was] in his mouth.	he hath done no injustice, and no guile is in his mouth.	But he was with the rich after his death : Because he had done no violence, Neither was deceit found in his mouth.
10 But it pleased Jehovah that the disease should crush him; when thou makest his life a sacrifice for guilt! He will see children, [he will] long live, and the charge of Jehovah will be successful in his hand!	10 But Jehovah is pleased to crush him with sufferings! If he will offer himself a sacrifice for sin, he shall see his posterity, he shall prolong his days, and the gracious purpose of Jehovah shall prosper in his hand.	10 But Jehovah was pleased to bruise him; He put him to grief: Verily, if he make himself a sacrifice for sin, He shall see his seed, he shall live long, And the pleasure of Jehovah shall prosper in his hand.
11 Free from sufferings, his soul will be delighted with the sight; Through his discernment, my righteous servant will make many righteous; and their sins he will bear.	11 The effects of his soul's pain he shall see, and shall be richly satisfied. By his knowledge my righteous servant shall make many righteous, and shall take away their iniquities.	11 After the sorrow of his soul, he shall see it, and be satisfied; By the knowledge of himself shall my Righteous Servant justify many : For he shall bear their iniquities.
12 Therefore give I him a share among mighty ones, and with strong ones will he share booty; for this, that he poured out his life unto death, and was reckoned with sinners; while yet he bore the guilt of many, and became answerable for sinners.	12 Therefore I will give him his portion with princes, and with mighty men he shall share the spoil: because he yieldeth his life to death, and is numbered with transgressors : yea, the sin of many he beareth, and intercedeth for transgressors.	12 Therefore, I will divide for him a portion among the great; And with the strong he shall divide the spoil ; Because he poured out his soul unto death, And was numbered with transgressors, And bare the sin of many, And made intercession for the transgressors.

ADDITION TO NOTE A.—Part I. Lect. I. p. 25

DESCRIPTIVE CHARACTER OF THE PSALMS

" The main subjects of these sweet songs are the glorious things of the
Gospel, as is evident by the interpretation that is often put upon them, and
the use that is made of them, in the New Testament."—Jonathan Ed-
wards.

" Divine wisdom has given to these songs of Zion not merely their matter
but their structure ; and has so united the former with the latter, as to
make it impossible to convey the one without strictly retaining the other.
The poetry of the Psalms is a poetry not of words but of thoughts.   It
consists in an exquisitely artificial connection, not of sound with sound and
syllable with syllable, but of one idea with another.   Let any other poetry
be translated verbatim, and the poetical character, as consisting in the
measure and cadence of the original words, is forthwith lost.   Hebrew
poetry, on the contrary, can be preserved only by the most exactly literal
translation : you destroy its peculiar character just as much by turning it
into measured verse as you destroy the character of Greek or Latin poetry
by turning it into simple prose.   No human ingenuity could give to a
rythmical version that accuracy of arrangement, that luminousness of
meaning, that beautiful adjustment of one member to another, that unstudied
dignity and unlabored magnificence, which continually present themselves
in the literal translation.   This is so obvious a fact, as to make it appear
wonderful that it has not been adverted to.   The more so, as one of the
great purposes of Divine wisdom, in adopting this peculiar species of poetry,
appears to have been, that it might not lose its poetical form in passing from
one language to another ; but that by a simple rendering of word for word,
its treasures might be shared, and its excellence enjoyed, by every age and
by every nation."—Alexander Knox.

INDEX

I—PRINCIPAL MATTERS

IV—AUTHORS QUOTED OR REFERRED TO

V — PASSAGES OF SCRIPTURE QUOTED OR REMARKED ON